How Values Education C;
Student and Teacher Wel

Presenting Values Education as a solution to major challenges in education such as student disengagement and teacher burnout, this book provides a wealth of practical advice about how to implement the Education in Human Values approach in schools, promoting wellness and improved educational outcomes.

Values Education is a worldwide movement and comes in several forms. This book explains the need for and nature of values education, provides practical, easy strategies for implementing the Education in Human Values (EHV) approach, and outlines the educational theories that underpin it. The practical strategies in this book can be implemented in small increments in all aspects of school life. The focus is on both student and teacher wellbeing. The methods can also be used by teachers to address their own professional and personal challenges and to help them cope with difficult situations that cannot be changed.

Written for teachers, teacher educators, and teachers in training, this book is the one-stop-shop for gaining a better understanding of values education, how it can support whole-school wellbeing and how to implement it effectively.

Roger Packham has over 40 years of experience in research and education, including a review for UN-Habitat of an EHV-based project and as a team member improving village-level wellbeing in India. He was the Deputy Chair of the Australian Sathya Sai School Board and the past Director of the Australian Institute of Sathya Sai Education.

Margaret Taplin has over 30 years of experience as a lecturer and researcher in teacher education. She has written several books and numerous articles about practical applications of EHV and led projects to introduce and develop EHV in primary schools in Mainland China, supported by the Hong Kong Institute of Sathya Sai Education.

Kevin Francis has over 44 years of experience as a counsellor, teacher, and facilitator in teacher education and positive psychology. He has conducted many workshops about the practical applications of EHV and introduced and developed aspects of EHV in State and Catholic educational systems.

How Values Education Can Improve Student and Teacher Wellbeing

A Simple Guide to the 'Education in Human Values' Approach

Edited by Roger Packham,
Margaret Taplin and Kevin Francis

Routledge
Taylor & Francis Group
LONDON AND NEW YORK

Designed cover image: Phoenix Pastro, graphics illustrator

First published 2024
by Routledge
4 Park Square, Milton Park, Abingdon, Oxon OX14 4RN

and by Routledge
605 Third Avenue, New York, NY 10158

Routledge is an imprint of the Taylor & Francis Group, an informa business

British Library Cataloguing-in-Publication Data
A catalogue record for this book is available from the British Library

ISBN: 9781032764757 (hbk)
ISBN: 9781032764733 (pbk)
ISBN: 9781003478607 (ebk)

DOI: 10.4324/9781003478607

Typeset in Galliard
by KnowledgeWorks Global Ltd.

To teachers and students around the world who are living and practising human values.

Contents

List of Illustrations

List of Tables

Contributors

Kevin Francis, B. App Sc., Dip. Ed., Grad Dip. (Ed. Couns.), M. Soc. Sc. (Couns. & Psych.), was a professional educator and teacher for 44 years, with a focus on teaching/counselling from 1978 to 2016 in both State and Catholic schools in Australia. During these years, he mentored, taught, and privately tutored hundreds of students in their final year of high school studies. He was also on various school boards, both as a parent representative and as a staff representative. He started his interest in EHV in the early 1980s and has been involved in values education since then for all age groups, running many youth groups and values education workshops in state and private schools across Australia. He has been a keynote speaker at educational conferences, both nationally and internationally. Kevin has run successful and well-received Anger Management, Positive Psychology and Mindfulness workshops, and parenting workshops based on positive psychology and human values. Kevin is a strong advocate for the Sathya Sai Ceiling on Desires Programme, a sustainable approach to living, relating it in practical terms to EHV principles.

Bob (Robert) Molloy, B. Sc., T.S.T.C., had a teaching career in Melbourne, retiring as a deputy head of a large secondary school. He taught mathematics and science. Following his wife, Roz, he took up EHV with enthusiasm, running after-hours and weekend groups for children and adults on the principles and practices of EHV. On his retirement in 1998, he took up the post of principal of the newly established Sathya Sai Primary School. This was a voluntary position which Bob held for 7 years. As the school expanded, he was responsible for the daily implementation of EHV across the school, including the day-to-day EHV training of the teaching staff. He did this for 21 years. During this period, he was also highly influential in introducing EHV across Australia.

Roz (Roslynne) Molloy, Dip. Nursing, had a career as a nurse in Melbourne. She encountered EHV and encouraged Bob to join her in teaching it to different groups. Roz and Bob are seen as a strong partnership in spreading EHV in Australia. When Bob accepted the job of Principal of the Sathya Sai

Primary School, she took on the Bursar role, again in a voluntary position. She has played a joint role with Bob in the EHV training and implementation of its principles across the school, as well as in training workshops across Australia.

Krish (Krishnamurthie) Naidoo, B. Comm. (Acc.), Grad. Dip. (Teaching), M. Ed. Dip. H.V., Cert. IV in Training and Assessment, has worked as an Auditor both in South Africa and as an academic, having lectured in Business Studies in New South Wales Technical and Further Education and at the University of Newcastle, Australia. He was the Inaugural Principal of the Australian Sathya Sai High School. Krish has also been responsible for offering an Introductory Course in EHV to teachers, parents, and other community members across Australia.

Selvanie Naidoo, M.H. Sc. (Ed.), B. Nurs., Dip. Mn., Dip. H.V., worked as a Nurse Educator for 15 years and is employed in the Faculty of Health at the Southern Cross University, Australia. Previous to this education role, she worked as a Registered Nurse in Intensive Care Units in South Africa, Brisbane, and Sydney, and as a Nurse Unit Manager (High Dependency Unit) in Newcastle, NSW. Selvanie has conducted workshops for health professionals, including two-day EHV-based workshops. Between 2005 and 2007, she participated in an Advanced Diploma in Human Values programme, conducting a research study in a high-dependency hospital unit, showing that managers who practice EHV are better able to retain their staff. From 2017 to 2018, Selvanie provided EHV lessons to high school students at the Sathya Sai College, Australia.

Roger Packham, B. Sc. (Hons.), M. Sc., M. Ed., Ph.D., at the end of 2003, after a 28-year research and teaching career at Western Sydney University, Roger moved into an Adjunct Associate Professor role. He has published more than 30 refereed journal and book chapters, edited two academic books, as well as over 70 keynote talks, conference papers, general articles, and consultancy reports. He has been the leader and/or participant in a number of curriculum development and rural development projects around the world. In 2013, he was part of a three-person team that conducted a review for UN-Habitat of their EHV-based '*Human Values for Water Sanitation and Hygiene Education*' (HVWSHE) project throughout Asia. In the 1990s, through retirement, he was the Head of the UNESCO APEID (Asia and the Pacific Program of Educational Innovation for Development) Centre at Western Sydney University. Since 2012, he has been working with a research team in 15 villages in India to improve village-level wellbeing through participative, values-based, sustainable groundwater management: The World Bank and the Government of India are using the results for a US$1 billion groundwater sustainability initiative across several Indian States and many hundreds of villages. Roger has served as the Director and later the Deputy Chair of the Governing Board of the Australian Sathya Sai School and as the Director of the Institute of Sathya Sai Education Australia (ISSEA).

Margaret Taplin, Ph.D. (Education), originally, a primary school teacher, Dr Taplin has over 30 years of experience as a lecturer and researcher in teacher education, curriculum, and pedagogy. Currently, she is an independent education consultant in Australia and Hong Kong. Her main interest is in supporting mainstream teachers to integrate EHV into their existing teaching practices. Since 2003, Margaret has been responsible for a series of projects to introduce and develop EHV in primary schools in Mainland China, supported by the Institute of Sathya Sai Education (ISSE) of Hong Kong. Margaret has written many articles about EHV for mainstream teachers and four books published by the ISSE (Hong Kong): *To Teach Not to Punish: A Human Values Approach to Classroom Discipline* (with Anita Devi); *Silent Sitting: A Resource Manual; Teacher Survival: A Practical Human Values Approach to Professional Fulfilment and Happiness; Education in Human Values Through Mathematics: And Mathematics Through Education in Human Values.* Currently, Margaret is conducting research investigations into the impacts of EHV on teachers' wellbeing, and the factors that influence teachers' adoption of EHV in their teaching.

Foreword

What is education for? As it happens, people differ sharply on this question. It is what is known as an 'essentially contested concept'. Like 'democracy' and 'justice', 'education' means different things to different people. Various factors can contribute to a person's understanding of the purpose of education, including their background and circumstances. Ideology also shapes our answer to the question, particularly around issues such as ethnicity, gender, and social class.

For a long time now, the predominant response to the question has been 'to prepare people for work', but not exclusively so. Typically, people attempting to answer the question, particularly policymakers, tend to hedge their bets. Whilst education is still intended to help people get jobs, the more pragmatic intention is to fully develop citizens, including their capacity for work, thereby enabling economic and social responsibility. A charitable reading of this response is that we still have the economic goal as the pragmatic outcome, but we also want our children to have engaging and meaningful careers. We don't just want them to work for money but to enjoy what they do. We want them to be fulfilled as well as productive contributors to their society.

Increasingly, however, such answers are wearing thin. Changed social and cultural pressures are requiring a rethink about the purposes of education. There is a paradigm shift underway. There are several reasons for this. The nature of work itself, its function in the global economy, and the skills and competencies needed to undertake it are increasingly different from those of the recent past. In this regard, many current practices are clearly unrealistic and need rethinking because they do not develop the skills required for the 21st century: Skills that are based primarily on 'deeper learning' like critical thinking, problem-solving, and teamwork, including skills such as interaction, collaboration, processing information, and managing people. Furthermore, statements about the purposes of education are usually parochial in nature and often somewhat euphemistic; frequently mentioning things like the nation's excellent and innovative education that facilitates individuals, through learning, to achieve their full potential and contribute to the country's social, economic, and cultural development. The authors of this book take a broader view about the purposes of education.

One simply needs to look around to see how misplaced parochial and euphemistic statements about the purposes of education are. Humankind currently finds itself facing literally a set of life-or-death challenges. We are on course for unprecedented environmental destruction through global warming and natural resource depletion. Population and consumption trends predict that we shall overshoot the earth's carrying capacity within the century. Humanity is at war with itself in escalating numbers of regional, ethnic, and religious conflicts. The global economy and many institutions have fallen prey to the short-sightedness of a mostly economic agenda. Inequality, domestic violence, youth suicide as well as child abuse and neglect are now at epidemic proportions. Fifty-four per cent of the human race now lives under autocratic rule. Humankind, it seems, is currently intent on tearing itself apart. These circumstances require repurposing education. Because, as Barack Obama prophetically wrote in his recent book in reference to today's world 'of global supply chains, instantaneous capital transfers, social media, transnational terrorist networks, climate change, mass migration, and ever-increasing complexity':

> We will learn to live together, cooperate with one another, and recognize the dignity of others, or we will perish.
>
> (Obama 2020, p. XVI)

The authors of this book recognise the truth in this sentiment and suggest that education providers need to shift their emphasis away from just fitting people for work and personal fulfilment to a more holistic approach to education designed to produce people capable of not only meeting Obama's challenge but also with the skills and competencies needed to succeed in a globalised world. Their vision is for a values-based approach to education (VbE) that is focused on the development of students' character. They are not alone in such a vision.

Worldwide, interest in, and experimentation with, VbE has grown exponentially over the last decade. VbE has taken a significant hold in Europe, India, United States, Latin America, and parts of Asia, including Australia. Arguably, its growth can be attributed to the extent to which VbE both contributes to the development of people with the caring and empathic dispositions that can meet Obama's challenge and, at the same time, develop the skills and competencies best suited to a globalised world with its ever-changing demographics and rapid technological advancements, so that students will be prepared to face the associated challenges and be able to seize the new and exciting opportunities they present. This worldwide movement comes in several forms including the new Values Pedagogy, Character Education, Values Education, Living Values Education, and Human Values Education. In the pages that follow, the authors spell out both the need for repurposing the education enterprise worldwide as well as offering practical advice about how to implement one particular approach consistent with that repurposing. They call this approach, *Education in Human Values (EHV).*

Ron Toomey, Emeritus Professor, Victoria University, Australia
Terence Lovat, Emeritus Professor, University of Newcastle, Australia

Acknowledgements

When complete, the draft manuscript was reviewed by Dr Tom Scovill, an educator from the United States, Ms Jenny Monson, a psychologist from Western Australia, and Professor Hymon Johnson from the Education Faculty of Antioch University, United States. We would like to thank them for their comments and reviews, which enabled us to improve the first draft in a number of ways. Subsequently, Professors Terrence Lovat, past Dean of Education at Newcastle University, Australia, and Professor Ron Toomey from the Education Faculty of Victoria University, Australia, read the draft manuscript from a broad Values Education perspective and also gave very useful and supportive comments. We were gratified when they both accepted our request to write a Foreword to the book.

Thanks go to our main illustrator, Phoenix Pastro, and also to two long-standing secondary teachers and advocates of EHV, Seelan and Sherleena Chetty, for their early contributions to shaping the concepts for the book.

Roger Packham's wife, Donna MacKenzie, played an irreplaceable role in critiquing his chapter contributions and then the final proofreading of the whole book. Her support and encouragement throughout the project were energising and appreciated by all. We would also like to thank Margaret Van Hennekle for proofreading some of the chapters. Any remaining errors are those of the authors.

Introduction

Roger Packham and Margaret Taplin

This book has the aim of improving education through the promotion of student and teacher wellbeing, while also helping to alleviate some of the issues currently facing schools, teachers, and parents. Some of these reported issues include disengagement, students thinking teachers don't care, teachers struggling to cope, and many students not being interested in learning. The 'old' ways of teaching are not working well anymore for either teachers or students, so it has become a fundamental task to find new ways to cope better with these issues. It is these authors' hope that improved relationships with teachers, with students, with parents, and with the wider community can eventuate through values education. This book shares strategies that can help to make a difference; however, it does not claim to be the *only* way that works. It is not a panacea, but it is a contribution, based on long experience, as an addition to what is already being done. It is the hope of the authors that teachers who read this book will find strategies that they are realistically able to try out, and that if they do, these will work for them as well as for other beneficiaries, including parents, the wider community, and businesses.

The approach to be described is called *Education in Human Values* (EHV), and is one of a number of values education programmes, such as wellness approaches and holistic education approaches, aimed at creating a better future for recipients and practitioners. All such approaches serve the same purpose of bringing some peace and harmony into people's lives.

EHV, as introduced in this book, works best when all of its aspects are included. However, using any part of the framework in conjunction with other approaches can be particularly powerful. At a time when teachers are under pressure from the multiple roles they are expected to play and the difficulties many of their students bring to class, the last thing they want is another 'add-on' to their commitments. The EHV strategies described within this book can be implemented in small increments in all aspects of school life and – more importantly – offer simple, practical strategies that teachers can use in their own lives to help them to change the professional and personal problems that can be changed and to cope better with those that cannot be changed.

DOI: 10.4324/9781003478607-1

Here are two example comments from teachers who used EHV in their teaching practice and who attended a workshop that focused on the use of EHV philosophies and strategies to help them to cope with work-related stress:[1]

> *I have more power to turn the situation around than I thought.*
>
> *Some of these (EHV) practices had almost become habits even before I attended the workshop. However, the workshop helped to reinforce them and now they appear to be more powerful. I find them very useful in leading me through a life that sometimes appears to be rather chaotic. Every day I am so preoccupied with work and there is hardly any space for reflection. With such (EHV) practices I know what are the most important things in life and living, and there is always a temple for retreat inside me.*

This book is intended for teachers and teacher educators primarily, but also for school leaders, parents, and community members. It is a practical and pragmatic guide based on sound educational theories that are also introduced and discussed. An important purpose of this book is to suggest some ways in which teachers can incorporate values education, in this case EHV, into existing programmes, and to give them the confidence to do so. Values education has always been an important part of the curriculum in Australia and most other countries. In Australia, values education has been well-researched through a Federally funded programme from 2003–2011.

This particular EHV approach to values education has the full name of *Sathya Sai Education in Human Values*, named after its founder, Sathya Sai Baba, who was an inspired Indian teacher and philanthropist. The EHV programme has been used widely around the world, both formally and informally. Formally, it is practised in model Sathya Sai Schools in over 30 countries and in the school systems of many countries under a range of political, religious, cultural, and educational ideologies. This book provides examples of such formal use of EHV from several countries, including Australia, China, Kenya, Zambia, and Ireland.

While EHV has many similarities with other values education programmes, it has many unique aspects not covered elsewhere. These include the following: Its focus on addressing teacher wellbeing by encouraging teachers to practise the strategies of EHV in their own lives, the programme called *Ceiling on Desires*, the regular use of 'silent sitting', the importance of the unity of thought word and action – or heart, head, hands – as well as others that will be described in the following chapters.

The *National Framework for Values Education in Australian Schools* emphasised that its nine values were a 'framework' not a 'cage'. Likewise, EHV is based on a framework (not a cage) of five core values – Love, Truth, Peace, Right Action, and Non-violence. EHV is concerned with holistic improvement, seen as the development of the physical, cognitive, emotional, social, and spiritual dimensions of a person in an integrated way, and with inter- and intra-personal growth; this implies the interactive development of all five dimensions and all five core value categories. The framework allows for schools/teachers to identify the associated values that are important for their contexts and wider culture. Teachers using EHV have found that when they are able to develop the concepts/language of these five core value categories, they find it easier to understand the particular values/values aspects that they choose to teach.

Teachers are sometimes overwhelmed with trying to understand the deeper meanings of desired values, so often they give up, or only pay lip service at a surface level, rather than getting to the deeper understanding that is what brings about changes in students (and themselves).

The authors are all members of the *Institute of Sathya Sai Education* (ISSE), an international group of teachers, teacher educators, and concerned community members who want to help to make a difference to 'healing society's ills'. Its aim is the research, development, and implementation of EHV in all its forms, and ISSEs have already had a lot of positive impact in many countries. This book and a companion online certificate course on EHV, also aimed at the professional development of teachers and teacher educators, are contributions to the ISSE aims.

EHV has now been adapted for use in more than 160 countries. The programme is concerned with human excellence and the all-round development of the individual. Our work, as educators, is to explore the best ways of bringing out human excellence in schools without creating extra pressure for teachers and school leaders: We hope this book will assist in achieving this.

0.1 Using This Book

The following chapters of this book will elaborate more deeply and pragmatically on ideas regarding values and Character Education. The aim is to convey a comprehensive understanding of these concepts and methods, and how to implement them for the benefit of all concerned – particularly teachers, students, and parents.

It is appreciated that some readers will have specific needs, so the following chapter outlines will enable you to go straight to the relevant chapters of interest. Others may want to weave your own way through the book, following the ideas that particularly appeal. Many will just read it sequentially, but this outline will still be useful for going back to the ideas you might want to implement first. Implementation of the ideas is a key concern for the authors, and to this end, each chapter either includes or concludes with some practical suggestions for implementation through *Action Learning*, a concept that is introduced at the end of Chapter 3.

0.1.1 Chapter 1: Can Values Improve the Anthropocene?

Values education helps to provide people of good character who can improve the changing world in which we live, with all its social issues. More importantly, such people can better deal with the unintended consequences of the Anthropocene. This chapter describes the Anthropocene and the associated issues of concern and uses examples to show why values education can help by supporting a positive view of human nature – that people are cooperative more than competitive, and that kindness and altruism can change how we think and act. The chapter then looks at how values education can be implemented, particularly through the EHV approach. The EHV model is outlined, together with its underlying philosophy of *Educare*, meaning to draw out from within.

0.1.2 Chapter 2: Re-discovering and Promoting Values through EHV

This chapter introduces why *values education* is important, and uses the example of nationwide research from Australia to show how governments see its importance. The same is true for most educational systems, yet many teachers are unsure about how best to incorporate values into their normal, everyday teaching practices, so the link is made to EHV. The chapter goes on to look at models of and the science behind the human mind, in order to understand how values influence learning and behaviours. Supported by Australian values-education research, the chapter then looks at important components of values education, including *neuroscience and learning*, *Social and Emotional Learning* (SEL), and *positive educational practices*, and their links to EHV. The chapter concludes with a section on *service learning* and how important this is for putting theory into practice in values education.

0.1.3 Chapter 3: What Is the Right Thing to Do?

How can you help children and adolescents to go beyond *knowing* what is right and what is wrong, to *choosing* to do the right thing? What do we mean by *right* and *wrong*? Why and how do we call some things *good* and some things *bad*? What is worth striving for, what makes a life worth living? The chapter discusses the nature and roles of ethics, morals, values, and virtues in our decision-making about the 'right' and the 'good'. Emphasis is placed on the key role of human values, and of reflecting critically on how we make judgements to improve the choices we make. Also discussed are the ethical systems of today, deontology, utilitarianism, emotivism, and virtue ethics that can guide the actions we take to help or teach others. This is then linked to the origins and ethical nature of the *EHV* model, and that *EHV* helps students to acquire habits of virtue that facilitate the development of 'right' actions. Finally, *Action Learning* is introduced as a way of trying out ideas for incorporating ethics and EHV into your practice.

0.1.4 Chapter 4: Values Acquisition and the Language of Values for Teaching EHV

The primary concern of this chapter is with the importance of a 'language of values' for Character Education since this is an essential prerequisite to integrating values into all aspects of life. The goal is for individuals to learn about and develop in the *affective domain* – feelings, emotions, and attitudes – so the chapter begins by looking at three models for the acquisition of *affect*: The *Krathwohl et al. Taxonomy*, the *Trans-Theoretical Theory of Change*, and *Gardner's Theory of Multiple Intelligences*. Also illustrated is how the *EHV* model aligns with these three models, explaining why a 'language of values' is a key feature of *EHV*. The development of *affect* requires individuals to reflect on their own inherent human values, as well as having a cognitive understanding of what the values are and a vocabulary to rationalise and explain their decisions. The five human values that form the foundation of *EHV* – *Love, Peace, Truth, Right Action,* and *Non-violence* – are discussed here, together with a number of value aspects for each. The chapter concludes with some specific examples of children's and adolescents' conversations to illustrate the importance of the language of values for all ages and stages of acquisition.

0.1.5 Chapter 5: The Ongoing Search for Meaning

It is argued in this chapter that our values help to lead individuals to an understanding of the purpose of their lives and to overcome obstacles that can get in the way of achieving this purpose. The chapter explores goals for personal life, for society, and for the environment. Such an understanding of a goal-focused life is needed if we are to become persons of good character. One important goal is to develop a sense of self-identity, a sense of 'Who am I?' The practice of *EHV* helps to remove confusions and contradictions around the goals of life and brings harmony to any individual's thoughts, behaviours, and actions.

0.1.6 Chapter 6: Reappraising Character

This chapter starts by inviting the reader to reflect on *people of good character* in order to arrive at a deeper understanding of what it means to be a person of good character. The evolution of the concept of character across the centuries and cultures is outlined, and character is considered in relation to the seven general capabilities of the *Melbourne Declaration* of Australian State and Federal education ministers, as reflected in Australian school curricula. The distinction is made between the promotion of *character* and of *wellbeing*, the latter being the more commonly addressed in schools. Theories of moral and character development are discussed, and ways to enact these in schools and other situations are described. The chapter concludes with a summary of the essence of *EHV* in relation to the theories and practices of Character Education.

0.1.7 Chapter 7: The Lifelong Nature of Values-Based Education

Here it is asserted that the development of character through a growing awareness and practice of human values is not a finite process, but rather one of *holistic lifelong learning*. Such learning is seen as the development of human potential through a continuous process which stimulates and empowers individuals to acquire all the knowledge, values, skills, and understanding they will require throughout their lifetimes. They need to be able to apply these with confidence, creativity, and enjoyment in all roles, circumstances, and environments. Engaging in lifelong learning encourages the improvement of our own quality of life and sense of self-worth by paying attention to the ideas and goals that inspire us. It is an ongoing journey of identifying personal interests and needs, engaging in exploration and research about how best to address these needs, showing commitment, and making time and space while reflecting on progress. *EHV* aims to promote holistic lifelong learning in the whole person through the development of their physical, intellectual, emotional, social, and spiritual domains.

Chapters 8, 9, and 10 give very practical suggestions for incorporating values education into school programmes using *EHV*.

0.1.8 Chapter 8: Methods for Teaching EHV

This chapter gives specific examples of how the *EHV* teaching strategies of silent sitting, quotations, stories, songs, mind-mapping, creative visualisation, and interdependent group activities are employed to promote and strengthen the learner's conceptual understanding of key human values. It is suggested that this is best achieved through regular sessions that focus specifically on values education; hence, it is referred to as the *Direct method*. Examples of lesson plans are given for all grade levels from K-10, and the changing nature of these programmes as the child matures is also discussed and illustrated. This chapter is a must for readers who want to find out how to implement EHV in their schools.

0.1.9 Chapter 9: Integrating Values into Current Practices: The 'Hidden' Curriculum

Discussion of the methods used to expose students to the values that are inherent in *all* curriculum subjects concurrently with that subject's content, known as the *Indirect method*, is the focus of Chapters 9 and 10. Through this indirect method, the conceptual understanding of values education is strengthened, and learners are encouraged to appreciate the importance of values education in every aspect of life. A key purpose of these two chapters is to illustrate that it does not have to be time-consuming or difficult to integrate values education across the curriculum. This chapter addresses the 'hidden curriculum', which includes modelling of teachers' own values, sharing with students how their values affect and enhance the teachers' own lives, and some suggestions about how to give *praise*, *feedback*, and *discipline* in values-based ways. Finally, taking advantage of 'teachable moments' is discussed.

0.1.10 Chapter 10: Integrating Values into Current Practices: Overtly through the Curriculum

This chapter continues the discussion of methods used to integrate values messages into curriculum subjects concurrently with that subject's content, using the *indirect method*. Practical examples are given for a range of subjects: Science, Mathematics, Geography, Political Science, Physical Education, Art, and Literature. This chapter also provides practical examples to illustrate how the teaching strategies described in Chapter 8, silent sitting, quotations and affirmations, storytelling, songs, interdependent group activities, and reflective questioning can be integrated across the whole curriculum in such a way that students are simultaneously learning about the topic under consideration and being challenged to practise and reflect on the underpinning values. The appendices provide real examples of values lesson plans and a values lesson plan template.

0.1.11 Chapter 11: Maintaining Positivity through EHV

This chapter looks at Positive Psychology, which is a way to enhance life skills. Practical examples are given of how this relates to values education and how it can be used to promote character development using EHV's approach to the teaching and practice of human values. In particular, Positive Psychology can be used to help alleviate many mental and emotional difficulties experienced by students, including self-esteem issues, anxiety, depression, stress-related problems, and interpersonal issues. The chapter provides positive examples of using these strategies from the author's personal experience of teaching and counselling practice, particularly in a school Wellbeing Centre. The work of Seligman, Jampolsky, and Ruiz provides focus to show how these approaches can be used to promote the pleasurable life, the engaged life, and the meaningful life.

0.1.12 Chapter 12: Curbing Excesses: Placing a Ceiling on Desires

This chapter describes a unique concept of *EHV*, known as *Ceiling on Desires*. All humans are driven by *desires/needs*, these often cause conflicting and demanding choices, this leading to conflict within us if the desires/needs are thwarted or denied. The *Ceiling on Desires* programme is not about denying or stopping these necessary desires, but rather reining them in, to manage them and to support more contented lives. The chapter explores the psychology and philosophy of needs and desires and relationships to character and personality development. The role of neurotransmitters is discussed, these driving the seeking of new things and experiences. The chapter looks at Freud's concepts of *Id*, *Ego*, and *Superego*, and Maslow's hierarchy of needs. Practical strategies are then discussed, with examples, for placing a *Ceiling on Desires* for food, for money, for 'internal' and 'external' energy, and for time, which includes modern media usage.

0.1.13 Chapter 13: Learning Partnerships to Enhance Values-Based Education

This chapter examines the vital role of the partnerships between parents or other primary carers, teachers, and students if values education in schools is to fully realise its aim. That aim is to provide the community with people of good character to develop and improve society. The development of children who will possess and act upon ethical sensibilities ideally begins when they are young. Students spend most of their time at home, so values education is not the sole responsibility of the school, albeit schools play a vital role. Since parenting styles are not homogeneous, schools often represent the best hope for students to fulfil their potential and flourish as contributing members of society. The chapter looks at the nature of the school/parent interaction, and how partnerships can be organised and developed. Consideration is given to how school leaders and other stakeholders can play their parts through a holistic approach to organising and running their school, and how the school interacts with its wider community. Clear guidelines to develop and implement strategies to support all aspects of these partnerships for values education are given, with specific examples of schools implementing such strategies.

0.1.14 Chapter 14: Character Education through EHV in Practice

This chapter concludes the book, describing how the principles of values education through *EHV* have been incorporated into a worldwide school system of model *Sathya Sai Schools* and other partnership schools that have adopted EHV on a whole-school basis. Anecdotes are given about the impacts on students, teachers, and their families. There are around 40 Sathya Sai Schools in 30 countries outside India and over 100 in India, established to demonstrate how the EHV principles can be implemented to develop people of good character serving their communities. All use EHV techniques described in Chapters 8, 9, and 10. This chapter also describes the organisation and operations of the schools and introduces the Australian Sathya Sai College. A brief history is given of this college's development from starting with nine children, to its current primary and secondary campuses offering K-12 values-based, character-building education. Specific examples are given for EHV teacher professional development and the use of communities of practice in the planning and implementation of EHV. Thus, values education through EHV will support the wellbeing of all involved, and help teachers to remember why they became teachers in the first place.

0.2 Concluding Comments

The first idea for this book took shape in November 2019 on a plane journey from India to Australia. Roger Packham had just stepped down as Director of the Australian Institute of Sathya Sai Education due to his deteriorating eyesight. He was seeking a new challenge given that he could no longer drive, and travel was limited: He drafted a working title and nine proposed chapters for a user-friendly book about EHV that linked EHV to the wider education literature. He contacted a small group of experienced colleagues with the idea, and all were excited to join the venture – these are the listed contributors. The group met in Queensland just as the COVID outbreak was beginning, and the shape of the book and the nature of the chapters emerged from three productive days of dialogue. The number of chapters eventually expanded to fourteen, each with a nominated lead author. The whole team met on a monthly basis via Zoom to critique the chapters as they were developed. Final writing and editing were done by the editor and the two associate editors.

The authors hope you will both enjoy and be inspired by this book. Above all, we hope it gives you more confidence and provides you with useful tools to implement values education. We hope that EHV becomes a normal part of your activities as an educator, a teacher, a parent, or in other community or workplace roles. By implementing these ideas, you will be able to play your role in equipping humanity to better deal with the vital issues that are impeding a more harmonious and flourishing life for all, and particularly to improve both the current social concerns and the issues of the Anthropocene that can threaten our very human survival as well as that of other species.

Thank you for reading our book, and we hope that it will mark the beginning of an important journey for you.

Note

1 M. Taplin, *Teacher Survival: A Practical Human Values Approach to Professional Fulfilment and Happiness* (Hong Kong: Institute of Sathya Sai Education, 2008), vii.

Chapter 1

Can Values Improve the Anthropocene?

Roger Packham and Margaret Taplin

1.1 Introduction

Values education is needed for the traditional reasons of educating people of character who will ensure a harmonious society, one that can deal in better ways with many of the current social issues and helps to promote the wellbeing of all. Notwithstanding this vital rationale, it is also the contention of this book that the issues of the *Anthropocene* (the current geological age, the period during which human activity has been the dominant influence on the Earth) are dramatic and require a values-based approach if they are to be improved such that humans and all other life can be sustained. As will be developed below, such issues must be addressed urgently; education holds a key role if society as we know it is to be sustained, rather than doomed.

World change is a topic on the minds and in the hearts of many people at this time, particularly the issues of climate change, COVID-19, and other potential pandemics. World events appear to be spiralling into ever greater manifestations of negativity, and many who hope to change the world with more positive actions and intentions are frustrated by the apparent lack of effect of their good work. In recent times, we have seen the rise of fundamentalism in many religions, which seems in many ways to be a manifestation that is exactly the opposite of the more peaceful, spiritual world that many are seeking to create. There are issues of mental health, of young people lacking direction, of drug taking, domestic violence, inequality, poverty, racism, and racist attacks.

To understand the process of world change, it is necessary first to understand the current times we live in. Never before have human beings been more interconnected. The acceleration of communications technology has created what is, for many, a global community where individuals are increasingly aware of the whole of humanity. The teaching that 'we are all one' is rapidly manifesting itself, as the reality of our interdependence and interconnectedness reveals itself.

The extreme imbalances in our world are also being revealed, and it is no longer possible to shut out the reality of the large human family of which

DOI: 10.4324/9781003478607-2

we are all a part. It is no longer possible to make someone else 'the other'. Philosophies, ideologies, or religions that attempt to make another group of people 'the enemy' are now being exposed for what they are. Change is badly needed in a world where most people lack basic resources for survival, and a relatively small number of people have an overabundance of resources.

A *system* can be seen to be comprised of everything that creates and sustains it. Any visualised system that is in harmony leans towards health, wellbeing, and sustainability. If any system is in disharmony, it will lean towards illness, disease, suffering, and collapse. Everything is interconnected and interdependent. Viewing the whole Earth as an interconnected ecosystem recognises the delicate balance between animals, plants, land, atmosphere, and bodies of water. If all of the parts of a system are in harmony, then the whole system will be in harmony. Disturb one thing, and a disturbance will be created that ripples through the whole system, and its effects will be unpredictable and possibly unintended. This principle applies to any and all visualised systems. For example, it applies as equally to an individual human being as it does to a family, community, or the environment. So 'care' must be taken to consider all actions and to take things as a whole, always keeping in mind that *nature* can survive without humans, but humans cannot survive without nature – humans are a part of nature.

The scientific consensus is that, while humans have been changing the Earth for at least 10,000 years, around 1950 a new geological epoch was entered known as the *Anthropocene*. The key feature of the Anthropocene is that humans have caused dramatic, complex, uncertain, and unpredictable effects on the biosphere, the atmosphere, the hydrosphere, and the geosphere, together with all important biogeochemical cycles, such as those of carbon, nitrogen, and phosphorus. This has enormous implications for life as we know it for both humans and other flora and fauna. Governments are struggling to find ways to improve this situation, and it seems that the only way out is to embrace a return to traditional human values, particularly by parents and educators.

To fully appreciate this proposition, it is necessary to understand more about what is meant by the *Anthropocene*, and how it has been affected by human behaviour. Technology alone will not solve these issues; there needs to be some grounding in values to ensure that technology is used wisely and well. The subsequent section will develop this argument about why values education is needed in the context of the Anthropocene.

1.2 The Anthropocene

Many readers will already be familiar with what is meant by the *Anthropocene*; however, for those less familiar with this term, here is a summary overview of what it is and its consequences.

The Oxford English Dictionary defines the word as:[1]

> *Relating to or denoting the current geological age, viewed as the period during which human activity has been the dominant influence on the environment, climate and ecology of the earth.*

Humans are leaving a clear, globally identifiable marker in the rocks. Humans have also caused many changes to the Earth, which will be outlined below, and both of these concepts have, beginning in 2008, led to calls for the Anthropocene epoch to be named as a new interval of geological time. In 2009, the *International Congress on Stratigraphy* (ICS) Subcommittee on Quaternary Stratigraphy appointed an *Anthropocene Working Group* (AWG) to make the case for this new epoch of geological time.[2] The scientific consensus today has already recognised the Anthropocene, so for the AWG, it was not whether, but when, and on what basis, the Anthropocene might be recognised within the *Global Time Scale.*

The most unambiguous basis for a global *isochronous*[3] stratigraphic marker is the spread of radioactive fallout from nuclear weapons testing, beginning in 1945. While this provides a clear marker from 1950 on, many believe the Anthropocene began much earlier. Candidates for the start of the Anthropocene include: The late Pleistocene megafauna extinction around 30,000 years ago; the emergence and spread of agriculture around 11,000 years ago; rising atmospheric methane from rice production around 5000 years ago; widespread anthropogenic soils[4] around 2000 years ago; the formation of a global trade system around 500 years ago; and the start of the industrial era around 200 years ago.[5] Deciding which of these to choose seems to be more a matter of values than of science.

Expressed in biological terms, it is the human capacity for niche[6] construction which caused Earth's transformation into the Anthropocene. From the 1990s onwards, there has accumulated a large body of scientific evidence that human activity is altering Earth's functioning as a system. More than half of the terrestrial biosphere has been transformed by human use, including urban areas, villages, croplands, and rangelands. No longer is there a real meaning to the idea of a 'natural habitat' or 'natural ecosystems': All of nature and its ecosystems have been transformed by human society in some way or another. It is astonishing that, today, 90% of Earth's total mammalian biomass is composed of humans and domesticated animals.[7]

While it is too early to know what an Anthropocene state of the Earth might ultimately be like, including its relative stability and how long this epoch might last, as Ellis[8] reports, many effects have already been documented by scientists. Earth's biogeochemical cycles are being disrupted, and all such changes are beyond natural variability. Human activities are changing in concert with changes to Earth's atmosphere, lithosphere, hydrosphere, biosphere, and the climate. Human use of land is reshaping Earth's ecology, eroding productive soils, diverting water to farms and cities, eliminating natural habitats, and driving species extinction. Humans are also causing global changes in the flow of rivers to the sea, transforming natural habitats, and reducing biodiversity. The oceans are becoming more acidic and polluted with plastic, and with fertiliser run-off from agriculture. Humans are producing vast numbers of industrial chemicals that are not found in nature, and many of these are untested for side effects beyond their use for which they were developed (*unintended consequences*), such as '*PFAS*' – Polyfluoroalkyl substances, used for firefighting in plastics, and everyday products such as packaging, clothing, carpets, cookware, etc., but which are also thought to cause cancer. There is an enormous growth in the production of plastic, something that is not found naturally and is entirely man-made.

An important concept here is that of a 'tipping point', the crossing of which might force Earth out of its stable Holocene-like state that was typical of the earlier geological time epoch. The potential of these tipping points has increased consistently since the 1950s due to a *great acceleration*[9] of human influence on all aspects of both earth systems science and social life. One measure of these changes is the *Planetary Boundaries Framework*[10] that raises the possibility of catastrophic changes in Earth's systems. Human social systems have also emerged as a planetary force within earth systems science; some are calling this an *Anthroposphere* (cf. Biosphere, Atmosphere, etc.).

While people are worried about what some see as a 'bad Anthropocene', it needs to be remembered that more food is now produced per person, even without significant increases in the global area of land used for agriculture. Unfortunately, scientists agree that current methods of farming are not sustainable and need to change and become more regenerative.[11] People also live longer on average, are healthier, less violent, are better educated, and have access to opportunities unimagined by our ancestors.

Concomitantly, human wellbeing is generally improved at the same time that our society is rapidly producing a hotter, more polluted, less biodiverse, and less predictable planet. While there was a massive increase in the population from 1950 onwards, population growth is now slowing possibly stabilising in a few years' time. However, human demands for food, water, energy, and other environmental resources are continuing to grow due to wealthier populations making greater demands on Earth's resources.

Different people and different societies use and transform their environments differently. A particular way of life is shaped by Earth's societies, not by its biology. Inequalities within and among societies, resulting from competitive sociopolitical and their associated economic processes, have been seen as the causes of many of Earth's transformations, both positive and negative, by producing massive social inequalities which are far more important than industrialisation in their effects on Earth's systems.[12] Different societies use and transform environments very differently, particularly wealthy, urban dwellers who, for example, emit ten times more carbon into the atmosphere than the rural poor. In fact, the Earth's poorest billion people emit almost no fossil carbon at all.

1.3 Responding to These Issues

So, the questions now are what can be done? Who is responsible? Who should act? There is no obvious political constituency or government infrastructure prepared to take on the task of managing these *wicked*[13] social-environmental challenges. While the *Montréal Protocol*[14] overcame the problem of the ozone hole in the atmosphere, such global agreements are rare and difficult to achieve, as can be seen in the debate over reducing atmospheric carbon emissions to avoid catastrophic climate change.

Many believe that humans can develop a conscious, intentional teleologically oriented (goal-directed), approach to guide Earth towards better outcomes. Others argue for an emphasis on our obligations (our commitments) to others such as parents, friends, work colleagues, or the poor and needy, but also for the Earth itself; this is known as Duty ethics or Deontology. These issues will be explored more in Chapter 3.

Rutger Bregman has described what he believes to be a *radical* idea, that *most people deep down are pretty decent.*[15] Unfortunately, most people think that everyone will only look after themselves when panic breaks out, that humans by nature are selfish and governed by self-interest. This view drives the headlines that are read each morning and the laws that govern lives. Yet Bregman provides a realistic alternative to this pessimistic view, based on overwhelming evidence that demonstrates the opposite; neighbours help each other, and people are willing to give their lives even for perfect strangers. While this truth has been shown over and over again by every branch of science, is corroborated by evolution, and confirmed by everyday life, it is still not accepted by rulers, is denied by many religions and ideologies, and ignored by the news media and most histories of the world.[16]

Bregman presents case after case of real-world examples, as well as scientific and psychological research, to support his argument. However, it is still true that most people believe others 'cannot be trusted', and hence that is how they act.

Ultimately, a person will get what that person expects to get, so to tackle this false belief is one of the greatest challenges of our time if all the issues of social ills and the Anthropocene described above are to be improved. The place to start is with our own view of human nature. As humans *are complex creatures with a good side and a not-so-good side*,[17] the question is which side do we turn to? This is beautifully illustrated by the story of *The Two Wolves*, a popular legend of unknown origin, possibly Cherokee Indian:

> It is a story of a grandfather using a metaphor of two wolves, one good and one bad, fighting within him to explain his inner conflicts to his grandson. When his grandson asks "which wolf wins?" the grandfather answers, "whichever wolf I choose to feed is the one that wins".[18] We need to feed the good wolf within us.

Educators need to 'feed the good wolf' and support the positive view of humankind that humans are cooperative rather than competitive, that human kindness and altruism can change how we think and act, as a foundation for achieving true change in our society. This is a key aim of values education, to stand up for human goodness despite the cynicism that this may bring out in others, and the fact that it may need us to stand up against the 'powers that be' since it can threaten their powers. The assumption that people are selfish and act like beasts or worse, while believing that civilisation is a flimsy veneer that will crack at the merest provocation, has lasted for a long time and is still prevalent today. Evidence such as that described by Bregman shows this view of humankind, and this perspective on our history is unrealistic. A new world awaits if we revise our view of human nature to what science, psychology, anthropology, and the like have shown. If we believe that most people are decent and kind, everything changes, and a complete rethink can occur about how we organise our schools, prisons, businesses, and democracies, as well as how we live our own lives. This more realistic view of human nature will have major implications for how individuals interact with others and how young people are educated about this truer view of humankind in order to create a better world.

Humans need to think bigger than their individual lives to imagine the operations of an entire planet, together with its potential changes over time scales longer than human societies have existed since their emergence. Individuals need to appreciate that it is the sum of *their own* individual actions that cause, or overcome, the issues faced by humanity. But for this to come about, it is critical for individuals to realise that these issues are not for 'others' to deal with and that *every* person's actions do make a difference. Until now, we do not seem to have been very successful in encouraging a critical mass of people to examine their own behaviours and to want to make changes. Humans can still shape a future in which both humans and non-human nature thrive together. However, this needs to be a values-based approach if it is to succeed. It is the loss of values, such as respect for nature and for each other, and the increase in individualism and selfishness, that are contributing to the adverse Anthropocene social and personal issues.

From time to time in history, various threats have occurred that have forced us to re-examine and go back to our traditional values, such as the United Kingdom responding in the 1940s to the threats of food shortages during World War II, dealing in the 1980s with the need to avoid certain chemical sprays and gases to repair the hole in the ozone layer, and especially saving lives and health in 2020 during the COVID-19 pandemic. But these have mostly been short-term solutions or partial ones, and mostly we have tended to slip again once the crisis has been contained; for example, the United Kingdom is again dependent on imports for more than 50% of its food, and the world is failing to deal with the climate emergency. Care must also be taken with such terms as 'traditional values': It is widely believed that when Gandhi was asked what he thought about Western Civilisation, he supposedly replied, 'It would be a good idea'. Many scholars and others across the world believe that 'our traditional values' include human subjugation, apartheid, and resource exploitation and expropriation. Some European nations are in the process of returning artefacts to African countries, and some in the USA, Canada, New Zealand, and Australia are returning 'stolen' lands and artefacts to indigenous peoples.

What is needed is a sustainable desire to change that is rooted in the hearts and consciences of individuals and their innate values that will be explored in Chapter 3. One such example of a values-based approach to change for the better is the *Mondragon Corporation*, Spain's seventh biggest industrial group. This €15bn corporation acts as the parent company to 111 small, medium-sized, and larger cooperatives, and is the outcome of a project launched in 1956 by a catholic priest, Don José María Arizmendiarrieta. He spent a number of years educating young people about a form of humanism based on solidarity and participation, and the importance of acquiring the necessary technical knowledge, before creating the first cooperative, that then led to today's corporation. Its values include inter-cooperation, grassroots management, corporate social responsibility, innovation, democratic organisation, education, and social transformation. Over the years, these have been embodied in a series of operating rules approved on a majority basis by the *Cooperative Congresses*, which regulate the activity of the Governing Bodies of the corporation, the grassroots Cooperatives, and the Divisions they belong to, from the organisational, institutional, and economic points of view as well as in terms of assets.[19]

A second example closer to home is that of Cathy McGowan and her election as an independent to Australian federal parliament in 2013 for the Victorian rural seat of Indi, achieved on the basis of community-based, values-led politics.[20] Her focus was on valuing her entire community and listening to the needs of all members in order to help empower them to create sustainable change, thereby causing politics to change for the better. She retired in 2019 but was replaced by another independent candidate with the same values and community-based approach. Cathy is now supporting similar values-based community groups to support nine independent candidates in political arenas around Australia in an attempt to make politics more participative for all people.

However, these examples are still not enough. There is a need for much more widespread, concerted effort, and, as argued in this book, it points to the need for a unified approach that needs to be a priority of education systems. There is a need for a values education that draws on the good work that is being done already and expands it, not as a separate speciality within education, but as a responsibility of all of society, enabling all educators to incorporate values into the whole school environment. This was the aim of the Australian Federal Government project that ran in the early 2000s and demonstrated many benefits.[21] So how might incorporating values education into schools be developed further today?

1.4 Implementing Values Education

Values education, also referred to as Character Education, is not a new idea. In fact, most education systems promote values education as expressed, for example, in the Australian *goals of education*,[22] and the Australian Government's 'Values Education for Schools' website.[23] However, it is often the case that educators and parents are not fully aware of how to actually '*do*' values education, and often feel it is the responsibility of the other party, or some third party such as a religious or other community organisation (scouts, guides, etc.).

To date, the focus of values education has been to develop citizenship and people of character, with the aim of ensuring the wellbeing of all and a harmonious society. The hope has been that, through values education, society can be improved. It also needs to be recognised that technology alone will not solve society's issues, particularly those of the Anthropocene: Rather technology grounded in a values-based community approach will be the way forward, as argued at the start of this chapter.

An example of the kind of values-based approach to technology being proposed here was the successful *UN-Habitat Human Values-based Water Sanitation and Hygiene Education* (HVWSHE) programme that ran in Africa, Asia, and Latin America from 2002–2012. It was a part of the effort to achieve the water and sanitation targets of the internationally agreed *Millennium Development Goals*.[24] Water is a particularly critical issue, with its declining availability for irrigation and the depletion of groundwater, both threatening sustainable supplies of food. There is also the issue of the pollution of water from fertiliser application, together with bad sanitation, threatening clean, and healthy water supplies to communities. This is particularly so in urban areas, where half the world's population now lives. Concern for clean water is reflected in the huge increase in bottled water consumption over recent years and the associated problem of discarded plastic bottles. These issues will not be overcome by technology alone. As a consequence, for example, the HVWSHE programme of the UN-Habitat stated:

> *Through the approach of Human Values-based Water, Sanitation, and Hygiene Education, we can promote a better understanding and practice of these concepts as a key social, economic, and environmental resource as well as facilitating the emergence of a new water management ethic. Experience has shown that human values-based education can be used as a strategic entry point for supporting positive attitudinal changes amongst students, teachers and all those involved in the educational process. The implementation of Human Values-based Water Sanitation and Hygiene Education will help achieve*

> *an all-round development of nations. Thus, education has a direct relationship with sustainable development.*[25]

An example of how this can be done is a values-based approach that has been incorporated into the Managing Aquifer Recharge and Sustaining Groundwater Use through Village-level Intervention (MARVI) project[26] that started in 2012 and is continuing and expanding still in 2024. MARVI aims to improve the livelihoods of villagers in rural Rajasthan and Gujarat in India (soon to expand to several other Indian States, to SE-Asia and elsewhere) through a greater understanding and valuing of groundwater. This understanding and valuing leads to the sustainable use of groundwater in agriculture, rather than its unsustainable overuse as is currently the case in much of India and other parts of the world.

All teachers are aware of the need to address all three learning domain areas,[27] the *affective* (emotions, feelings, and values) as well as *cognitive* and *psychomotor* competences, to achieve a holistic education for their students. Impediments to teachers introducing values and Character Education in their classrooms include time and curriculum constraints, as well as a lack of understanding about exactly what and how to teach in the area of *affective* competences. However, there are many opportunities to teach the principles of human values through all curriculum subjects and topics, with the added advantage that schools do not have to abdicate in any way their responsibility to teach the academic (cognitive) and other skills; however, it does require that they rethink the ways in which they do this.

> ***One important purpose of this book*** is *to suggest some ways in which teachers can incorporate values education into existing programmes, and to give them the confidence to do so.*

By engaging parents and other community members as a part of the process, it becomes possible for whole school communities to make a difference by first enhancing their own understanding and changing themselves. A framework that enables this to be done effectively is the Education in Human Values (EHV) programme. This programme was founded in India by Sathya Sai Baba, a renowned Indian teacher. Now there is a university on the site of the original programme, with four constituent colleges on different campuses, and more than 100 schools in India are using EHV. The EHV programme (in 2023) is also operating in 37 model schools in 31 other countries around the world, as well as in numerous projects in mainstream schools and community groups in 160 countries. Additionally, the EHV programme is supported by national education department policies in several countries. It is a secular programme that is concerned with putting character development and values more firmly into education and developing all domains of the student's personality: Cognitive, physical, emotional, social, and intrapersonal/spiritual.

The EHV model is based on eliciting five human values that are seen as universal and interdependent, that are already inherent in all of us, and that are traditional to all cultures: *Truth*, *Right Action*, *Peace*, *Love*, and *Non-violence* (these are discussed more fully in Chapter 4).

A fundamental principle of EHV is that all teaching needs to be based on Love and that the teacher's example in 'living' the values is the most critical component. Therefore, it is hoped that this book will give some insights about how teachers can become values educators as well as role models in all aspects of their teaching and other interactions with their students.

1.5 The EHV Model

In this section, a brief description of the rationale for EHV will be given.

The goals of EHV are:

- To bring out human excellence at all levels: Character, academic, and 'being', leading to self-awareness, self-confidence, self-motivation, and being 'fully' conscious
- The all-round development of the child (the *heart* as well as the *head* and the *hands*)
- To help children to know 'who they are'
- To help children to realise their full potential
- To develop attitudes of selfless service.

Jumsai[28] has described the essence of the EHV model as being that, through the five senses, the mind receives and processes information from the environment in order to create awareness and understanding. The subconscious stores the memories of everything that is experienced and feeds these memories to the conscious mind when automatic responses are insufficient to deal with a particular situation and a decision needs to be made about how to act. The conscious mind may then control the individual's thoughts and actions and will also enable the colouring of perceptions of events that happen. The superconscious mind is the source of wisdom, knowledge, conscience, and 'higher' consciousness. In a holistically balanced person, these three levels of the mind interact to contribute to the physical, intellectual, emotional, social, and spiritual wellbeing of the individual. Chapter 2 further elaborates on these ideas.

Jumsai[29] proposed that there are two important ingredients for healthy interactions to occur. The first is to free the three levels of the mind from extraneous 'chatter', to enable enhanced concentration and memory. The second is to ensure that the information that then becomes stored in the various levels of the mind is positive, healthy, and constructive, since its retrieval will have such significant effects on the individual's thoughts and actions. These, in turn, contribute to the presence or absence of holistic wellbeing – this concept is expanded in Chapter 2 and further in Chapter 11, which deals with the role of positive psychology in education.

The EHV model is a simple but effective means of ensuring that these two essential ingredients occur. The above-mentioned five values of Truth, Right Action, Peace, Love, and Non-violence are all interrelated and interdependent. *Love* is in fact considered to be the basis of character and encompasses all of the other values: Love in thought is Truth, Love in feeling is Peace, Love in understanding is Non-violence, and Love in practice is Right Action.

1.6 Transformation through EHV

Transformation is viewed here as the process whereby the power of Love is suffused into the thoughts that arise in the mind so that what is seen, heard, and done is good. For example, we are all being 'programmed' constantly by the environment around us, our past experiences, television, social media, advertising, and the like. If these are negative, it is this negativity that can fill our minds, unless the negative aspects are substituted by positivity. Negative programming is difficult to revoke, as the mind operates to reinforce what is already in the subconscious. Yet, 'reprogramming', if necessary, can be achieved through inculcation of the five human values and their development and daily practice; this can help to establish the values in the conscious and subconscious levels of the mind. When such a development of the mind is achieved, thought, word, and action will be unified by the conscience – metaphorically this is called *head*, *heart*, and *hands*. This is the transformation that EHV can achieve.

1.7 EHV Teaching Approaches for Drawing Out Inherent Values

There are several teaching approaches that are particularly useful in drawing out the values inherent in children. These will be described in detail, with examples, in Chapters 8, 9, and 10. Here is an overview of the five key ones:

1. A fundamental component of EHV is *silent sitting*, which has some commonalities with the currently popular practice of mindfulness. Silent sitting refers to encouraging pupils to sit quietly and allow their minds to relax for a few minutes, particularly at the beginning of a lesson, to make them feel more focused and peaceful. Often, this time is used to listen to soft, relaxing music. Silent sitting is frequently combined with *guided visualisation*, which can be used in various ways to promote students' understanding of and reflection on their own values.[30]

2. The use of *quotations or positive affirmations* is also an important component of the EHV programme, based on the idea that children's thinking can be influenced by regular exposure to positive statements. The teacher can select quotations that are relevant to the child's age, interests, and culture. Quotations can be displayed every day and used as a basis for discussion, or can simply be left for the students to read for themselves.
3. The EHV model encourages teachers to utilise opportunities to tell *stories and anecdotes* about famous people, heroes, and ordinary people who have demonstrated the kinds of values under consideration. By regular exposure to stories of such people, and reflection on the values portrayed in relation to their own lives, the pupils will come to value the good qualities described and then to use them as a framework to draw on when the need arises.
4. *Music and song* are valuable ways of promoting inner peace and emphasising positive values. These days, with concerns that young people are exposed to many negative values through song, there needs to be a counterbalancing by the use of music and songs that promote positive feelings and celebrate aspects of the five key human values.
5. *Group activities* are important. Apart from the fact that current research about teaching suggests that pupils can come to better understanding if they have the chance to work together in pairs or small groups,[31] this methodology allows for the development of unity, co-operation, mutual regard, and creative conflict resolution, all of which are essential if people are going to be able to live together in peace and harmony. In EHV, group activities encourage collaborative interdependence, with members each contributing their own strengths and talents, thereby illustrating the concept of 'strength in unity'.

1.8 Using EHV

While it is appropriate to utilise the EHV model in teaching directly about values concepts, and many teachers are using it successfully in this way, it is also very easy – and important – to adapt the principles to existing classroom practices, thus empowering all teachers, irrespective of their subject specialisations, to be teachers of values. There are two ways in which the EHV model can help to achieve this:

1. The first is by integrating the values and the teaching methodologies into existing curricula. This can be done by the careful selection of appropriate examples and recognition of 'teaching opportunities' to promote values education without needing to make any changes to the syllabus. (See Chapters 9 and 10 for more details.)
2. The second way in which the EHV model can be incorporated into existing classroom practices is by addressing contemporary problems that exist in

schools, such as discipline problems, pupils refusing to work, bullying, and lack of respect for authority. The EHV programme empowers teachers to examine themselves and to think about how they might be able to reflect the major human values in their own behaviour, particularly their interactions with students and colleagues. In so doing, they can enhance their own mental health and wellbeing, their resilience to cope with the stresses of teaching, and to improve the ways in which their pupils respond to them.

1.9 Educare

Educare is the term used to exemplify the philosophy of education that underpins EHV. The word itself is a Latin term that is the root of our word *education* and means 'to lead out'. It is concerned with bringing out the values and spirituality that are inherent within the individual's higher levels of consciousness.

The following statement, based on the teachings of the founder of EHV, Sathya Sai Baba, outlines the essence of *Educare*:

> ***Educare*** *is not the learning from books by rote, to be vomited in the examination halls. But it is the learning from life, which is absorbed into living and transforming. This gives a new meaning to dull mathematics and geography, a new vitality to language, cosmic understanding to science and an enhanced beauty to music and art. It is not to be stuffed from without into the ears of innocent children. Rather it comes from within. It is the release of the inherent intuition ..., which is within every individual. ... Educare is also the art of ensuring a perfect constant balance of the five elements within, by managing the mind and the inputs from the five senses.... In other words, a harmony between thought, word and deed has to be achieved .... Educare is when we have sensitized ourselves, when we sensitize our children to begin to respond and become caring people.*[32]

When properly applying the principles of ***Educare,*** the pupils:

- are encouraged to appreciate the five basic human values of Truth, Right Action, Peace, Love, and Non-violence as essential to the development of character
- learn about the cultures and customs of other people along with their own, in order to appreciate the unity of all humans
- acquire decision-making skills, which help to facilitate the development of moral actions
- develop a sense of responsibility for the consequences of their actions, their duties to others, and to act with regard for the rights, life, and dignity of all
- develop self-discipline and self-confidence as necessary to promote the fulfilment of their potential, this being achieved by enhancing their moral, physical, social, spiritual, and academic achievements

- develop the value skills needed for personal, family, community, national, and world harmony
- develop caring attitudes towards all forms of life and to value the need for preservation, conservation, and general care of the environment

To bring out these qualities, teachers need to regularly examine all of their activities and interactions with their pupils by reflecting on the questions:

- Does this go to the child's heart?
- Does this have practical application?
- Does this help the child transform?

In conclusion, the ideals of EHV and *Educare* can be summarised as follows:

> *Does **Educare** entail a new curriculum or a new course content? Once again, the answer is 'No'. The answer lies in our implementing this philosophy in our lives. Am I able to control my desires? Am I conscious of the inputs of the five senses in my mind? Am I able to turn my mind inside in reflection? Am I able to experience the power of love within? These are the questions that all of us have to ask. Because we are not communicating knowledge, we are not communicating words, what we are really communicating is experience.*[33]

The students are taught two important life messages. One is that whatever thoughts come into their heads, they think about and examine them in their 'hearts' (the conscience) before they act. This is referred to as ***3HV***, the harmony of the three Hs, ***head***, ***heart***, and ***hands***.

The other life message taught is *concentration and inner stillness*. The main ingredient for this is Love, and through Love students are helped to become self-reliant, self-confident, and self-sacrificing.

It is not easy to measure all the outcomes of EHV quantitatively because the transformations that come about in children are often very subtle and qualitative, and quite often do not emerge fully until they have left school and entered into adult life. Even as adults, like the rest of us, they will still make mistakes, but the big gift given to students by *Educare* is that they can pick themselves up from their mistakes and move on. As Sathya Sai Baba said:

> *The character of the children must be made strong and pure. Give them all the confidence they need to become good, honest, and self-reliant children. It is not enough if they learn something by which they can make a living. The manner of living is more important than the standard of living. The children must also have reverence for spirituality, their culture, their educational attainments, and their country. They must learn well their mother tongue, so they can appreciate well the great poetical works and epics written by the seers of their land. This will give them valuable guidance in the stormy days ahead.*[34]

Notes

1 https://public.oed.com/blog/june-2014-update-new-words-notes/ accessed 1-7-2021.
2 Erle C. Ellis, *Anthropocene: A Very Short Introduction (Very Short Introductions)* (Oxford, UK: Oxford University Press, 2018).
3 An '*isochronous*' marker represents a *chronostratigraphic* unit (the age of rock strata in relation to time) that can be identified at multiple sites around the world at the same time, rather than a '*diachronous*' unit varying in age from place to place.
4 An Anthropogenic soil is a soil which has been profoundly modified or constructed by humans.
5 Ellis, *Anthropocene,* 2018.
6 *Niche*: A habitat supplying the factors necessary for the existence of an organism or species.
7 Ellis, *Anthropocene,* 2018.
8 *Ibid.*
9 Will Steffen, Wendy Broadgate, Lisa Deutsch, Owen Gaffney, and Cornelia Ludwig, "The Trajectory of the Anthropocene: The Great Acceleration," *The Anthropocene Review* 2, no. 1 (2015): 81–98.
10 Will Steffen, Katherine Richardson, Johan Rockström, Sarah E. Cornell, Ingo Fetzer, Elena M. Bennett, Reinette Biggs, Stephen R. Carpenter, Wim de Vries, Cynthia A. de Wit, Carl Folke, Dieter Gerten, Jens Heinke, Georgina M. Mace, Linn M. Persson, Veerabhadran Ramanathan, Belinda Reyers, and Sverker Sörlin, "Planetary Boundaries: Guiding Human Development on a Changing Planet," *Science 13* 347, no. 6223 (2015): 1259855.
11 National Academy of Sciences, *The Challenge of Feeding the World Sustainably: Summary of the US-UK Scientific Forum on Sustainable Agriculture* (Washington, DC: The National Academies Press, 2021).
12 Ellis, *Anthropocene,* 2018.
13 A wicked problem is a problem that is difficult or impossible to solve because of incomplete, contradictory, and changing requirements that are often difficult to recognise.
14 http://environment.gov.au/protection/ozone/montreal-protocol accessed 1-7-2021.
15 Rutger Bregman, *Humankind: A Hopeful History* (London, UK: Bloomsbury Publishing, 2020).
16 *Ibid.*
17 *Ibid.*
18 https://en.wikipedia.org/wiki/Two_Wolves#:~:text=The%20story%20of%20the%20Two%20Wolves%20is%20a,a%20metaphor%20of%20two%20wolves%20fighting%20within%20him accessed 1-7-2021.
19 https://www.mondragon-corporation.com/en/about-us/ accessed 27-7-2021.
20 Cathy McGowan, *Cathy Goes to Canberra: Doing Politics Differently* (Australia: Monash University Press, 2020). Also, the Podcast *Doing Politics Differently – Unleashing the Power of the Community* https://cidsel.podbean.com/e/doing-politics-differently-unleashing-the-power-of-the-community/ accessed 20-7-2021.
21 http://www.curriculum.edu.au/values/val_vasp_final_report,30121.html accessed 1-7-2021.
22 http://www.curriculum.edu.au/verve/_resources/National_Declaration_on_the_Educational_Goals_for_Young_Australians.pdf accessed 1-7-2021.
23 http://www.curriculum.edu.au/values/ accessed 1-7-2021.
24 https://www.un.org/millenniumgoals/ accessed 1-7-2021.

25 https://unhabitat.org/sites/default/files/download-manager-files/Facilitators%20and%20Trainers%20Guidebook%20on%20Human%20Values-based%20Water,%20Sanitation%20and%20Hygiene%20Classrooms.pdf accessed 1-7-2021.
26 http://www.marvi.org.in/ accessed 1-7-2021.
27 There are three main domains of learning, and all teachers would know about them and use them to construct lessons. These domains of learning are the ***cognitive*** (thinking), the ***affective*** (social/emotional/feeling), and the ***psychomotor*** (physical/kinaesthetic) domain.
28 A. Jumsai Na Ayudhya, *The Five Human Values and Human Excellence* (Bangkok: International Institute of Sathya Sai Education, 1997).
29 *Ibid.*
30 For more in-depth examples of silent sitting, see: https://issea.org.au/wp-content/uploads/2020/08/Silent-Sitting-comp.pdf accessed 29-12-2022.
31 A. Schoenfeld, "Metacognitive and Epistemological Issues in Mathematical Understanding," in *Teaching and Learning Mathematical Problem Solving: Multiple Research Perspectives,* ed. E. A. Silver (Hillsdale, NJ: 1985), 361–379; Lawrence Erlbaum, and National Council of Teachers of Mathematics (NCTM), *Curriculum and Evaluation Standards for School Mathematics* (Reston, Virginia: NCTM, 1989), and E. Von Glaserfeld, *Radical Constructivism in Mathematics Education* (Netherlands: Kluwer, 1991).
32 V. Srinivasan, *Inaugural Address 1, Sri Sathya Sai Educare.* In: Proceedings of the International Convention of Sri Sathya Sai Bal Vikas Gurus 2–4 July, 2001, Prasanthi Nilayam, India. Page 5. https://www.sathyasai.org/education/reports/reporteducare.pdf accessed 20-7-2021.
33 N. Pandya, *Five Elements of Nature, Five Human Resources and Five Human Values.* In: Proceedings of the International Convention of Sri Sathya Sai Bal Vikas Gurus 2–4 July, 2001, Prasanthi Nilayam, India. Page 23. https://www.sathyasai.org/education/reports/reporteducare.pdf accessed 20-7-2021.
34 Sathya Sai Baba, *Sathya Sai Speaks* (Prasanthi Nilayam, India: Sri Sathya Sai Sadhana Trust, July 22, 1994), Vol. 27 (21).

Chapter 2

Rediscovering and Promoting Values through EHV

Roger Packham and Margaret Taplin

One of the goals of this book is to help teachers to understand better what values education is, how to incorporate it into their teaching, and the benefits to be gained from doing this. To this end, this chapter begins with a specific example, from within the Australian education system, of some extensive research into the practice and use of values education.

2.1 The Australian Perspective

It is the policy of the Australian Federal Government[1] to have all schools (public and private) introduce comprehensive values education programmes. In Australia, the various state governments (rather than the federal government) have responsibility for implementing education and educational policies, but again, each state education system has values education as a mandated part of the curriculum. Values education is seen as a principle of curriculum organisation, with values shaping the whole schooling experience, including planning, managing, and organising the total school curriculum, the teaching and learning opportunities, and especially relationships between and within staff, parents, and students (see Chapter 13 for more on this). For Education in Human Values (EHV) as for much of values education, the heart of the approach is wellbeing, achieved through the holistic education of the student: This encompasses *intellectual*, *physical*, *emotional*, *social*, and *spiritual* wellbeing;[2] it also needs to be noted that often it is only religious schools that include the spiritual in this grouping, yet it is important for all students, secular or religious. The issue seems to centre on how spirituality is viewed in a secular situation, so a clarification of what is meant by this and each of the other four aspects of education for wellbeing is presented in Box 2.1.

From this it can be seen that the spiritual dimension is important for all schools, and while all five are seen to be closely intertwined, EHV very much includes spiritual wellbeing.[3]

To improve the understanding of values education, and to support its implementation, the Australian Federal Government *Values Education Project*[4]

DOI: 10.4324/9781003478607-3

Box 2.1: The Dimensions of Wellbeing for EHV

Intellectual Dimension

Intellectual wellness encourages creative, stimulating mental activities. The mind needs to be continually inspired and exercised, just as the body does. People who possess a high level of intellectual wellness have active minds and continue to learn. Intellectually, well people use the resources available to expand their knowledge and improve their skills.

Physical Dimension

Physical wellness encompasses a variety of healthy behaviours, including adequate exercise, proper nutrition, and abstaining from harmful habits such as drug use and alcohol abuse. Developing such healthy habits will not only add years to a lifespan but also enhance the enjoyment and quality of those years.

Emotional Dimension

Emotional wellness is a dynamic state that fluctuates frequently with other dimensions of wellness. Being emotionally well is typically defined as possessing the ability to feel and express human emotions such as happiness, sadness, and anger in appropriate ways. It means having the ability to love and be loved and achieving a sense of fulfilment in life. Emotional wellness encompasses optimism, self-esteem, self-acceptance, and the ability to share feelings.

Social Dimension

Social wellness refers to the ability to interact successfully in the global community and to live up to the expectations and demands of personal roles. This means learning good communication skills, developing intimacy with others, and creating a support network of friends and family members. Social wellness includes showing respect for others and oneself and contributing to the local community and to the world.

Spiritual Dimension

Spiritual wellness involves a set of guiding beliefs, principles, or values that help give direction to a life. It encompasses a high level of faith, hope, and commitment to individual beliefs that provide a sense of meaning.

was initiated and ran from 2003 to 2011. It involved qualitative and quantitative research about values education, with the first step of the project in 2003 involving 50 schools. This provided an evidence base for the *National Framework for Values Education in Australian Schools*;[5] it was emphasised that this was a 'framework' not a 'cage' and was made up of a set of nine core values so that within this framework a school could develop its own particular values set. In 2004, the project was further funded with a $30 million budget allocation to build a 'National Values Education programme' that was guided by the earlier framework. Many useful and evidence-based findings emerged; for example, some interesting outcomes relating to learning were:

- Effective learning is as much about *affect* and *social dynamics* as about *cognition*.
- Learning needs to include communicative competence, empathetic character development, self-reflection, and self-knowing. These are all just as central to intellectual development as the recall of facts and figures.
- Values education is not a moral imperative, but it is of pedagogical importance.
- Academic success is a by-product of a whole-person approach to learning (see the five dimensions in Box 2.1).
- A cognitive/affective/sociality nexus is needed to engage the whole person, not just the cognitive person.
- This is why trust, care, and positive relationships have such an impact on learning in general.
- Learning requires a trustful supportive ambience concerning the ethics and aesthetics of relationships, particularly with the teacher(s).
- There needs to be an explicit discussion about values in ways that draw on students' deeper learning and reflections.
- Values education transforms patterns of feelings, behaviour, resilience, and academic diligence of students.

Subsequent chapters of this book explore the implementations of many of these insights in the specific context of the values education programme that is the focus of this book, EHV (Education in Human Values). However, in this chapter, the focus is on a feature of the research[6] that refers to quality teaching as being composed of the following three elements:

1. ***Quality of the teaching*** – seen as intellectual depth, communicative competence, capacity for reflection, empathetic character, self-management, and self-knowledge.
2. ***Values education*** – including strong positive relationships, positive dispositions to learning (learning to love learning), emotional and spiritual space, and a calm teaching and learning environment.

3. ***Service learning*** – achieved by crafting ways of teaching that practise the values, as well as learning about the values that the school community has agreed upon.

All three of these were supported by the following three *pillars*:

- Neuroscience research
- Social and emotional learning (SEL)
- Positive educational practices

The researchers noted that:

> *As schools give increasing curriculum and teaching emphasis to values education, students become more academically diligent, the school assumes a calmer more peaceful ambience, better student-teacher relationships are forged, student and teacher wellbeing improves and parents are more engaged with the school…Rather it seems clear that the fit between values education and quality teaching is better described not as one having an impact on the other, but rather as the two of them being in harmony.*[7]

The report on the project concluded that:

> *Teachers need to imbue their various scaffolds*[8] *with the school's core values, whether that be through the subjects they teach, other school-wide instructional techniques or other dimensions of the school's infrastructure of policy, practice and relationships.*

For EHV, the core values framework are Love, Truth, Peace, Right Action, and Non-violence, as will be discussed more fully in subsequent chapters, particularly in Chapter 4. EHV was introduced in Chapter 1, and here it needs to be emphasised that EHV goes further than the Australian values education project by the overt inclusion of the physical and spiritual dimensions of wellbeing as being critically intertwined with the cognitive, emotional, and social dimensions. There is also a focus in EHV on the link between the metaphorical *Head*, *Hand*, and *Heart*, in other words actions (hand) follow from thinking and planning (head), and these actions reflect the values and spiritual commitments (heart) of the person acting.

At this point, readers might like to think about the 'scaffolds' used in their own teaching or parenting practice to imbue the students with their school's or their personal core values. Take a few moments to jot down your ideas.

Before looking deeper into the three pillars supporting values education, the chapter will next look pragmatically at some ways to better understand the *mind* since, as all teachers know, it is the mind that must be developed and transformed through education. Presented here are two approaches that have been used to help understand both how the mind works and the role of values education to transform it in beneficial ways. Following this, more recent research findings will be outlined to help in the understanding of the mind from a learning perspective. The chapter will then return to examining more closely the three pillars identified in the Values Education Research Project.

2.2 The Human Mind

The mind is the driving force in unfolding reality; we are always using our minds at every moment of life. Understanding how the mind works can result in better relationships, improved work, and health, and can assist in the improvement of all aspects of life. Above all, it can help a teacher or parent to better understand what they are doing in teaching and guiding others. This is demonstrated in the following two models.

2.2.1 *Thurman Fleet Model*[9]

Dr Thurman Fleet described how the body takes actions to get results, yet the body is influenced heavily by the mind. The subconscious and conscious minds work together as a team; key relevant neuroscience aspects of this are explained later in this chapter. The conscious mind considers relevant information, holds one thought at a time, makes decisions, and generates awareness. The subconscious mind runs on autopilot, has no filters, and is where beliefs, feelings, and memories are stored. It magnifies dominant thoughts and has the greatest influence on our actions. The subconscious mind interprets thoughts literally and responds with actions. The subconscious mind is like a watchman, only letting things into the mind that it is authorised to allow, while the conscious mind lets the subconscious mind know what is wanted by overriding thoughts when required. The subconscious mind takes our thoughts and feelings and finds a way to put them into action. You must be careful what you wish for, since if you are not specific enough, the subconscious mind will give you what you want but not necessarily *exactly* what you are looking for!

People receive information from their environment, whether it be from their friends, family, authority figures, or the media. When they take ideas from the environment, they develop beliefs. These learned beliefs go into the subconscious mind and then beliefs become habits. For example, if your friend told you that Nancy was very friendly and popular, and you take this opinion as truth, it will go into your subconscious mind. When you meet Nancy, you will act according to your learned belief: You might be gracious, feel very good, and overall be happy when around her. The same relates to being surrounded by peaceful people, peaceful stimuli, and a loving environment versus being surrounded by negativity, anger, and violence: This will go to your subconscious mind if you accept it as truth. Psychology has long established the connection between beliefs and actions, showing that beliefs form our habits, and we act accordingly. If there is a belief different from the one we have internalised, we create internal conflict and may reject that belief even if the truth is right in front of us. Unless we bring our beliefs to consciousness, our subconscious mind will run the show. Thus, when we accept opinions and influences from our surroundings, they will impact the way we live our lives.

Experiences and responses of past behaviour are also stored in the subconscious, even if they are contradictory and inconsistent. This aspect of the mind can be seen as a servomechanism[10] that is good at discrimination and lets in only what is consistent with what is already stored there, like the watchman at a gate. Because of contrary experiences in the stored 'files' of memories and experiences, behavioural responses will also be inconsistent. For example, if a child is told to be 'seen and not heard' and has been reprimanded in the past for responding to questions from visitors, he or she will not respond when asked questions by someone new, even if told it is 'OK to talk freely'. Figure 2.1 illustrates the above ideas.

The Thurman Fleet model helps to understand the functioning of the mind, how control can be gained, and how the stored 'files' of past behaviour can be changed for the better. To gain such control, inputs from the five senses also need to be controlled, something that can be described as 'Ceiling on Desires' (see Chapter 12). In addition, the practising of desirable values diminishes the inappropriate behaviours stimulated by the mind. Getting past

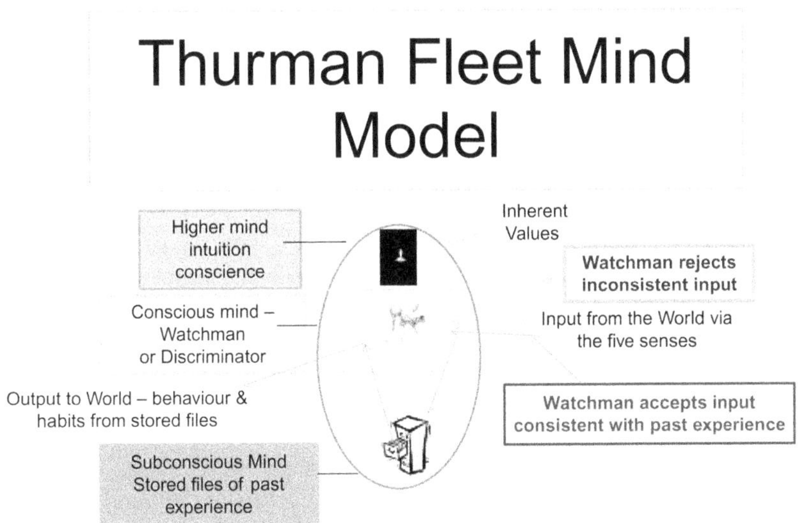

Figure 2.1 The Thurman Fleet Mind Model[11]

the mind's 'watchman', that is improving the mind by practising mindful discrimination, involves a number of alternatives described here with metaphorical illustrations:

- Rushing in and pushing the watchman aside through a strong emotional experience. This could be an epiphanous moment or a traumatic experience.
- Learning ways of disguising the values (from the watchman) via a process acceptable to the watchman, for example, by embedding the values in an activity children enjoy doing, such as storytelling or singing.
- Wearing the watchman down, for example, by consistent and constant repetition of particular values messages, for example, direct and indirect teaching approaches, as described in Chapters 8, 9, and 10.

Through these processes, teachers can modify the 'files' of past poor behavioural responses and replace them with values-based conduct. (Examples can be found in Chapter 11 on Positive Psychology.)

2.2.2 *Jumsai Model*[12]

The second model is one developed in his doctoral dissertation[13] by Art-Ong Jumsai Na Ayudhya (Jumsai), a Thai scientist, parliamentarian, and EHV teacher and trainer, explicitly to help teachers understand and practise values education. In his description of the essence of the EHV model, Jumsai described that, through the five senses, the mind receives and processes information from the environment in order to create awareness and understanding. With his model of the mind, Junmai differs from that of Thurman Fleet, by including an extra level, the super-conscious, the source of inspiration and intuition.

These ideas were later developed into the model of Figure 2.2 to illustrate the learning process and the role of human values in learning and actions.

The subconscious stores the memories of everything that is experienced and feeds these memories to the conscious mind if a decision needs to be taken when automatic responses are insufficient to deal with a particular situation. The conscious mind then controls the individual's thoughts and actions and will also enable the colouring of perceptions of events that happen. The superconscious mind is the source of wisdom, knowledge, conscience, and 'higher' consciousness. In a holistically balanced person, these three levels of the mind interact to contribute to the physical, cognitive, emotional, social, and spiritual wellbeing of the individual.

Jumsai proposed that there are two important ingredients for this healthy interaction to occur. The first is to free the three levels of the mind from extraneous 'chatter', to allow enhanced concentration and memory, and to enable the conscious mind to retrieve deeper levels of thinking and problem-solving. The second is to ensure that the information that then becomes stored in the

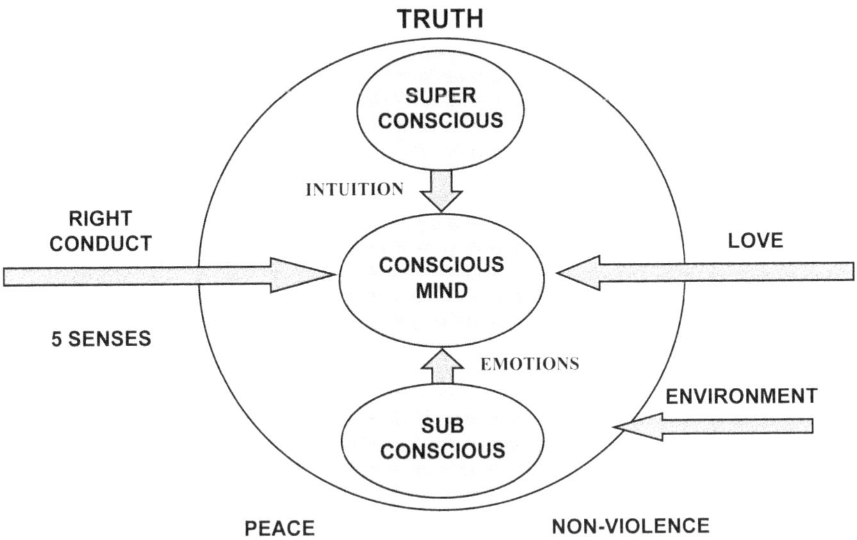

Figure 2.2 Model of the Human Values Integrated Learning Concept[14]

various parts of the mind is positive, healthy, and constructive since its retrieval will have such a significant effect on the individual's thoughts, feelings, and actions. These, in turn, contribute to the presence or absence of holistic wellbeing – this concept is expanded in Chapter 11, which deals with the role of positive psychology in education.

The EHV model is a simple but effective means of ensuring that these two essential ingredients occur. It promotes five human values, Truth, Right Action, Peace, Love, and Non-violence (that are discussed more fully in Chapter 4). The ultimate goal is to develop the 'whole' student, not only the cognitive and physical aspects.

As summarised by Jumsai:

> *Stimuli are received through the five senses. The stimuli have to be interpreted into something meaningful. This is done by retrieving data from the subconscious mind which contains past experiences and memory. The conscious mind then becomes aware and understands the stimuli received. This awareness and understanding is then stored in the subconscious mind and reinforces the memory. In education, the Human Values Integrated Instruction is applied. This requires involvement of friends, teachers, parents, and the community as well as the creation of an atmosphere of peace and love in the school. Human values are an integral part of all subjects and all activities in the school. Thus, not only subject matter but also human values are stored in the subconscious mind. This will influence future interpretation of outside stimuli received.*

2.2.3 *Recent Findings from Cognitive Science*

There has been a great deal of psychology and neuroscience research into the mind in recent times. These findings[15] now enable further insights into the human mind and how it operates beyond the above two models drawn from earlier research, intuition, and experience that allowed for the development of the earlier models.

Dr Mark Solms[16] and Dr Antonio Damasio[17] have studied brain structure and identified a small piece of brain tissue which is our emotional centre – this is basically what controls our emotional behaviour. From this, it can be seen how values work – they are emotional responses to our daily situations and experiences. Jumsai's model shown in the previous Section 2.2.2 has the five values with arrows pointing in. What can be said now is how these actually function and influence/are influenced by the mind.

A key feature of any living organism is its ability to respond to changes in its environment in ways that enhance its survival, and learning, and education can also be understood from this perspective. For all multicellular organisms, and more particularly for humans, this ability is described as *homeostasis* – the maintenance of a stable internal environment in the face of a changing external environment. Homeostasis consists of concrete physical and chemical constraints applied to the life processes such that these processes operate within certain parameters. These homeostatic constraints and processes have been developed by the organism through trial and error to select naturally available behavioural solutions to a number of problems of life management; hence, some understanding is useful to recognise how learning occurs. Both cooperation and competition help to select the organisms that exhibit the most productive strategies, but in addition, humans can think and feel through life processes in their minds, both subconsciously and consciously, and can, to some extent, deliberately select the approach to deploy to respond to environmental changes. Humans can also learn how to respond better in the light of experience, including several behavioural emotions of benefit, such as altruism, passion, admiration, awe, and gratitude. These can be taught in families and schools as a deliberate human strategy. Additionally, they can be encouraged, trained, and practised in an individual's society. Education, in the broadest sense of the term, achieves this through the creation of healthy and socially productive environments that give prominence to ethical and civic behaviours, and encourage moral virtues such as honesty, kindness, empathy, compassion, and gratitude, as well as the EHV human values of Love, Truth, Peace, Right Action, and Non-violence.

The human condition encompasses two worlds. One is made up of the nature-given rules of life regulation and homeostasis that are regulated through pain and pleasure. Humans are not conscious of the rules concerned here and are only conscious of the 'pain' or 'pleasure' outcomes. Humans have nothing to do with the way natural selection has operated for aeons to build the apparatus of affect that largely governs our social and individual lives through the limitation of pain and the enhancement of pleasure. However, we can use the human mind to reflect on knowledge, think it through, manipulate it intelligently, and invent all sorts of responses to nature's rules. Damasio[18] sees culture and civilisation as the results of these efforts. We can direct and deliberately counter our genetic mandate when we refuse to act on our desires for food or sex or resist the impulse to punish another, or when we follow an idea that runs counter to a natural tendency such as depleting natural resources, as is occurring in the Anthropocene described in Chapter 1. Also required to achieve this resistance to natural impulses is a set of goals capable of transcending immediate homeostatic needs to both inspire and elevate the mind as it projects into the future (see Chapters 5 and 12).

The human mind has two systems[19] for responding to environmental change. ***System one*** operates automatically and quickly, with little or no effort and no sense of voluntary control.

System two requires mental effort for activities that include complex computation and consciousness. The operations of System two are often associated with the subjective experience of agency,[20] choice and concentration. A key function of System two is to monitor and control the thoughts and actions of System one, suppressing or modifying some while allowing most to be expressed directly in behaviours, habits, and reflexes.

System one is impulsive and intuitive, while System two is capable of reasoning and is cautious and only comes into play due to particular triggers: It is looking for anything new going on, or a threat or other stimuli that attract attention. Such assessments are carried out automatically and unconsciously, with System two determining whether extra effort is required since the aim is to minimise the expenditure of energy by the mind to reduce the need for additional food. Too much effort from System two can also lead to *cognitive strain*, which reduces the effectiveness and abilities of this system. Teachers and parents are intuitively aware of this if they try to 'push' learners too much.

Another function of *System* one is to maintain and update a model of a *personal world* – the body and its context, which represents what is normal in the environment, that world around the individual. The model is constructed by associations that link ideas and memories of circumstances, events, actions, and outcomes that occur with some regularity, either at the same time or within a relatively short interval. As these links are formed and strengthened, the pattern of associated ideas comes to represent the structure of events in that person's life, and it determines their interpretation of the present as well as their expectations of the future. This is an important consideration for values education, as it now becomes apparent that developing these patterns in the most beneficial way is an important aspect of education and a key concern of EHV. System one generates impressions, feelings, and inclinations that, when endorsed by System two, become beliefs, attitudes, and intentions, all expressed as reflexes, habits, and behaviours. Thus, EHV will develop the beliefs, attitudes, and behaviours beneficial to the individual and society.

Skilled intuitions arising from the super-conscious are used by System one after adequate training, thereby creating a coherent pattern of activated ideas in associative memory, linking a sense of cognitive ease to impressions of truth, pleasant feelings, and reduced vigilance. However, System one neglects ambiguity and suppresses doubt and can substitute and respond to an easier question rather than a difficult one that the mind then overlooks at its peril. System one is not very sensitive to *quantity* and responds more strongly to losses than to gains; hence, most people have an aversion to loss, such that problems requiring decisions are framed narrowly and in isolation from other problems. This again emphasises the importance of establishing beneficial habits and responses to common situations within System one as early as possible in the growing child.

Intelligence is not just only the ability to reason but also the ability to find relevant material in the mind's memory, and to deploy the mind's attention when needed, rather than just leaving things to the automatic responses of System one. In this sense, intelligence becomes a form of engagement where the learner is more alert, more intellectually active, less willing to be satisfied with superficially attractive answers, and more sceptical about their intuitions. Training to pay appropriate attention, rather than simply letting things happen automatically, can improve executive control in the mind and thus intelligence.

2.2.3.1 *The Role of Consciousness*

An interesting question to ask is why the conscious, subjective aspects of System two arose at all, rather than allowing everything to happen purely subconsciously[21] and automatically. The answer requires a deeper understanding of the mind and how it functions. A purely functionalist view of consciousness can explain the anatomy and physiology of the brain, but not how *qualia*,[22] such as experiences of redness or of beauty, arise in the mind. Perception and learning can go on without conscious awareness; indeed, they do so for more than 90% of cognition. Recent research[23,24] has proposed that consciousness is a way to improve homeostatic responses to environmental change. Conscious awareness is *feeling*, and feelings arise *within* the body, so conscious awareness gives more options to adjust homeostasis, to keep it within its dynamic limits, it is monitoring the body. In this way, conscious awareness gives a competitive advantage in evolutionary terms. Feelings only arise in the body when automatic responses do not have the desired effects on homeostatic deviations and are thus a way of monitoring the *internal* environment of the body and its needs; in the same way, as the five senses – sight, smell, sound, taste, and touch – monitor the external environment. It is a kind of sixth sense, where *affect*, or feeling, enables the body to become aware of itself. For those who would like to read more, please refer to Appendix 2.1.

Now we can see the key role of values in all of this, most importantly the development of unconscious automatic responses to the environment that are referred to elsewhere in this book as *habits* that need to be developed so that virtuous actions predominantly occur. The earlier this starts the better, as the child's brain is developing these habitual responses that go beyond the innate drives. Equally, values need to be a key part of the choice-making process in consciousness when automatic responses are not functioning well (System two), so that resulting actions can develop new habits to be built into the long-term memory and better enable the learning of improved automatic responses.

Memory is the ability to take in information, encode it, store it, and retrieve it at a later time. The three main forms of memory storage are sensory memory, short-term memory, and long-term memory. Sensory memory is all within the subconscious and allows for the retention of impressions of sensory information – smell, sight, sound, taste, and hearing. This is how such senses as a smell or a sound can trigger 'flashbacks'. Short-term memory, unlike the other two stores, lasts for a very brief time, and can only hold 7 ± 2 pieces of information at once. It is one role of the EHV method of 'silent sitting' (see Chapter 8) at the start of a lesson to help to clear this memory and make it ready for the lesson that will unfold. Long-term memory storage, like sensory memory storage, can last for very long periods of time. Explicit and implicit memories are two different types of long-term memory; *implicit* memories are of sensory and automatised behaviours, while *explicit* memories are of information, episodes, or events. Sensory memory is not involved in higher cognitive functions like short- and long-term memory are, but relevant pieces of information can be extracted from sensory memory by short-term memory and processed by *working* memory.

Working memory is the term psychologists use for the 'processing space' in the mind/brain when a person computes information. Working memory is the processing space between the memory storage areas of sensory/short-term and long-term memory. It constructs meaning from inputs from sensory and short-term memory, thereby influencing what can be stored in long-term memory. However, it has limited capacity that can vary from person to person, thereby affecting learning ability. The capacity of working memory also increases with age up to adolescence and can be increased through increased efficiencies in the strategies used to compute information, thereby increasing learning capacity.

The following Box 2.2 and Figure 2.3 present a summary of this section. Box 2.2 summarises the potential links of EHV to this mind/body model, while Figure 2.3 illustrates all the ideas in a single model that is relevant to learning and values education.

Box 2.2: How EHV Can Influence the Mind/Body Model

1. The super-conscious is the source of intuition and our conscience; it is attested by many[25] that to 'seek inside' ourselves gives answers to important issues, to concerns, and to dilemmas, including moral dilemmas; this is what turning to the super-conscious represents.
2. It is the belief of EHV that Love resides in and comes from the super-conscious, and as Love is the basis of all five values, they are inherent in all humans.
3. The values influence what we sense through our five senses, and hence what the body/mind responds to. Practising values helps us to respond better to our environment.
4. Feelings arise in the body and keep the mind informed about the state of the body. Feelings arise in response to a change from what is innately determined as 'normal'. When triggered, these feelings give rise to emotional responses which are generally automatic, arising from *System one*. The body learns from the behavioural responses these emotions trigger, and if continued, the responses become habits. By understanding and practising values, the mind can learn to override what it detects as inappropriate responses by triggering *System two*, thereby developing improved habits.
5. It is these learned and improved responses that then become more useful habits.
6. By monitoring the behavioural responses to both sensory and feeling inputs, the mind can improve its 'model of context and body' to help establish better responses to inputs.
7. These monitoring and response effects are also stored in memory, again affecting how the mind responds to inputs.
8. By 'stilling' the mind through techniques like *silent sitting* and meditation, the mind becomes calmer and better able to react by not responding too quickly, and considering all options based on the *model of context and body*, memories of past events and associated responses, and considering the option from potential effects from different responses.
9. A calm mind can also learn better through the evaluation of options and the use of all aspects of the mind.
10. A key aspect of the mind is to have time to incorporate its learned values into automatic and learned responses.
11. The more our sensory and long-term memories are loaded with values-based memories, the better our automatic and thoughtful responses will be.
12. Short-term memory can be cleared through the EHV method of *silent sitting*, and thus made ready for new learning.

13. Using visualisation can draw on and add to sensory and long-term memory.
14. By the regular practice of values and learning from thoughtful responses, improved habits and reflexes are developed in association with the monitoring of responses, better models of context and body, and appropriate memory selection; then quick, automatic responses based on values are forthcoming.

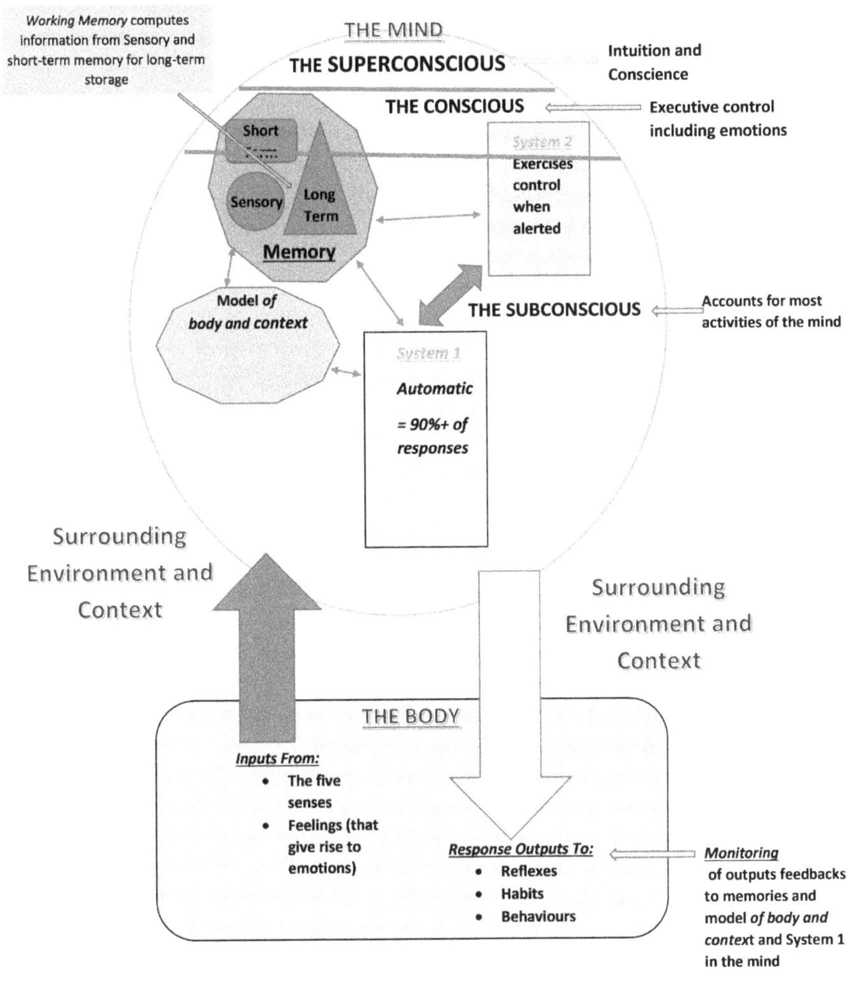

Figure 2.3 A Model Depicting Key Aspects of the Mind from a Learning and EHV Perspective

The chapter will now return to the outcomes of the values education research described earlier that proposed the 'three pillars' that underpin quality teaching – neuroscience research, social-emotional learning, and positive educational practices. Each of these will now be looked at in more depth.

2.3 Neuroscience Research Supporting Values Education and Student Wellbeing

Learning, as discussed in Section 2.2.3, is an interaction between the individual, the environment, and his/her abilities that is a combination of environmental and genetic constraints and possibilities. Learning can depend, therefore, on the type of learning experiences provided and the social-emotional ambience fostered.

Therefore, effective values education is contingent on the dynamic interaction of the cognitive, affective, social, physical, and spiritual dimensions of the teaching/learning environment. The other chapters of this book elaborate on how to do this, using EHV while there are also published papers demonstrating EHV in practice, for example, with 62 schools in five provinces of China over a ten-year period.[26]

Neuroscience has given substance to this nexus of interacting dimensions that most teachers are aware of from practice, but unfortunately many 'urban myths' surround the topic of neuroscience.

In one research project,[27] teachers from different countries around the world were asked to answer which of the following questions were *true* or *false*. Please pause here for a moment and consider your own responses. Do you answer 'yes' or 'no' to each question?

1. We mostly use only 10% of our brains.
2. Individuals learn better when they receive information in their preferred learning styles, e.g., visual, auditory, or kinesthetic.
3. Short bouts of coordination exercises can improve integration of the left and right hemispheric brain functions.
4. Differences in hemispheric dominance (left and right brain) can help to explain individual differences amongst learners.
5. Children are less attentive after sugary drinks and snacks.
6. Drinking less than six to eight glasses of water a day can cause the brain to shrink.
7. Learning problems associated with developmental differences in brain function cannot be remediated by education.

Responses from teachers in the different countries revealed that, for the first five questions, between 44–93% of teachers thought they were *true*, and even for the last two questions the range was from 5–50% believing them to be *true*. The countries included the United Kingdom, the Netherlands, Turkey, Greece, and China, thereby eliminating some potential anomalies due to ethnicity or geography. So how did your responses compare to these?

Unfortunately, *all* are *false* – they are *neuromyths*. Two other common beliefs are that 'there is a difference between male and female brains, 'Mars and Venus', and the concept of 'unconscious learning', but again both are not supported by research findings. In contrast, neuroscience *has* shown the following to be true about brain function:

- It is improved by physical exercise
- It improves with use
- It requires adequate sleep for creativity, memory, and the acquisition of skills
- A short sleep after learning improves performance
- Learning causes structural changes in the brain via synaptic interconnections of the neurons
- The development of brain function is not a series of steps like a ladder, but rather an interactive web of multiple strands that is supported by practice

All of these points have been taken into account where possible in the processes of EHV, although some are dependent on the individual teacher's class management. How EHV incorporates these will become clearer in later chapters, particularly Chapters 8, 9, and 10 for EHV teaching techniques, and Chapters 3 and 5 for other aspects. EHV methods support the need for a holistic approach to learning that covers all five dimensions of cognitive, physical, emotional, social, and spiritual.

Neuroscience has particularly illuminated teenage development, showing that as children move into their teenage years, there is improved information processing, improved executive functioning, long-term planning becomes available, metacognition commences, self-evaluation and self-regulation can be improved, and the coordination of affect and cognition can be seen (see below). However, teenagers take increased risks due to the different rates of development of the *limbic* system, the areas of the brain associated with *affect*, together with the developing pre-frontal cortex (associated with cognition), which controls the emotional impulses. Adolescents reach adult functioning of cognitive abilities around age 16, but psycho-social maturity is between ages 26 and 30. Thus, the educational focus needs to include the strengthening of internal controls, such as by self-paced learning, the critical evaluation of transmitted knowledge, meta-study skills, and a supportive learning environment, all features of the EHV process. Empathy and compassion are refined at this time, as are the related behavioural choices enhancing the five human values of Truth, Right Action, Peace, Love and Non-violence through explicit discussion. Methods that help achieve this are described in subsequent chapters of this book.

2.3.1 Memory, Emotion, and Cognition

Learning is the process by which new information about the world is acquired. Memory is the process by which this information can persist over time. The two are interlinked, as has been discussed above in relation to the mind. The more synaptic connections between the brain neurons that are formed, the more stable the memory becomes. For education, this is encouraged by engaging multiple senses, and across curriculum areas, as well as by students personalising the learning, e.g., by linking to material already learned and by the students using it in practice, what is termed *experiential learning*.

Emotion and cognition are not operationally separated in the brain but work seamlessly together. Emotion acts as a 'rudder' to guide and stabilise a learner's behaviour and decisions once there is recognition and recall of knowledge that is relevant, either consciously or unconsciously. Academic tasks are never emotionally neutral, and engaging students in real-world social realities helps to bring into relief the interaction between values and the 'Head/Heart/Hands' of action. This is an important point for values education: Values acquisition needs to be situated in the reality of every aspect of a learner's daily life, with plenty of opportunity to reflect on their experiences, and not just confined to 'moral education' classes.

Cognitive engagement does not mean the absence of emotion, nor does it occur in a social vacuum. Emotion (affect) is important to decision-making and the transfer of learning to other contexts. The social context will also influence the uptake of values and attitudes, and this is an important aspect of EHV and its commitment to group activities and other teaching techniques (see Chapter 8). These ideas have also been developed and researched[28] by neuroscience. The researchers describe the emotion/cognitive nexus as follows:

> *The evolutionary shadow cast by emotion over cognition influences the modern mind... Emotional thought can be conscious or nonconscious and is the means by which bodily sensations come into our conscious awareness. High reason and rational thought also contribute to high-level social and moral emotions to form the specialized branch of decision making that is ethics. Motivated reasoning works in a similar manner and refers to the process by which emotional thoughts gain additional significance through the application of rational evidence and knowledge. In the other direction, rational evidence can be imposed upon certain kinds of emotional thought to produce the sort of automatic moral decision making that underlies intuitive notions of good and evil. .... Emotional thoughts, either conscious or nonconscious, can alter the state of the body in characteristic ways, such as by tensing or relaxing the skeletal muscles or by changing the heart rate. In turn, the bodily sensations of these changes, either actual or simulated, contribute either consciously or non-consciously to feelings, which can then influence thought.*[29]

Effective teaching involves responsiveness to students' emotions. Teachers can foster emotional connections to the curriculum content to establish relevance, particularly by looking for how knowledge can be applied to real-world situations (see also Chapters 9 and 10 for examples from EHV). One way to achieve this connection is to utilise service-learning opportunities, as discussed later in this chapter.

2.3.2 *Imitation*

This is a very important dimension of learning that operates via *mirror neurons* in the brain's pre-motor cortex that fire on observing an action performed by another. All humans are predisposed to imitating those around them; thus, teachers need to demonstrate *how* to know as well as impart *what* to know. For this reason, teachers' values, beliefs, and attitudes towards teaching and learning are just as important to the learning process as the material being taught. Students will also imitate their chosen role models, so teachers might encourage students to select good ones. A teacher who is punctual and well-prepared for a lesson generally finds that students imitate this. When teachers demand deadlines for work, students respect those teachers who get that work back to them within short periods of time, illustrating their own adherence to deadlines.

Imitation alone, however, does not, of course, solely explain learning. Creativity and imagination also require good decision-making together with helping learners to be inventive. The pre-frontal cortex can exercise inhibitory control of imitation, but this is hard for young children to achieve since it develops through adolescence.

2.3.3 *Summing Up*

In conclusion, neuroscience research in relation to teaching and learning has demonstrated:

- The nexus of cognition, affect, and sociality for learning
- The interaction of the learner and the physical/social environment
- Internal motivation and engagement with learning are contingent on finding emotional affinity with the subject matter
- The role of mirror neurons, and hence the critical role of the teacher in modelling and mentoring
- Teachers' beliefs and values are significant ingredients in the learning environment, particularly in regard to caring, support, and competence
- Learning is best facilitated by multi-sensory teaching practices so information can be cross-referenced to what has already been learned
- The importance of real-world/service learning

EHV and its modelling of values by teachers helps to scaffold cognitive, emotional, and social dimensions, as well as taking most of these neuroscience findings into account. An example here might help:

> A point of contention in many schools is tidiness of the school yard and litter. Schools often use picking up litter as a punishment or consequence of unacceptable behaviour. When teachers on yard duty cheerfully invite students to help clean up an area, then start to pick up litter themselves before any students have responded to their request, a significant number of students usually quickly mirror the modelling of the teachers.[30]

This behaviour can also be mirrored by the general student body when student leaders also take up this mantle of modelling right action.

2.4 Social and Emotional Learning to Support Values Education and Student Wellbeing

This section concerning *SEL* (Social and Emotional Learning) builds on from the previous one, thereby further illustrating the intertwining within the brain/mind of emotions and cognition. This is something that good teachers and good schools are well aware of and strive to provide through emotionally supportive environments for learning. Some principles relating to SEL have been developed from research,[31] demonstrating that individuals can only reach their human potential within a community, but they also need to know the norms, rules, and values of that community and have the skills to interact effectively within it. Effective learning is a holistic process involving the integration of mind and body (see also Chapter 5). There is a need, therefore, to avoid compartmentalising the cognitive as separate from the social, affective, and spiritual domains. Research as well as several government reports nominate SEL skills as competencies that are important for students to have, and that these skills also facilitate academic achievement by strengthening their abilities to learn. As already discussed, EHV is a holistic approach that develops cognitive, physical, emotional, social, and spiritual aspects of education, and so SEL is naturally a part of this values education approach. EHV endorses SEL, yet also believes that the cognitive, physical, and spiritual aspects of learning are also important.

Erikson's[32] *stages of emotional development* are useful to consider in regard to SEL, since they are important not just for children but throughout the whole of life. Erikson identified the following emotional development stages:

1. *Trust V Mistrust* – children need to feel they can always depend on their teacher, parent, or carer for help when needed, the same applying to other supervisors.
2. *Autonomy V Shame and doubt* – children need to be given opportunities to make choices and decisions within their sphere of competence in order to gain self-worth and confidence in themselves and their abilities. A balance

is needed between challenge and structuring activities within their *ZPD* (Zone of Proximal Development[33]). This requires skill from the teacher.

3. *Initiative V Guilt* – teachers can 'scaffold' children to research their ideas and explore interests to stimulate their inherent creativity and intrinsic motivation, while also developing self-esteem. Service learning has an important role to play in achieving this, as discussed later in this chapter.

These stages are not just maturation issues that can be left to occur naturally as the child ages. Deficiencies of SEL may not be developmental delays or deficits rather they may be areas that need promoting just as much as cognitive, physical, and spiritual areas need promoting. Appropriate 'scaffolding' can help children to control and label their emotions, to produce a sense of inner peace by such simple actions as asking them to wait their turn, or, more deeply, by sharing how responding to challenging situations from a position of inner peace has helped in their 'right action' choices, and by getting them to look after their physical environment and each other: The EHV technique of silent sitting (see Chapters 8, 9, and 10) can assist with this. These social/emotional skills are just as vital as counting, reading, and colour recognition.

Values education is important in developing SEL, and thereby a school environment that supports SEL development as well. One tool that can be used here is for the teacher, parent, or carer to correct a bad behaviour or an emotional outburst by, at the appropriate time when the child is able to be reasoned with, asking 'What value would have been useful to practice here?' thereby assisting the child to become more self-aware while also promoting that value as useful to that child.

Five clusters of SEL that have been identified as needing to be developed through education are:

1. Self-awareness
2. Self-management
3. Social awareness
4. Relationship skills
5. Responsible decision-making

These SEL skills are also features of Emotional Intelligence. People with Emotional intelligence[34] (EQ) perform better in various aspects of life than those with less EQ due to their ability to maintain cooperative and mutually satisfying relationships. Classroom contexts that optimise SEL are characterised by an emphasis on cooperation, assertion, responsibility, empathy, and self-control. When psychological needs are met, particularly Trust, Autonomy, and Initiative (see Erikson's stages outlined above), the result is intrinsic motivation in learning and self-regulation of behaviour in line with the ideals of EHV.

SEL skills taught at the *early primary* school stage are those of listening, sharing, cooperation, negotiation, and compromising, all of which are readily related to the values of EHV. There can also be a need to help cope with emotions by using cognitive (thinking) rather than behavioural strategies to deal with stressful situations. More is said on this in later chapters of this book.

At the *late primary and early high* school stages, the skills required are learning to act autonomously, maintaining friendships, and preserving a balance of independence and interdependence, thereby helping to establish a stable sense of personal identity, which includes further development of inner peace. How teachers (and parents and carers) listen and talk with children, solve problems, cooperate, and manage internal and interpersonal moments are ongoing lessons or 'teachable moments' from which children (and teachers and parents/carers) can also learn.

EHV provides a natural context for SEL. Like the *National Framework for Values Education in Australian Schools*,[35] EHV encourages schools to use a bottom-up approach as to which values to target and how they might be taught within a set of guiding principles, and this is looked at in detail in later chapters (e.g., Chapter 4). EHV has the Five Values as key guiding principles.

2.5 Positive Educational Practices Supporting Values Education and Student Wellbeing

This topic will be touched on only briefly here, as it is dealt with extensively and with several practical examples in Chapter 11. However, it needs to be noted that this 'third pillar' is also fully integrated with the other two pillars discussed in the previous two sections, all three being enmeshed components of a whole that supports values education.

A key principle of positive educational practices is to believe that all students are capable of success given supportive circumstances. Beyond this, Australian research[36] has developed a framework called *PROSPER* to assist in the establishment of positive educational practices that include *p*ositive emotions, positive *r*elationships, engagement, accomplishment, and personal and emotional wellbeing, all to enable individuals to flourish and for institutions to thrive. The *PROSPER* acronym components are:

- ***Positivity*** – encouraging positive skills, experiences, and emotions
- ***Relationships*** – social skills and social values to encourage positive relationships throughout the school
- ***Outcomes*** – facilitating experiences of outcomes and achievements
- ***Strengths*** – taking a strengths-based approach, where the strengths are both of character and of ability
- ***Purpose*** – fostering students' sense of purpose and meaning
- ***Engagement*** – enhancing students' opportunities for engagement in terms of *flow* during an activity – highly focused, effortless attention, or concentration
- ***Resilience*** – supporting students to develop the skills and attributes that underpin behaviours

PROSPER is underpinned by positive psychology, the scientific study of the conditions and processes that contribute to optimal functioning in individuals and institutions (see Chapter 11). It helps to ensure a focus on identifying, building, and enhancing each individual's positive qualities and skills, rather than trying to repair what is not working. It concentrates on what that individual's strengths and capabilities are, rather than their deficits, while highlighting what is going well, rather than what is not working. A *strength* in this context is a natural capacity for behaving, thinking, and feeling in a way that promotes both inner peace and successful goal achievement. While clearly, there is still a need to understand and manage weaknesses, this is just not the main focus.

Other aspects that are developed include helpful and rational thinking skills; distancing skills adaptive to context; encouraging the use of humour and optimistic thinking skills; and seeking assistance when needed. Gardner's multiple intelligences[37] can also be useful here (described in Chapter 4). Also, the values of compassion and respect are important, and they lead to empathy, fairness, and honesty. Meaning and purpose can be enhanced by service learning, peer support programmes, exercises like the 'Circle of friends',[38] student participation in school-wide leadership and decision-making structures, such as through classroom councils, sports teams, as well as arts, music, and drama groups. These ideas are extended in Chapter 13.

To conclude this chapter, we return to the three themes identified in the Australian values education research project. Of the three components identified (see start of chapter), *quality teaching* and *values education* are both explored in more depth in the subsequent chapters of this book; thus, it only remains to discuss *service learning*. It also needs to be emphasised that in EHV, service learning goes further and is more important than is generally found in discussions about this concept, as is elaborated in the next section.

2.6 Service Learning

One of the most important fundamental components of EHV is to encourage students to engage in selfless service, not for the sake of reward but for giving service to others for its own sake. The benefits of this are not only to the recipient of the service but also to the person who is giving it since it develops attitudes of altruism and compassion. The founder of EHV emphasised the maxim:

> *Love all, serve all.*[39]

In a talk about service he also said:

> *Rendering Service selflessly with a compassionate heart is true Service. One is bound to attain peace if one serves in a friendly spirit.*[40]

Service learning is a pedagogy that is growing in popularity, particularly in higher education but also in schools. The key idea underpinning service learning is that it combines the academic learning that occurs in curriculum subjects with the opportunity to apply this learning in a practical context that helps others in need of the service. Students apply what they have learned in their curricula to developing and implementing meaningful service projects. Reflection on what they are learning about their subject knowledge, about themselves, and about their service recipients, is an essential component both during and after the service experience.

Examples of service-learning projects at higher education level can include:[41]

- Electrical engineering students developing and working with local engineering students to install and implement low-cost energy infrastructures for developing regions,
- Business students developing and implementing business projects for underprivileged communities,
- Education students helping primary school students with specific reading difficulties,
- Optometry students providing eye care and vision health to disadvantaged people in the community.

At school level, some examples are:

- Creative writing: Write a children's reading book, then read and give away books to children in hospitals and to community partners.[42]
- Environmental science: Clean up a vacant lot and landscape with native vegetation.[43]
- Mathematics: Students in algebra classes study real-life applications of mathematics such as calculating mortgage payments, car payments, and credit card payments, and provide a walk-in workshop for other students and the wider community.[44]
- Community-based service projects: Students perceive gaps in the service projects currently provided by society and initiate their own projects to address these gaps.

2.6.1 *Transformative Effects of Service Learning*

EHV is concerned ultimately with the holistic transformation of the individual. Lam[45] described six ways in which students can transform as a result of service learning:[46]

- ***Civic***: Develop or expand their sense of social responsibility and citizenship.
- ***Social***: Change their ways of dealing with people around them.
- ***Intellectual***: Rethink their presuppositions or attitudes towards knowledge and problems, or engage in related metacognitive development.
- ***Cultural***: Reflect on their stereotypes and bias towards people from different backgrounds, and display understanding and respect for others' cultures.

- ***Personal***: Reflect on their previous self-concepts, lifestyles, meaning of life, and future paths.

Spiritual transformation is a sixth dimension, described by Kiely[47] as:

A movement toward deeper (un)conscious understanding of self, purpose, society, and greater good.

The following comments are from a group of primary school children who participated in a lunch-time service project to knit rug squares for the elderly.[48] Most of the children had been unable to knit previously, so the learning that occurred in this case was the learning of this new skill. As well as the rugs that were produced, a secondary service-related outcome of the activity was that the older children helped the younger ones to develop their skills. It was a particularly valuable experience for some troubled students:

- *It was fun because I love helping others. When I made a mistake, it was easy to fix.* (Jarrod, 9 years old, a child with very special learning needs who had a rare experience of success through the knitting project)
- *I taught Trent and Kael* (other boys) *to knit, and I brought a lot of wool. I liked teaching people to knit. It gave me something to do. I wasn't getting into trouble. I loved helping people.* (Jesse, 10 years old, a boy who had difficult times in the playground and had sometimes been involved in bullying)
- *It makes you feel warm and fuzzy inside to do something for others.* (Georgie, 10 years old)

2.6.2 *How Does EHV Interface with Service Learning?*

So why is it that service learning, when implemented in the framework of EHV, can bring about positive results? In attempting to answer this question, let us take a look at some of the components of EHV that can be mirrored in a service-learning project:

- ***Love***: The key value underpinning service learning is Love. This value is manifested as the sense of compassion and empathy that students develop for the 'less fortunate' people who are the recipients of their service.
- ***Equality***: An understanding of equality emerges when students offer service, without any sense that one is a more important group member than any other, and without any thought of 'what's in it for me'. This is a practical manifestation of personal peace and has some elements of the value of *Truth*.
- ***Creativity***: Creative activity is an essential component of character development: As a means of expression, for relaxation and enjoyment, to build

self-confidence and co-operation, to teach discrimination, to encourage responsibility, to strengthen concentration, to develop co-ordination, to bring out inner talents, to encourage discipline, patience, and perseverance; and to develop skills, which are all aspects of *Right Action*, ultimately leading *to Non-violence.*[49]

- ***Unity of head, heart, and hands*:** From an EHV perspective, service-learning projects can engage all three: The *head*, as the students concentrate on the new skill they are learning; the *heart*, as the ultimate goal is to provide something to help the needy; and the *hands*, as these are busily occupied with carrying out the task.

If reflections on the service learning focus not only on the academic learning but also on these aspects of human values, service learning can be a powerful way to bring about holistic transformation in learners.

2.7 A Last Exercise

For a better understanding of these ideas, think of a service-learning project you could implement, on your own or with others, as a parent, carer, or a teacher. Perhaps, carry this project out with your family, your class, or your friends. If necessary, it can be 'short and sweet', yet more extensive projects, if possible, can be particularly impactful.

Once completed, reflect on the outcomes of what you did from as many different perspectives as you can, as described above in Section 2.6.

Appendix 2.1: Consciousness and Its Role

Despite a common belief, it has now been shown that the brain's cortical structures are *not* the source of consciousness, rather cortical consciousness arises from structures in the brainstem, the most ancient part of the brain, and more particularly from the *Reticular Activating System* (RAS): The RAS is aroused by feelings, and this creates consciousness. Thus, an *affect* (feeling or emotion) is an extended form of homeostasis and a part of a self-organising system, the human body in this case, that aims for survival within a changing environment. The environmental changes are registered by the brain as *needs*, and various categories of needs have been identified, such as the bodily needs of hunger, thirst, and temperature, as well as seven innate needs[50] with their own built-in responses that happen automatically – *SEEKING*, *RAGE*, *FEAR*, *PANIC*/GRIEF, *LUST*, *CARE*, and *PLAY* – that have identifiable responses to particular needs. Each need is an individual one with its own values or *valence* that relate to increasing or decreasing deviations from the homeostatic norm, so they are felt either as pleasure or pain. Each of the feelings that arise activates a predicted programme of automatic responses that aim to return the deviation to dynamic equilibrium through the innate instincts or reflexes, supplemented by learning from experience. However, these different needs have to be prioritised and balanced, and it is here that there is choice so that education can play a role. This balancing of needs and feelings through choice aims to ensure that the critical ones are dealt with to maintain homeostasis. For example, is it more important to run from a potential predator or to quench one's thirst?

The various needs are prioritised by a mid-brain structure, the *decision triangle* that then passes information on to the *Peri Aqueductal Grey* (PAG) in the brainstem and the needs are ranked by the PAG with signals of pleasure or unpleasure, being displayed as a two-dimensional map in another part of the brain (the sub-cortical superior Caligulea). This triggers cortical action programmes to unconsciously unfold, based on expected contexts determined by a hierarchy of prediction from the model of the person (discussed in the main part of this chapter) located in the cortical forebrain. Working memory in the cortex also minimises error by initiating trial-and-error actions in thought and then in reality. By selecting reliable choices in this way, adjustments are then made to long-term memory and to the model of the person to allow for more automatic responses in similar future situations (see Figure 2.3). The aim here is to make as many reactions to change in the environment as automatic as possible, which is why more than 90% of reactions to such changes are achieved subconsciously.

Notes

1 http://www.curriculum.edu.au/values/val_about_values_education,8679.html accessed 10-12-2021.
2 https://www.pdhpe.net/better-health-for-individuals/what-does-health-mean-to-individuals/meanings-of-health/dimensions-of-health/ (accessed 11-12-2021). Here the *intellectual* is referred to as the *mental.*
3 M. Taplin, "A Model for Integrating Spiritual Education into Secular Curricula," *International Journal of Children's Spirituality* 19, no. 1 (2014): 4–16.
4 http://www.curriculum.edu.au/values/val_vegps1_final_report,16381.html accessed 11-1-2022.
5 DEST 2005: http://www.curriculum.edu.au/verve/_resources/framework_pdf_version_for_the_web.pdf accessed 30-12-2021.
6 T. Lovat and R. Toomey, "The Evolution of Student Wellbeing Pedagogy and Its Implications for Teacher Education – Chapter 1," in *Teacher Education and Values Pedagogy: A Student Wellbeing Approach,* eds. R. Toomey, T. Lovat, N. Clement, and K. Dally (Australia: David Barlow Publishing, 2009).
7 T. Lovat, R. Toomey, K. Dally, and N. Clement, Project to Test and Measure the Impact of Values Education on Student Effects and School Ambience. Report for the Australian Government Department of Education, Employment and Workplace Relations (DEEWR) by the University of Newcastle, Canberra, Australia, 2009.
8 ***Scaffold***: Teachers provide successive levels of temporary support that help students reach higher levels of comprehension and skill acquisition that they would not be able to achieve without assistance.

9 Thurman Fleet, *Rays of the Dawn: Natural Laws of the Body, Mind and Soul*, 2nd ed. (Concept-Therapy Institute, 2000).
10 ***Servomechanism***: An automatic device that uses error-sensing negative feedback to correct the action of a mechanism, such as a thermostat.
11 Developed and drawn by Bob and Roz Molloy for EHV teacher training.
12 A. Jumsai Na Ayudhya, *The Five Human Values and Human Excellence* (Bangkok: International Institute of Sathya Sai Education, 1997).
13 Jumsai Na Ayudhya, Art-Ong. *A development of the human values integrated instructional model based on intuitive learning concept*: A dissertation submitted in partial fulfilment of the requirements for the degree of Doctor of Philosophy in Curriculum and Instruction, Department of Secondary Education, Faculty of Education, Chulalongkorn University, Thailand, 2003. https://issea.org.au/research/higher-degree-dissertations/ accessed 12-12-2021.
14 Jumsai, *The Five Human Values and Human Excellence* (1997).
15 See references below to Damasio; Solms; and Kahneman.
16 M. Solms, *The Hidden Spring: A Journey to the Source of Consciousness* (Profile Books, 2021).
17 A. Damasio, *The Strange Order of Things: Life, Feeling, and the Making of Cultures* (Pantheon, 2018).
18 *Ibid.*
19 Daniel Kahneman, *Thinking Fast and Slow* (Macmillan, 2011).
20 ***Agency***: Action or intervention, especially such as to produce a particular effect.
21 In this chapter, the term *subconscious* is being used as a synonym for *unconscious*, the complex of mental activities within an individual that proceeds without his awareness. Sigmund Freud, the founder of psychoanalysis, stated that such unconscious processes may affect a person's behaviour even though he cannot report on them. https://www.britannica.com/science/unconscious accessed 12-12-2021.
22 ***Qualia***: A quality or property as perceived or experienced by a person.
23 Damasio, *The Strange Order of Things*, 2018.
24 Solms, *The Hidden Spring*, 2021.
25 V.Frakl, *Mans Search for Meaning*, Ebury Publishing, UK, 2011. *B. Courtney, The Power of One, Penguin* Australia, 2006.
26 M. Taplin, "A Model for Integrating Spiritual Education into Secular Curricula," *International Journal of Children's Spirituality* 19, no. 1 (2014): 4–16.
27 P. Howard-Jones, "Neuroscience and Education: Myths and Messages," *Nature Review Neuroscience* 15 (2014): 817–824. https://doi.org/10.1038/nrn3817 accessed 01-11-2021.
28 H. Immordino-Yang and A. Damasio, "We Feel, Therefore We Learn: The Relevance of Affective and Social Neuroscience to Education," *Mind Brain and Education* 1, no. 1 (2007): 3–10. https://onlinelibrary.wiley.com/doi/10.1111/j.1751-228X.2007.00004.x accessed 20-12-2021.
29 *Ibid.*
30 *Ibid.*
31 K. Dally, "The Second Pillar of the Student Wellbeing – Chapter 3," in *Teacher Education and Values Pedagogy: A Student Wellbeing Approach*, eds. R. Toomey, T. Lovat, N. Clement, and K. Dally (Australia: David Barlow Publishing, 2009).
32 Erickson's stages of emotional development: https://www.simplypsychology.org/Erik-Erikson.html accessed 20-11-2021.
33 L. S. Vygotsky, *Mind in Society: The Development of Higher Psychological Processes* (Cambridge, MA: Harvard University Press, 1978). https://www.simplypsychology.org/Zone-of-Proximal-Development.html#:~:text=Vygotsky's%20Definition%20of%20ZPD&text=%22the%20distance%20between%20the%20actual,86 accessed 22-12-2021.

34 *Emotional Intelligence.* https://www.helpguide.org/articles/mental-health/emotional-intelligence-eq.htm#:~:text=Emotional%20intelligence%20(otherwise%20known%20as,overcome%20challenges%20and%20defuse%20conflict accessed 20-11-2021.
35 National Framework for Values Education in Australian Schools (2005). http://www.curriculum.edu.au/values/val_national_framework_for_values_education,8757.html#:~:text=The%20National%20Framework%20was%20agreed,education%20authorities%20and%20Australian%20schools accessed 11-1-2022.
36 T. Noble and H. McGrath, "PROSPER: A New Framework for Positive Education," *Psych Well-being* 5, no. 2 (2015).
37 H. Gardner, *Frames of Mind: The Theory of Multiple Intelligences* (Hachette UK, 2011).
38 http://circleofriends.org/program-description/ accessed 17-11-2021.
39 Sathya Sai Baba, *Sathya Sai Speaks* (Prasanthi Nilayam, India: Books and Publication Trust, July 18, 1989), Vol. 22.
40 Sathya Sai Baba, *Sathya Sai Speaks* (Prasanthi Nilayam, India: Books and Publication Trust, November19, 1987), Vol. 20 (26).
41 https://www.polyu.edu.hk/sllo/about-sllo/vision-and-mission/ accessed 27-12-2021.
42 https://servelearn.co/blog/10-creative-service-learning-projects-to-inspire-your-students/ accessed 11-1-2022.
43 https://www.ethicsed.org/project-ideas-for-service-learning.html accessed 29-12-2021.
44 http://www.rhsroughriders.org accessed 29-12-2021.
45 Lam Hiu Yu, *Transformative Learning in International Service Learning.* Unpublished Dr. of Education thesis, The University of Hong Kong, 2021.
46 *Ibid.,* p. 95.
47 R. Kiely, "A Chameleon with a Complex: Searching for Transformation in International Service-Learning," *Michigan Journal of Community Service Learning* 10, no. 2 (2004): 5–20, p. 11.
48 M. Taplin, Unpublished reflections collected from an Australian primary school.
49 A. Jumsai and L. Burrows, *Sathya Sai Education in Human Values Handbook for Teachers* (Bangkok: Sathya Sai Foundation of Thailand, 1991).
50 Solms, *The Hidden Spring,* 2021.

Chapter 3

What Is the Right Thing to Do?

Roger Packham

3.1 Introduction

This chapter will look at issues concerning how we decide what is right and what is wrong. Most people intuitively know the difference between what is right and what is wrong, the issue is *choosing* between right and wrong. As a teacher or a parent, how can you help children and adolescents to *choose* to do the *right* thing and not the *wrong* thing? What do we mean by right and wrong; why and how do we decide to call some things *good* and some things *bad*?

One day your teenage son is coming home on the train, and he notices a wallet under the empty seat opposite him. He picks it up, looks inside, and sees there are some banknotes, some credit cards, a driver's licence, and other personal effects. What is the right action that he should now take? Will he choose to take that action?

Your daughter has recently joined a netball club, and she has been practising hard and looking forward to being part of the competition team. She comes home from practice and tells you she has not been selected for the team this Saturday: What do you do now, what do you choose to say to her, and why?

As a teacher, you are on playground duty, and you notice a new child (aged around eight) who has recently joined the school and is sitting on her own eating lunch. Nearby, there are two or three tables of friends eating lunch while chatting and laughing: What is the right action to take now?

These are just a few of the many, many issues facing parents, carers, and teachers every day; some are simple, some are far more complex: How do we decide what is the right thing to do, how do we help children and teenagers to learn what is the right thing to do, and how do we help them to both *know* what is the right thing to do, but, more importantly, to *choose* the right thing to do?

To be able to resolve or at least improve some of these issues, it is necessary to first delve a little deeper. The really fundamental questions of our lives are not questions of fact or of finance, but questions of ***value***. What is it that gives something genuine value? What is worth striving for, and what makes a life worth living? Without values, one could know all the facts and not even know

DOI: 10.4324/9781003478607-4

which facts were important. Therefore, reflections on life's 'forking paths' (our choices) and recognising the importance of *values* in understanding matters of fact are key to living a good life.

> Values are inescapable for human creatures like us. A life guided by some form of values is essential. The fact is that we do hold strong positions regarding values, such as the value of *commitments* and *justice*. Another of our values is a commitment to *truth*. Without such commitments, trade and commerce would quickly become unworkable, and families and society could not function: If you tell me an appointment is at such-and-such a time, I need to be able to assume you are being truthful. Similarly, there is widespread community outrage if unjust behaviours are exposed. To be fully rational *human* creatures, reflecting critically on our own values is necessary, and thus parents and teachers need to help children and teenagers to learn to reflect on their values in order to learn how to choose wisely. Such reflection can help us become the best human beings we can be. As the founder of EHV said: *Raising the standard of living must also mean raising ethical, moral, and spiritual standards. Then only can education lead to progress in human values and harmony in social life.*[1]

This chapter will explore answers to some of these questions and, together with the rest of this book, will give tools that can be used to help to promote good actions, to help ourselves and others, particularly children and adolescents, to be the best human beings they can be. The chapter will explain what values, ethics, and morality are, together with some theories that underpin them, and how these theories can be enacted. It will be taking a 'Western' approach to these issues and will show where Education in Human Values (EHV) fits into these theories, while also discussing how EHV evolved and developed as a very practical way of promoting right thoughts and right actions.

3.2 Ethics, Morality, and Values

The questions above come under the topic of *ethics and morality: ethics* looks at how humans *ought* to act, as well as searching for definitions of 'right action' and the 'good life'. Such answers are not simple as there is no single absolutely agreed definition of ethics; your own judgement is always the ultimate decider: This is because a definition of ethics will depend on the sociocultural and political context. Thus, for example, in the ancient Greek tradition of Aristotle (384–322 BC), ethics was first conceived as relating to the concept of the 'good life', and inquiries were directed towards discovering the nature of happiness and how it could be obtained. Later, a quite different orientation arose from the Judeo-Christian tradition, where the ideals of 'righteousness before God' and the 'love of God and neighbour' were the subject of ethics rather than the happy or pleasant life. In the Middle Ages, Thomas Aquinas combined both of these views into his ethical system based on *virtues*. More recently, many have argued that what is *right* is 'what makes me feel good' (*emotivism*), or recognising and fulfilling our duties (*deontology*), or the *consequences* of our actions, hoping that optimising these will lead to greater utility or happiness (*utilitarianism*).

Often, we feel we are faced with the difficult task of deciding on the relationship between 'doing what is right' and 'being happy' or choosing between what our *desires* are or what our *rationality* tells us to do. For example, should I buy that new shirt or new dress, or use the money to save for emergencies? One choice might make me happy now, while the other may be more prudent by 'saving for a rainy day'. How can I use my particularly human capacities to decide without feeling disappointed with myself? This chapter aims to help to unravel these dilemmas, describing the nature and dynamics of ethics in our current 21st-century context.

In addition to the definitions given above, ethics is also the branch of knowledge that deals with moral standards, and thus ethics applies both to individuals and to society. Hence, it is closely associated with political philosophy, that branch of knowledge that looks at how society should be organised, what society is, what justice is, and the like.

So, what about *morality*? Many see the terms *ethics* and *morality* as interchangeable, with ethics denoting the *theory* of right action and the greater good, while morality indicates the *practice* that is the right or the wrong of a particular human action in a particular context. The concern of ethics is to critically examine the underlying principles of morality: Morality is more prescriptive in nature than ethics. It tells us what we *ought* to do and asks us to follow the right way. The objective of morality is to equip people with a body of *norms* (rules, standards, and values) that make for peaceful and collectively satisfying coexistence. This thereby facilitates our living together and interacting in ways that are productive for the realisation of the general benefit or *good* of our community. Examples of such moral maxims include those that prohibit the taking of innocent life, theft of property, those that require some large degree of truthfulness, and at least some significant measure of altruistic benevolence. Box 3.1 summarises the concepts of value, ethics, and morals.

Any particular society wants to keep alive the values it considers worthwhile and to aim for the improvement of the moral quality of the particular community. Morality aims to guide our actions by *reason*, thereby giving us a picture of what it really means to be a *morally upright* person in a particular context.

> *The years of student life must be saturated with cooperative activity, social service, eager search for truth and readiness to sacrifice one's interests for the good of those who are less fortunate. Moral and spiritual values have to be honoured as much as, if not more than, economic and material values. Life must be a harmonious blend of these values, with emphasis on moral strength.*[2]

Box 3.1: Defining Values, Ethics, and Morals

1. A ***Value*** is the regard that something is held to deserve. It is the importance, worth, or usefulness of something. It also refers to principles or standards of behaviour; one's judgement of what is important in life. Your values are the things that you believe are important in the way you live and work. They (should) determine your priorities and, deep down, they are probably the measures you use to tell if your life is turning out the way you want it to. The word *value* is currently dominated by its economic sense of: *The quality of being most useful.* This gives rise to judgements of worth, a fair equivalent for something or someone's usefulness or importance. Today, this judgement is often made in *monetary* terms; indeed, this was the original meaning of the word: Up until the 18th century, the word 'good' was used rather than the word 'value'.
2. ***Ethics*** deals with such questions as: Why are some things considered *right* and others *wrong*? Why do we say some things are *good* and others *bad*? How do we decide how to act in a given situation that requires some judgement? Ethics gives the principles on which morals are based.
3. ***Morals*** can be defined as standards or norms of behaviour and are developed over time within communities. Morals provide the rules: Standards and values that make for a peaceful and collective coexistence in a particular context.

3.3 Human Values

From the above, it can be seen that values, ethics, and morals are all closely intertwined. They guide how we live and how we feel about how we are living. Furthermore, they also help create the society we are inevitably a part of. All creatures are aware of their environment, enabling them to act in ways that enhance their survival and optimise their wellbeing. Humans are different from other creatures in that their intellectual abilities, particularly speech and rationality,[3] present them with a range of ***choices***. What *should* we do? How *should* we organise society? What is right? On what basis can we choose between different courses of action? How should we understand the idea of *justice*? It is this rationality that means there are ***Human Values*** of special interest. All these questions lead to the study of ethics and political philosophy, but the focus in this chapter is on ethics and its links to our values, human values, and morals. While the chapter will not go into political philosophy, it should never be forgotten that the proper role of politics is to enact laws that promote ethical and moral behaviour in citizens.

We can say that, whether we know it or not, we are always using some kind of ethical system to make judgements. Perhaps we use the same system all the time, or perhaps we use different systems in different circumstances. Either way, *critically reflecting* on how we make judgements helps us to improve our learning and thus our satisfaction about the actions we take in our lives and the actions we can take to help or teach others.

Current ethical viewpoints can be understood better from a historical development perspective. In the 'Western' tradition ethical questions were first discussed by the ancient Greeks with the key figures being Socrates, Plato, and Aristotle, although there were others before and after them. Their ideas guided the field of ethics right through to the *enlightenment* in the 16th and 17th centuries. The original ideas were shaped and extended to fit the emergence of Christianity, most notably by St Augustine in the 5th century and then St Thomas Aquinas in the 13th century, with the latter developing Aristotle's ethical concepts to fit the Christianity of St Augustine. Thomas Aquinas is considered to be the foremost philosopher for the 2000 years following Aristotle. The enlightenment of the 16th and 17th centuries moved away from the authority of the church and the 'kings and nobles' to a belief in science and rationality independent of theology, and eventually to a secular society with a separation of church and state. From this movement emerged two new ethical systems – principles to guide action – the first developed by Emanuel Kant and known as *deontology* or *duty* ethics, and the second, being particularly attributed to David Hume, Jeremy Bentham, and John Stuart Mill, and known as *utilitarianism* or *consequentialism*. In the 20th century, the ethics of *emotivism* (later referred to as *expressionism*) became the commonest way of deciding what is right, whereby if individuals thought something was 'good' if they approved of it, they thereby felt others should also approve of it.

These systems dominated ethical thinking through to the 21st century, and it should be particularly noted that such systems aimed at presenting individuals with overarching ethical principles of action, enabling them to make 'good' choices in any situation. One point needs emphasising; however, these systems are concerned with the ***act*** rather than the individual ***actor***, while the original ethical system arising particularly from Aristotle and Aquinas, now known as *virtue ethics*, is concerned with the ***individual human*** – individuals' characters or dispositions to *act virtuously* rather than following all-encompassing ethical principles to guide them in how they act. Many writers have pointed out that some situations create dilemmas between different act-based ethical principles, making decision-making difficult and not at all 'all-encompassing'.

The idea of the 'virtuous individual' largely avoids these dilemmas and has been reflected in numerous writings about how to *act well* since ancient times. Here is one example from the *Tao The Ching* by *Lao Tzu*, a Chinese philosopher from two thousand years ago:[4]

What is well planned cannot be uprooted.
What is well embraced cannot slip away.

Your descendants will carry on the ancestral sacrifice
for generations without end.

Cultivate Virtue in your own person,
And it becomes a genuine part of you.
Cultivate it in the family,
And it will abide,
Cultivate it in the community,
And it will live and grow,
Cultivate it in the state,
And it will flourish abundantly.
Cultivate it in the world,
And it will become universal.

Hence, a person must be judged as a person;
A family as a family;
A community as community;
A state as state;
The world as world.
How do I know about the world?
By what is within me.

What can inform the special human quality of 'reason' in such a virtue ethics system? Reason can be viewed as being made up of three parts: *Comprehension*, *judgement*, and *rationality*. Here *comprehension* is analogous to 'light' in that it is a flash of instant understanding, while *judgement* has to be considered over time, and *rationality* is analogous to the computer – working things out systematically and logically from first principles. The approach that is used in EHV is the application of self-evident first principles as the basis for judgement and rationality, these being five universal human values – or 'goods' – that can be found within all cultures and religions:

Love
Peace
Truth
Right Action
Non-Violence

This approach also follows the view of Scheler[5] that values form a hierarchy, and that lower values gain their power from higher values. These ideas have also been discussed by Schutz,[6] and, in connection with the location of aspects of the values hierarchy on different sides of the human brain, by McGilchrist.[7]

Scheler's lowest level of his values hierarchy begins with the *senses*, where something is pleasant or unpleasant, is useful or useless; at this level, things only have a value if they please or have utility. The next level Scheler saw as 'values of life', such as bravery, loyalty, and humility, or their opposite, such as cowardice, self-seeking, small-mindedness, treachery, and arrogance. Next

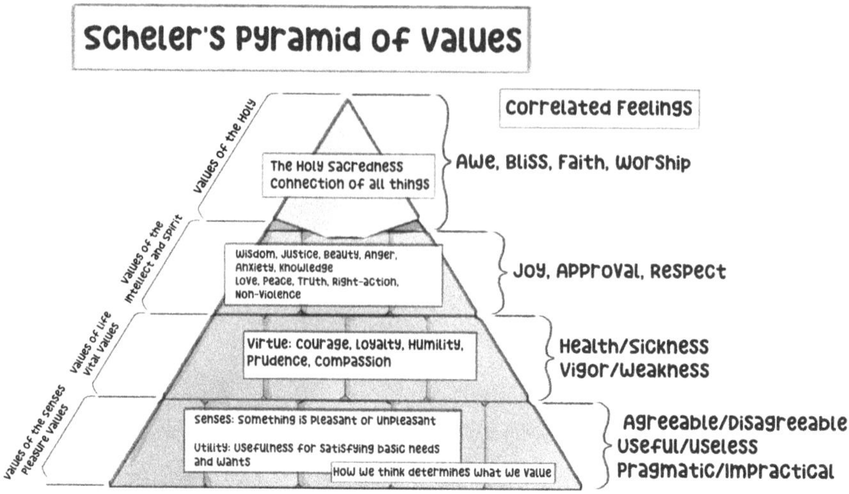

Figure 3.1 Sheler's Pyramid of Values

in the hierarchy come 'values of the intellect and spirit', and this is where the EHV human values of Love, Truth, Peace, Right Action, and Non-violence can be seen to fit alongside Sheler's concepts of justice and beauty. The final level was seen by Scheler to be 'the holy', also called by others as sacredness, or the connection of all things. Scheler's hierarchy is illustrated in Figure 3.1.

For McGilchrist[7] the right hemisphere of the brain builds on lower-order values to embrace higher-order values, all of which require effective or moral engagement with the world. In contrast, the left hemisphere dismisses higher-order values in favour of lower-order values – it either reduces everything to its utility value or rejects it. This is a concern for McGilchrist as he believes our society has become left-brain dominant and needs to correct this and become more balanced. A focus on the higher-order values of Love, Truth, Peace, Right Action, and Non-violence would assist in achieving this.

These five human values are accessed via *intuition* (see Chapter 2), thereby contributing to our 'reasoned' judgements, rationality, and associated decisions. They are already within us, but to be consciously aware of them, they often need to be drawn out through education, practice, and reflection, thereby helping us to form habits and develop good characters that will enable us to choose right actions.

3.4 Twenty-first-century Ethics

How do people make ethical decisions today? While they may not be aware of it, they are constantly using one of a number of ethical approaches. The most prevalent one in use is called *expressionism*,[8] earlier known as *emotivism*. It is based on 'going with our feelings', denying the possibility of ethical knowledge that might guide our actions, with the belief that ethical terms are used to express certain feelings that are not useful beyond these feelings. Ultimately, it simply leaves people to make ethical decisions based on their *feelings* rather than any principles. As we all know, our feelings often deceive us through a lack of complete understanding of them or a complete understanding of the situation that gave rise to those feelings. I recall an advertisement on TV that showed a scruffy young man running towards an old lady who was clutching her handbag to her chest with a look of fear on her face – we were led to feel horror and disgust that this young man was trying to snatch the bag of a defenceless old lady. The camera then panned back, and we could see that in fact the young man was running to push the lady away from under a suspended platform above her, where a worker was about to lose control of some paint tins which were close to falling on the lady below. The scruffy young man was not a thief but a hero! Our feelings as onlookers were deceived until we had a bigger picture.

Many people tend to think of ethics as a list of 'dos and don'ts' that effectively become rules of action, much in the style of the 'Ten Commandments'. This approach suggests that if we try hard enough, we should be able to come up with a set of rules for today's society and conditions to guide all our actions. However, this approach is not as simple as it might first seem, as can be explained by looking at another area of learning for children, namely language acquisition. A child picks up knowledge of a language by the age of three or four by experience alone. Hundreds of linguists have been working for decades to formulate that experience into rules that could be followed to understand that language, and they are still a long way from success. We learn all our everyday practices, such as language, housebuilding, farming, or music, by mastering bodies of *practice* rather than by learning rules,[9] and the same applies for learning about ethics. All these practices are underpinned by theoretical knowledge that helps with the mastery of the practice, and this is also the case for ethics. However, it must always be remembered that the development of good habits through practice is key to knowing and choosing ethical actions. To look for a set of rules about how to decide the right thing to do is like looking for a theory of how to decide what to believe.

A child of eight will develop habits through being given clear guidelines to follow and then being corrected where necessary in a loving way using the language of values (see Chapter 4). A teenager needs to understand the reasons behind the guidelines as a part of developing ethical habits, and the reasons need to come from an ethical adult. With young adults, the situational context is key, since they will have begun to internalise their ethical habits due to practice and experience, such that they can start to discriminate between what might be right in one situation and wrong in another without needing external support. In all age groups, while the underlying ethical theory helps, it is learning by reflecting on practice in real-world situations, guided by ethical adults when required, that enables the development of good habits.

There are three ethical theories with clear underlying principles. The first is most often seen in use by politicians today. It emphasises the 'greatest amount of pleasure (or good) for the greatest number of people' and is called *Utilitarianism* or *Consequentialism*. Unfortunately, this is inadequate because issues regarding *justice*, individual *rights* and the ethical force of *commitment* are not included. This system will also be influenced by context and luck.

The second ethical system places emphasis on our obligations (our commitments) to others, such as parents, friends, work colleagues, or the poor and needy. This is known as *Duty ethics* or *Deontology* (from a Greek word meaning *duty*) and was first developed by Emanuel Kant (1724–1804), the German enlightenment philosopher. The core ethical focus for Kant was the 'good will'. For him, the value of the 'good will' is independent of its consequences. In this view, the core of morality is immune to luck.

The third system is that of *Virtue ethics*. The underlying principle here is that individuals need to develop good characters by practising *habits of virtue*, so that they will be able to act virtuously spontaneously in any particular situation. This is a development of Aristotelian/Aquinas ethics that re-emerged in the second half of the 20th century.

Science, for Aristotle, was a reasoned capacity for acquiring *knowledge*, while Art was considered to be the reasoned capacity to *make things*. The intellectual virtue appropriate to ethics was *practical wisdom*, a reasoned capacity for *action*. For both Aristotle and more recent ethicists, *practical wisdom* was a form of ethical perception rather than a set of rules. It is a moral skill rather than an artistic or technical one: A person with practical wisdom knows what to do and the reasons behind any decision. In our fast-moving, complex, and bureaucratic society, rather than focusing on what can be done by ourselves as individuals, the tendency is to follow rules. As any decision taken can have profound consequences on the happiness and wellbeing of self and others, developing a 'guiding compass' of practical wisdom provides additional help to just following rules. Such wisdom is reliant on a capacity to perceive a situation and to consider what the appropriate response should be. Rather than mechanically following rules, the individual needs to know themselves, be able to discriminate as to when to act, when to feel, when to desire, and in what ways: This is what practical wisdom achieves.

Wisdom as such is the ability to know what is true or right, often considered as 'common sense' or the collection of one's knowledge. One simple example is that 'the tomato is a fruit', however, you cannot use it in fruit salad as biologically it is a fruit yet culturally it is a vegetable. *Practical* wisdom, however, involves more than just wise knowledge; it is a special kind of practical reasoning regarding how to live well, happily, or virtuously and of recognising truth. If you want to improve a problem, you need to find out the details of the issues of concern. It requires a degree of self-awareness and being perceptive about others, as well as self-reflection, in order to assess our motivations and failures. Indeed, it is more important to understand than it is to be 'right'. Sometimes you may be required to 'bend the rules'. In reference to practical wisdom, it has been said that:

> *A wise person is like a jazz musician—using the notes on the page, but dancing around them, inventing combinations that are appropriate for the situation and the people at hand.*[10]

The idea of balancing competing considerations is also important in virtue ethics since different types of values can come into conflict. Examples include obligations to other people or institutions; constraints deriving from the *rights* everyone has as stated in various international declarations and laws; effects on other people's welfare; and, what often seems to be, the perfectionist ends of values. There are right and wrong ways of balancing these values, rights, and responsibilities, and *practical wisdom* is the rational capacity for doing so. Such practical wisdom will enable an individual to tap into her or his intuition (see Chapter 2) to give guidance that enables the better understanding of friends, family, and others. It will lead to a better understanding of the goal of any activity, and enable adaptation to any given situation, while also ensuring the awareness of and adjustment to changing environments. There will also be an awareness of the social norms of the context, and thus behaviours will be modified accordingly. Such practical wisdom is learned and developed through experience and practice, through listening to others, by caring, and by acting honestly and fairly. It combines reason with emotion.

EHV is an example of virtue ethics because it aims to enable students to acquire habits of virtue and decision-making skills which help to facilitate the development of ethical actions, while also developing the value skills needed for personal, family, community, national, and world harmony. For EHV, it is the goal that whatever thoughts come into the heads of students, they will think about and examine these thoughts in their conscience before acting on them. While EHV develops a sense of responsibility for the consequences of actions, as well as for duties to others, and acting with regard for the rights, life, and dignity of all persons, it is always the development of virtuous habits that is prime and that leads to these desired outcomes.

There can be cases in which people do the right thing for the wrong reasons; for example, one can do the 'right' thing by voting; however, it could be for the wrong reason, such as voting for a candidate because they are charming rather than for their policies. Similarly, there are cases in which people do the wrong thing despite pure motives, such as having to lie to protect someone. At the base are things of genuine value, the 'good' things. Actions that are motivated by an attempt to produce 'good' are right actions. Traits of character that result in 'right' actions are called *virtues*, and actions based on virtues express values in practice.

Utilitarianism and virtue ethics are both based on a concept of the 'good' while duty ethics is built on the concept of the 'right'. Any practical system of ethics will have to incorporate considerations of both the *good* and the *right*, since ethics is a complex of both, even though such theories appear incompatible. EHV is such a practical system: It develops a sense of responsibility for the consequences of actions as well as for duties to others. At the same time, it is the development of virtues and virtuous habits that is considered most important.

Complicating matters further, there are two radically different ways in which a life can be thought of as 'good', as originally proposed by Aristotle. There are first those lives that we *envy* – such as a life of adventure or of accomplishment, as in sporting fields, in business or in the arts and sciences. The second are lives that we *admire* – lives of self-sacrifice and dedication, lives well spent: Examples here would be Martin Luther King, Gandhi, Mother Teresa, Eddie Mabo, and the like.

Is happiness among the things that are praised, or among the things that are prized? Admirable lives are 'lives of virtue'. Enviable lives are good for their bearers, yet if it were only a life full of subjective pleasures and nothing else, it would be merely the life of a supreme spectator. Real contact with other people, hard work, and achievement all require self-sacrifice. A life without elements of the admirable would not be fully enviable. Individuals can resolve the tension between the enviable and the admirable life not in the abstract but only in the course of living, and also by reflecting on the values held that drive actions. This is another goal of EHV, which aims to educate students so that they are admired and envied because of their actions and their interactions, their self-awareness and their self-sacrifice, their strength of character, and their humility.

Utilitarianism offers too simple a picture of our ethical lives, saying in effect that the only morally significant relationship between my neighbours and me is that of them being possible beneficiaries of my action. But they may also stand to me in relationships of promises – the promise of creditor to debtor, of wife to husband, of child to parent, of friend to friend, of fellow countrymen to fellow countrymen and the like. In any situation, there are usually a number of demands on you: These obligations are what you should do, all things considered. What the individual has to do is to study the situation as fully as possible and then to weigh up all the considered options. In the particular situation and circumstances, one of these options will be more important than others, and the individual will decide that to do *this* duty is the most important thing to do in that situation at that time.

When making comparisons between different obligations, no general rules can be laid down. A person can only realise that a great deal of importance needs to be given to the duties of keeping our promises, of repairing wrongs we have done, and of returning the equivalent of services we have received. The process of balancing is something that has to be learned through practice and it is what the teaching of virtue ethics and EHV tries to do. Such practising results in the formation of habits of virtue that produce people of character. People of character have practical wisdom, enabling them to evaluate holistically all situations and thereby to act virtuously – they will do the right thing.

3.5 The Rebirth of Virtue Ethics and the Origin of EHV

Virtue ethics and EHV both re-emerged in the first case, or emerged for EHV, in the mid-20th century and came into their own in the 21st century.

3.5.1 Rebirth of Virtue Ethics

In 1958, two Oxford University postgraduates, Elizabeth Anscombe[11] and Philippa Foot,[12] wrote papers that challenged the (then) current view of ethics, based on emotivism, deontology, and utilitarianism, all of which were trying to provide universal principles for ethical action in every situation. Their view argued instead for a 'case-by-case' view of ethical phenomena that looked at ethical issues from their history and context. They tried to understand, rather than make assumptions about, the relevant ethical issue. Their ideas were further developed by Alasdair Macintyre in his seminal work 'After Virtue'.[13] He argued that ethics had lost its grip on any clear notion of the human *Telos* – the human goal, the picture of human wellbeing that furnishes ethical life with its objective. He supported Aristotle's view that the goal of human life was happiness, where happiness was seen as ***human wellbeing***, or a fulfilling human life. This led to a widespread revival of what is now known as ***virtue ethics***.

Virtue ethics treats ethics as being concerned with one's whole life, not just for those occasions when something with a distinctly 'moral' quality is at stake. Rightness is about what we are doing, while virtue is about how we are living. The ***virtues*** are those character traits that are essential to living a fulfilling human life, a life in which a person both cares about the right things and has the wisdom and skills to act intelligently about those things. A virtuous person expresses his or her virtue through action, but the establishment of any rules of right action is largely a secondary matter; it is presupposed that ***practical wisdom*** is possessed by the person of virtue. This kind of ethics begins not with the question, 'What is the right thing to do?', but with the question, 'What is the best way to live?', such as living sustainably, or helping others who are in need, or caring for your family: It is concerned with what to do with one's life and how to make it a happy one.[14] It involves reflecting on what sort of person one wants to be and what sort of ***character*** to develop. It consists both of caring about the right sorts of things and of having the wisdom and practical skills to judge and act successfully with respect to these things. Such skills come through education, practice, and experience, much like many life skills such as becoming a good doctor, a good artist, or a good parent. These are all features of EHV, which is a form of virtue ethics as discussed earlier in this chapter. EHV is a method of teaching and learning these practices.

3.5.2 The Origins of EHV

How did EHV arise? Coincidentally to the re-emergence of virtue ethics in the West, EHV was emerging in India, also in the 1950s, and had its origins in the teachings of Sathya Sai Baba, an Indian teacher, whose mission was *to impress upon humankind the crucial importance of leading moral lives by the practice of the universal Human Values of Love, Truth, Peace, Righteousness and Non-Violence.*[15] The most distinguishing feature of this educational system is the philosophy that helping students develop good character is equal in importance to fostering the development of skills that will help them earn a good living.

As the EHV programme expanded, demonstration schools were established in many countries in the world with the philosophy of incorporating values into existing curricula. There are now around 40 such demonstration Sathya Sai schools in about 30 countries around the world, including one in Australia, as well as many partnership schools and a whole range of informal programmes aimed at developing children and adolescents with good character.[16]

This immediate focus on the implementation of EHV in practice in both formal and informal settings marks a contrast with the Virtues Education movement in the West, even though they share similar philosophical principles. The virtue ethics movement has tended to focus more on its philosophy and theory, although now more programmes are being developed to put the ideas into practice in educational settings.[17]

While EHV is clearly located within the tradition of Virtues philosophy, even though its founder did not suggest this, EHV still develops the consideration of consequences, fulfilling duties, and being aware of emotional responses as valuable educational outcomes. However, these outcomes are always to be achieved through the development of character in students, through an understanding of, and the developing of the habits of a wide range of virtues. More is written on the details of the EHV programme elsewhere in this book, but two key features of the EHV programme are its holistic approach to education as described in Chapters 2 and 7, and its particular teaching techniques that are elaborated in Chapters 8, 9, and 10 of this book.

3.6 Educating the Ethical Mind

To educate the ethical mind, it is important to consistently use a language of values. The 'language of values' is made up of simple everyday words. All areas of the curriculum have their own specialised language – think of the language used by mathematics, physics, chemistry, geography, art, and the like. Values education is no different, and the use of a 'language of values' is critical to the development of character and an understanding of how to act for the *right* and the *good* and is a key part of EHV. While the language of values only uses familiar terms, the values vocabulary is not used as generally or as frequently as is required for successful values education. This topic is discussed more extensively in Chapter 4 of this book.

> It is ideal if a language of values can be taught to children and adolescents from preschool onwards, with the aim of developing good habits leading to good character. The language of values would be used throughout all lessons and all school and home activities as far as is possible. Such a language will bring out the values either being used (or not being used) in particular situations, and how appropriately these particular values have been used in that context thereby supporting the development of good habits. It is important to always remember *Do not treat 'Human Values' as a separate curricular assignment. Then, it will become dry and uninspiring. It must transform the way of life and should not stop with imparting information. It must be imparted more through example and practice rather than by books and formal teaching.*[18]

The ethical mind is one of five minds identified by the Harvard University professor Howard Gardner.[19] He describes someone with an ethical mind as *being able to abstract crucial features of their role at work and as a citizen, and acting consistently with those conceptualizations, striving toward good work and good citizenship.*[19] In addition, Gardner notes that *the developing of the ethical mind occurs after an individual has developed the ability to think conceptually and abstractly about their role as a worker and as a citizen. For example, asking yourself questions such as what kind of person, employee, or citizen do I want to be?*[19]

Thus, the development of these abilities is a crucial role for teachers and parents. Acting in an ethical way presupposes strength of character, and such character development requires supportive relationships with friends, family, parents, grandparents, teachers, community leaders, sports coaches, and the like.

Children and adolescents need exposure to role models – individuals as well as institutions – that exemplify desired character traits. Sometimes, these role models can be 'ideal', examples whom the children and adolescents may not know personally but whom they can admire from afar. But Gardner believes that the most effective examples are individuals who are known personally and who, while not immune from human foibles, regularly exhibit the desired character traits. Needless to say, our current society does not always support the propagation of such positive role models. Gardner points out that it *is difficult to behave ethically when so many rewards - monetary and renown - are showered on those who spurn ethics but have not, or at least have not yet, been held accountable by the broader society*,[19] but this simply highlights the need for better values education that will produce people of character who will improve society. More will be covered in Chapter 6 on education for the development of character and the implementation of EHV (Chapters 8, 9, and 10).

3.7 Action Learning – Putting Theory into Practice and Practice into Theory

It is to be hoped that as you have been reading this chapter, ideas have come to you as to how to put these theoretical ideas into practice in your own contexts. A good way to try ideas out is through *action learning*. Action learning follows a cycle of reflecting on what you want to do and why you want to do it based on your experience and theoretical ideas, planning how you might go about putting a change proposal into practice, implementing that plan, and then evaluating, reflecting on, and learning from the results. This leads to the cycle beginning again, as illustrated in Figure 3.2.

While this can be done by oneself, there are advantages to doing it with another person or a small group, as this brings in different worldview perspectives and ideas, thereby enriching the whole process.

You will get more ideas on the implementation of values education using EHV in subsequent chapters, and these chapters will also conclude, where appropriate, with similar suggestions for acting on the ideas contained in that

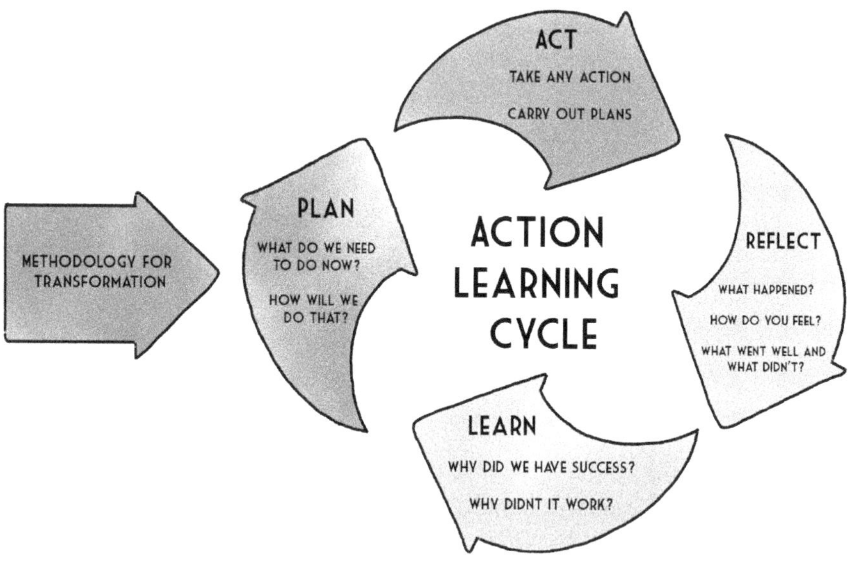

Figure 3.2 The Action Learning Cycle

chapter. As an introduction, here are some of the things that you might consider doing:

- Provide reading material that illustrates values in action. These could be biographies of famous people of character, or of people exhibiting particular character traits such as courage, empathy, forbearance, trust, etc.
- Illustrating mathematical, historical, scientific, and other topics with stories that have a value focus. You will find details and examples in later chapters, but one example might be rather than just saying 'NSW was set up as an English penal colony', you might also ask how you think it would feel to be a prisoner sent there from England? Thereby encouraging the development of empathy.
- Ensuring as far as possible that any books children and adolescents read convey the right messages and discussing these books with the readers to draw out the values they illustrate.
- When disciplining children and adolescents, doing so in a positive way that draws on a language of values.[20]
- Using music and songs to both provide a desired environment and to illustrate values ideas; once you start looking for these, they can be found everywhere, for example, the Bob Dylan song '*Forever Young*'.
- Individual or group planning of EHV lessons, direct or indirect.

The list is endless, and space prevents further examples. These are just a few ideas to start you off, and more will follow as you read on through this book. The important thing is for you to select something of interest for which you have enthusiasm. The authors hope that whatever you pick is enjoyable and useful to you as a teacher or parent.

Notes

1 Sathya Sai Baba, *Sathya Sai Speaks* (Prasanthi Nilayam, India: Books and Publications Trust, March 8, 1981), Vol. 15 (3).
2 Sathya Sai Baba, *Sathya Sai Speaks* (Prasanthi Nilayam, India: Books and Publications Trust, April 1, 1973), Vol. 12 (1).
3 *Rationality*: The quality or state of being agreeable to reason; having reason or understanding, where reason is a statement offered in explanation or justification.
4 Tao Lao Tzu, *The Ching Number 54*, trans. John C. H. Wu (Boston, MA: Shambala, 1989).
5 M. Scheler, *Formalism in Ethics and Nonformal Ethics of Values: A New Attempt towards the Foundations of an Ethical Personalism,* trans. M. S. Frings and R. L. Funk (Evenstone, IL: Northwestern University Press, 1971).
6 A. Shutz, "Max Scheier's Epistemology and Ethics: II," *The Review of Metaphysics* 11, no. 3 (1958): 486–501.
7 I. McGilchrist, *The Master and His Emissary: The Divided Mind and the Making of the Western World*, 2nd ed. (London: Yale University Press, 2018).

8 A. Macintyre, *Ethics in the Conflicts of Modernity: An Essay on Desire, Practical Reasoning, and Narrative* (Cambridge: Cambridge University Press, 2016).
9 *Ibid.*
10 Barry Schwartz, *TED Talk* "Our Loss of Wisdom" (2009). https://www.ted.com/talks/barry_schwartz_our_loss_of_wisdom#t-71062.
11 G. E. M. Anscombe, "Modern Moral Philosophy," *Philosophy* 33, no. 124 (1958): 1–19.
12 P. Foot, "Moral Arguments," *Mind* 67, no. 268 (1958): 502–513.
13 A. Macintyre, *After Virtue: A Study in Moral Theory* (USA: Duckworth, 1981).
14 Macintyre, *Ethics in the Conflicts of Modernity*, 2016.
15 Sri Sathya Sai World Foundation, *Global Overview of Sri Sathya Sai Education*, Ch. 1 (California, USA: Sri Sathya Sai World Foundation Arcadia, 2007), p. 3. https://www.sathyasai.org/about-us/education/global-overview accessed 12-1-2022
16 *Ibid.*, Ch. 4. http://sathyasai.org/files2007/GlobalOverview/Chapter4_30Jun07.pdf accessed 12-1-2022.
17 One example is the character education program developed by the Jubilee Centre of the University of Birmingham, UK. https://www.jubileecentre.ac.uk/ accessed 12-1-2022.
18 Sathya Sai Baba, *Sathya Sai Speaks* (Prasanthi Nilayam, India: Books and Publications Trust, December 31, 1984), Vol. 17 (31).
19 H. Gardner, *Five Minds for the Future* (USA: Harvard Business Review Press, 2009).
20 For detailed information on this topic, see: M. Taplin and A. Devi, *To Teach Not to Punish: A Practical Human Values Approach to Discipline* (Hong Kong: ISSE Ltd., 2004). https://issea.org.au/wp-content/uploads/2020/08/To-Teach-Not-to-Punish.pdf accessed 9-8-2022.

Chapter 4

Values Acquisition and the Language of Values for Teaching EHV

Roger Packham, Margaret Taplin, Kevin Francis, Bob Molloy, and Roz Malloy

4.1 Introduction

This chapter commences by looking at how values can be acquired and internalised in such a way that they can be used continually and without thinking consciously about them. This is an important point since many values education programmes adopt the more common approach of providing a list of principles, pillars, values, or virtues, which are memorised, or around which themed activities are planned. Rather, it is the internalisation of a language of values that Education in Human Values (EHV) sees as important, and that is explored here. The chapter also suggests how parents and teachers can facilitate this process of acquiring and internalising values. The chapter goes on to examine two key aspects involved in implementing values education:

- A language of values
- A framework for acquiring values

Outlining why these two features are important and then clarifying their meaning.

A fully implemented values education programme needs the following features as well, but these will be the subject of subsequent chapters:

- Techniques for teaching values (see Chapters 8, 9, and 10)
- Role modelling (see Chapters 8, 9, 10, and 13)
- A school culture based on values (see Chapters 13 and 14).

4.2 Values Acquisition

A key feature of EHV is that it is concerned *not* with imposing external values but rather with 'eliciting' or 'drawing out' values from within the individual. To understand more about this process, it is useful to consider a general model of how *affective domain*[1] factors, such as feelings, attitudes, emotions, and values, are developed. The Krathwohl, Bloom, and Masia Taxonomy[2] of the *Affective*

DOI: 10.4324/9781003478607-5

Domain is a longstanding model for the acquisition of affective factors, including human values, and it can be a useful model for teachers and parents wanting to help learners develop fully internalised value sets to guide their lives.

Table 4.1 gives a summary of the five main levels of this taxonomy (column 1) with a focus on values acquisition. The second column has been adapted from an online source[3] to present verbs that show a relationship to the acquisition of human values. In the third and fourth columns are guides to the roles the learner (column 3) and the teacher (column 4) can play in eliciting human values at each stage. The word 'learner' has been used here to indicate that this process is equally applicable to children and adults.

4.2.1 Consistency with Other Models

To understand further about how the process of eliciting human values may evolve, two other models are examined here. One is the *Trans-theoretical Theory of Change*,[5] which gives us an indicator of the stages an individual typically goes through in order to bring about behavioural change. The other is Gardner's model of multiple intelligences,[6] which helps our understanding about how to facilitate change and values acquisition in learners.

The Trans-theoretical Model (TTM) of behavioural change is derived from different theories of psychotherapy, thereby giving rise to its name. TTM assesses an individual's readiness for such behavioural change, such as adopting values as a guide to action. The TTM theory of change consists of five main stages: *Pre-contemplation* (not ready to change), *Contemplation* (getting ready to change), *Preparation* (Ready to change), *Action* (current change action), and *Maintenance* (Monitoring the change).

- At the *Pre-contemplation* stage, the individual is not yet acknowledging that there is a problem behaviour that needs to be changed. Here, individuals learn about values and the potential benefits of behaving in a values-based way, through being mindful of how they currently make decisions to act, and the benefits of changing their behaviour.
- *Contemplation* – Individuals who are at this stage are beginning to acknowledge that there is a problem but are not yet ready or sure of wanting to make a change. They are debating the pros and cons of a behavioural change, so need to learn about the kinds of people they could be if they were to change, especially learning from role models who exhibit that values-based behavioural change. It can be argued that this aligns with the Krathwohl *et al.*[7] *Receiving* stage; in order to move from pre-contemplation to contemplation, the individual first needs to become aware of the values concepts and their meanings.
- At the *Preparation* stage, individuals are ready to change and are willing to take small steps towards values-based behavioural change. Here, they might tell family or friends that they want to change as a way of getting support

Table 4.1 Krathwohl *et al.* Taxonomy[4] Adapted for Values.

Category	*Examples and keywords (verbs)*	*Role of the learner*	*Role of the teacher/ facilitator*
Receiving Phenomena: Awareness, willingness to hear and tolerate new ideas.	Acknowledge, describe, identify, name, understand, use.	Aim to understand the meaning and role of values. Listen to talk about values from teachers, parents, and others. Describe the values prominent in their lives.	Describe the core values and some values aspects. Talk about the benefits of following values. Expose learners to the values through their actions.
Responding to Phenomena: Active participation. Attend and react to a particular phenomenon. Compliance in responding, willingness to respond, or satisfaction in responding (motivation).	Comply, conform, discuss, present, tell.	Know the rules and show some commitment to practising them. Comply with values behaviours. Begin to use values in daily life, with or without prompting.	Talk about and expose learners to a range of values. Provide opportunities for learners to demonstrate values in use, directly or through scenarios. Model values in the teacher's/parent's own behaviour.
Valuing: The worth or value a person attaches to a particular object, phenomenon, or behaviour. This ranges from simple acceptance to the more complex state of commitment. Valuing is based on the internalisation of a set of specified values, while clues to these values are expressed in the learner's overt behaviour and are often identifiable.	Appreciate, demonstrate, initiate, justify, respect, share the ideas.	Demonstrate belief in the use of a range of values and their benefits for self and others. Propose a plan for social improvement in their life and follow through with commitment. Willing to be perceived by others as practising and believing in certain values. Become more proficient in using a range of values and relinquish old behaviours. Support, debate on the complexity of behaving with values.	Continue to talk about, model and expose learners to the values but also encourage them to reflect and debate about the implications for their own lives. Ask learners to share experiences and encourage open debate about any issues raised.

(*Continued*)

Table 4.1 (Continued)

Category	*Examples and keywords (verbs)*	*Role of the learner*	*Role of the teacher/ facilitator*
Organising: Organising values into priorities by contrasting different values, resolving conflicts between them, and creating a unique value system. The emphasis is on comparing, relating, and synthesising values.	Adhere, compare, defend, generalise, explain.	Recognise the need for balance between freedom to do whatever comes to mind and appreciating when values-based behaviour is more appropriate. Apply values consistently to real-life ethical issues. Accept responsibility for own behaviour. Relate a new value concept to those already held and bring it into a harmonious and internally consistent system. Discuss and develop their own theories about what the values mean to them in their own lives.	Continue to talk about, and expose learners to the values, but also encourage them to think about how the values can be applied in all aspects of their daily lives.
Characterising ***(Internalising Values):*** Possession of a value system that controls one's behaviour. The behaviour is pervasive, consistent, predictable, and, most importantly, characteristic of the learner.	Consistency, discriminate, revise, serve, solve.	Show self-reliance and self-confidence in practising values, even in the face of opposition. Display a commitment to ethical practice on a daily basis. Revise judgements and behaviour in light of new evidence. Act consistently in accordance with the values he/she has internalised in a wide range of complex contexts. Aim to value people for what they are, not how they look. Avoid/resist behaviour that goes against the values even under peer pressure, apply the values to solve problems or resolve conflicts, and can clearly be seen to be applying the values consistently in daily life. Learners at this stage are being true to themselves and who they really are – living by what they really believe to be right.	Be a consistent role model. Provide feedback on observed behaviour. Discuss ethical dilemmas and allow learner to choose from possibilities.

for adopting values-based behaviour. They need to be encouraged to think about how they might feel when acting differently. The better prepared they are, the more likely the change will be sustained. It is suggested that, as this begins to happen, the learner moves towards Krathwohl's *Responding* stage, in which she/he begins to be committed to the idea of values as a guide to behaviour. In the next level.

- *Action*, the learners are coming to value the ideas, so the behaviour actually changes. At this stage, they need to learn ways to keep up the values-based changes through being aware of situations that might discourage them and thinking positively about themselves and their successes. They need to avoid people and situations that might ethically challenge the values they are aiming to adopt.
- The fifth stage is *Maintenance*, when the behaviour change is maintained. Individuals need to be aware of all situations and, where possible, avoid ethically difficult situations. They need to learn how to cope with stress and stressful contexts caused by ethical challenges, to share their experiences, and to get feedback and support from people they trust who exhibit values-based behaviours. This appears to be a demonstration of the Krathwohl *et al.*[8] *Organisation* and *Characterisation* stages.

Turning now to ***Howard Gardner and his development of Multiple Intelligences***,[9] it should be noted that Gardner extended his concepts in a number of subsequent publications.[10] His ideas have been accepted widely by practising educators, as they move away from a focus on the single intelligence of *IQ*[11] and academic achievement to first acknowledging *EQ*,[12] and then to eventually include eight intelligences and the methods for developing them. These concepts marry very well with the principles behind EHV and its teaching techniques (see Chapters 8, 9, and 10). Gardner's eight intelligences and their link to EHV are explained in Table 4.2.

These components were developed further,[13] and the authors looked at the applications and development of Multiple Intelligences and the five Minds in Practice. In Gardner's own words:

> *When we speak about good work, we speak of work that is excellent in quality – first rate; work that is engaging – personally meaningful, something that you really believe in and want to do; and work that is ethical – work that constantly thinks about its implications for others, for the broader community. We talk about it as being responsible or ethical.*[14]

Gardner went on to say:

> *And while these are all connotations of the word 'good' in English, we now think of them as an intertwined triple helix of three Es: Excellence, Engagement, and Ethics.*[15]

Table 4.2 Gardner's Multiple Intelligences

Identified intelligence	*Brief descriptor*	*How used in EHV*
1. Linguistic	*Word smart*	Use of storytelling, writing journals, and discussion of values being presented
2. Mathematical	*Number/ reasoning smart*	Reflection on scenarios and engagement in problem-solving using values within the scenarios
3. Spatial	*Picture smart*	Artwork, creation of posters, creating spatial designs for role plays, and dramatic interpretations to illustrate values
4. Body-kinaesthetic	*Body smart*	Expression of values through movement, e.g., dance, dramatic performance
5. Musical	*Music smart*	Development of values concepts from listening to and composing values-based songs
6. Interpersonal	*People smart*	Interactions with others in values-based ways, engagement with other students, teachers, and parents
7. Intrapersonal	*Self-smart*	Awareness of self, e.g., use of silent sitting and positive affirmations; development of self-awareness through ethical examination and empathetic reflection of values (see Chapter 10)
8. Naturalistic	*Nature smart*	Engagement in caring for the physical world and investigation of sustainability issues through values-related programmes such as Ceiling on Desires (see Chapter 11)

Gardner acknowledged that, upon more reflection and research, there should perhaps be a fourth E, *Empathy*. EHV provides a solid platform for individuals to become engaged actively in excellent work, which is indeed highly ethical and promotes empathy towards others.

4.2.2 *Insights from the Three Models*

By considering the TTM and Multiple Intelligences theories together with that of Krathwohl *et al.*,[16] it can be concluded that all of these models essentially point to processes of gradual growth in values acquisition:

- This growth is from a simple understanding of a single value linked with other values to the incorporation of these values into an internalised value set that can guide behaviour in a range of contexts.
- It requires the understanding of appropriate processes to facilitate continuing growth that develops all aspects of the learner's intelligences.

- It is helped by splitting growth in values acquisition into named stages and then using the ideas of multiple intelligences to ensure all the learner's needs are facilitated as well as possible.

It should also be recognised that the '*stages*' are simply arbitrary, albeit useful, divisions in a continuum, and that a learner needs to start a values-education programme by first learning about and reflecting on the meaning and role of a range of individual values; for EHV these are the five core values of Love, Peace, Truth, Right action, and Non-violence, together with their various value aspects, as discussed below. Encouragement by teachers, parents, and significant others to build these into a value system that is internalised by the learner is key to success.

The process of values acquisition is always done by the learners themselves, yet facilitated in a range of ways to develop all the individual learner's various intelligences by teachers, parents, and significant others, until such time as the learner has the ability and confidence to act independently. In this process, role modelling by teachers and parents is of critical importance. The process is the same for a young child in a kindergarten class or an older child, adolescent, or adult who is starting to acquire and act upon the language of values.

4.3 The Language of Values

Every subject taught, including each of the Key Learning Areas (KLAs), has a basic vocabulary, a language which expresses, defines, and captures the scope and uniqueness of that particular subject area. Values education is no different; it also needs a vocabulary which allows people to manipulate and tease out an understanding of values through an awareness of social behaviour, emotions, and other affective domain issues.

A crucial thread running through the entire process of eliciting values and transforming the individual's behaviour is the language of values. This is something that recurs at all stages of education (K-12 and beyond), although the way in which the language is used changes as the learner matures. With the Krathwohl *et al.*[17] *Awareness* stage, for example, the concern is with introducing a values vocabulary to describe the relevant human values, and hence aiding learners to begin to understand values as well as acquiring them as valuable concepts. This can be achieved by the *direct method* of teaching EHV (see Chapter 8). Once the values concepts are understood and the individual has the values vocabulary to talk about them and discuss them, total immersion in a values-enriched environment facilitates further development towards a whole *characterisation* (as per the affective domain stage) of a value system (or set) for the individual. The *indirect, or integrated*, approach to incorporating the values language into all aspects of the curriculum (see Chapters 9 and 10) and creating a *school-wide values culture* (see Chapter 13) helps students to see the importance of values in all aspects of their lives, helping them to begin to use them naturally. At this stage, using the values vocabulary to talk about issues enables the learner to reflect on the significance of the values concepts and thereby come to appreciate them more. The onus is put onto the learner to evaluate their own behaviour through using the language of values that they have acquired. For example, when a student commits a misdemeanour, it is often enough to ask the question, 'How might the outcome have been different if you had remembered to practise your values? Which value/s would have helped?'

Reflective questioning that encourages students to think and talk about what the values mean in their daily lives (see Chapter 10) is crucial at this stage to encourage them to recognise the consequences to themselves and others of accepting or rejecting values-based behaviours in their own lives. Through this process of constant reflection, students can move to the stages of *Organisation* in the affective domain hierarchy, and then *Characterisation*, where they are able to use the values to guide their actions spontaneously and consistently in any context.

In other words, the progression from direct lessons about the values concepts to a whole-school values culture enables *values words* to be developed into *values thoughts* before they then become consolidated as *values actions*.

4.4 A Values Framework

While the language of values only uses simple, everyday words with which most people are familiar, the values vocabulary is not used as generally, as frequently, or with as much conscious focus as is required for successful values education. The EHV programme has a basic framework of five core or prime human values – *Truth*, *Right Action*, *Peace*, *Non-violence*, and *Love*. These five relate to our interactions with all of life, and such a framework is needed so as to capture, in a simple way, all the areas of our interactions between our 'outer' and 'inner' worlds. In the words above the entrance doors of Plato's Academy, it helps all to '*Know Thyself*.[18]

4.4.1 The Five Core Human Values in History

Historically there were four *cardinal*[19] virtues – identified since the time of Plato (428–348 BC). These were:

- ***prudence***, sometimes called *wisdom*, which is the ability to discriminate appropriately, and that equates to *Truth*.
- ***fortitude***, also called *courage* which is the ability to confront fear and uncertainty, and that equates to *Right Action*.
- ***temperance***, sometimes called *restraint* which is the practice of self-control and moderation, and that equates to *Peace*.
- ***justice***, also called *fairness*, which equates to *Non-violence*.

These were added to in the Christian era around 300 AD onwards with the three Christian virtues of *faith*, *hope*, and *charity*, all of which are equated with *Love*.

Virtues and values are intertwined, effectively as practice and theory, in a person of good character, and more will be said about this in Chapter 6. For Aristotle (384–322 BC), all virtues were defined as a '*golden mean*' between an *excess* and a *deficiency* of actions. For example, courage was seen as a 'golden mean' between rashness and cowardice. However, Aristotle emphasised that this was not an *arithmetic* mean but a variable one dependent on particular situations and contexts.

4.4.2 The Five Core Human Values

People of good character have acquired virtues, summarised as the five core or prime values, as well as having developed *practical wisdom* through using them in a range of contexts (see Chapter 3). Such people will have learnt to discuss the meaning, breadth, and complexity of the values through the language of values, so they know what the right and good thing to do is, as a precursor to putting this right and good thing into actual practice.

As well as the historical links described, the five core human values align with a wide literature that suggests a balanced human being is one who has achieved health in five domains,[20] these being the *cognitive*, *emotional*, *physical*, *social*, and *spiritual* (see also Chapter 2). While EHV sees all five values as interconnected, associations can be made between each of these domains and each of the five core values in a similar way to the historical links outlined above. The cognitive domain can be associated with *truth*, the physical domain with *right action*, the emotional domain with *peace*, the social domain with *Non-violence*, and the spiritual domain with *love*. Yet in the same way that the five domains need to all be active and combine to make a whole healthy person, so too all five values also need to be present and interacting.

To clarify how EHV sees each of these core values, here is a summary for each of these five core values:

- ***Love***: *Love is selflessness. It is a form of energy which each individual transmits and receives every moment.*[21] Love is recognising oneness in all others. Love flows from the depth of the 'heart' or our 'being'. It affects all forms of life; it is something which grows with sharing.
- ***Truth*** is defined not only as free enquiry, open-mindedness, truthfulness, and honesty but also on a personal level as having oneness between thoughts, words, and deeds – in other words, integrity. At a wider level, it means realising the truth of equal value, and kinship of all human beings travelling on 'spaceship earth'. We are not separate islands but belong together as parts of an interdependent whole, which needs all of us co-operating with each other in order to function harmoniously.

- ***Peace*** can be defined in two ways: First, as the internal unity of feeling happy and at peace with oneself, free from conflicts and agitations which waste mental energy and impede both performance and happiness. Second, it can be defined as external peace in relationships with others and the world around, essential for united families and communities.
- ***Right Action:*** Right Action is used synonymously with *Right Conduct*, and involves choosing an action in keeping with one's conscience. It is conducive to one's own wellbeing and the wellbeing of all.
- ***Non-Violence*** refers to one's social obligations and general attitude of love towards the entire world and all its beings. The concept of Non-violence is not limited to the physical aspect and includes thoughts and feelings. One should not wish to harm anybody by thought, speech, or bodily action.

4.4.3 *Using the Core Values*

While the five core values are useful overarching ones, particularly for teachers in the classroom and parents in discussions with their children, when it comes to applying the language of values to particular situations, it is useful to be more specific. Thus, each of these five core values can be divided into *values aspects*. These values aspects of the core values when used in action equate to *virtues* (see Chapter 3), and it is the combined *habits of virtue* that make up a person's character, as discussed in Chapter 6. There is no specific number of these value aspects (virtues), rather EHV recognises that particular communities and cultures will decide on the value aspects that are relevant for them. Many values aspects can also be associated with more than one core value, dependent on the context and how the aspect is seen and used. This is not surprising given the earlier emphasis on all five prime or core values making an interconnected whole. As the founder of EHV says: *Human values can be listed as 50, 60, 70, 80 in all. But they can be better grouped under the following three headings, pure thoughts, pure words, pure deeds; thoughts, words and deeds coordinated with one another.*[22]

An initial list of such values aspects is useful in clarifying what is meant here, and so Table 4.3 provides examples. It will also be seen in subsequent chapters of this book (particularly Chapters 8, 9, and 10) how EHV explores each of these value aspects in detail to help learners gain a clear understanding of their breadth, depth, and the use of any particular one of interest.

The following are a few examples of students using the language of values in real-world situations, in order to clarify what is being proposed as the *language of values*.[23] Chapter 8 also looks at some of these value aspects in detail as an EHV teaching tool called *mind-mapping*.

Table 4.3 The Five Core Values and Associated Examples of Their Aspects

Core value	*Examples of aspects of these values*
Truth	Accuracy, curiosity, discrimination, honesty, human understanding, integrity, prudence, self-reflection, sincerity, wisdom
Right Action	Courage, dependability, determination, efficiency, endurance, fortitude, healthy living, independence, initiative, perseverance
Peace	Calmness, concentration, contentment, equanimity, forbearance, optimism, restraint, self-discipline, self-esteem, temperance
Non-violence	Benevolence, co-operation, concern for ecological balance, fairness, justice, respect for diversity, respect for life, respect for property
Love	Compassion, charity, consideration, faith, forgiveness, hope, humaneness, interdependence, selflessness, tolerance

4.4.4 Examples Using the Language of Values

4-year-old: Truth/Right Action/Non-violence/Discrimination: Distinguishing between good choices and bad choices, and to act on the good choices between what we should and shouldn't do.

Example: When Johnny used the 'F' word, Peter was able to tell him, 'That was a "bad choice" word'. (Sathya Sai Preschool, New Zealand)

4-year-old: Right Action/Love/Non-violence: Considering the feelings and needs of others.

Example: When Johnny used the 'F' word, the teacher asked him to think about how it might have hurt Peter's ears to hear it. She asked, 'Was that a **good choice**, to say something that made Peter's ears hurt?' Johnny was able to reply that it was not a good choice and to say sorry to Peter for hurting his ears. (Sathya Sai Preschool, New Zealand)

4-year-old: Right Action/Non-Violence: Acting on the right thing to do; being prepared to stand up for what they believe is right.

Example: Two boys were fighting. Harry went to intervene and stop them. Because Harry was usually the one causing trouble, he was blamed, and the teacher was going to punish him. Angela had seen what was happening, so she told the teacher that it had not been Harry's fault. (Sathya Sai Preschool, New Zealand)

4-year-old: Truth/Love: Seeing the good in others.

Example: Susy and Jane had a fight in the sandpit. Susy was broken-hearted because her best friend had hit her. When questioned by the teacher, Susy was able to say that the good things about Jane were .... Jane was able to say that the good things about Susy were ...... This helped them to be able to make up and be friends again. (Sathya Sai Preschool, New Zealand)

3-year-olds: Love/Empathy for a friend: Seeing the best in others.
Example: The teacher asked the children to 'Look at your friend. How can you tell if your friend is happy?'
Children's answers included: 'She smiles'. 'She is talking kindly'. 'She is sharing'. (Sathya Sai Preschool, New Zealand)

4-year-olds: Peace/Inner silence: Feeling peace in the heart.
Example: In a music lesson, the children were ringing bells to play a tune. The teacher asked them to hold the bells to their hearts between rings to still the sound. She asked them to put the sound into their hearts to make their hearts happy. One child spontaneously held her bell to the teacher's heart to make her heart feel happy too. (Sathya Sai Preschool, New Zealand)

Year 5 students: Peace: Using silent sitting to maintain inner peace.
Examples: 'If I am in a bad mood at home, I will do silent sitting by myself. My mood changes very quickly and I recover my equanimity'.

> "I was trying to do a painting at home, but it was not going well. I became angry and destroyed the painting. My father saw me and reminded me to do silent sitting. After silent sitting I became calm, and I did a very good painting".

> "When I encounter an unhappy situation, I seek a place of calmness to calm down".

Year 8 student: Right Action/Non-Violence: Acting according to conscience; choosing right from wrong, even despite peer pressure.
Example: 'I stopped doing many of the bad things I was doing at home. Instead of laughing and mocking at me, my friends now admire me. Some are drunkards and they have nowhere to go'. (Sathya Sai School of Zambia)

Year 8 students: Love/Right Action: Forgiving friends.
Example: 'Earlier this year, I had a very big fight with a friend. It was very upsetting and sad. In the end, we both showed the value of forgiveness and forgave each other. We now have a better relationship than ever'. (Sathya Sai School of Australia)
Example: 'A few months ago, I used the value of forgiveness to get over some old friendship issues. We reconnected and forgave each other, and our friendship is now even stronger than it was before. I consider this value to be quite important to me, as these people have now helped me through a lot and are always there for me, and I really appreciate them. I think that if you've been trying to fix old relationships and you've been thinking about reconnecting with old friends, it's worth it'. (Sathya Sai School of Australia)

Year 8 student: Right Action/Truth: Being honest and not making excuses.

Example: 'I did not want to hang out with a friend one weekend, and instead of choosing to make up an excuse, I decided to be honest with my friend. In the end, they respected my honesty, so in the end, everyone felt good by displaying the value honesty'.

Year 9 student: Right Action/Non-Violence: Acting according to conscience; choosing right from wrong, even despite peer pressure.

Example: A group of adolescents indicated that they either choose their friends carefully from amongst those who do not engage in destructive behaviours or try to tell their friends not to participate in destructive behaviours. (Sathya Sai School of Thailand)

Year 9 student: Right Action/Non-Violence: Acting according to conscience; choosing right from wrong, even despite peer pressure.

Example: 'Many students don't obey their mother or teacher. I can tell them to be good/do good. They listen to me and then they stop because they believe their friends more than their parents'. (Sathya Sai School of Thailand)

Year 9 student: Peace/Self-confidence: Facing fears.

Example: 'Peace lived as self-confidence helps me practise facing new things and be confident facing my fears'. (Sathya Sai School of Australia)

Year 9 student: Peace/Love: Generating happiness.

Example: 'My family has given me a lot of love, as well as everyone else around that I know. Knowing how loving people can make me happy, and that happiness can be turned into love, then that love can be given to other people'. (Sathya Sai School of Australia)

Year 10 student: Right Action/Non-Violence: Acting according to conscience/choosing right from wrong, even despite peer pressure.

Example: 'They ask me to join [drugs and smoking] but I don't, I just say no. Sometimes I say I'm busy. But I go to 'healthy' entertainment with them'. (Sathya Sai School of Thailand)

Year 12 student: Right Action/Non-Violence: Acting according to conscience/choosing right from wrong, even despite peer pressure.

Example: 'I found out that what I was doing was useless and everything was pointless in my life. I remember the nights I spent crying with regret and pain that I had wasted my life. I've always been glad that I came here .... I know my life has been changed in my devotion to helping others'. (Sathya Sai School of Zambia)

Year 12 student: Love: Practising gratitude.

Example: 'The value of love lived as gratitude has supported me through my character development and striving towards academic excellence. The senior years of high school have been challenging but the thing that helped me to overcome this was finding time to sit down and think about what I was grateful for. I go to a beautiful school, the teachers are always there to support us as students, and I have had the privilege of being educated in the human values. I practise this exercise whenever I become overwhelmed, and it has contributed to the dissipation of my anxiety which I needed to have strategies to manage'. (Sathya Sai School of Australia)

Year 12 student: Right Action: Developing independence and responsibility.
Example: 'Throughout life we are faced with challenges, even more so as young adults. Independence is a value that has allowed me to grow. I have recently realised as I age and now become an adult, I have more independence and responsibility. It is important that you display these values as it allows you to expand your horizons and develop your character. Independence has allowed me to maintain a level head when becoming an adult'. (Sathya Sai School of Australia)

4.5 Final Activity

Now it is time for you, the reader, to consider ways of putting these ideas into practice, using the method that was introduced at the end of Chapter 3, *action learning*.

Here are a few ideas to consider, and hopefully you have been inspired to formulate and try others for your particular context:

- What stage of the Krathwohl *et al.* model do you think you are at personally in regard to the growth of your own values? What can you do to move to a higher stage if you did not nominate the *Characterisation* stage?
- Think of how you might talk to a young person using the language of values. What happens when you try this out?
- Pick one aspect of one of the five core values and aim to follow it in all your actions for a day or more, and reflect on what occurs.
- Think of some value aspects that you can add to Table 4.3 that are relevant to yourself and your particular context, then try using one of them in some way.

4.6 Conclusion

Through becoming increasingly effective and efficient in using the language of values, such as is taught in EHV, learners will become more competent to discuss the meaning, breadth, and complexity of the five core values, as well as a contextual range of values aspects of these core values. Such a learner will develop *practical wisdom*, as discussed in Chapter 3, through using and reflecting on these values in a range of contexts. In this way, the learner will not only know what is *right* and *good* to do, but they will choose to ***do*** what is *right* and *good* because they have come to value such action as a part of 'who they are'. Such a development needs good values-based education, together with as much support as possible from peers, parents, teachers, and other role models, and will be explored further in subsequent chapters of this book.

Notes

1 The *affective domain* involves our feelings, emotions, and attitudes. This domain includes the manner in which we deal with things emotionally, such as feelings, values, appreciation, enthusiasms, motivations, and attitudes. Other domains in '*Bloom's taxonomy*' are the *Cognitive* and *Psychomotor*.
2 D. R. Krathwohl, B. S. Bloom, and B. B. Masia, *Taxonomy of Educational Objectives: The Classification of Educational Goals. Handbook II: Affective Domain* (New York, NY: David McKay Co., Inc., 1973).
3 http://www.nwlink.com/~donclark/hrd/Bloom/affective_domain.html accessed 5-4-2021.
4 *Ibid.*
5 J. O. Prochaska and C. C. DiClemente, *Handbook of Psychotherapy Integration: Oxford Series in Clinical Psychology*, 2nd ed., eds. J. C. Norcross and M. R. Goldfried (Oxford, UK: Oxford University Press, 2005), 147–171.
6 H. Gardner, *Frames of Mind: The Theory of Multiple Intelligences* (London, UK: Hachette, 2011).
7 Krathwohl *et al., Taxonomy of Educational Objectives*, 1973.
8 *Ibid.*
9 Gardner, *Frames of Mind*, 2011.
10 H. Gardner, *Five Minds for the Future* (Harvard Boston, MA: Business School Press, 2006); H. Gardner, *Changing Minds* (Harvard Boston, MA: Business School Press, 2006); H. Gardner, *Truth Beauty and Goodness Reframed* (Basic Books, New York: 2011); H. Gardner, *The Unschooled Mind* (Basic Books, New York: 2011).
11 ***IQ*** stands for Intelligence Quotient, a number representing a person's reasoning ability (measured using problem-solving tests) as compared to the statistical norm or average for their age, taken as 100.
12 ***EQ*** stands for Emotional intelligence (otherwise known as emotional quotient or EQ) is the ability to understand, use, and manage your own emotions in positive ways to relieve stress, communicate effectively, empathise with others, overcome challenges, and defuse conflict.
13 H. Gardner (with B. Damon, M. Csikszentmihalyi, and others), *Good Works: Theory and Practice: The Good Works Project* (2010). https://goodworksproject.org/ accessed 15-1-2022.
14 H. Gardner, *Good Work: Aligning Skills and Values: A Conversation with Daniel Goldman and Howard Gardner* (Florence MA: More than Sound Publishers, 2012). https://open.spotify.com/album/5rv7FaYETDlOjb4H9gnEvV accessed 15-1-2022.
15 *Ibid.*
16 Krathwohl *et al., Taxonomy of Educational Objectives*, 1973.
17 *Ibid.*
18 This comes from: Plato, *Phaedrus*, trans. Alexander Nehamas and Paul Woodruff. From Plato: Complete Works, ed. by John M. Cooper (London, UK: Hachette, 1997).

19 ***Cardinal***, meaning of the greatest importance, or fundamental.
20 The literature cites between four and seven domains. Five domains have been extracted from this literature, see for example: https://www.verywellfamily.com/definition-of-domain-3288323, and https://allwork.space/2019/05/how-to-address-the-7-dimensions-of-wellness-in-the-workplace/ accessed 15-1-2022.
21 Sathya Sai Baba, *Sathya Sai Speaks* (Prasanthi Nilayam, India: Books and Publications Trust, May, 1994), Vol. 27.
22 Sathya Sai Baba, *Sathya Sai Speaks* (Prasanthi Nilayam, India: Books and Publications Trust, August 31, 1981), Vol. 15 (20).
23 Actual examples from schools provided by Dr Margaret Taplin.

Chapter 5

The Ongoing Search for Meaning

Selvanie Naidoo

5.1 Introduction

As long as the art of living has not been mastered, mistakes are bound to be made that transgress laws of nature, hence the 'ups' and 'downs' of life. Lives are constantly affected by worldly conditions. For humans, there will be stages of a journey during which challenges cannot be avoided. However, we can learn to confront and manage these challenges, with the secret of success being an understanding of a person's own life. As the saying goes, *The journey of a thousand miles begins with a single step.*[1]

To fulfil one's chosen goals and to achieve a conscious flourishing life, one needs to have harmony at the four levels of human living, namely the individual, the family, society, and the natural environment. To understand the goal of human life, one has to first understand oneself, one's aspirations, and one's happiness. Second, there is a need to understand the other parts of nature, their interconnectedness and coexistence, and the role of human beings as part of nature (see Chapter 1).

An understanding of a goal-focused life is needed and can be achieved by a person of good character, which is an important goal of Education in Human Values (EHV).

Chapter 3 presented an understanding of the theories of values, ethics, morality, and practical wisdom, as well as how EHV is embedded in these theories. It also gave insight to allow for differentiation between *knowledge* and *wisdom*, where knowledge is about facts and information, while wisdom cannot be learnt and comes from an openness and willingness to learn from practical life experiences. It is something that should unfold through education and is an aim of EHV.

An example to illustrate this point (on a lighter note) is that knowledge is being aware that a tomato is a fruit and wisdom is about not adding the tomato to a fruit salad!

EHV enables learners to understand their personal needs and to visualise personal goals, aiming to guide learners in a direction that will help them to

DOI: 10.4324/9781003478607-6

fulfil their goals in life, removing confusions and contradictions to bring harmony to thoughts, behaviours, and actions.

5.2 Self-Identity

5.2.1 *Who Am I?*

If you have asked yourself this question, 'Who am I?' you would probably have answered with a first name, followed by a surname, the city where you were born, your relationships, or perhaps your profession, etc. When you were born, you did not arrive with a name, you acquired a name, and this very name became your identification or label. As you journey through life you acquire more labels, such as son of…, sister of…, friend of…, qualification, nationality, or even change labels, such as Ms to Dr or student to teacher. Individuals become attached to these labels and forget who they really are. It is essential to understand that each person is unique and authentic, is connected to every other, and is certainly a part of the universe.

> The founder of EHV says about this, *'You are not one person but three: The one you think you are; The one others think you are; The one you really are'.*[2]

From the time of birth, the question arises, 'What do we expect from life and what does life expect from us?' There is awareness that the interval between birth and death is all of life's experiences, so these additional questions arise over and over during a lifetime: 'Are you this body? Are you making mistakes? Do you have this disease? Are you a mother? Are you a son? Etc.' However, the body, the mistakes, the diseases – all of these roles have the capacity to change and, therefore, cannot be the authentic *you*.

From time immemorial, people have believed themselves to be the bodies that they have been given, and so they are affected by whatever happens to these bodies, whether they are happy or sad. They try to make happiness linger and try to avoid unhappiness. Very simply, the principle is that whatever people believe, they will be affected by, and whatever they believe does not belong to them will not affect them. Finding a scratch on a new car will cause upset if it is thought that only yesterday this new car gave so much happiness and has now brought sadness because of the damage. However, if you do not have this attachment to the new car, you will not be as affected by it being scratched. There is a part of everyone that is indefinable and changeless, that does not get lost or change with age, disease, or circumstances. This authenticity we are born with, we will live with, and will die with.[3] Further, it has been stated[4] that a key lesson in life can be to find our authentic, unique selves and to see authenticity and uniqueness in others. No one has ever experienced the world in the way a particular individual has, taking into consideration each person's history and life's events. However, it is only when 'who you are' is truly discovered that this uniqueness can be celebrated. The goal then is to access that potential, keeping the parts of an identity that continue to serve a person well, and shedding the old, habitual pieces that constrain them. As Margaret Mead said: *Always remember that you are absolutely unique. Just like everyone else.*[5]

The great renaissance artist Michelangelo was once asked how he created sculptures such as the *Pieta* or *David*. He explained that he imagined the statue already inside the block of rough marble, then chipped away the excess to reveal what had always been there. The marvellous statue, already created and eternally present, was waiting to be revealed (Michelangelo's *Pieta*[6]). Like Michelangelo's subjects, each one of us has this unique person within us waiting to be revealed. When we feel more connected from within, we discover that we need to live life not just on the outside, which is our outer world, but also from the inside, which is our inner world.

There are changes throughout life from childhood to adulthood. Children are dependent on their parents, and the child's whole world is mainly home and school. With the transition to adulthood comes maturity, and the world expands. To be comfortable with this outer expansion, there has to be an inner growth, which means developing control over the inner world of intellect and mind. This is when the purpose of education is realised, first and foremost in developing the skills to control the 'inner worlds' (intellect and mind) and, second, for education to bring out the best in that person. This should be made a priority in our lives.

5.2.2 The Outer World

The *outer world* is everything surrounding a person that is visible. It is made up of the *environment; places* – home, school, shops, beach, sporting fields; *people* – family, friends, relatives, and pets; *activities* – sport, music, games, travel, dance, functions, and events; and finally *objects* – smart phones, iPad, wireless headphones, online apps, TVs, video games, and online gaming. An example[7] of some of the problems that can occur with outer-directed persons is when things are not happening according to their expectations. Their reaction can manifest as anger, fear, sadness, depression, anxiety, or terror, and blame for this unhappiness can then be placed on others; complaints may be made about their life's situation. While looking to others for approval, they succumb to pressure, feeling that they have no choice in their own life's circumstances; they also feel they are at the mercy of others because of their dependence on the outer world (people, objects). They often make excuses for themselves with statements such as 'It's not my fault…', 'Don't blame me…' or they feel inadequate and make statements such as 'I should have done…', 'I should not have done…'. Everything starts with the individual. If people perceive the world as volatile, they will look for evidence to validate this. Other people may see life as wonderful, and attract pleasant experiences as a result.

Here is a story from the *Charleston Gazette Mail*[8] called 'Is your environment out of control?':

Last week, I was in a healthcare environment that is usually a peaceful place to visit. As a result of extremely polarized political views from their patients, however, their waiting area had become polluted. It got to the point that the professionals felt like they had lost control. Patients were spewing venomous comments, and others were retaliating.

This situation didn't arise overnight, and it will likely take a while to change. I suggested, though, that the practitioners look at how this had developed into such a downward spiral. Were they subconsciously projecting their own strong political views? Or starting to get defensive—or feel on edge—when they knew certain patients would clash?

This had built up to such a fever pitch that it was starting to cause a lot of stress in their environment and take a personal toll on them. We talked about ways to diminish these negative charges and how they could look at the situation as a disease—and vow they weren't going to be 'hosts' for the disease. Mind you, these are very positive people. And they found themselves unintentionally going down a rabbit hole—feeling powerless over the situation. We examined some ways to right the ship.

They disconnected the TV in the waiting room. Patients were arguing over which cable news station was on, so this took away their ammo. They agreed to declare their work environment as a stress-free zone by returning to their former environment as an oasis—here patients could come to escape their everyday pressures. They are looking for ways to divert the negative energy—having some funny stories on hand or sharing cute videos from YouTube.

You teach people how to treat you. And these professionals had unwittingly allowed their environment to become a place where this behaviour is OK. Well, it's not OK.

With consistent practice, I'm confident they can get their environment back to a more peaceful place over time. They have to be willing to commit to this daily discipline, though. I'm sure their patients will test them.

Are you listening? Our inner world is always talking to us. For the most part, though, we're not listening. According to author Carole Mandi, when your inner world is in disarray, the best thing to do is to stop and figure out

> what is happening on the inside. If you're unhappy with what your outer world is reflecting, then something has to give, explains Mandi, and it has to start internally. Just like the health care office with the toxic waiting room, it will likely take some time for your new thought patterns to take hold. And that's perfectly OK. At least you're moving in the right direction.

This illustrates a person's outer world reflecting the inner world. It is necessary to spend time building the 'inner world' and then the outer world will flourish, just like a garden that you look after carefully, watering and nourishing the bulbs and seedlings day after day, so that one day it yields luscious, rich, and beautiful flowers.

5.2.3 The Inner World

What is the 'inner world'? It is the place where individuals are able to gain insights about themselves and how they operate in the world, where true feelings can be uncovered and the 'shadow self' met. It is here that connections to the 'inner child' can be made, and the place where forgiveness of the self and others occurs. It is here that a person can learn to let go of the past and choose to grow into a 'new self'. The more self-awareness that you have about who you are, why you behave in the way you do, what motivates you, and what inspires you, the more self-control there will be over how your life is shaped going forward.

Where is this inner world? The *inner world* cannot be seen; it is a very special place and belongs solely to the individual. It is also called 'within' or the 'heart'. The 'inner witness', or *conscience*, is found in the inner world and prompts one to be honest. Within the inner world are *emotions* and *feelings*, such as happiness, sadness, confusion, excitement, nervousness, etc.; *memories* of the past, whether good or bad, past experiences; *life goals*, such as career, sports, and aspirations for change or transcendence. Inner-directed people have a strong sense of personal worth and self-control of their states of mind and happiness. Everyone can do this if responsibility is taken for inner-world development.

In reality, the facts of the past cannot change. However, how these facts are viewed, how individuals feel about them, and the stories that they tell themselves about these situations *can* change. These changes affect experiences of the past, which can impact on memory (see Chapter 2), and it is these memories that are part of the individual and shape them as the person they are today. This kind of change can be called *inner transformation*.

How can the inner world be developed? It can happen through having self-control over thoughts, emotions, and breathing, achieved through practices such as *silent sitting*, *breath awareness*, and *meditation* (see Appendix 5.1), all of which help to develop inner peace and happiness. Breath is the very essence of life; it is like a biological barometer that measures the emotional state of being. If you are calm and relaxed, you will breathe slowly and rhythmically. If you are angry, your breathing becomes fast and irregular. Appendix 5.1 provides examples of strategies to still the mind and strengthen the inner world.

It is important to identify what is of value to a person by them exploring their inner world. Consider how much time is spent in the outer world as compared to the time spent in the inner world. Then ask the questions, 'Who Am I? What are my goals or aspirations? What is the process of fulfilling these aspirations?' A journal would be a good way to record the daily processes and progress made.

Attitudes towards life have been influenced by parents, culture, teachers, and the environment and, based on these, attitudes and judgements are made about oneself. This then determines one's mental strength and inner strength. This inner power comes from how much one loves oneself and this is expressed through self-confidence, self-esteem, and fearlessness. For example, if you have a positive opinion of yourself, the opinions of others will not matter. Also, if failure in a task occurs, it will not shatter you, rather you will accept it as a 'learning experience'. When a person lives in love this will be expressed to others as caring, compassion, understanding, tolerance, kindness, and love. When energy is spent in this way, results can be seen in lives that are meaningful and filled with positive energy from within. The same can be said for the work done with children, spending hours of time with them to help them learn and grow. These positive qualities indicate great inner strength, resulting in inner transformation.

5.2.4 Emotions, Emotional Intelligence (EI), and Emotional Hijacking

Emotions exist within individuals all the time, and it is difficult to erase them. However, when the intellect takes charge with full awareness, it becomes possible to maintain emotional balance by consciously minimising negative thoughts. A metaphor could be 'to drive away darkness (negative emotions) in a room, switch on the light; where there is light, darkness disappears spontaneously'.

The concept of *Emotional Intelligence* (*EI*) describes the ability to identify, understand, and manage emotions. One of the concepts is that of the *emotional hijack*. In the words of Goleman.[9]

> *An emotional hijack refers to a situation in which the amygdala, the part of the brain that serves as our emotional processor, hijacks or bypasses the normal reasoning process.*

This is illustrated in Figures 5.1 and 5.2. Emotional hijacking can be triggered in some people by physical things such as bad smells, someone chewing

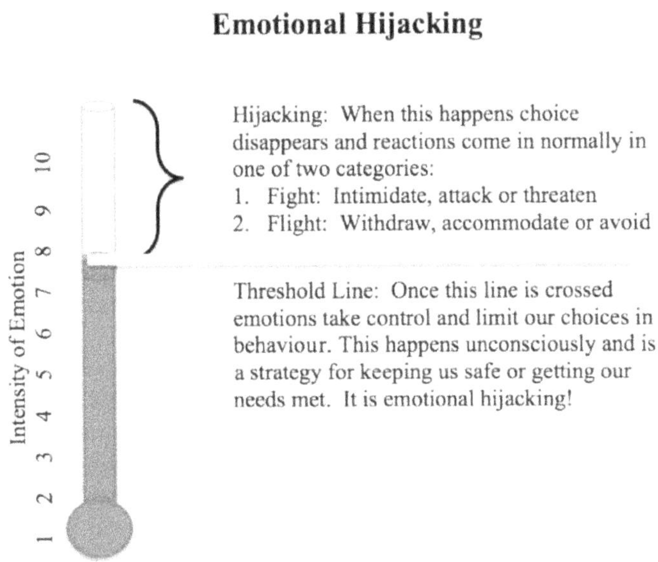

Figure 5.1 Emotional Hijacking[10]

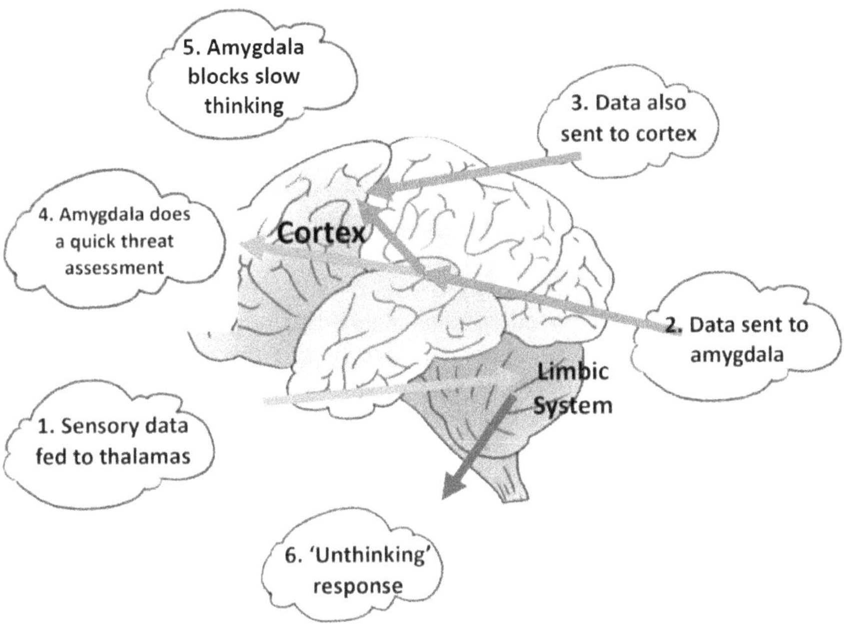

Figure 5.2 The Process of Emotional Hijacking[10]

with an open mouth, or someone cutting in front of your car whilst driving (road rage). Remember that becoming a victim of emotional hijacking is avoidable, and that increasing EI to achieve this is absolutely possible.

EI helps to build stronger relationships, to succeed at school and work, and to achieve career and personal goals. It can also help individuals to connect with their feelings, turn their intentions into action, and to make informed decisions about what matters most. EI can be improved with the regular practice of self-controlling emotions and staying calm rather than overwhelmed. To do this, it is first necessary to be aware of one's own emotions as well as the feelings of others. Without an objective sense of 'who we are' and what drives oneself, it is nearly impossible to be emotionally intelligent.

Figure 5.3 illustrates the behaviours to be expected from people with a low or high EI. The conclusion from this figure is that the goal is to be self-aware in relation to emotions. To attain peace of mind, one article explains[11] that a person needs to use their intellect to still the emotional outbursts pouring out from some of the mind's emotions. Like a wave, these outbursts have periodic ups and downs in the same way we experience pleasure and pain, happiness and suffering, elation and depression, all of these alternating all the time.[12]

Goleman[14] also states: *Once we're aware of our emotional responses as we're having them, we can start to regulate how they influence our actions. There are 3 emotions that most people find hard to regulate: anger, anxiety, and sadness.* One's efforts should be devoted to reducing the peaks and the troughs of emotional outbursts until the wave no longer exists and, finally, becomes peaceful, as Figure 5.4 demonstrates.

5.2.5 *Unity of Thought, Word, and Deed (3HV)*

The unity of thought, word, and deed in EHV is called 3HV, representing the three values of, Head Value, Heart Value, and Hand Value.

5.2.5.1 *Head*

The 'head' is to be understood or referred to as the location of the five senses, namely the eyes, the ears, the nose, the tongue, and the skin, through which information is received and transmitted. The external world enters the human body not just through the mouth and nose (such as when eating or breathing), but also through the other senses (ears, eyes, and skin). From birth until death, all experiences about the external world are gained through these senses (see Chapter 2). The five senses are windows to the outside world, but they also draw attention outward, forcing the acceptance of outside influences.

The mind plays a great role in all individuals, from children to adults, and is an important concept in the 'head'. What is the mind? This was discussed in Chapter 2, but here it can be seen as a bundle of thoughts. What are thoughts?

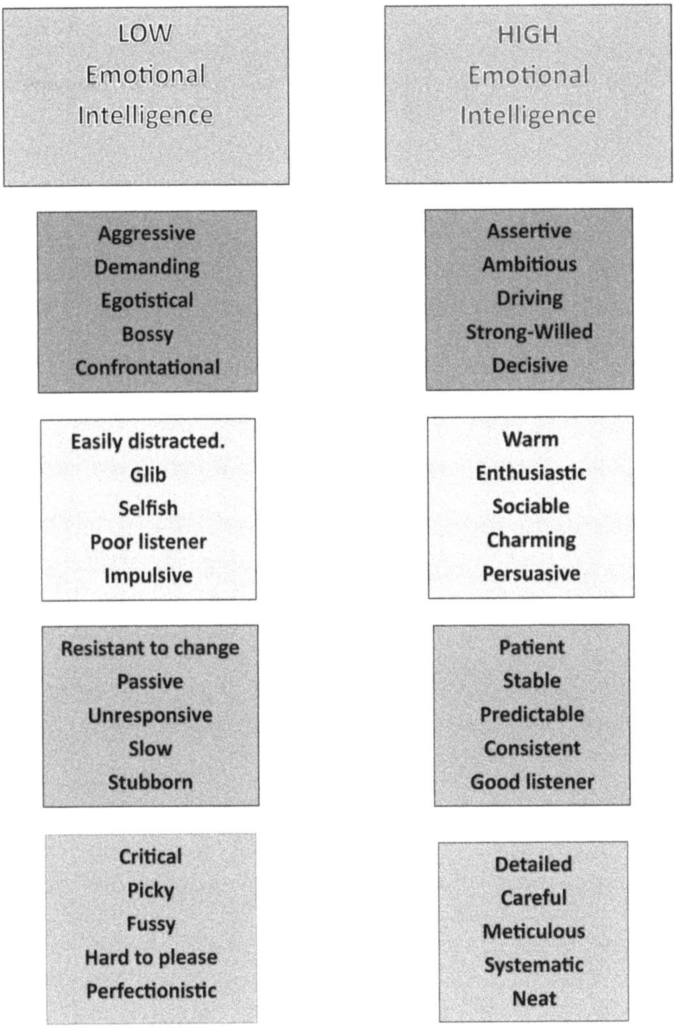

Figure 5.3 Different Responses to Same Inputs Based on EI Levels[13]

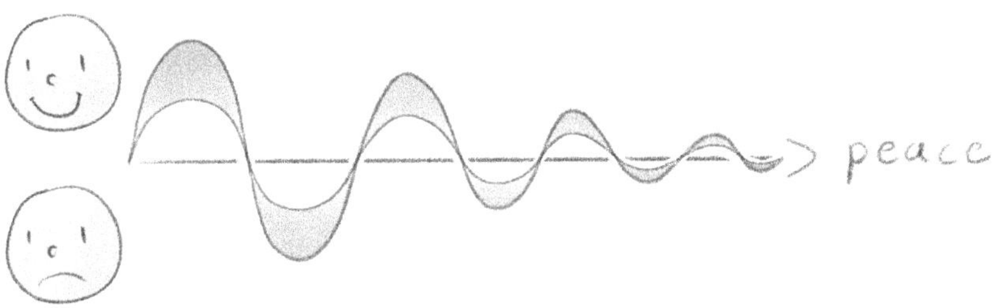

Figure 5.4 The Balance Needed to Find Peace[15]

They are bundles of desires. Thoughts thus turn into desires, desires give rise to cravings, and when cravings are strong, actions follow (see Chapters 2 and 12). No sooner do these attributes of nature and our senses start interacting, than the mind comes into play.[16]

5.2.5.2 *Heart*

The metaphor of the 'heart' represents the *conscience*, and thoughts should be directed through the conscience; this 'spiritual heart' is the seat of human values. In Chapter 2, this was located in the super-conscious part of the mind. One of the most admirable aspects of the 'heart' is the power of discrimination. Despite general thinking that this power of discrimination lies in the 'head', it is the 'heart' that has the capability to analyse which thoughts are right and which are wrong. If the thought is good, the 'heart' will approve it, and then it can be acted upon (metaphorically) by the *hands*.[17] Why is it that consulting the *heart*/conscience is often forgotten? This is because of being in a hurry, or choosing to deliberately not go by the *heart/conscience*! Why is it that sometimes the 'voice' of the *heart* is not obeyed? The *heart* always speaks the truth, and the truth can be a bitter pill, leading to being afraid to accept it and preferring to embrace a more superficial life. Outside influences, such as peer pressure or blindly following others' habits, can also be contributing factors to such negative behaviours.[18]

5.2.5.3 *Hands*

A common saying is 'one's fate is in one's hands'. How can destiny be in one's hands? The human hand is full of flexibility and dexterity, and can perform a variety of actions, such as expressions of love, hate, rejection, acceptance, victory, and failure. Hence, it is the 'hand' that determines one's destiny. How can the purity of the 'hand' be brought out? Purity of the 'hand' is directly associated with the 'heart' and the 'head'. Together they make *3HV* (head value, heart value, and hands value). The 'hands' must carry out the tasks emanating from the 'head' and approved of by the 'heart' in a careful, respectful, disciplined, and committed manner.

Each person has the power to control everything said, felt, thought, and done. It has been stated[19] that truly free people are those who not only have knowledge of their 'inner worlds' but also have control over them. One should always act in accordance with one's conscience; ideally, what is wanted is that the *head*, *heart*, and *hands* operate in unison, and it is the conscience that lets a person know when this is not happening. Harmony in thought, word, and deed will be the sign of a holistically educated person; thus, control and proper regulation of the *head*, the *heart*, and the *hands* is the hallmark of a person of character.

5.3 The Goal of Life

With regard to life, Sathya Sai Baba has said *Life is a challenge meet it, Life is a dream realise it, Life is a game, play it, Life is love enjoy it,*[20] a great set of ideas to follow. Now that there is an understanding of self-identity, of *who we really are* and our *inner and outer worlds*, there are some further questions to be asked:

- What is life? (purpose)
- What do you want from life? (goal)

How often do people really stop to think about these questions, and what might be their conclusions?

Exercise

- Spend a few moments thinking about the questions above, and jot down some responses.
- If you came to a conclusion, have you pursued this goal (what you want from life) or have you ignored it, or were you not prepared to change your way of life?
- Where has life led you thus far, and what is your present state of 'being'? Are you happy, content, and at peace with yourself, the people around you and the world?
- If not, perhaps a reassessment of your life and state of 'being' is required so that your purpose and goal of life can be fulfilled.

There is a process to reach the goals in life, especially when setting personal goals. First, you need to take stock of where you are at present and make an honest assessment of where you have succeeded and where you have failed. This could be related to finances, career, or relationships. It is only then that you can determine how to move forward. It is important to be aware that things can change along the way as life moves on, as new people are met, fresh experiences happen, new ideas are encountered, and you grow older. When changes are made, personal values transform, and so does the sense of purpose, which means these need to be worked on continually.

Goals need to be simple, measurable, realistic, relevant, and timely. One of the biggest challenges in meeting any goal, whether it be related to productivity, waking early, changing a habit, exercising, or just becoming happier, is finding the motivation to stick with it. Sticking with a goal for long enough almost always gets one there eventually; it just takes patience and motivation. Long-term goals are aspirations, desires, and dreams. Short-term goals allow day-to-day progress on the big, life-enhancing changes that are wanted.

5.3.1 *Short-Term Goals*

Short-term goals are the processes required to reach long-term, aspirational goals, and here again, they can vary with individuals. Here are some examples:

- Walking on the beach or in nature with the family every weekend for an hour
- Writing in a journal every night before sleeping
- Checking recycling bins weekly to make sure appropriate items are in them
- Waking up at 6 am daily; practising mindfulness/meditation at 0615 and exercising at 0630-15 minutes each
- Once a month, helping to feed the homeless

Exercise

Write down some short-term goals for yourself

5.3.2 *Long-Term Goals*

Initially there is a need to ask exactly what the long-term goals are. The answers will vary depending on the individual and the four levels of human living mentioned earlier: Self, family, society, and environment. Here are some examples:

- to live a happy and balanced life – mentally, physically, emotionally, socially, and spiritually
- to provide love, comfort, and quality time for the family
- to make life significant by living it to its fullest
- contributing to making the world a better place for all living beings and the environment
- to serve the less fortunate in society and so improve their lives

Exercise

Write down some long-term goals/aspirations for yourself

Having short-term goals is like driving in the dark with the headlights on; as long as what is in front can be seen, the destination can be reached safely; they guide what to do now. Long-term goals are the maps and blueprints; they show what is to be achieved in the future.

5.3.3 *Goals and Choices*

One of Ralph Waldo Emerson's quotes states that: *We need to be useful, to be honourable, to be compassionate, to make some difference, and to have lived and lived well.*[21] Within all people is the power to make a life significant, regardless of nationality, ethnicity, capabilities, and opportunities. Discipline and determination help everyone to reach goals. The goals of human life differ for each individual. Some believe that there is a need to strive for that which will give enduring happiness and not just transient pleasures.

According to Aristotle:[22] *Happiness is a final end or goal that encompasses the totality of one's life. It is not something that can be gained or lost in a few hours, like pleasurable sensations. It is more like the ultimate value of your life as lived up to this moment, measuring how well you have lived up to your full potential as a human being.* This requires the making of choices, some of which may be very difficult. Often the 'lesser good' promises immediate pleasure and is more tempting, while the 'greater good' is painful and requires sacrifice. It may be easier and more enjoyable to spend the night watching television, but you know that you will be better off if you spend it researching for your university assignment or some similar goal (see also Chapters 3 and 12).

Developing a good character (see Chapter 6) requires a strong effort of inner strength to do the right thing, even in difficult situations. Remember, the past is gone and is beyond control, but the future is yet to come, and it is in every single being's hand; therefore, the need is to focus on the present. In every moment, a person can be seen to be either in a state of *love* or in a state of *fear*. When in a state of fear, the brain's 'fight or flight' system is activated, and survival is the focus: Higher reason and morality cannot be used in such a situation as the animalistic portion of the brain is in control, as described earlier in this chapter as 'emotional hijacking'.

Through the simple but powerful practice of inner strength, the ability to shift out of fear and expand into love can occur, leading to an increased focus on the present moment. Each moment can now be seen as a precious opportunity to choose love over fear. Every time that choice is made, a person travels further along their journey to a better life.

5.4 The Purpose of Life

Life is meant to be lived with purpose. Having a purpose can guide the journey through life with a sense of direction. As the paradoxical saying goes, 'If we fail to plan, we plan to fail'. Decisions that are made influence behaviours and help to create goals. For example, some people may consider their purpose connected to a successful career while for others their purpose lies in their responsibilities to their family or friends, or perhaps both. Life is not meant only to be happy but also to have value, to be productive, to make a difference, and to be able to show at the end that one did live a meaningful life. All humans are aware that they have to go through the life cycle of birth, growth, sickness, and death, and this can be compared[23] to a candle burning brightly and then being extinguished; as the following quotation from Hunter S. Thompson infers, all lives can be meaningful, *Life should not be a journey to the grave with the intention of arriving safely in a pretty and well-preserved body, but rather to skid in broadside in a cloud of smoke, thoroughly used up, totally worn out, and loudly proclaiming 'Wow! What a Ride!'.*[24]

5.4.1 Lessons in Life

This is a story[25] that was narrated by Stephanie, a woman in her early forties:

> One Friday afternoon I was driving from Los Angeles to Palm Springs. There was freeway traffic, however I was anxious to get to spend a relaxing weekend with friends. At the outskirts of Los Angeles, the cars in front of me came to a standstill.
>
> As I came to a stop behind a long line of cars, I glanced in my rear-view mirror to discover that a car behind me was not going to stop. In fact, it was hurling towards me with tremendous speed. I realised that the driver was not paying attention and that I was going to be hit and hit hard. I knew that given his speed and the fact that I was nose-to-rear with the car in front of me stopped, I was in great danger. I realised in that moment that I might die!
>
> I looked down at my hands and clenched on the steering wheel. I had not consciously tightened them; this was my natural state, and this is how I lived life. I decided that I did not want to live that way, nor did I want to die that way.
>
> I closed my eyes, took a breath, and dropped my hands to my side. I let go. I surrendered to life and to death. I was then hit by an enormous force. When the movement and noise stopped, I opened my eyes, I was fine. The car in front of me was wrecked, the car behind me was demolished. My car was compacted like an accordion.
>
> The police told me I was lucky I had relaxed, for muscle tension increases the likelihood of severe injury. I walked away feeling I had been given a gift. The gift was not that I had survived unhurt, it was greater than that. *I saw*

how I had been living life and was given the opportunity to change. I had held life with a clenched fist, but now I realised that I could hold it in my open hand, as if it were a feather resting on my palm. I realised that if I could relax enough to release my fear in the face of death, I could now truly enjoy life. In that moment, I felt more connected to myself than I ever had before.

Stephanie learned a lesson, not about death but about living and life. It is when people are pushed to the edge of life that they see life most clearly. Why wait until the end of life to learn the lessons that could be learned now?

5.4.2 Increasing Self Awareness

There is a need for all of us to become more self-aware in our daily lives. Essentially, this means that more attention is paid to the emotions that are experienced, resulting in a better understanding of why personal actions are taken. The more that is known about personal habits, the easier it becomes to improve on those habits. Self-awareness results in self-improvement, which means that the 'right thing' will be looked for, and that will result in right actions.

Having self-awareness results in a sharper realisation of personality, including your individual strengths and weaknesses, thoughts, beliefs, emotions, and motivations. How does one increase self-awareness? Here are some suggestions:

- *Silent sitting:* Taking even just five minutes to sit quietly and follow the breath can help a person to feel more conscious and connected for the rest of the day
- *Mindfulness*: To focus the mind and observe thoughts
- *Slowing down*: Live the present moment at a slower pace
- *Looking at yourself*: Objectively, factually, and not influenced by personal feelings
- *Keeping a journal*: Ideally daily, for self-inquiry and self-reflection
- *Writing down your goals*: Short-term and long-term, together with plans and priorities
- *Eating well*: A well-balanced diet
- *Limit screen time*: Keeping phone, computer, and television time in check
- *Exercising:* Cardiovascular and stretching exercises are ideal tools to focus your energy
- *Enjoying nature*: Spend time in nature whenever possible
- *Selfless service:* Serve the needy in any way you can
- *Listening to music:* Music helps increase energy and focus

Understanding that *energy flows where attention goes*[26] is the first step towards the mindful achievement of goals. With this powerful concept in mind each day, training with the above tools can develop a focus on the positive aspects of life's experiences (see Chapter 11), and enhance mindfulness and living in the present. By starting to attract more of what is wanted in life, an understanding emerges of the power of focusing the mind on the goals that matter most. Personal thoughts and interpretations begin to change by developing self-awareness, and this change in mental state will also alter the emotions and increase EI. This is an important factor in achieving overall success. In this state of wellbeing, a start is made to becoming more responsible, and being fully responsible is to be fully conscious, a paradigm shift in ways of thinking and living. The educational process of EHV supports such a transformation, with one report stating that *EHV raises the level of awareness of our human purpose on earth and aims to lift morality to a higher level by igniting the conscience of humanity through living life consciously rather than drifting along unconsciously, with the key outcome being the transformation of humanity to a more flourishing life for all.*[27]

For some individuals, the purpose of life is to serve others, yet in doing so there needs to be no expectation of 'something in return'; rather the intention needs simply to be purely for the purpose of reducing another's misery and should benefit both the giver and receiver. Service to others is most effective when it is sincere and done from the heart, without any expectations. Only then does it become metaphorically 'fruitful' and, as the saying relates, 'trees do not eat their own fruit'. Service activities help to teach that human beings need not only to use their minds, bodies, and speech for themselves but also to help others, thereby contributing to society. This section is summarised by the following anonymous quotation: *When you learn how to live a meaningful life, everything you do and everything that happens for you has a purpose.*

5.5 Understanding the Journey to the Destination

5.5.1 Journey and Destination

Life is a journey filled with lessons, hardships, heartaches, joys, celebrations, and special moments that will ultimately lead to a destination. How people react to what they are faced with determines what kind of outcome the rest of the 'journey through life' will be like.

When referring to a 'journey' what is meant is a focus on the process (journey) rather than a focus on the destination (goal): The 'destination' is the vision and end goal. Therefore, enjoy the process towards reaching the goal. It also means being fully aware of the change process and the things that need to be addressed along the way. Very often there is a need to be flexible and adjust the initial goals if the process leads to somewhere different. By embarking on a process of change through a journey towards a goal, the initial understandings about the goal and associated expectations might change, so, 'destination' as well as 'journey' also calls for a continuous examination of the present situation in relation to a goal.

5.5.2 *Quality of Thoughts*

Some see the key mission of life as being the attainment of a happy and flourishing life, one that ends the 'miseries' of existence. Most people are constantly searching for happiness, but often fail in its pursuit. Also, a glimpse of happiness does not last forever since unhappiness and challenges cannot be prevented from occurring. Mahatma Gandhi told us to *Keep your thoughts positive because your thoughts become your words. Keep your words positive because your words become your behaviour. Keep your behaviour positive because your behaviour becomes your habits. Keep your habits positive because your habits become your values. Keep your values positive because your values become your destiny.*[28]

Referring to this quote, how do thoughts become beliefs? It is a chain reaction, as our *thoughts* lead to our *feelings*, which lead to our *actions*, which lead to our *results*. ... As results lead to repeated improvement, thoughts become *beliefs*, and beliefs then become automatic thoughts that drive our behaviours, which then become our *habits* (see Chapter 2). The quotation above expresses how the quality of thoughts shapes lives. As the past has created the person of today, the present thoughts will create the person of the future. In a similar vein, Chuck Danes said *Do not under-estimate the Power of Thoughts. Just as water has the power to shift and change earth's landscape, your thoughts have the power to shift and change the landscape of your life.*[29]

So how do people 'watch their thoughts'? What does it mean to watch thoughts? It is simply the practice of slowing down, paying attention, and noticing what is being thought about before reacting impulsively to unconscious thoughts (see Chapter 2). Here is an example of this practice:

> After a hard day's work, a friend, Angela, had made a scrumptious savoury dish for dinner. Preparation and cooking time would have been approximately two hours. Her five-year-old daughter had been helping to set the dinner table and took it upon herself to carry the savoury dish from the kitchen to the dining table. Just as she was about to place the dish on the table, she misjudged placement and the dish fell off the table, crashing to the ground. Food was splattered everywhere. When

Angela saw the mess, blood rushed to her head and anger began to well up through her body. Exhausted after a stressful day at work and cooking for two hours, her thoughts were rapid and irrational. They were so dramatic and with rage that it made the situation worse. At this point, she paused long enough to watch her thoughts and realised **YES**, this incident was unfortunate; however, it was an accident and could be sorted out in a couple of minutes.

Angela watched those raging thoughts for just a few seconds, and what she saw was how different her thoughts were from 'who I am'. The thoughts were caught up in ego and anger and not ones that offered any solution, or any way to ease the situation (recall Figures 5.1 and 5.2 showing the neural pathway for this emotional hijack/response). She realised those thoughts actually meant nothing and were not even true. She was not compelled to act them out; however, she could observe them and not give into these thoughts.

This flash of insight diffused the emotion immediately and allowed her to choose deliberate, conscious actions that helped her comfort her daughter and get things cleaned up. As good as this practice was, however, it did not give her one single idea about what to cook for dinner that night! A situation that clearly could have gone off the rails and become more difficult had she reacted to her initial thought flares. Thankfully, it actually became a way to connect with her family. Now this awareness has become part of her daily life as Angela realised the quality of her thoughts will determine her destiny, just as illustrated in the quotes above.

Much of daily life is taken up by habits that have formed over a lifetime. An important characteristic of a habit is that it's automatic, and not always recognised as a habit of behaviour. Daily activities are performed in almost the same way, so patterns of improved behaviour allow goals to be reached by repeating what worked, thus helping the 'journey' towards a peaceful and meaningful life that reaches its destination.

Finally, let us remember that *Without Goals, and Plans to reach them, you are like a ship that has set sail with no destination.*[30]

5.6 Overcoming Obstacles to Goals

5.6.1 Loss of Focus

Clarity, passion, and determination are needed after goals have been set and then they are bound to be achieved. However, these goals may need adjustment as particular obstacles present themselves. It is easy to say that changes need to be made but to actually do the work is very different. It is necessary to decide what kind of priorities are given to particular goals; otherwise, intentions will get lost amongst other daily activities. Giving up before results are seen is a symptom of impatience, the enemy of change. In today's digital world, most people struggle to allow for the time it takes to reach a goal. In other words, *minds* clarify the goals; 'hearts' provide the fuel; and determination will keep the journey going.

5.6.2 The Conflicting Human Condition

A setback to reaching goals can be overcome by the appreciation, or understanding, of the human condition. Achieving such understanding gives the ability to appreciate every aspect of behaviour. In effect, one of the greatest goals of life is coming to terms with the contradictions between such experiences as happiness and sadness, goodness and badness, elation and depression, and pleasure and pain. These alternating emotions come from the senses through the mind (see Chapter 2).

Jumsai[31] developed a model of the mind as discussed in Chapter 2. In this, the mind receives and processes information arising from the environment, using the five senses, in order to create awareness and understanding. The *subconscious* mind stores the memories of everything that is experienced. It feeds these memories to the *conscious* mind to control the individual's thoughts and actions and to obscure some perceptions of events that occur. An example would be an accident at the traffic lights, in which a young child experiences the feelings of anxiety, fear, and panic. The same feelings may surface every time that former child, now an adult, approaches traffic lights, since this experience is lodged in the subconscious. However, such techniques as meditation and conscious awareness can lessen the feelings of anxiety, fear, and panic. The *super-conscious* mind is the source of wisdom, knowledge, and conscience. In a well-balanced person, these three levels of the mind – the subconscious, conscious, and super-conscious – interact together to contribute to the physical, mental, emotional, social, and spiritual wellbeing of the individual.

In everyday behaviour, why are humans often competitive, aggressive, and selfish when clearly the ideals of life are to be the complete opposite, namely cooperative, loving, and selfless? One explanation is that: *the human condition is the set of characteristics, key events, and situations that compose the essentials of humanexistence, including birth, growth, emotionality, aspiration, conflict, and mortality.*[32] Some examples of human needs and desires are for air, water, food, shelter, clothing, sleep, reproduction, love, belonging, respect, self-esteem, freedom, recognition, and self-actualisation. From an individual point of view, it could be interpreted that people believe something to be true, based on their personal experiences, and most people seldom go on to see the complete picture before coming to a conclusion.

In other words, people form opinions based on incomplete knowledge. There is a famous Jain parable about *The Blind Men's View of an Elephant*.[33]

> A group of blind men encounter an elephant for the first time. Each of them touches different parts of the elephant. Not knowing what an elephant is like, each of them comes to a different conclusion based on his own experience. One blind man touches the elephant's side and claims that the elephant is like a wall. Another blind man touches its leg and exclaims that the elephant is like a tree. The other blind men touch the tusk, trunk, ear, and tail and believe that the elephant is like a spear, snake, fan, and rope, respectively. They argue over what the elephant is like, based on their experience of the animal. The message of the story is that all 'facts' can have many interpretations, and the whole can be different from its parts. In the story, each blind man touches only a part of the elephant and believes it to be the whole elephant. They base their opinions of what an elephant is on their knowledge of the animal, which is not complete. The story demonstrates that there may be a range of 'truths and mistakes' and thus there is a need for communication and the respect for different perspectives.

How are obstacles such as this, obstacles that prevent goals from being reached, overcome? This chapter has described how life and living are seen as a combination of mental and physical processes, and that these processes are constantly in a state of change and unpredictability. For example, the physical body is subject to changes in size, shape, hairstyle, or complexion, changes that are quite visible and noticeable. However, changes, which occur in the mind or mental processes, are more subtle and often more dynamic. By making a conscious effort and carefully observing thoughts, ideas, and concepts, it is possible to become aware of and to experience how rapidly these thoughts are subject to change. In one moment, we can say 'Yes' and in the next moment we can say 'No', depending on the state of the mind. The need is to train the mind to observe the functioning of the mental and physical processes, thereby realising that person's true nature. It is at this point that an enquiry occurs about the meaning and purpose of life.

5.7 Goals for Society

Society incorporates individuals and everyone around them, whether the individual is involved directly with those around or not. Everyone needs society to ensure wellbeing; however, the only thing society truly expects of the individual is to contribute to it positively. All individuals are just tiny little specks in the universe, yet every single person matters. Think of all of the individuals who made real impacts in history; they were just little specks who felt the need to take a stand. Think of what would happen if more people tried to take a stand. What would the world look like? Imagine if just 5% of the population tried to be like some of the great leaders from the past, such as Mahatma Gandhi, Mother Theresa, Nelson Mandala, or Martin Luther King Junior; the world would be so much better. Many people believe, because there are so many problems in the world, if more people had the courage and ambition to try to help, these problems could be reduced or alleviated altogether. As Margaret Mead famously said, *Never doubt that a small group of thoughtful, committed, citizens can change the world. Indeed, it is the only thing that ever has.*[34]

Social goals are described as the goals that connect individuals or groups to their immediate world, in order *To make an impact, to create values, to affect lives, to provide or preserve social amenities or infrastructure, to solve social problems, and/or to protect the natural environment.*[35] Therefore, the need is to learn to live cooperatively with others, sharing all joys and sorrows, and to be forbearing, not overbearing. When everyone spends time together in harmony, society will be happy and safe, will be like a well-knit family, and will strengthen others to be resilient. Jealousy, anger, hatred, and greed disintegrate society and make it fall into disorder and distress. Individuals must resist these disruptive forces that lie within us all, and that keep individuals away from extending cooperation and mutual help. Inculcating discipline within the mind and conscience will enhance the journey towards complete peace.

Exercise

Make notes in response to the following, and then decide if you want to make any changes in your life:

- What do you currently do for your community?
- Are you part of a volunteer organisation or do you volunteer your time to help others?
- How many hours per week do you spend volunteering?
- Do you donate money to charity? How much and how often?

5.8 Goals for the Environment

Sustainability and the aim of reducing impacts on the environment as much as possible are the challenges for setting environmental goals. There is a need to move to a 'circular economy' that eliminates waste by reusing it. Humans consume water, energy, the forests, and many other parts of the environment, resulting in increased consumption, the creation of millions of tons of greenhouse gases, and waste, such as plastic and paper that end up in landfills or polluting the waterways and oceans. The forests that are destroyed are the natural environmental filters that keep humankind alive (see Chapter 1).

Humankind has immense power to destroy the planet and also has the power to save it, by each person choosing to set their own environmental goals. Many people around the world are making such small lifestyle changes to save the environment, and as one website says, *While these changes are small, in combination, the impact is **Big**.*[36] Some of the long-term goals that can be considered for the environment are:

- learn how the natural world works,
- understand how humans interact with the environment,
- determine how individuals affect the environment, and then find ways to deal with these effects,
- learn about regenerative agriculture and how to support it by practising it, or supporting those that do practise it.

Some examples of short-term environmental goals include:

- A focus on reducing energy use – check power bills
- Conserving water consumption – check water bills
- Reducing car fuel – walk or cycle rather than drive
- Buying environmentally responsible products
- Planting trees thereby helping to reduce ozone levels and store carbon
- Recycling – compost, recycle cans and bottles, and the like
- Buying fresh food rather than processed products
- Avoiding food waste – check what gets thrown out
- Buy food grown by regenerative agriculture

Most of these environmental goals simply involve a small change in the way we do things, and, while they may only have small impacts on their own, in combination with many other small changes in the way things are done, a large impact on the environment will result.

5.9 Taking Action by Setting Goals

Whether goals are big or small, they are the stepping-stones to a happier life. However, the way goals are set can make a difference to achieving them. An important part of being human is having goals for the things that are to be achieved, and then working towards their accomplishment.

The path towards them may not always run smoothly or be easy, but having goals, whether large or small, is part of what makes life good. It gives a sense of meaning and purpose, points the direction to go, and gets an individual interested and engaged, all of which supports overall happiness. The physical act of writing down a goal makes it real and tangible, and then there is no excuse for forgetting about those goals. The word '*will*' needs to be written in front of these goals, rather than '*would like to*' or '*might*'. Tracy provides useful guidance for the way to develop goals such that your work/life balance remains appropriate as well, and the following box draws on those guidelines[37] for the goal-setting process:

1. 'WHAT' GOALS. What Do You Really Want to Accomplish in Life?
Remember that learning how to be happy is one of the most important skills you can learn in life. Proper time management and goal-setting techniques are simply tools to help you dedicate time towards achieving your goals.
2. 'WHY' GOALS. Why Do You Want to Achieve Your Goals?
To make sure that your goal is motivating, write down why it's valuable and important to you. Personal, family, and health goals are the *most important goals of all* in determining your happiness and wellbeing. This should be your true aim and purpose in life.
3. 'HOW' GOALS. How Do You Achieve Your Goals?
By Goal setting, learning, and practising new skills and behaviours you achieve the 'WHAT' in order to enjoy the 'WHY'.

It is important to work on all three types of goals simultaneously so that you can keep your work-life balance and continue moving onward and upward. Thinking positively about the future enhances our ability to create goals and consider the actions required to achieve them.

5.10 Conclusion

Maintaining a healthy work-life balance directly relates to good mental health, emotional wellbeing, physical health, and happiness. A well-balanced approach will allow for more efficient performance in all areas by reducing 'burnout' and boosting motivation to achieve goals. EHV particularly views the purpose of education to be for living a life with raised awareness through a focus on goals, rather than just being for establishing a career. EHV is a holistic process concerned with the purpose of life, and with the goal of unfolding human excellence. Yet the ultimate goal of EHV is to strive continuously to practise the five human values and to demonstrate them through living them. The practice of these five human values allows people to live in harmony as one global family, to see unity amidst diversity, and to live in joy and peace.

All adults need to be clear about their goals, the processes involved in setting, achieving, and sustaining them, and having the clarity, passion, and determination to follow them through. For teachers and parents, this will positively influence children, students, friends, families, and all aspects of the environment. The future lies before all and the door is wide open. Remember, only individuals can choose the path they wish to follow. As the past UN president, Kofi Annan, once said, *To live is to choose. But to choose well, you must know who you are and what you stand for, where you want to go and why you want to get there.*[38]

Appendix: 5.1: Stilling the Mind and Strengthening the 'Inner World'

Silent Sitting

- Sit comfortably and relax your eyes, you may wish to close them or lower your eyes to the floor, whatever helps you to move into a peaceful state of inner reflection.
- Keep the spine straight and also relaxed as this will allow a natural flow of energy up and down your body.
- Focus on your breathing. There is no need to be concerned whether it is fast or slow, just notice it without attempting to change it.
- Allow your breath to become deeper naturally, without forcing it.
- Allow any tension and busy thoughts to be exhaled with each breath.
- Feel yourself relaxing more and more … your mind becoming more and more still.
- Allow thoughts to pass like clouds, seeing them yet not following them.
- Remain in this stillness for a minute.
- When you are ready open your eyes gently.

Breath Awareness: Focus

- Be still. Breathe gently through your nose. Let your abdomen rise and fall with each breath. Keep your shoulders still. Continue to breathe as you feel all the restlessness and tension go away.
- You can pay attention to the sensation of coolness when you breathe IN and a very faint sensation of warmth when you breathe OUT.
- You will notice this inside each nostril on the wall that divides the two nostrils at the very tip of your nose.
- For the next few minutes, notice the sensation of coolness when you breathe IN and a sensation of warmth when you breathe OUT. Keep your awareness here. When thoughts arise observe them and let them pass like clouds.
- Now gently open your eyes and become aware of your surroundings.

Guided Light Visualisation

- Soft music can be played in the background during the exercise to facilitate relaxation. If feasible, have a lighted candle, and if not, imagine that there is a candlelight in front of you.
- Using your imagination, bring this light to the centre of your forehead.
- Imagine the head to be filled with light, and say: 'Whenever there is light, darkness cannot be present. I will only think good thoughts'.
- Expand the light to the centre of your chest. Imagine that there is a flower bud here.
- When the light reaches the flower bud, imagine you can see the petals opening into a beautiful flower. It is full of love, peace, and joy.
- Let the light expand down the two arms to the hands, let these hands be filled with light. Think, 'Let me do only good, kind and helpful things'.
- Now the light expands through the body and down the legs to the feet. Think, 'May my feet take me to places where I will be safe and in good company'.
- Be aware of the light in the head and in the mouth and tongue. Think, 'May I always speak the truth and only what is kind and necessary'.
- Slowly expand the light to the ears. Let the ears be filled with light. Think, 'Let me only hear good things'.
- Let your two eyes be filled with light. Again, concentrating on the light, and thinking, 'Let me see the goodness and beauty all around'.
- Imagine that the light is radiating from your being to surround your family, or whomever is in your home. They are now full of light. Think, 'May they be filled with peace'.
- Let light and love radiate out to your relatives and friends.
- Let it expand out into the whole world to all beings – people, animals, birds, fish, insects; to all plants – trees, grass, and flowers everywhere. To the rocks and to the earth itself. Think, 'Let the world be filled with light. Let the world be filled with love. Let the world be filled with peace'.
- Then spread the light out to the stars and to the whole universe.
- Remain surrounded by the beautiful light. Think, 'I am in the light … The light is in me … I am the light'.
- Now gently open your eyes and focus your attention on the lit candle, become aware of your surroundings.

The Light Visualisation is designed to encourage you to visualise your five senses, your thoughts, words, and actions, all being purified by an imaginary light that symbolises purity and wisdom.

Notes

1 Lao Tzu. https://www.goodreads.com/quotes/247448-the-journey-of-a-thousand-miles-begins-with-a-single accessed 16-1-2022.
2 Sathya Sai Baba, *Sathya Sai Speaks* (Prasanthi Nilayam, India: Books and Publication Trust, 2009), Vol. 42.

3 E. Kubler-Ross and D. Kessler, *Life's Lessons* (London, UK: Simon and Schuste, 2001).
4 D. Miller, W. Miller, K. Puzan, and P. Puzan, *Human Values at Work* (USA: Global Dharma Centre, 2005) https://www.globaldharma.org/hvw-home.htm accessed 31-1-2024.
5 Margaret Mead. https://www.brainyquote.com/quotes/margaret_mead_141040 accessed 17-1-2022.
6 Michelangelo's Pieta (2019) 1498–1500. http://www.michelangelo.net/pieta/ accessed 17-1-2022.
7 P. Dhall, *Sai Spiritual Education: Lesson Plans Group 3* (Canberra: Sri Sathya Sai International Organisation of Australia and Papua New Guinea, 1995).
8 L. Arnold, *Your Outer World Reflects Your Inner World: Live Life Fully* (Charleston: Gazette Mail, 2020, February 21).
9 D. Goleman, *Emotional Intelligence* (New York; Bantam Books, 2005). ISBN: 9780553383713
10 Adapted from Amygdala Hijack. https://www.progressivedairy.com/topics/management/you-got-emotionally-hijacked-now-what accessed 18-1-2022. Also see video https://youtu.be/GHnuyJFGVng accessed 18-1-2022.
11 Institute of Sathya Sai Education, Mumbai, *Towards Human Excellence. Book 2-The Five Human Values* (Mumbai, India, 2002).
12 *Ibid.*
13 Adapted from https://www.pinterest.com.au/pin/132363676525938747/ accessed 18-1-2022.
14 Goleman, *Emotional Intelligence,* 2005.
15 Adapted from: S. Shah, *Towards Human Excellence. Sri Sathya Sai Education for Schools. Book 2-The Five Human Values* (Mumbai, India: Dharmakshetra, 2000).
16 Institute of Sathya Sai Education Mumbai, *Road to Global Peace and Happiness* (Mumbai, India: Sri Sathya Sai Educare, 2001).
17 Handbook of Sai Spiritual Education in Canada, Sathya Sai International Organisation Canada, 2015.
18 Sathya Sai School of Kisaju, Kenya. *A workshop on 3HV* (2015).
19 *Ibid.*
20 Sathya Sai Baba, *Sathya Sai Speaks* (Prasanthi Nilayam, India: Books and Publication Trust, 1999), Vol. 32 (18).
21 J. Maxwell, *The Power of Significance* (New York, NY: Hachette Book Group Inc., 2018).
22 Aristotle. *Nicomachean Ethics,* ed. Hugh Treddenick (London: Penguin, 2004).
23 J. Griffith, *Freedom: End of Human Condition* (Duffys Forest, NSW, Australia: Fedmex Pty Ltd., 2016).
24 Hunter S. Thompson. https://www.azquotes.com/author/14615-Hunter_S_Thompson accessed 18-1-2023.
25 E. Kübler-Ros and D. Kessler. *On Grief and Grieving* (New York, USA: Scribner, 2014).
26 T. Robbins, *Where Focus Goes, Energy Flows.* https://www.tonyrobbins.com/career-business/where-focus-goes-energy-flows/ accessed 22-1-2022.
27 D. Miller, W. Miller, K. Puzan, and P. Puzan, *Human Values at Work* (Global Dharma Centre, 2005). https://globaldharma.org/hvw-home.htm accessed 22-1-2022.
28 Mahatma Mahatma Gandhi.: https://www.goodreads.com/quotes/1163097-keep-your-thoughts-positive-because-your-thought-become-your-words accessed 22-1-2022.
29 C. Danes. http://www.abundance-and-happiness.com/the-power-of-thoughts.html accessed 22-1-2022.

30 Fitzhugh Dodson. http://www.quoteland.com/author/Fitzhugh-Dodson-Quotes/4176/ accessed 22-1-2022.
31 Jumsai Na Ayudhya, Art-Ong. *A development of the human values integrated instructional model based on intuitive learning concept*: A dissertation submitted in partial fulfilment of the requirements for the degree of Doctor of Philosophy in curriculum and Instruction, Department of Secondary Education, Faculty of Education, Chulalongkorn University, Thailand, 2003. https://issea.org.au/research/higher-degree-dissertations/ accessed 12-12-2021.
32 E. Valea, *The Human Condition in World Religions* (n.d.). https://www.comparativereligion.com/man.html#12 accessed 24-1-2022.
33 T. van der Breggen, *The Blind Men and the Elephant.* http://apologiabyhendrikvanderbreggen.blogspot.com/2009/01/blind-men-and-elephant.html
34 Margaret Margaret Mead. https://fiercekindness.com/margaret-mead-quotes-and-more/#:~:text=Margaret%E2%80%99s%20most%20famous%20quote%20is%20probably%20this%3A%201,Just%20like%20everyone%20else.%E2%80%9D%20Margaret%20Mead%20More%20items accessed 19-1-2023.
35 L. Ho, *How to Create Social Goals to Make an Impact in the World* (2020). https://www.lifehack.org/864435/social-goals accessed 19-1-2023.
36 Anon. *Achieving Goal Setting Success* (2007). https://www.achieve-goal-setting-success.com/ accessed 24-1-2022.
37 B. Tracy, *Goals! How to Get Everything You Want – Faster Than You Ever Thought Possible,* 2nd ed. (Oakland, CA: Berrett-Koehler Publishers, 2010).
38 Kofi Kofi Annan. https://www.goodreads.com/quotes/257475-to-live-is-to-choose-but-to-choose-well-you accessed 25-1-2022.

Chapter 6

Reappraising Character

Roger Packham

6.1 Introduction

This chapter discusses what is meant by the terms *Character* and *Character Education*, and then looks at how Character is developed in individuals, as well as the practice of Character Education today. It needs to be noted that the term *Character Education* is used more commonly in the USA and the UK, while *Values Education* is the common term in Australia and India; other countries will use one or other of these two terms, and sometimes they are used interchangeably. The importance of character has been emphasised by the founder of EHV who said: *Character is the hallmark of humanity. Teachers must dedicate their learning and wisdom to the great task of uplifting pupils to higher levels of knowledge and action. The virtues they help inculcate in their pupils are essential for the uplift of society. Every student must endeavour to equip oneself for serving society with skill and knowledge. When virtues are rooted in the heart, every being shines in full glory.*[1]

The chapter starts by asking you, the reader, to explore your own understanding of the terms *Character* and *Character Education*, and then builds up the reader's learning and understanding by introducing a number of definitions and descriptors from a range of published sources. By completing this first exercise, you will be able to compare your ideas with what is subsequently presented. It is hoped that by the end of the chapter, you will have found further ideas that you might want to try out in practice.

6.2 Exercise

Think of and name some people you know, or some famous people you are aware of, whom you consider to be 'people of good Character', and then jot down some answers to the following questions:

- What are the qualities of this person/these people that indicate good Character? That is, how do you recognise a person of Character?

DOI: 10.4324/9781003478607-7

- What is your understanding of how Character develops?
- In your view, do our schools currently develop Character as you would wish? If *no*, what could be done about this?

Remember, there are no 'right answers', there are only your own views.

6.3 Why Talk about Character Education?

A central focus of EHV is the development of Character. While academic achievement to the best of a learner's ability is undoubtedly an important aim of education, a person cannot be educated fully without Character development; these two need to go hand in hand, as demonstrated by the research conducted in the *Australian Values Education Project* as described in Chapter 2. In the USA, Character Education is a government educational policy as well as the reason for a number of specific programmes of education. Both the Clinton and George W. Bush administrations made it a central focus of their educational policies. Schools that have infused Character Education into their curricula and cultures have found improved academic achievement, behaviour, school culture, peer interaction, and parental involvement.[2] They have reported dramatic transformations, with pro-social behaviours such as cooperation, respect, and compassion replacing negative behaviours such as violence, disrespect, apathy, and underachievement. Researchers have found that *Positive Action*, a programme that teaches social and emotional skills and character development in elementary schools, can improve academic test scores by as much as 10% on national standardised mathematics and reading tests.[3]

While academic achievement is not the main goal of Character Education programmes, it is obviously an important outcome for schools, and it is encouraging to note that such programmes can have positive outcomes for academic achievement. For example, in a two-year programme to implement EHV in primary schools in a province of China,[4] over the duration of the project, the average monthly test scores of the experimental EHV classes increased slightly more than the scores in parallel classes not doing EHV. The researchers considered that this was probably related to the students' improved concentration. This offered encouragement to teachers that Character development did not detract from and, in fact, could enhance academic results.

In the UK, there is a government-funded *Jubilee Centre for Character and Virtues* that promotes Character Education in schools throughout the UK.

It is also the case that if the mottos of many schools or their statements of aims/goals, are examined, it will usually be found that there is reference to Character development or issues closely associated with Character and values.

In the review of the Australian curriculum (2014), it was recommended that the curriculum should place 'more emphasis on morals, values and spirituality'. While already being addressed in schools, these ideas can be strengthened through a greater focus on Character. The *Melbourne Declaration* set out the educational goals for young Australians and said that students should be taught to *understand the spiritual and moral dimensions of life, enabling them to act with moral and ethical integrity.*[5] The Australian curriculum review suggested that this has been neglected and states that the curriculum fails to adequately reflect the Melbourne Declaration's belief that a well-rounded, balanced education should deal with the moral, spiritual, and aesthetic education of students.

These views do not necessarily reflect what is really happening in schools. The curriculum requires schools to teach students ethical understanding as one of seven 'general capabilities' that sit across the curriculum.[6] The teaching of morals, values, and spirituality in schools is often left to be done implicitly, and teachers are often unsure how best to approach these topics, yet they are critical for the development of Character. Regarding the teacher's own character, *Your Character is the best tool for the profession you have entered upon; your learning is of course valuable, but one can excuse a little less of it; Character on the other hand must be 100 per cent.*[7]

Character Education is about helping students grasp what is ethically important in situations and how to act for the right reasons, so that they become more autonomous and reflective. This involves them in deciding the kind of people they wish to become and in learning to choose well between alternatives. Every day in schools, teachers and students discuss a range of matters regarding honesty, truth, loyalty, and a range of other virtues. Many schools promote wellbeing which, while distinct from Character Education (see Chapter 11), has the potential to be connected to the development of Character. Clearly, there is considerable potential for the revitalisation of Character Education in schools.

In 2005, the 'National Framework for Values Education in Australian Schools'[8] was agreed to and endorsed by all the State and Territory Ministers of Education and then distributed to all Australian schools. The Framework recognises the Values Education policies and programmes already in place in education authorities and schools. It also recognised a significant history of Values Education in both government and non-government schools, drawing on a range of philosophies, beliefs, and traditions. To support this initiative, a well-funded 'Values Education project' was sponsored by the Australian government[9] and continued over a ten-year period (see Chapter 2). It involved a range of schools throughout the country and resulted in the refereed publication of many materials and findings.

However, effective Character Education takes time and intentionality to get it right. Teachers often think, with everything else they need to focus on as educators, 'How can we fit character education in as well?'. However, when students are taught to accept responsibility for their actions and that their actions matter, they spend more time on task instead of disrupting the class, giving teachers more time to teach. It also gives teachers more peace of mind and helps them to be able to cope better with the pressures of the job.[10] Character Education is not an 'add-on', it is instead a powerful and necessary method of school reform. It can help educators to fulfil their fundamental responsibility of preparing young children for their futures by supporting and fostering caring, respectful, achievement-minded school environments. Comprehensive and effective Character Education begins when members of the school, along with the local community, come together to determine the core values that they share (see Chapter 4). These values then become the foundation for all that the school does, including the curriculum, teaching, strategies, school culture, and extracurricular activities (see Chapter 13). This can then be infused into the broader community, where parents want their children to be happy, healthy, and to have peace of mind, as well as to develop good Characters that enable them to be both good citizens and to prosper in the workforce and generally in life. Character is something that is valued by parents, teachers, and societies. Thus, it is important to consider what it is, how it develops, and how it can be taught.

6.4 What Do We Mean by Character and Character Education?

6.4.1 *Character and Personality*

The term *Character* refers to an individual's distinctive mental and moral or ethical qualities. It is the aggregate of features and traits that form an individual's unique nature. Character has been viewed by the group *Character Counts* as being made up of 'six pillars':[11]

1. Trustworthiness
2. Respect
3. Responsibility
4. Fairness
5. Caring
6. Citizenship

Whether you agree with these 'six pillars' or not, they help with an understanding of what is meant by *Character*. A person's Character is a set of 'learned behaviour traits' that determine whether the individual will effectively achieve goals, be forthright in dealing with others, and obey the laws and rules of the community. Character relates to attitudes and values and should not be confused with *personality*. Personality refers to individual differences in characteristic patterns of thinking, feeling, and behaving, and although Character is related to personality, it is not the same thing. Personality primarily consists of *inborn* traits, while Character consists of *learned behaviour*. Both may vary with the situation or circumstances, yet Character is typically learned from parents, teachers, and friends. This learning comes from being taught directly or from observations of others. Since it is learned, a person's Character can also change over time.

To illustrate the difference, there is no possibility of a person having a *dishonest* personality; honesty is a positive Character trait and dishonesty is a negative one, but there may be a tendency towards breaking the law if you have a rebellious personality – although, thankfully, rebellion is often simply a phase that young people go through. Whether people have introverted or extroverted personalities, their Characters are concerned with their attitudes towards doing difficult tasks, dealing with other people, following the rules of their culture and context, and respecting those of other cultures. Character and personality are related, but they are not the same thing. The reason there is interest in the development of Character and in Character Education is precisely because Character may be changed purposefully and deliberately.

6.4.2 *Character Education*

Character Education is often seen as the process by which people convey moral values to others, so it is important to note at this point that while many Character Education programmes attempt to impose character values externally, in EHV the focus is always on eliciting the values that already exist within the learner but may be latent and require cultivation and practice; this is an important component of the philosophy of *Educare* that underlies EHV (see Chapter 1).

A useful definition of Character Education comes from the *Jubilee Centre for Character and Virtues*,[12] which describes it as follows:

> *Human flourishing is the widely accepted goal of life. To flourish is not only to be happy, but to fulfil one's potential. Flourishing is the aim of character education, which is critical to its achievement. Human flourishing requires moral, intellectual, and civic virtues, excellence specific to diverse domains of practice or human endeavour, and generic virtues of self-management (known as enabling and performance virtues). All are necessary to achieve the highest potential in life. Character education is about the acquisition and strengthening of those virtues: the traits that sustain a well-rounded life and a thriving society.*

This view of Character Education demonstrates clear links between this chapter and Chapter 3 of this book, where virtues and their link to values ethics and morals are discussed, and more particularly, how people's virtues form their characters. It also links to Chapter 5 that discusses the goals of life.

Another view of Character Education comes from the USA,[13] where there are extensive resources available to support government policies in this field:

> *Character education is an educational movement that supports the social, emotional, and ethical development of students. It is the proactive effort by schools, districts, communities, and States to help students develop important core ethical (recognizing what's right) and performance (doing what's right) values such as caring, honesty, diligence, fairness, fortitude, responsibility, grit, creativity, critical thinking, and respect for self and others. Character education provides long-term solutions to moral, ethical, and academic issues that are of growing concern in our society and our schools. Through character education, students learn how to be their best selves and how to do their best work while making school a place where students and educators feel comfortable and able to work. Character education has always been an essential part of our (USA) schools' mission. In fact, since the founding of our nation's public schools, character development was always an integral part of schooling along with academics. Today's character education movement is a re-emergence of that important mission.*

Again, the links to Chapter 3 of this book are clear from this statement; it can be seen that, effectively, Character Education is a way of enacting the ideas and theories discussed in Chapter 3. The focus on social and emotional learning is also worth noting (see Chapter 2), as this area has been recognised as an important component of holistic education (see Chapter 7) and is also an important part of EHV.

6.5 An Overview of the History and Cultural Contexts of Character

The concept of a 'good' Character varies in time, place, and culture. A quick illustration is that the ancient Greeks in the time of Homer saw *courage* and *bravery in battle* as paramount, while Protestants in Europe in the 18th and 19th centuries saw *hard work* and *thrift* as indicative of good Character. However, these societal norms are still underpinned by the same concepts of Character, Character development, and Character Education as described in this chapter.

'Western' and 'Eastern' cultural traditions differ in respect to the qualities that are regarded as 'good' Character. According to traditional Western thought, a happy person must have *virtuous traits* of Character. Aristotle emphasised moderation in all things, albeit relative to the situation. For him (as described in Chapter 3), the key to finding this balance was to recognise the value of developing one's rational powers and then using rationality to determine which actions were appropriate in which circumstances. The key traits of interest were the four cardinal virtues (discussed in Chapter 3) that were taught to all Greek citizens, with a person exhibiting through action the Character traits that were admired by their society.

Eastern thought, however, generally views the nature of humans at birth as quiet and calm, but when affected by the external world, it is also their nature to develop *desires*. When these desires are not controlled properly (as discussed in Chapter 12) and the conscious mind is distracted by the 'material world', it is thought that there is a loss of the *true* self, and natural reason can be disturbed or even destroyed. From this can arise rebellion, disobedience, cunning, deceit, and general immorality. For example, in China, a hallmark of Confucian thought[14] was an emphasis on tradition, family, and study, resulting in a heavy scheme of *obligations* and intricate *duties* for one's many social roles that aim to control these adverse tendencies.

Another example of an Eastern philosophy that focuses on the absence of desires is Taoism, where the theme is that of *harmony with nature* and, if achieved, desires should be relatively few and easy to satisfy. Taoists believe that, unfortunately, socialisation creates a plethora of desires for 'social goods' such as status, reputation, and pride, thereby creating attitudes of resentment and anger that can incite competition and then violence. The way to social order for Taoists is for people to eliminate these socialised ambitions through being open-minded and listening to all kinds of ideas and suggestions, which is also an ideal of Western democracy.

Although Western and Eastern thoughts seem to value the actions of people of Character in different ways, both clearly see Character as being made up of certain traits that express themselves in desirable actions performed by those who are 'good' citizens.

In Australia, first nation peoples have rich traditions of relationship with *country* (location and environment), family traditions and structure, together with their community, which make up their Character as well as their identity.[15] These beliefs have long been suppressed, largely ignored or at best given token recognition.[16] The need to better understand their values, culture and resultant Character has never been more obvious. Good Character Education based on more universal, inclusive Human Values could help in this endeavour.

Disturbingly, many psychological experiments of the late 20th century[17] purported to have shown that, even if humans do have noble tendencies, they are likely to remain narrow 'local' traits that are not unified with other traits into a wider behavioural *pattern of being* unless this has been part of their specific Character Education. This highlights the need for good Character Education from an early age.

6.6 An Overview of Moral (Hence Character) Development

Two distinct traditions of moral/Character development emerged in the 20th century, 'socialisation' perspectives and 'cognitive development' approaches. Historically, socialisation theories were the first to emerge, conceptualising moral development primarily in terms of children's internalisation and compliance with adults' and societal rules and requests. These approaches originally focused on the development of *conscience* through guilt and internalised behaviour, typically measured in terms of compliance. Further work, for example by Hoffman,[18] has emphasised the positive affective and behavioural components of morality, including empathy and prosocial behaviour. Additionally, tendencies towards care and cooperation need to be considered, as they have been shown to be rooted in our biological make-up and to come from a more feminist perspective.

Cognitive development theories started with the work of Jean Piaget (1896–1980), which focused on the development of children's moral judgement. Piaget viewed children as active in their own development, constructing moral knowledge through reciprocal interaction with their environment. Piaget's work was developed further by Lawrence Kohlberg (1927–1987), who proposed a more extensive 'stage theory' of moral development. Kohlberg[19] held that the process of stage change occurs gradually as a result of the efforts of individuals to resolve the contradictions or conflicts that result from the application of their moral understandings to actual moral situations.[20] He found that development was enhanced when individuals were drawn into discussions about moral conflicts and were asked to provide both solutions and justifications for their positions. These views are reflected in Character Education approaches today, as discussed below.

Kohlberg's stages considered the way people organise their understanding of *virtues*, *rules*, and *norms* and how they integrate these into moral choices. Kohlberg divided moral intelligence into three levels, each with two stages. The first two levels, *pre-conventional* and *conventional*, broadly align with those of Piaget. Kohlberg's third stage, *post-conventional*, included notions of individual rights against the majority, justice, and appeal to universal principles. These ideas are illustrated in Figure 6.1.

The determinants for right or wrong for each of Kohlberg's Moral Stages are as follows:

- In the pre-conventional stage (up to the age of 7), right or wrong is defined by the punishment associated with a particular action, which implies the chosen action is wrong.
- For the conventional stage (most teenagers and adults), the choice is determined more by what is rewarded and doing what others think you should do. Doing the right thing is what pleases others, so moral choices and the concepts of right and wrong are determined by the majority. Issues of law and order become important as a duty to society, so most are compliant with a degree of respect for authority.
- For 10–15% of people over 20, the concepts of social contracts and agreed universal ethical principles mean individuals answer to their own consciences or sense of deeply held morality, which are seen as more important than the laws of the land.

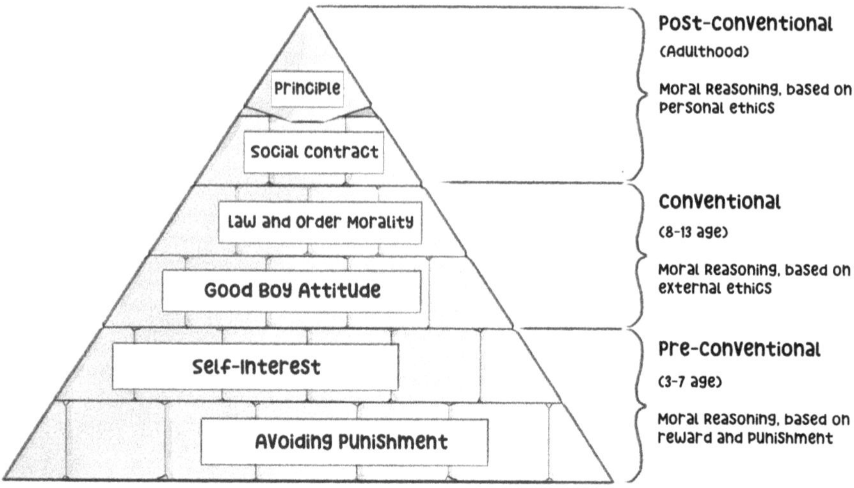

Figure 6.1 A Representation of Kohlberg's Six Stages of Moral Development (Adapted from https://i.pinimg.com/originals/50/f6/75/50f67520fb0a82fbe9fa30e67bd07f2d.jpg)

The theories of both Kohlberg and Hoffman propose that, by taking on the perspectives of others, we develop morally. The most plausible position in moral motivation seems to be neither 'affective primacy' (Hoffman's position) nor 'cognitive primacy' (Kohlberg's position) but rather a kind of co-primacy, where both empathy and justice are examples of primary motives.[21] In this way, contemporary approaches to moral development integrate thoughts, emotions, and behaviours and stress the importance of social interactions, and it is these ideas that are needed to guide actual educational practice, with EHV as a prime and easily accessible example. Further, the rise of evolutionary-based accounts of moral development has led to more research with infants and studies incorporating neuroscience, thereby improving the understanding of the complex nature of moral development.[22]

The practical implications for Character Education of this improved understanding of moral and Character development will be discussed below. While the implementation of Character Education using EHV has not been underpinned by these theories, since EHV has arisen from practical teaching experiences, its methods are very compatible with the implications of these theories. However, in EHV, the prime way to achieve moral development has always been seen as being a focus on how best to incorporate the five human values into all aspects of the school and the curriculum, particularly through modelling by teachers and the school community (see Chapter 12).

6.7 What Is Character Education Today?

Unless knowledge is transformed into wisdom, and wisdom expressed in character, education is a wasteful process.[23]

Around the mid-20th century, two popular Character Education methods arose: *Values clarification* and *cognitive developmental* moral education. Values clarification did not tell learners what values they should have; it simply provided the means to discover what their values were. It was criticised for promoting 'moral relativism' among students, which is the view that any value that an individual 'feels is right is right', similar to *emotivism* as described in Chapter 3. Similarly, there is little evidence that moralising to children or giving them direct instruction in moral principles has much effect. Unfortunately, too many programmes that say they are developing Character and call themselves 'Character Education' seem to be aimed at promoting good manners and compliance with rules rather than with the development of students with strong, independent Characters.[24]

There are dozens of Character Education programmes available to schools and businesses today, and a common approach to many of these is to provide a list of 'principles, values, or virtues' to be memorised, or that form the basis of themed activities. Too frequently, there is little evaluation or assessment of these programmes, something that needs to be addressed for all Values Education programmes. As the aim of Character Education is for individuals to have self-motivating characters, it is from the *affective* domain of feelings and emotions that the basis of any evaluation of progress needs to come. As discussed in Chapter 4 of this book, Krathwohl's taxonomy[25] is useful here as it charts the shift of feelings and emotions (the *affect*) from an *external* orientation to an *internal* one. A good Character Education programme would benefit from the use of this taxonomy.

As described in the previous section of this chapter, a person's Character develops over time and is formed in many ways. One way is through exposure to the actions and attitudes of others, particularly those whom the person has come to care about and trust; another is through engaging in moral actions, such as service to others; and a third way is through open and thoughtful dialogue about the complexities of moral situations and alternative responses to those situations. All of these approaches are incorporated into EHV.

The essential challenge for education is to help students *want* to grow as moral beings and to equip them with the *internal* resources to act effectively on that desire. Educators also need to help learners develop a deep regard for themselves and for others, and an abiding commitment to core values as epitomised in those of the EHV programme – Love, Truth, Right Action, Peace, and Non-violence.

Students of good Character need the resolve to live by and speak up for what they believe while also hearing, understanding, and accommodating the beliefs of others. The outcome will be students who better understand and commit to developing skills for putting values into action in life's complex situations.

Character Education programmes need to engage and inspire students' hearts as well as their minds, and this requires that schools get better at meeting their students' basic needs for safety, belonging, competence, and autonomy. Students will bond to a school in the same way, and for the same reasons that infants bond to their mothers who capably provide for them. In other words, students will care about a school's goals and values when that school cares for them. When students feel connected to a school and the people in it, they learn better.[26] EHV and other good Character Education programmes enlist students as active participants in creating a caring and just environment in the classroom and in all aspects of the school. The challenge for the school is to become a 'safe space' in which students are able to practise age-appropriate versions of the roles they must play in later life, and deal with the related problems and complications that will inevitably arise. The goal needs to be a total school culture (see Chapter 12) in which all people in the school, including teachers, administrators, and support staff, as well as students, treat one another and visitors to the school with kindness and respect, and collectively encourage the implementation of values in every aspect of life.

The best forms of Character Education, particularly EHV, also involve students in honest, thoughtful discussion and reflection about the moral implications of what they see around them, what they are told, and what they personally do and experience in their own lives. When guided by a trusted adult, these opportunities to talk and think about social and ethical matters enable every student to come to a clearer, stronger sense of what really matters, and 'who I want to be'. A school must work to see that the goals and values it professes are embodied in what it does, and that its policies and procedures reflect the values it wants its students to embrace. Its discipline policies must be fair and humane[27] and provide opportunities for students to reflect on the values underpinning their decisions. The school must deploy its resources equitably, and ensure that accomplishments of many kinds are honoured, not just the most academically and athletically gifted,[28] and that recognition is given to students who demonstrate exemplary Characters. The following specific suggestions for classroom and school practices that promote students' Character growth have been drawn from the literature:[29]

- Class meetings in which students, with the teacher's help, get opportunities to set class goals and group rules, plan activities, assess their progress, and solve common problems.
- Ethics-rich academic classes in which students go beyond facts and skills to consider the moral and social implications of what they are learning, most

obviously in social studies and literature, but also in the sciences, mathematics, and the arts (see Chapters 9 and 10).
- Cooperative learning groups, in which students collaborate on academic tasks and have regular opportunities to plan and reflect on the ways they work together (this is one of the methods of EHV as discussed in Chapter 8).
- Class discussions on ethical dilemmas of age-appropriate issues of relevance to the learners. Successful discussions will see members actively engaged in efforts to reconcile competing moral arguments, with the goal of arriving at a shared moral position.
- Promoting a caring and values-based environment within the classroom and the whole school, marked by compassionate engagement and acts of kindness towards others, along with the capacity to accept care directed towards oneself.
- 'Buddies' programmes that regularly bring together individuals and whole classes of younger and older students to work one-to-one on academic, service, and recreational activities.
- Inclusive, whole-school events involving students and their families at school in ways that capitalise on their diverse backgrounds and personal experiences, such as a 'family heritage week' or an 'international food day'.
- Service-learning opportunities inside and outside the school that enable students to contribute to the welfare of others as an integral part of their learning. Two factors are important here: Some degree of choice as to the nature of the particular activity a student will take part in since this is important for student motivation; and that the activity be linked to a period of reflection where students can share their feelings and experiences and connect those experiences to their own social values and sense of self.[30]

When implemented well, these community-building approaches to Character Education become an integral part of a school's overall improvement efforts (see Chapter 13). They are woven intentionally and seamlessly into the school's pedagogy and its daily routines. They are not regarded as add-ons. Character Education ought not to be seen as a threat to an emphasis on academic performance; in fact, the opposite is the case since it helps to achieve academic goals. Educators have reported that subjects become more interesting to students when they can focus on ethical and social issues embodied in the subject matter (see Chapters 9 and 10). It also helps students to better understand themselves and 'who they are'. A school that prepares its students to be citizens by emphasising academic performance at the expense of ethical, social, and emotional development will not be good for society.

6.8 Activity

Now please go back and review your initial responses to the first activity (Section 6.2) at the beginning of this chapter, and then respond to the following:

1. From what you have gained from reading this chapter, how do you think adults might be inspired to transform their accustomed ways of seeing, thinking, and acting to achieve their own higher-level moral development?
2. Can you think of some ways that improved Character habits can be developed, those habits exhibited by the outstanding 'people of good Character' that you nominated in that first exercise, and the kind of people that all look up to?
3. Use the *action learning cycle* presented at the end of Chapter 3 of this book to implement and reflect on one or more of these ideas in your school, home, business, or workplace.

6.9 Concluding Comments

Early in this chapter, it was noted that Character Education and Character development are a central focus of EHV. This chapter has reviewed key aspects of Character, Character development, and Character Education from the literature. The chapter will now conclude with a summary of the key aspects of the EHV Character Education programme featured throughout this book, followed by a list of the *ideal* outcomes that EHV is aiming to develop in learners and to which those using it aspire. It is felt that this provides a goal for educators and parents aiming to develop Character in all learners. Each of these ideal features has attached to it a related virtue that is also a good character trait and a value to enact.

6.9.1 *The Key Aspects of EHV*

1. Proposes a framework of five core human values – Truth, Right Action, Peace, Love, and Non-violence, which are seen as the essence of human nature.
2. Assists in eliciting these five human values from within a person.
3. Views the end of education as Character, and the end of Character as wisdom.
4. Is transformational in the development of Character in individuals.
5. Promotes the unity of 'Head', 'Heart', and 'Hands' by emphasising the importance of the unity of, and harmony, among one's thoughts, words, and actions.

6. Strongly encourages all participants – teachers, parents, and students – to live the values they espouse.
7. Helps to highlight *unity in diversity*, promoting peace, understanding, and harmony within the individual and society.
8. Has a defined pedagogy with seven teaching techniques that are implemented both directly and indirectly (see Chapters 8, 9, and 10).
9. Aims for the development of Character as well as for academic excellence.

6.9.2 *Ideal Outcomes from an EHV Programme*

Here are some ideal characteristics of a person graduating from an EHV programme, with each of these exemplified by a good Character trait, or 'value aspect' of the five core values:

- Uses discrimination to distinguish between good and bad, right and wrong: Can distinguish between truth and falsehood. (*Discrimination*)
- Tries to put self in the position of the 'other', and evaluates actions against that background. (*Empathy*)
- Engages in good actions and does good deeds. (*Caring*)
- Talks sweetly without anger. (*Equanimity*)
- Engages in harmony of head/heart/hands – Uses the *conscience* to examine thoughts and ideas before putting them into action. If it is good and will harm no one, go ahead; if it is not good, put it aside; if not sure, do nothing until sure. (*Thoughtfulness*)
- Uses his/her abilities in harmony with the universal values of society. (*Calmness*)
- Is not affected by the ups and downs and challenges of life; can cope with being sad, unwell, angry, or unhappy, and recognise this as part of a fully lived life for a human being. (*Resilience*)
- Is sufficiently 'whole' and peaceful on the inside so as not to be mentally 'tossed about' by changes in circumstances or people around him/her. (*Tolerance*)
- Feels love for self and others. (*Interdependence*)
- Gives respect to all. (*Respect*)
- Forgives others and forgives himself/herself. (*Forgiveness*)
- Recognises their own uniqueness and how to use it for the benefit of self and others. (*Self-awareness*)
- Able to see the beauty in all the imperfections of life and in everything else. (*Compassion*)
- Is in touch with her/his own deep inner resources and intuitive superconscious mind; Is in touch with 'who I am'. (*Self-awareness*)
- Shows commitment to his/her values system. (*Commitment*)

- Does his/her best without undue concern for the results of his/her actions. (*Resoluteness*)
- Recognises unity in all beings – fundamental unity beneath the superficial differences in world cultures. (*Interconnection*)
- Shares in others' joys and sorrows as if they were his/her own. (*Sensitivity*)
- Stands by his/her own values even if under pressure from others to go against them. (*Dedication*)
- Trusts in own inner strength rather than depending on externals like relationships and material things for happiness and sense of self-worth. (*Confidence*)
- Thinks before acting. (*Consideration*)
- Feels gratitude. *(Appreciation)*

It is hoped that this chapter has clarified for you the ideas and practices of Character and Character Education, such that you adopt applicable ideas for use in your daily activities.

Notes

1 Sathya Sai Baba, *Vidya Vahini,* Ch. 18 (Prasanthi Nilayam, India: Sri Sathya Sai Sadhana Trust, 2010), 51.
2 Character.org. https://www.character.org/ accessed 15-06-2021.
3 Character Counts. https://charactercounts.org/ accessed 5-2-2022.
4 M. Taplin, Unpublished data collected from primary school teachers participating in a two-year EHV program in China, 2013.
5 Melbourne Declaration on Educational Goals for Young Australians (2008) see: https://www.academia.edu/63984060/Melbourne_Declaration_on_Educational_Goals_for_Young_Australians accessed 26-1-2024.
6 A. Peterson, "What Sort of People Do We Want Young Australians to Be?" *The Conversation*, October 23, 2014.
7 Sathya Sai Baba, *Sathya Sai Speaks* (Prasanthi Nilayam, India: Books and Publications Trust, September 5, 1968), Vol. 8 (31).
8 http://www.curriculum.edu.au/values/val_national_framework_for_values_education,8757.html accessed 15-06-2021.
9 http://www.curriculum.edu.au/values/values_homepage,8655.html accessed 15-06-2021.
10 M. Taplin and L. Li, "Teachers' Perceptions of Silent Sitting as a Buffer to Their Problems," in *A Human Values Pathway for Teachers,* ed. S. Parakaharan (Singapore: Springer, 2021), 125–150.
11 The six pillars of Character. https://charactercounts.org/character-counts-overview/six-pillars/#:~:text=The%20Six%20Pillars%20of%20Character%20are%20trustworthiness%2C%20respect%2C,specific%20order%20and%20using%20the%20acronym%20%E2%80%9CT.R.R.F.C.C.%E2%80%9D%20%28terrific%29 accessed 15-06-2021.
12 http://www.jubileecentre.ac.uk/ accessed 15-06-2021.
13 http://character.org/about/faqs/ accessed 15-06-2021.
14 History of Character Education. https://www.k12academics.com/educational-programs/character-education/history accessed 15-06-2021.

15 Korff Jens, *Aboriginal Culture Essentials* (2018). Download eBook from: https://www.creativespirits.info/aboriginal-culture-essentials#buying-options accessed 4-2-2022.
16 https://www.creativespirits.info/ accessed 4-2-2022.
17 The Stanford Prison experiment. https://en.wikipedia.org/wiki/Stanford_prison_experiment#Experiments_in_the_United_States accessed 15-06-2021.
18 Martin L. Hoffman, *Empathy and Moral Development: Implications for Caring and Justice* (Cambridge: Cambridge University Press, 2000).
19 L. Kohlberg, "Essays on Moral Development," in *The Psychology of Moral Development* (San Francisco: Harper and Row, 1984), Vol. 2.
20 L. Nucci, "Moral Development and Education," in *International Encyclopedia of the Social & Behavioral Sciences*, 2nd ed. (2015), Vol. 15. http://dx.doi.org/10.1016/B978-0-08-097086-8.92152-4 accessed 15-06-2021.
21 J. C. Gibbs, *Moral Development and Reality: Beyond the Theories of Kohlberg and Hoffman* (Thousand Oaks, USA: Sage, 2003).
22 *Ibid.*
23 Sathya Sai Baba, *Sathya Sai Speaks* (Prasanthi Nilayam, India: Books and Publications Trust, July 19, 1979), Vol. 14(28).
24 E. Schaps, E. F. Schaeffer, and S. N. McDonnell, "What's Right and Wrong," in *Character Education Today* (Washington, DC: The Character Education Partnership, 2001). https://www.character.org/ accessed 4-2-2022.
25 D. R. Krathwohl, B. S. Bloom, and B. B. Masia, *Taxonomy of Educational Objectives: The Classification of Educational Goals. Handbook II: Affective Domain* (New York: David McKay Co., Inc., 1973).
26 E. Schaps, E. F. Schaeffer, and S. N. McDonnell, "What's Right and Wrong," 2001. https://www.edweek.org/leadership/opinion-whats-right-and-wrong-in-character-education-today/2001/09 accessed 15-06-2021.
27 M. Taplin and A. Devi, *To Teach, Not to Punish: A Practical Human Values Approach to Discipline* (Hong Kong: Sathya Sai Education in Human Values, 2004). https://issea.org.au/wp-content/uploads/2020/08/To-Teach-Not-to-Punish.pdf accessed 4-2-2022.
28 E. Schaps, E. F. Schaeffer, and S. N. McDonnell, "What's Right and Wrong," 2001. https://www.character.org/ accessed 4-2-2022.
29 *Ibid.*
30 *Ibid.*

Chapter 7

The Lifelong Nature of Values-based Education

Selvanie Naidoo, Roger Packham, Kevin Francis, and Margaret Taplin

7.1 Introduction

Lifelong learning requires learning about ourselves, our ongoing development, and the valuing of our unique gifts in order to use them to help ourselves and others. It involves learning continually how to become more and more healthy in the ways we deal with conflicts and problems, and learning how to love and appreciate ourselves and others. Henry Ford said, *Anyone who stops learning is old, whether at twenty or eighty. Anyone who keeps learning stays young.*[1]

The aim of this chapter is to recognise the importance of lifelong learning and incorporate such learning into all domains of life, but particularly our internalised value systems (see Chapter 4). Humans have a natural drive to explore, learn, and grow; therefore, lifelong learning inspires and encourages the improvement of the quality of life so that these goals can be met. The 21st century is calling for major transformations, both personal and societal, in work, learning, and development.

The concept of lifelong learning is said to have been introduced in Denmark as early as 1971[2] to describe the ongoing processes of education and learning throughout one's life. The reality is that most people have goals or interests outside their formal schooling and employment, so the role of lifelong learning to support this is explored here within the context of Education in Human Values (EHV), the focus of this book. Like all aspects of life, learning about human values and how we can apply them in our lives is a lifelong process – there is always something more to discover. EHV is simply structured to foster and cultivates universal Human Values common to all cultures and creeds.

7.2 Holistic Education Approach to Lifelong Learning

Two aspects are discussed below to elaborate on what 'holistic education' means. The first comes from a United Nations 1996 report that had a major influence on education at many levels and throughout the world. The second is drawn from the values education literature and looks at how lifelong education needs to influence all aspects of the human personality, not just the intellectual

DOI: 10.4324/9781003478607-8

or the skills dimensions. The 21st century is calling for major transformations, both personal and societal, in work, learning, and development.

7.2.1 Four Pillars of Education

It has already been established in earlier chapters that EHV is a holistic process. The UNESCO *Delors Report*[3] proposed an integrated vision of holistic education based on two key concepts, 'learning throughout life' and the 'four pillars of learning' that encompass learning:

- to know
- to do
- to be
- to live together

In support of these, the practice of EHV helps to raise the level of awareness of our human purpose, aiming to lift values to a higher level by living life consciously rather than drifting along.

Learning to know strives to combine a sufficiently broad general knowledge with the opportunity to work in depth on a small number of subjects. This also means learning to learn so as to benefit from the opportunities that education provides throughout life. In relation to lifelong EHV, the human values can be understood at ever-deepening levels for those who wish to engage in ongoing enquiry.

Learning to do aims to acquire not only an occupational skill but also, more broadly, the competence to deal with many situations and to work in teams. It also means *learning to do* in the context of our various social and work experiences. As we move through life, we can be engaged continually in the process of exploring how the human values can be lived and practised in all aspects of our lives in order to bring about better outcomes for ourselves and those around us.

Learning to be has the goal of developing one's personality so as to be better able to act with ever greater autonomy, judgement, and personal responsibility. In that connection, a holistic education must not disregard any aspect of a person's potential: Memory, reasoning, aesthetic sense, physical capacities, communication skills, and, underpinning all of these, our ever-evolving human values. The following section returns to these ideas.

Learning to live together aims to develop an understanding of other people and an appreciation of interdependence – carrying out joint projects and learning to manage conflicts, all in a spirit of respect for the values of pluralism, mutual understanding, and peace.

As viewed by Delors, this renewal of emphasis on values in education needs to be seen as much more than *a longing (of the world), often unexpressed, for an ideal and for values....*[4] Rather, it needs to be viewed as an imperative that, as the world has gradually come to realise, is required to eliminate increasing violence, religious and cultural intolerance, and fatalism that characterise today's society. For this to happen, any process of lifelong learning needs to foster values that can promote the unity and integration of people in a culturally plural society. More importantly, as espoused eloquently by the Delors Commission, education needs to provide a clear and practical process of translating these values into daily reality, at both individual and societal levels. Education needs to 'uplift' minds and spirits in some measure, in a transcending way. The Commission went on to say ... *the survival of humanity depends there.*[5]

7.2.2 Holistic Learning and the Domains of Human Personality

A holistic approach to lifelong learning also entails gaining insights about life from the multiple domains of the human personality: *Intellectual*, *physical*, *emotional*, *social*, and *spiritual*. In today's society, a focus on holistic learning through all of these domains is needed to initiate true growth and prosperity.[6] This, in turn, can lead to the development of well-balanced and harmonious individuals with well-integrated personalities.

As discussed in earlier chapters, human values education develops excellence in all the domains of the human personality in a balanced and integrated manner, with the overall aim of promoting good character. These domains and their links to human values are explored in Table 7.1, and connect directly to the ideas presented in Chapter 4. The table depicts the 'Ideals of Education' mapped to the five domains of the human personality, which manifest in the five core human values of EHV. Some aspects of these core values have been added as examples.[7] The authors from whom this table has been drawn also noted that, in order to develop a complete personality, the relative values of

Table 7.1 The Ideals of Education Mapped to the Five Domains of the Human Personality

	Ideal of education	*Domain of personality*	*Human value promoting excellence*	*Examples of values aspects*
1	Knowledge	Cognitive/ Intellectual	Truth	Self-Awareness, Integrity, Assertiveness
2	Skill	Physical	Right Action	Self-Confidence, Peer Pressure, Responsibility
3	Balance	Emotional	Peace	Fearlessness, Resilience, Focus, Reflection
4	Vision	Social	Love	Forgiveness, Empathy, Human Dignity
5	Identity	Spiritual	Non-violence	Social Awareness, Global Awareness, Environmental Awareness, Unity of Faiths

Knowledge, Skill, Balance, Vision, and Identity grow into absolute values with Love at the root. As has been discussed before, Love is the undercurrent of all human values (see Chapter 4), and the founder of EHV said *When your thoughts emanate from a mind purified by Love, they will result in Right Action. When Love becomes part of your experience, thought and action, you get Peace. When we comprehend Love clearly, Non-violence will result automatically. So, Love is the unseen undercurrent binding all the four values.*[8]

On the *Intellectual Level*, the ideal follows the quest for *Truth* and encourages an enquiring mind. It acknowledges the importance of both rational methods of enquiry using clear reasoning and also intuitive, creative capabilities. This view considers that when Truth is understood, all are seen to be connected. Whatever is done to others is being done to the doer, as the same life-force permeates all things. Thus, helping and protecting everything around also protects the individual.

On the *Physical Level*, words and actions are trained to follow informed and unselfish ethical choices through *Right Action*, the aim being to encourage the best possible application of the human will, strengthened by control over selfish, greedy, or agitating impulses. Once Right Action is practised, it is possible to see good in everything, hear positive things, speak kind words, and perform acts of service for the benefit of all.

On an *Emotional Level*, the ideal, *Peace*, is seen as a sense of calm and equipoise which enables one to handle any situation. It does not suppress negative thoughts or feelings which pass through the mind, and it does not identify with these thoughts or waste mental energy. Instead, such Peace retains a calm stance and concentrates on positive thoughts, feelings, and solutions (see also Chapter 1). Therefore, by keeping this mental balance, both performance and happiness are enhanced. To promote *Non-violence*, we all need to work for peace. Peace is the opposite of anger, hatred, envy, jealousy, and attachment. All these emotions cause disharmony, disunity, and violence.

On the *Social Level, the ideal* is defined as including a sense of identity with all. *Love* becomes a natural, instinctive way of life and there is a feeling of kinship with all of creation. Love permeates all the human values, since pure love will create *Peace* both within and without, whilst love in action is *Right Action*, and love in the heart develops *Non-violence.*

The *Spiritual Level* aims at uncovering the potential inherent in everyone for steady, selfless *Non-violence.* This attitude is not just an emotional feeling or an intellectual attitude but is closer to a sense of identity with the concept of Love. This type of Love is independent of circumstances or returns and gets satisfaction from caring actions. Acting for the sake of others and giving without wanting anything in return will promote *Non-violence.* Non-violence is the culmination of all human values and results in excellence of character. The practice of Non-violence brings about the development of the total personality. If people are to live in harmony with their surroundings, they must learn not to violate nature; they must learn to conserve and protect their environment. They must respect all life, plants, and animals; otherwise, they may upset the delicate balance of nature, resulting in a calamity for the human race, as illustrated by the issues of the Anthropocene outlined in Chapter 1. At the same time, the world has limited resources, so learning to conserve is vital (see Chapter 12).

The most important manifestation of this whole integrated human personality is Character, and that is the goal of the EHV programme. The core human values provide the framework for Character, which in turn manifests as unity in thought, word, and deed, in selfless service and in Love for all. Character confers the ability to exercise objectivity and a sense of personal responsibility to attain the common goals of society. Information, knowledge, and skills gained through education are important tools, but these become ineffective when the personality lacks Character.

Human beings have an extraordinary inner worth that should be nurtured to fruition and fullness. Mahatma Gandhi's definition that *Education is an all-around drawing out of the best in child and adult body, mind, and spirit*[9] demonstrates excellent consistency with this point of view. Clearly, the emergence of this inner worth is an ongoing process that can be refined and enhanced constantly throughout life if we allow it.

7.3 What Is Lifelong Learning?

Lifelong learning, as the name indicates, implies learning through all stages of life, from cradle to grave. In addition, lifelong learning is the development of human potential through a continuously supportive process which stimulates and empowers individuals to acquire all the knowledge, values, skills, and understanding that they need so they can apply them with confidence, creativity, and enjoyment in all roles, circumstances, and environments.[10] Lifelong learning can also be interpreted as engaging people in a broader sense during their school years, post-school studies, working lives, and even when retired. Here, however, we are talking specifically about lifelong learning of what it means to be a happy and fulfilled human being of good character. The story in the box below is a real-world example.

It is important to stress that lifelong learning is not just lifelong schooling or studying! The concept stresses the importance of people taking responsibility for their own learning, and there are a wide range of ways in which this can be done. Lifelong learners recognise the need for ongoing learning, are motivated to engage in the process and have the necessary confidence and learning skills to achieve their learning goals. Lifelong learners of values reflect critically on their actions and interactions, think about what they are doing, contemplate ongoing development of their own values frameworks, and have positive impacts on the values of others. They also accept life's ups and downs as opportunities to develop and practise values.

The concept that learning to live a values-rich life is a lifelong process needs to be introduced at secondary school level or even earlier, helping to develop in students the characteristics that will make this learning an integral and valued part of their lives after they leave school.[11] Encouraging self-directed learning will help them to become lifelong learners. Seeing their teachers practising human values in their own lives and benefiting from doing so can help students to understand that EHV is for life, not just for the school years. In fact, it is well beyond their school years that learners change and grow.

Lifelong Character Learning in Practice – *Howard Gardner*[12]

For the developmental psychologist Dr Howard Gardner, lifelong learning is not just a philosophy but a practical necessity. He continues throughout his working life to refine his *Theory of Multiple Intelligences* and expand on its implications, particularly in relation to interpersonal, intrapersonal, and existential intelligence. His interest in lifelong learning meant that he progressed his work from the theoretical concept of multiple intelligences to putting them into practice and context in his most recent works in such publications as '5 Minds for the Future', 'Truth Beauty and Goodness Reframed', and 'Good Work: Theory and Practice'. In this third publication, he has edited the work of a group of researchers who have related the values of Excellence, Ethics, and Engagement to ongoing education and learning based on his Multiple Intelligences. The necessary development of character through values is evident in these later publications, suggesting Gardner himself as an excellent exemplar of the concept of a lifelong learner.

Lifelong learning is best described as being voluntary, with the purpose of achieving personal fulfilment through informal or formal education. Lifelong learning helps people to become better at what they do by keeping open minds, increasing wisdom, and keeping pace with the changing world. Ultimately, everyone is responsible for one's own learning, and any undertaking will be driven by the values the learner holds.

7.4 The Process of Learning and the Influence of Values

Humans of all ages have a drive to understand their own particular personal universes in some way, triggered by the experiences they encounter and the values they hold. We all need to learn from experience to develop our values frameworks, but this needs to go hand-in-hand with learning about our universe and about *how* we learn. This section explores the holistic process of learning and developing values within the previously described cognitive, physical, emotional, social, and spiritual domains. A quote from the physicist Stephen Hawkingis pertinent here: *We are just an advanced breed of monkeys on a minor planet of a very average star. But we can understand the Universe. That makes us something very special.*[13.]

When it comes to acquiring knowledge from experience in order to use it to improve lives, then the framework used is open to choice. Generally, young learners do not think about having such frameworks, or what some call 'worldviews' but very often neither do adult learners. However, reflecting on choices and the framework/worldview used to make a particular choice is an important part of learning. A critical influence on a framework is the value system the individual has developed; consequently, a good values education can have a dramatic influence on how and what people learn and the actions they take as a result of that learning. Their framework provides a reference from which knowledge is developed and then used. Reflection can also reveal different *ways of knowing.*

It is possible to differentiate at least four ways of knowing: *Propositional, practical, tacit,* and *inspirational.*

- *Propositional* knowledge is probably the most familiar to everyone, being encountered in formal learning situations that present *facts* relevant to what we need to know.
- With *practical* knowledge we learn the skills required to achieve some end.
- *Tacit* knowledge is that which cannot be written down easily and is difficult to transfer from the holder to another; it is that *personal* knowledge that cannot be codified and requires personal contact for others to acquire it from the person who has it.
- Finally *inspirational* or *intuitive* knowledge is the knowledge people have without understanding how it was acquired; it is important, however, that such knowledge is tested against evidence and conscious reasoning, even though these have not been used to acquire it.

All four can be combined by practising *experiential learning*, as described in Figure 7.1.

When putting all of these types of knowing into action, learners are all embedded in their own worlds, trying to make sense out of these worlds in order to take action to improve them or resolve problematic issues. Clearly, judgements about what action to take are value-laden, so being aware of the values held and reflecting on them helps improve decisions. This highlights the importance of values education and the interconnection of values and lifelong learning.

There are also different 'levels' of learning. At the first, the cognitive level, the challenge for learners is to become increasingly aware of how they are immersed in the world, about the issues involved and how issues might be improved.

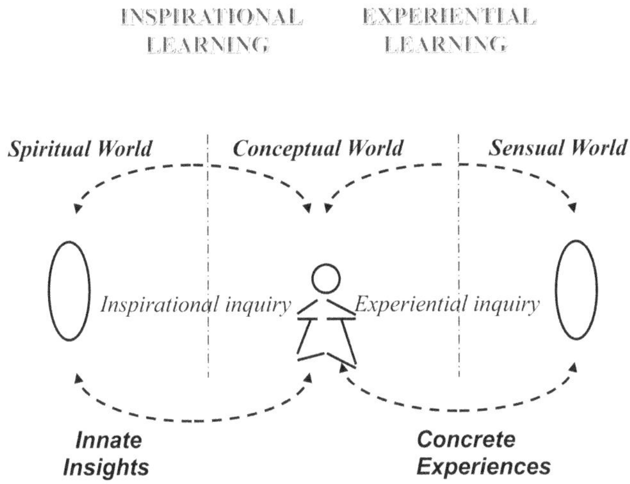

Figure 7.1 The Holistic Learning Process[14]

At the second level, the metacognitive, an expansion of consciousness, enables learners to interact and interpret the world better as they reflect on how they are going about looking at and working on their issues of concern. Are there other perspectives they might take? Are there other processes and methods they might use?

At the third level, the epistemic level, improved integrative consciousness that incorporates the learners' value systems allows them to process ideas better and to interact with the world more ethically. Figure 7.2 illustrates all these ideas combined into what can be called a 'Learning Holon'.

Learning in a group is often an advantage: First, there is the fact that different members of the group will have different learning styles, enabling the group to learn better as a 'whole system' than individual learners on their own. Additionally, at the (first) cognitive level, learners in the group have the opportunity to expand their knowledge and skills by learning from the practical, the tacit, and the propositional knowledge of the other learners, thereby improving their own competences and how they each go about cognitive learning. Thus, learners are encouraged to join or form groups interested in their issues wherever the context allows. One of the community programmes developed from EHV, called 'Sai Lifestyles', is concerned with putting human values into practice to resolve issues in daily life. In the programme, younger participants learn from their elders within workshop groups while the older members learn from the younger group members during their discussions and interactions about their experiences of leading values-rich lives and resolving problems and issues more effectively.

Learners' dispositions to learn are undoubtedly affected by the cultures in which they find themselves. Culture is not just content to be learned but a *context* of learning in which values and meanings of a learner's experiences are

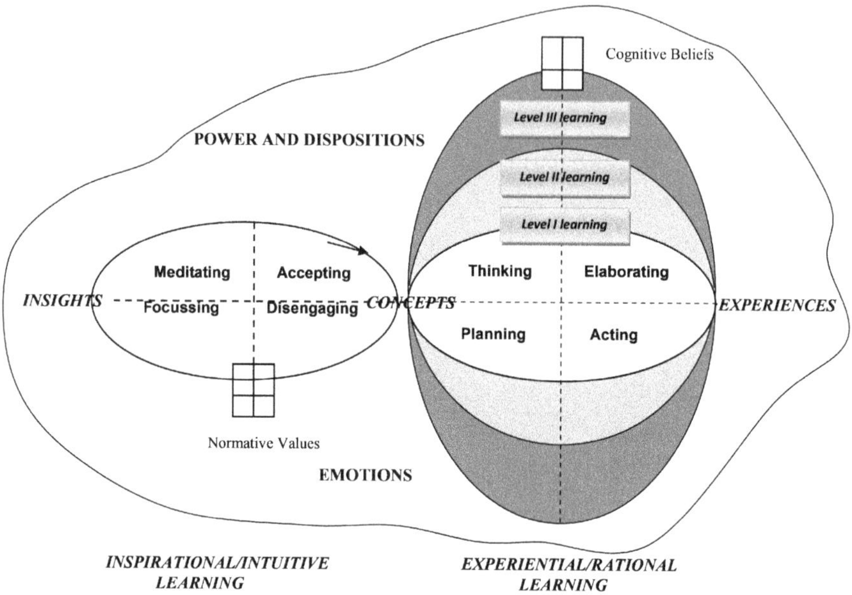

Figure 7.2 The Learning Holon[15]

interpreted. Dealing best with cultural issues requires a community of learners in which multiple ways of learning take place. Culture is the 'toolkit' for sense making and communicating; an example of this toolkit is the language used in a particular context, as well as the local knowledge, beliefs, and values shared by the people of that local culture. In his discussions about experiential learning, Kolb[16] emphasised the importance of what he called 'learning spaces'. He described these as the physical, cultural, institutional, social, and psychological dimensions that can be adjusted to optimise learning. These ideas apply to learners of all ages and are relevant to school, tertiary, and adult learning situations. Power relationships also influence all of these aspects, while dispositions to learning and the *learning spaces* can be seen as the manifestations of the intertwining of power relationships and other external factors with internal bodily responses of the learner.

Good learners can create a sense of self, which means a sense of agency, or the ability to get something done on their own. A sense of self also requires the development of the conceptual system that organises the interactions that the learners have with their world, markedly influenced by the values they hold and the values that are developed as a result of the learning undertaken: Nothing is ever value-free.

Returning to optimising learning at the cognitive level, cognition is something that goes on in the mind and is both conscious and non-conscious. However, the mind is not the same as the brain (see Chapter 2) and is no longer seen as being confined to the brain. The mind and consciousness are now considered to be not *things* but *processes*, a view developed independently by both Bateson[17] and Maturana and Varela[18] since the 1960s. This concept of cognition implicitly gives rise to a concept of mind that involves the entire process of life, including perception, emotion, values, and behaviour. It is a self-generating system that undergoes continual structural changes while preserving its pattern of organisation. Such a self-generating system couples to its environment structurally, that is, through interactions which trigger structural changes, but this coupling does not direct any changes specifically. Changes can include modifications of bodily behaviour on the basis of previous experience that is either valued or rejected, and this is what can also be called *learning*. In practice, this means that we learn with our whole bodies not just our brains, interacting with all aspects of our environment, including home, work, and leisure, not just the learning situation in isolation.

The mind is an embodied process of continuous modulations of the body, and there is no aspect of the body that is not a part of mind. It is the embodied mind that records the life history of the individual, yet most of this embodied knowledge is largely unavailable to conscious enquiry, so learners are unable to describe precisely what it is they are doing when, for example, they ride a bike or play a guitar, or see the funny side of a story; what was referred to earlier in this chapter as *tacit* knowledge.

All of this illustrates how the learning of values can help learners of all ages to deal better with the world in positive ways using the language and practice of values in all types and all levels of the learning process.

7.5 How Are Lifelong Learning Skills Developed?

Lifelong learning skills provide the foundation for living and working by enabling the pursuit of goals, both personally and professionally. The practice of learning from mistakes is one of the best lifelong learning skills anyone can master – turning mistakes into opportunities. So how are such skills developed, particularly when it comes to the ongoing development of human values?[19]

Initially, it is necessary for the learners to acknowledge their personal interests, goals, and, of course, values. There is a need then to reflect on what the learners are passionate about and what they visualise for their own futures (see Chapter 5). It is important to adjust and develop value systems continually as we encounter and deal with new issues; hence, identifying and developing awareness of values is an important component of identifying personal interests.

Committing to a decision to engage in a new learning initiative is the most important step. If realistic expectations have been set and there is self-motivation to see it through, the process should come naturally. To be a lifelong learner, it is necessary to be prepared to reflect on what is being learned and whether it has helped both the individual and others, and to consider the benefits of the learning.[20] It is here that the EHV technique of silent sitting (see Chapters 8 and 10) promotes concentration and frees the mind to focus on what is at hand, and it can play an important role. It is also important to mention that Silent Sitting is a useful tool to support lifelong learning of one's values. Often, as little as one minute is enough, either before deciding how to act in a particular situation or to reflect on whether different actions could have improved our experiences.

7.6 Benefits of Developing Lifelong Learning Skills

There are many benefits to be gained from participating in lifelong learning and matching our actions to our values. At times, almost everyone gets stuck in a routine, doing things simply because they have to be done, such as gardening, housework, or routine tasks in the workplace. It is necessary at times to find renewed self-motivation by figuring out what we find inspirational. This puts us back in the 'driver's seat' and is a reminder that we can really do things in life that resonate with our personal values, rather than ignoring or going against what we value, which is a key reason for life becoming difficult. Once goals and interests are recognised, reigniting what makes us 'tick' according to our values, boredom will disappear and life made more interesting, and this can open future opportunities. One never knows where one's interests will lead.

Becoming more knowledgeable or skilled in something will increase self-confidence in both personal and professional life. On a personal level, this confidence can stem from the satisfaction of devoting time and effort to learning and improving oneself, thus giving a sense of accomplishment. From a professional perspective, this self-confidence can be the feeling of trust in the knowledge and ability to apply what has been learned in a values-based and ethical manner.[21]

The following stories are from two Chinese teachers who, from their training to implement EHV in their classes, clearly embraced the values and methodology as part of their lifelong learning journeys.

Two Teachers' Stories

> I was feeling burnt out and restless....Therefore in my teaching I would always strive for perfection and always thought the students had grasped the complete knowledge as long as they obtained good test results. But the fact is not so. You pay very much, but the harvest is actually very little. Facing this fact, I had become excessively sad, excessively disappointed, and very tired. My teaching did not have any meaning. Then I started to participate in the values education training, and we became aware of the theory to; awaken the child's innermost feelings, thoughts and values', to 'help the children to know they all have special qualities', and that 'the deepest impression the student has is of the teacher's personality, not the knowledge which

she teaches'. All of this touched me in a very big way, and I blushed with shame when I recalled the past. Though I had thought myself to be a teacher, only pursuing the academic score was really superficial. I have learned the 'humanist' side of the work, to 'take the love as the starting point' even if the student's outcomes are not so good. I try as much as possible not to look at the superficial things but to discover the students' true intrinsic selves. As a result of my own values change, I now always set out to try to discover the students' happy side, maintain a happy mood in the classroom, and now I have finally found the work to be a joy, and my teaching to be happy.

(Teacher 1, EHV Experimental School, March, 2006)

I had a very serious problem of easily getting panicky, worried, irritated. When I got to know Educare (EHV) great changes took place in my mind. It has been like a light guiding me out of the darkness. Every day early in the morning I close my eyes and breathe deeply three times and fully concentrate on today's work.
I imagine my students sitting in the classroom and I put my focus on each student's face, imagining each of them as a beautiful flower or something beautiful. I then have a sense of love from my heart.
I feel full of strength and energy all over. Then the day's work goes smoothly – everything is under control, and I feel full of joy. Gradually I have conquered my panicky problem.
The values education has changed me and my relationships with my colleagues. Before I would speak extremely candidly and had not considered the feelings of the person I was speaking to. Now I have learned to pay attention to others' feelings, which has helped to build a harmonious atmosphere with colleagues. Many look from the other's point of view, render encouragement and assistance and respect each other equally as one respects one's own family members.

(Teacher 2, EHV Experimental School, March, 2006)

7.7 Conclusions

The final story, presented below, further inspires us to undertake lifelong learning, irrespective of our cultures or our ages. The story implies the importance of our living ethical and values-based lives, caring for and serving others through a recognition of the benefits of lifelong learning. This story is about the values-based lifelong learning of Nelson Mandela.[22]

Nelson Mandela: An Exemplar of Lifelong Learning

Through all his layers of education, Mandela exemplified dialogic lifelong learning that was life-wide, lifelong, and life-deep. This ongoing learning lay at the core of his personal and political transformation. A study of Nelson Mandela's educational experiences has revealed the global icon to be an exemplar of lifelong learning.

First, he learnt a lot about tolerance through dialogue with others. These included friends and mentors like Walter Sisulu and Anton Lembede in the ANC Youth League – but also Communists, who were both rivals and comrades. Second, he learnt about his own values through dialogue with himself. At crucial moments, he was able to reflect critically on what had happened and what it meant. Sometimes an uncomfortable encounter prompted this. Third, Mandela showed a continuing learning dialogue with the collective of the ANC. Its history, ethos, and policies were a constant reference point for him to refine his ways of responding to situations. Fourth, perhaps the most striking of Mandela's learning dialogues was with his changing context. He could read and respond to the signs of the times in very different settings – such as when re-entering public life as a septuagenarian in the 1990s in an extremely volatile national and global context, but as a clear exemplar of values such as Peace, Right Action, and Non-violence. One example of his learning about Non-violence was the way he used rugby as a vehicle to help lessen divisions between black and white South Africans and foster a shared national pride.

These four moments of Mandela's dialogic lifelong learning – dialogue with others, with self, with the collective, and with context – were not discrete. They interacted constantly. Nelson Mandela's life and writings reveal his fascination with a lifetime of learning about human values. His autobiography, *Long Walk to Freedom*, is written 'almost as a learning story'.

The world has entered a period in the history of humanity when, in the developed world during adulthood, free time often exceeds work time and will do so more and more. But education that continues for the duration of life, and in all areas of life, is incomplete unless learners also make it their own journeys of personal development and transformation. Learning cannot become lifelong and life-wide without being 'life-deep'.[23] People often learn things out of necessity yet, even then, they cannot do so unless they find personal meaning in what is being learned so that this knowledge can be assimilated actively and subsequently mobilised. The reality is that most people have goals or interests both within and outside of their formal schooling and jobs. This is part of what it means to be human; to have a natural curiosity and a need to learn. People develop and grow, thanks to this ability to learn. The EHV programme is best viewed not as an add-on or a separate activity; rather, it is to be seen as an investment in structuring the foundation for lifelong learning, promoting human excellence, and social cohesion, resulting in a society that truly prospers. Therefore, lifelong learning about how one's own human values will help to expand the capabilities and choices of all, enabling individuals and societies to cope with the new and as yet unknown challenges of the 21st century[24] and to become happier, more fulfilled human beings.

7.8 Activities

It can be good to become more conscious of your true current values because they are your best guide to how to live a better life. You can accomplish this 'values consciousness' by completing a *values and morals inventory* which will help you to examine what it is that you want for yourself and comparing these desires to the moral desires that society or your own higher principles (spiritual or humanist), have for you.

Most well-socialised people will find that there is a lot of correspondence between what you want and what society wants. If you are honest, however, you will sometimes find that there are areas and aspects of your life where society wants one thing from you, and you want something different.

To make the inventory, simply ask yourself what it is you want from life. Explore your wants and desires in depth:

- List what you value, what you want from life, and how you want to live.
- Also list what you think you are supposed to want and what other people who are important to you want for you.
- Look for two sorts of discrepancies:
  - Discrepancies between what you want and what society wants.
  - Discrepancies between what you want and where you are actually at.

Do this so as to determine if you are someone who largely lives out your values or if you are instead someone who does one thing and believes another.

If you act differently from how you believe you should, why is that so? What is stopping you from acting the way you want to act?[25]

Notes

1 Henry Ford. https://www.goodreads.com/quotes/tag/lifelong-learning accessed 23-8-2022.
2 From: Arrow Human Development, *The On-going Process in Peoples Life* (n.d.). http://www.arrow-training.com/index.php/en/what/life-long-learning accessed 23-8-2022.

3 J. Delors, *Rethinking Education, Towards a Global Common Good* (UNESCO Publishing, 1996). https://unesdoc.unesco.org/ark:/48223/pf0000232555 accessed 12-3-2022.
4 *Ibid.* https://en.wikipedia.org/wiki/Delors_Report accessed 31-3-2022.
5 *Ibid.*
6 S. Bhattacharjee and D. Bhattacharyya, "A Value Based Lifelong Learning – A Need of the Hour," *Scholarly Research Journal for Humanity Science and English Language* 4, no. 21 (2017).
7 *Ibid.*
8 Sathya Sai Baba, *Sathya Sai Speaks* (Prashanthi Nilayam, India: Books & Publications Trust, 1985), Vol. 18.
9 P. K. Jena, *Mahatma Gandhi and Basic Education.* Chapter 9 (Meerut, India: Anu Books, 2020), 57–63.
10 N. Longworth and W. K. Davies, *Lifelong Learning: New Vision, New Implications, New Roles for People, Organizations, Nations and Communities in the 21st Century* (London: Kogan Page, 1996).
11 J. Bryce and G. Withers, *Engaging Secondary School Students in Lifelong Learning* (Australian Council for Educational Research. LTD, 2003).
12 https://en.wikipedia.org/wiki/Howard_Gardner accessed 2-2-2023.
13 Stephen Hawking quote. https://www.goodreads.com/quotes/22524-we-are-just-an-advanced-breed-of-monkeys-on-a accessed 20-5-2022.
14 Modified from R. Bawden, "The Community Challenge," in *The Learning Response, Social Learning Systems and Communities of Practice* (London: Springer, 2010), 39–56.
15 Modified from R. Bawden, "A Paradigm for Persistence: A Vital Challenge for the Agricultural Academy," *International Journal of Agricultural Sustainability* 5, no. 1 (2007): 17–24.
16 D. Kolb, *Experiential Learning: Experience as the Source of Learning and Development,* 2nd ed. (New Jersey: Pearson FT Press, 2014).
17 G. Bateson (First published 1972), *Steps to an Ecology of Mind: Collected Essays in Anthropology, Psychiatry, Evolution, and Epistemology* (Chicago, IL: University of Chicago Press, 2000).
18 H. R. Maturana and F. J. Varela, *The Tree of Knowledge: The Biological Roots of Human Understanding* (Published by Shambhala, 1992).
19 L. Crockett, *6 Ways to Build Lifelong Learning Skills in Your Learners* (2021). https://blog.futurefocusedlearning.net/6-lifelong-learning-skills accessed 31-3-2022.
20 *Ibid.*
21 Valami, *Lifelong Learning* (2019). https://www.valamis.com/hub/lifelong-learning#lifelong-learning-benefits accessed 31-3-2022.
22 MacGregor Karen, *Nelson Mandela: An Exemplar of Lifelong Learning* (2015). Open Democracy. https://www.opendemocracy.net/en/transformation/nelson-mandela-exemplar-of-lifelong-learning/ accessed 20-8-2022.
23 S. Walters, "The Planet Will Not Survive If It's Not a Learning Planet: Sustainable Development within Learning through Life," *International Journal of Lifelong Education* 29, no. 4 (2010): 427–436. https://doi.org/10.1080/02601370.2010.488807 accessed 12-3-2022.
24 Bhattacharjee, "A Value Based Lifelong Learning," 2017.
25 Mental Help.net, *Values and Morals Clarification: Value Changes* (n.d.). https://www.mentalhelp.net/self-help/values-and-morals-changes/ accessed 24-5-2022.

Chapter 8

Methods for Teaching EHV

Bob (Robert) Molloy and Roz (Roslynne) Malloy

8.1 Introduction

This chapter will enable the reader to have an understanding of and insights about the methods of Education in Human Values (EHV) and how these can be used in schools in a *direct* manner (specific lessons on values) in order to develop cognitive awareness of human values concepts and how they may apply to daily life. EHV can also be taught through *integration across the curriculum*, and this will be the subject of the next two chapters (Chapters 9 and 10).

This chapter will enable readers to:

- Think about how values education may be missing or not emphasised in the modern curriculum.
- Have knowledge of the methods – the teaching techniques of EHV.
- Be aware that the principles and teaching strategies of EHV are suitable for lifelong learning (see Chapter 7), but that the methodology of using these strategies changes as students grow older.

While it is the responsibility of the whole community to instil and practise values, the role of parents and especially the school is of prime importance. Teaching values through a whole-school approach provides the common and essential thread, which unites a school and creates the focus for staff, students, parents, learning stages, key learning areas (KLAs), and outcomes. More will be said about this in Chapter 13. For the teacher in the classroom, when it comes to values there is no neutral stance, as the teacher cannot 'not teach values', whether directly or indirectly. All teachers promote values naturally as a matter of course in their teaching (the 'hidden' curriculum, see Chapter 9), but without a structured values programme this is usually done unconsciously and without focus, hence the need for a systematised programme.

Generally, education is structured around KLAs. Each of these KLAs is designed to produce a particular set of outcomes, skills, and competences. The ultimate goal is to produce functional citizens who can contribute to our

DOI: 10.4324/9781003478607-9

modern society in positive ways and in a broad range of disciplines. Examples of these KLAs are:

- *English*: The development of literacy
- *Mathematics*: The development of numeracy
- *Science and Technology*: Understanding of the physical world
- *Human Society and its Environment* (HSIE): Understanding of the social world
- *Creative and Practical Arts*: Developing creativity
- *Personal Development, Health, and Physical Education* (PDHPE): Developing a fit and healthy citizen

These KLAs aim at producing a skilled society that can achieve great feats, yet, without the appropriate guidance, citizens can also use these skills for selfish purposes and thus harm society. This, of course, is why values education is so important. In fact, for the many reasons explained in earlier chapters, there is a compelling argument for values to be embedded in the curriculum alongside the other KLAs.

For society to function, we need moral and ethical citizens. We could go a long way towards better achieving this by having an additional KLA, EHV, to give children a deep understanding of positive human values and a 'moral compass'. Chapter 14 describes some schools that have adopted this viewpoint. This chapter and the next two (Chapters 9 and 10) will show how to achieve this goal, first, here, through a *direct* approach focused on lessons specifically about values, in Chapter 9 by incorporating values education *indirectly* into the 'hidden curriculum' and in Chapter 10 by integrating values messages into subjects across the curriculum. This theme will be taken up again in Chapter 13, which is concerned with creating a values-embedded whole-school culture.

8.2 Prerequisites for Implementing Values Education

A Malaysian school practicing EHV says: *This program takes up the challenging vision, placing new emphasis on social, moral, and spiritual values in the curriculum, by eliciting the universal and timeless values of love, peace, truth, right conduct, and nonviolence.*[1] To implement values education, the following are required:

- A values framework – See Chapters 2 and 3 for a discussion of this, and Chapter 14 for some more examples of a school's values framework.
- A language of values that enables learners to understand the concepts of values, so they are able to recognise them when they see or practise them (see Chapter 3).
- Techniques for eliciting the values inherent in the individual.

- Opportunities to put values into practice and reflect on the outcomes of this in all aspects of daily life.
- Teachers' and other significant adults' role modelling of values.
- A school culture embedded in values (see Chapters 13 and 14).

None of the above are mutually exclusive; they form a holistic setting for values education. Also, there is a great deal of overlap and interaction between the direct and indirect teaching methods with these six essential components. In Table 8.1, these have been mapped onto both Krathwohl's

Table 8.1 Aspects of EHV Related to Krathwohl's Taxonomy and the Trans-Theoretical Model

Related aspects of EHV	*Link to Krathwohl's taxonomy*	*Link to Trans-Theoretical model*
Direct method	• *Receiving* phenomena • *Responds* to phenomena • *Valuing* (i.e., seeing those around us using the values in every aspect of daily life) • *Organisation* (i.e., examining and prioritising values as they arise in daily life) • *Characterisation* (i.e., pervasive, consistent, predictable values behaviour)	• Precontemplation • Contemplation • Preparation • Action • Maintenance
Integrated method	• *Receiving* phenomena • *Responding* to phenomena • *Valuing* • *Organisation* • *Characterisation*	• Precontemplation • Contemplation • Preparation • Action • Maintenance
Language of values	• *Receiving* phenomena • *Responding* to phenomena	• Precontemplation • Contemplation • Maintenance
Techniques	• *Receiving* phenomena • *Responding* to phenomena • *Valuing* • *Characterisation*	• Precontemplation • Contemplation • Preparation • Action • Maintenance
Opportunities to practise and reflect on all aspects of daily life	• *Responding* to phenomena • *Valuing* • *Organisation* • *Characterisation*	• Contemplation • Preparation • Action • Maintenance
Role modelling	• *Responding* to phenomena • *Valuing* • *Characterisation*	• Preparation • Action • Maintenance
Values-based whole-school culture	• *Valuing* • *Organisation* • *Characterisation*	• Preparation • Action • Maintenance

Taxonomy and the Trans-Theoretical Model (see Chapter 3 for details) to illustrate how they describe an individual's pathway to understanding and 'living' human values. The purpose of this table is to illustrate how important ***both*** the direct and indirect methods are, as well as ***all*** of the six components in order to succeed in bringing about real, sustainable, and desirable transformation in the characters of the students and the culture of the school.

Every KLA has its basic, specific vocabulary; a language which expresses, defines, and captures its scope and uniqueness. As discussed in Chapter 3, values education is no different. Again, the Malaysian EHV school notes that *The goal of the EHV programme is to foster the development of character into all aspects of the personality. Personality is fully integrated when there is consistency in thought, word, and deed … the EHV Programme defines five aspects of the human personality: the intellect, the physical, the emotional, the social and the spiritual. Each of these aspects corresponds [predominantly] to one basic human value.*[2]

The adjacent model considers how the five human values can be linked to the domains of our experience. The prime value is the highest expression of values in that domain. A holistically healthy child is balanced in all of these domains. As the founder of EHV said, *Love as thought is Truth, Love as action is Right Conduct, Love as feeling is Peace, Love as understanding is Non-violence*[3] (see Chapter 14).

8.3 Incorporating Values into the Primary School Curriculum: Grid of Values

A critical step in adopting human values in everyday life is to develop a cognitive and affective understanding of what values are. This is why the framework of the five human values has been broken down into example aspects, as can be seen in Table 8.2.

This grid, which is by no means exhaustive, is an example of value aspects of the five core human values that were chosen and used in an Australian primary school.[4] Understanding and articulating these aspects is the means by which our feelings are expressed, and control is gained over emotions and behaviour. This is the basis of moral literacy. These values aspects may be found under more than one core value, for example, *Sharing* can be connected to *Love* and also to *Right Action*. Once again this emphasises the interconnectedness of the five core human values.

It is not always easy to incorporate values education (such as EHV) as an additional KLA into the cluttered Primary School Curriculum, even though this has been done in some schools (see Chapter 14). So how can direct EHV lessons be fitted into the weekly timetable allocation? While it would be ideal to have short EHV lessons every day, that is not always possible, yet in most schools, it is possible to find at least 30 minutes per week to allocate to the direct teaching of human values. This can be consolidated and reinforced

Table 8.2 The Five Core Values and Examples of Their Aspects

Love	*Truth*	*Right Action*	*Non-violence*	*Peace*
Care	Curiosity	Courage	Citizenship	Self-Esteem
Compassion	Honesty	Determination	Cooperation	Balance
Consideration	Quest for Knowledge	Helpfulness	Teamwork	Calmness
Dedication	Self-Awareness	Kindness	Balance	Optimism
Empathy	Self-Esteem	Good Manners	Equality	Gratitude
Forgiveness	Understanding	Perseverance	Human Rights	Self-Discipline
Friendship	Trust	Respect	Interdependence	Concentration
Generosity	Persistence	Responsibility	Justice	Equality
Gentleness	Self-Reflection	Initiative	Loyalty	Happiness
Service	Truthfulness	Resourcefulness	Respect	Patience
Sharing	Discrimination	Organisation	Friendliness	Self-Acceptance
Tolerance	Integrity	Tolerance	Caring	Contentment
Patience	Spirit of Inquiry	Freedom of Speech	Forgiveness	Reflection
Sincerity	Intuition	Enthusiasm	Flexibility	Self-Respect

in weekly assemblies. If the school year consists, for example, of four terms each of 10 weeks, a direct EHV lesson could be delivered over two weeks as it requires at least one hour to equip students with a cognitive understanding of the values. In our experience, this method of delivery has worked well.[5]

The value aspects selected can be chosen collaboratively by staff at the beginning of each year or each term. Key factors that determine which value aspects will be taught explicitly for each particular year or term are:

- Behavioural needs of students (whole school and individual)
- Emotional needs of students (whole school and individual)
- Subject matter to be covered in KLAs
- Exposure and opportunity to meet KLA curriculum outcomes
- Parental concerns/needs
- Community concerns/needs
- Values aspects taught in previous term/year

Table 8.3 is an example of a *Values Planner* used in one school. This plan was linked to the KLA of *Human Society and Its Environment* (HSIE), although it could easily have been linked to other KLAs. In this case, the same values were introduced across the whole primary school, although they were treated differently for students in different grade levels as their understanding and ability to use the relevant language matured.

Table 8.4 is a second example. In this case, the value and associated quotation are displayed around the school.

Table 8.3 A Values Planner

	Term one *Cultures*	*Term two* *Change and continuity*	*Term three* *Social structures and systems*	*Term four* *Environments*
Values	Weeks 1–2 Love: Friendliness 'To have a friend you need to be a friend'	Weeks 1–2 Truth: Curiosity 'There's more to life than meets the eye'	Weeks 1–2 Truth: Self-Discipline 'Small steps, big goals'	Weeks 1–2 Truth: Awareness (environment) 'Love the world and the world loves you'
	Weeks 3–4 Right Action: Responsibility 'A safe self begins with me'	Weeks 3–4 Right Action: Understanding 'To understand others first I need to understand myself'	Weeks 3–4 Non-violence: Fairness 'Do as you would be done by'	Weeks 3–4 Right Conduct: Enthusiasm 'Enthusiasm is having a positive attitude to do the things that you do'
	Weeks 5–6 Non-violence: Respect 'If you look after your body it will look after you'	Weeks 5–6 Non-violence: Caring 'Caring people help the world to be a better place'	Weeks 5–6 Peace: Flexibility 'Flexibility means thinking of new ways of doing things'	Weeks 5–6 Non-violence: Persistence 'Turn your face to the sun and the shadows fall behind you'
	Weeks 7–8 Truth: Self-Confidence 'Know that you are a blessing to yourself, and you will be a blessing to others'	Weeks 7–8 Peace: Reflection 'Looking forward, looking back'	Weeks 7–8 Right Conduct: Service 'In the spirit of service, we make a difference'	Weeks 7–8 Peace: Acceptance 'We need to accept the things we cannot change and improve the things we can'
	Weeks 9–10 Peace: Sincerity 'To speak what is true and do what is right for you'	Weeks 9–10 Love: Appreciation 'Appreciation is the heart's memory'	Weeks 9–10 Love: Cooperation 'We may have come on different ships, but we are in the same boat now'	Weeks 9–10 Love: Joyfulness 'All people smile in the same language'

Table 8.4 A Values Planner with Quotations

Term 1	*Term 2*	*Term 3*	*Term 4*
Week 1 & 2 Non-violence as Cooperation *'Many hands make light work…'*	**Week 1 & 2 Love lived as Sacrifice** *'Think of others before yourself…'*	**Week 1 & 2 Right Conduct lived as Responsibility** *'Being responsible means that others can depend on you'*	**Week 1 & 2 Peace lived as Freedom** *'Freedom comes with boundaries…'*
Week 3 & 4 Right Conduct lived as Discipline *'Self-discipline means choosing to do what you feel is right…'*	**Week 3 & 4 Peace lived as Doing Your Best** *'Doing your best means never stop trying…'*	**Week 3 & 4 Non-violence lived as Fair Go** *'Do unto others as you would have them do unto you…'*	**Week 3 & 4 Truth lived as Self-Knowledge** *'Trust yourself. You know more than you think you do…'*
Week 5 & 6 Peace as Contentment *'Most people are as happy as they make their minds up to be'*	**Week 5 & 6 Non-violence lived as One-ness** *'We are a oneness universe. We are all connected…'*	**Week 5 & 6 Love lived as Kindness** *'Be kind whenever possible. It is always possible …'*	**Week 5 & 6 Love lived as Forgiveness** *'Forgive and forget'*
Week 7 & 8 Truth lived as Quest for knowledge *'The more we know the more we grow'*	**Week 7 & 8 Right Conduct lived as Hard Work** *'The secret of success is hard work'*	**Week 7 & 8 Peace lived as Forbearance** *'I want it now, but I can wait…'*	**Week 7 & 8 Non-violence lived as Consideration** *'A little consideration, a little thought for others makes all the difference'*
Week 9 & 10 Love lived as Friendliness *'Friendliness isn't a big thing; it is a million little things'*	**Week 9 & 10 Truth lived as Trustworthiness** *'Be true to your higher self'*	**Week 9 & 10 Truth lived as Concentration** *'Make each day your masterpiece'*	**Week 9 & 10 Right Conduct lived as Duty** *'In this life, it is actually your duty to live it as fully as possible'*

8.4 The EHV Teaching Techniques

Each fortnight, students are introduced to the vocabulary and concepts of one selected value aspect from the above plan. The following seven techniques (introduced in Chapter 1), in combination, provide a powerful teaching approach for developing these concepts. Chapter 2 explained how these techniques impact on different parts of the mind. Initially, it is encouraged to use all of these activities in a regular rotation, although it is also important to apply some flexibility and use them creatively so that students, particularly older ones, do not become bored with the same structure for every lesson. Experience has shown that, from upper primary school, introducing a thematic approach overcomes this, using whichever of these techniques lend themselves best to the chosen theme rather than using all of them in every lesson. The seven techniques are:

1. Silent Sitting
2. Mind Map
3. Storytelling
4. Quotations and Affirmations
5. Group Activity
6. Song/Music
7. Creative Visualisation

8.4.1 *Silent Sitting*

As stated in Chapter 1, this is an essential technique in the EHV programme. In order to learn, students need to be calm and concentrated. Silent sitting enables them to put aside distracting thoughts and to become aware of their inner feelings and the 'inner voice' of conscience and wisdom. They become aware that happiness and love come from inside themselves, not outside. In a direct EHV lesson, silent sitting is often used at the beginning of the lesson to prepare the students to absorb the message to be addressed. Many schools are introducing similar practices, such as mindfulness, meditation, and *apps* such as 'Smiling Mind'. There have been some studies on the effectiveness of such practices in schools.[6]

Students need an introduction to silent sitting and its purposes and benefits, starting with simple activities that can help them to become comfortable with this type of activity. One way to introduce the technique is to concentrate on the breath, and Appendix 5.1 provided examples.

In our experience, even young children are very accepting of this practice, and, within a short time, they are able to sit silently for one or two minutes. Some children are reluctant to close their eyes at first, but by addressing their concerns, gradually their confidence can be built up; never force them to do so. At first, as long as they are quiet and not disturbing others, just let them be, as in time most become comfortable with and even look forward to closing their eyes to shut out distractions. Here is an example from one teacher's practice:

8.4.1.1 Concentration on the Breath

Students sit quietly, close eyes and concentrate on the inner silence, letting all their thoughts go.
They are then told to concentrate on breathing, a slow breath in and a slow breath out.
Continue this for one or two minutes.
Then get them to open their eyes and be present in the classroom.

Another example:

Ask students to count their breaths over a period of time (e.g., 30 seconds). Then repeat and try to breathe fewer times.

8.4.1.2 Stilling the Mind

A further example uses guided visualisation to provide children with an experience of stilling the mind. While guided visualisation, as discussed in the following section, has a different role to play in developing students' conceptions of values, it can also have a role as a form of silent sitting to still the mind.

Example:

Close your eyes and imagine that you are in the countryside.
You lie down on soft warm grass. It is a safe place, and nothing can harm you.
Gaze up into the sky and see the clouds drifting by.
They take on shapes of animals, people, and things.
These clouds are the thoughts in your mind, let these clouds drift away and focus your mind on the clear blue empty sky.
Do not follow the clouds, your thoughts. Let them just drift away.
Focus on the empty blue sky.
Now let the children stay in this state for one to two minutes, depending on the age group. Then bring the children back to the classroom.

As children become more comfortable with this approach, the teacher can then just ask them to close their eyes for one minute of silent sitting.

It is suggested that all daily or weekly assemblies commence with a whole-school silent sitting activity. Not only can this be a way to settle the students down to start the day, but it can also generate a strong atmosphere of peace that can carry over into the day. Classroom teachers can use one/two minutes of silent sitting to focus the students' awareness. This usually occurs when they come in from recess, lunch, or outdoor activities. It may also be used if students are becoming unsettled during an activity or to demark a change of subjects; more is said about this in Chapters 9 and 10, in connection with using this technique more widely across the curriculum.

8.4.2 Quotations/Affirmations

These are positive statements of profound truth and wisdom. An example is, *To have a friend you must first be a friend.*[7] Used in direct lessons, these quotations are an easily memorised key to help students to understand and remember what a core value or one of its aspects means. The value and quote are discussed with the class. This is done through questioning, e.g., 'What does this saying mean to you?', and sometimes using a visual mind map (see description below).

Repeated use of quotations can programme, or reprogramme, the subconscious mind to promote good thoughts and habits, as described in the mind model shown in Chapter 2. They can be used to focus on the positive aspect of the value of the lesson and its importance in life (see the importance of emphasising goals in life, as described in Chapter 5). Quotations can be displayed throughout the school and discussed in the morning school assembly. Additionally, different quotations related to the same value might be selected for early childhood, primary school, middle school, and secondary school levels.

8.4.3 Mind Maps

As used in EHV, the *Mind Map*[8] consists of several prime questions, with the number of questions dependent on the maturity of the students. The students can extend these questions in a dendrogram. Examples of these prime questions used for the values Mind Map with students are:

1. ***What is it?*** – Develop a short dictionary-like definition.
2. ***What does it look like?*** – Explore what the students might see in practice when the value is displayed by someone else.
3. ***What does it do for me?*** – Explore how the student might feel when practising the value.
4. ***What does it do for others when I practise it?*** – Explore how students think others might feel when the students practise that value.
5. ***What is its opposite?*** – List any that are named.
6. ***What are the limits of the value?*** – Explore when the value might not be useful or appropriate in a context.
7. ***What are the challenges?*** – Examine what makes it difficult to practise this value.
8. ***What are the related values?*** – Discuss whether there are other similar or closely related values the students are aware of.

This is an activity for students to complete in small groups and then to share their responses with the class. Mind mapping can generate much discussion and thus needs adequate lesson time. It is a particularly useful activity for more complex values.

A mind map is a valuable, comprehensive way of grasping the scope and deeper appreciation of the value under consideration. Students will give

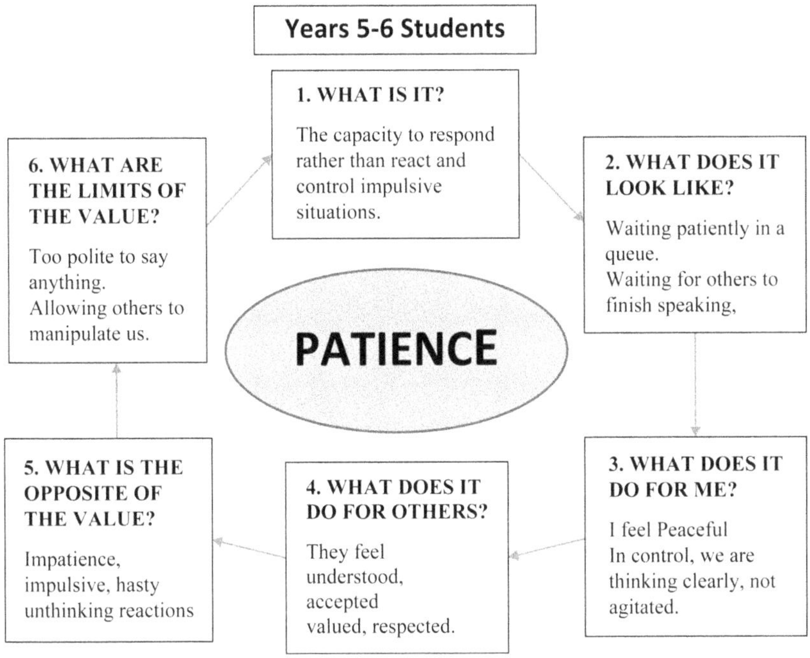

Figure 8.1 A Values Mind Map of Patience

responses according to their age levels and understanding, thus giving the teacher an indication of the level at which to pitch the lesson. Kindergarten children can be asked to respond verbally to the first four questions.

Mind mapping is also of great use as a whole-staff exercise to deepen the teachers' understanding of the weekly/fortnightly value, thereby giving confidence to staff no matter how experienced they may be.

It is a good idea to follow mind-mapping with creative visualisation (see below) to consolidate the concept in the students' minds and establish, or 'programme' an image of themselves drawing on this value when a situation calls for it.

Figures 8.1 and 8.2 are some illustrated examples of actual mind maps developed with students.

8.4.4 *Storytelling*

Stories are used to foster understanding of selected values. Storytelling is one of the oldest and most effective tools for teaching, as most people enjoy being told stories. The story can be presented through oral storytelling, literature, videos, pictures, guest speakers, documentaries, or various forms of multimedia.

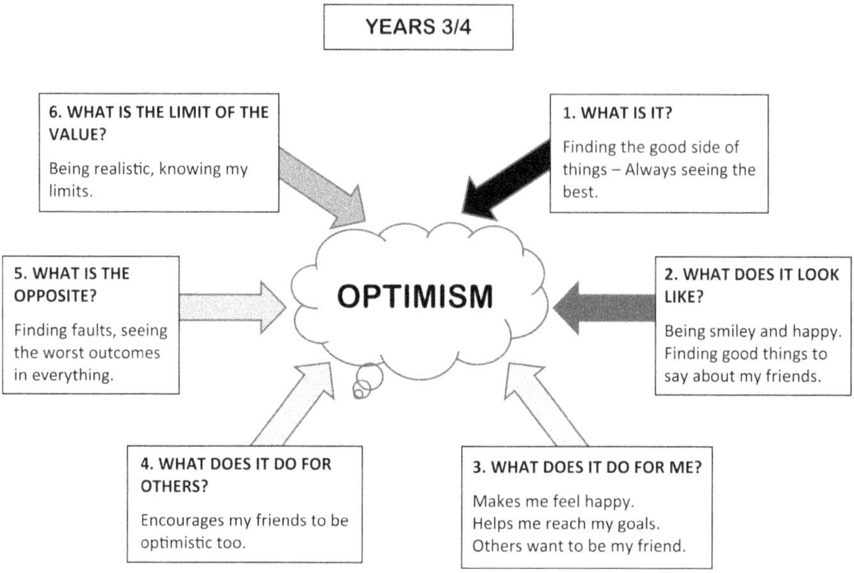

Figure 8.2 A Values Mind Map of Optimism

Every values aspect ideally has a story at its core. The story puts the value into a context and is the cocoon which carries it. Young people will likely remember the story, and hence the values message with it.

Discussion and questioning based on the story are essential to reinforce the student's understanding of the selected value. First, one or two questions are asked about content, but the main focus should be on how the students think the characters may have felt and how they, themselves, are feeling: For example, whether they have experienced what they think the story characters are feeling, whether they have practised the value reflected in the story, and, if so, what the effects were for themselves and others. Storytelling is incomplete without questions; keep in mind Bloom's Taxonomies[9] to determine the effect on the cognitive and affective domains.

Here are some examples of questions that might be asked:

- ***Cognitive Questions:*** Drawing out the facts, such as *Where…*, *What…*, *How many times…*, etc. (remembering, knowing, and understanding)
- ***Affective Questions***: Bringing out emotional intelligence and helping students to become aware of their feelings, such as *how you felt when* …. etc. (receiving, responding, valuing, organising, characterising)
- ***Experiential Questions***: Helping students to relate to the situations. Ask, *have you ever experienced a similar situation* …, *what would you do* …, *has anyone* … (application, analysis, synthesis, and evaluation)

Example 1: Story for children aged 5–7 years

'***Dinofours – I'm the Boss***', by Steve Metzger, Scholastic, 1998[10]

This story was used to illustrate the value of 'caring'. The aims were to raise the children's awareness of 'caring' in relation to their behaviours in the playground, classroom, and at home; to make them aware of subtle forms of bullying, e.g., name-calling and exclusion; and to realise that the value of 'caring' is absent in the behaviours represented in the story.

Questions:

- Who wanted to play?
- Who wanted to be boss all the time?
- Why did each child leave in turn?
- Why do you think this happened?
- Has something like this happened to you?
- What would you do? What can we learn from this about the value of 'caring'?

Example 2: Story for children aged 9–10 years

The Very Best of Friends by M. Wild and J. Vivas[11]

Two elderly people live and work on a farm. The old man is friends with his cat. The old woman is not very fond of the cat. The old man dies. The old woman and the cat become the best of friends.

Questions:

- How do we know that William was James' friend?
- How do we know that Jesse was not the cat's friend?
- How did you feel when William was not allowed in the house?
- How did Jesse become the cat's friend?
- What can we learn from this story about friendship?
- Who is a good friend to you, and why?
- What is something you have done recently to be a good friend to someone?

8.4.5 Group Activities

Group Activities provide a lived experience of a selected value. Such an activity will be designed to focus on class/student interaction so that the selected value is clearly on display through the activity. The activities are, naturally, age-related and designed for the class level. Examples might be games, role plays, co-operative tasks, group artwork, or community service. It is particularly valuable if these activities are interdependent, where students each add their unique contributions to strengthen the group's outcome. It is also important to create opportunities for discussions about the effectiveness of their contributions as good team members to promote strength in unity.

Examples:

Kindergarten and Grade 1: Drawing, cutting and pasting, placing pictures in order, co-operative displays. Children at this stage enjoy placing their own words/ideas on a paper tree display.

Lower Primary School: Role play for age level, board games, indoor games such as Freeze, group artwork.

Upper Primary School: More role play, debates, discussions, group artwork, service activities.

8.4.6 Music/Song

This technique does not need to take any more than five minutes; however, in our experience, students always look forward to it and enjoy it.

Why music and singing?

- It is enjoyable, calming, and uplifting.
- Appropriately selected music can decrease feelings of agitation, restlessness, and excitement.
- It removes barriers and encourages cooperation.
- It makes one feel joyful, happy, and as one with those around.
- Anything learnt through song is remembered and is easier to recall, so embedding the value in a song is a powerful tool for remembering the concept.
- Rhythm comes naturally to children.
- When a person feels good, the heart beats gently with a steady rhythm. When one is angry, the heart becomes erratic, yet by listening to calming music, it can be observed that the individual gradually calms down and relaxes. Music has been an integral part of human life since the beginning of recorded history.

It is important for songs to be age-related and that they reflect a values message. These can come from a wide variety of sources and are available through many media. There are also many *YouTube Videos* with values songs. Students might write and create their own songs as well. The values song for the fortnight can be played and sung at the weekly assembly.

Some guidelines for implementing this music and singing technique are as follows:

- Music has the power to change all levels of our consciousness, so it is important to select the right music.

- Choose most songs from the language and culture of the students in the class.
- Ensure that the songs have values messages.
- Words about the values being taught can be used to develop new words to well-known tunes/jingles, for example, *Kookaburra Sings*, *Mary Had a Little Lamb*, *Jingle Bells*.
- Children must understand what they sing.

Example:

(To the tune *Frere Jacques*)
Silent sitting
Silent sitting
Peaceful time
Peaceful time
Relax and take a deep breath
Make your body heavy
Quiet place
Peaceful space
Silent sitting
Silent sitting
Peaceful place
Peaceful place
(Written at Exeter Primary School, Tasmania, Australia)

8.4.6.1 Examples of Songs Used in Primary Campus, Sathya Sai School Murwillumbah, Australia

Week 1–2 – Truth – Quest for Knowledge

- The Drop of Water – *Sing 2005* Vol. 1 No. 22[12]
- Or I Believe – *Sing 2004* Vol. 1 No. 4
- Feed Your Brain – *Great Southern Song Book* 2001

Week 3/4 – Right Action – Responsibility

- More than Words – *Splitters*
- Infants – Helpful Humpty – *Virtues in Me* No. 17
- Helping You is Helping Me – *Virtues in Me* No. 18
- Universe's Daughter – *Sing 2002* Vol. 1 No. 16

Week 5/6 – Non-violence – Resourcefulness

- Reuse, Recycle – Jack Johnson
- Garden Song – *Sing 2001* Vol. 2 No. 11

Week 7/8 – Peace – Balance

- Heal the World – Michael Jackson
- Wet Day Blues – *Splitters Razzamajazz*
- With Our Own Two Hands – *Sing 2004* Vol. 2

Week 9/10 – Love – Gentleness

- A Better Place – *Splitters Razzamajazz* No. 14
- Early Childhood: Gentle Old McDonald – *Virtues in Me* No. 4
- I Can See Clearly Now – *Sing 2005* Vol. 2 No. 2

8.4.7 Creative Visualisation

Creative visualisation is a short technique, often only requiring one or two minutes. In direct EHV, it is often used at the end of the lesson, as it is basically the formation of mental visual images to support what has been covered in the lesson about the selected value. It is a different technique from silent sitting.

While silent sitting is concerned with stilling the mind, the creative visualisation technique in EHV refers to the practice of seeking to affect the outer world via changing one's thoughts and one's inner world (see Chapter 5). This technique also assists positive thinking (see Chapter 11) and is similar to a process frequently used by athletes to enhance their performances.

8.4.7.1 Example: Year 9 – Respect

Ask the group to sit comfortably, then close their eyes, and then say the following:

> Imagine you are at home after school doing your homework, so you can go out later. Your mobile phone rings. It is your best friend, Anna. She sounds really upset. She has been home sick for a week with flu. She has missed out on some vital work for her term assignment. She asks if you can help by coming around this evening and share your notes with her so she can catch up and complete her assignment. You hesitate and think 'Oh no', as you had planned to hang out with another friend this evening and you don't really want to go to Anna's. Then you think how upset she sounds, and you remember how much time she spent helping you to learn the dance steps that you found difficult. So, you say, 'OK. I'll come around and help you'. Anna sounds so relieved.

Then suddenly, you feel so good and happy, and it doesn't matter that you have had to postpone your plans. Allow yourself to focus for a few moments on this feeling of happiness that you are able to support your friend.

8.4.7.2 *Example Year 7 – Non-violence*

The narrative here is as follows:

Imagine you are walking on a clear sandy beach ...

The afternoon sun is shining behind you ... lighting up the whole beach in a shade of golden hue ...

The sun's rays are reflected back in the water in dazzling colours ...

You can see the sun's reflection in clear ripples ...

The water touching the sand gently ...

Suddenly you see a plastic bottle being tossed around by the waves...

You think about the damage that this plastic can cause to the creatures in the sea

You keep your eye on the plastic bottle until finally it is tossed onto the shore....

You quickly grab it and walk to the recycling bin and drop the plastic bottle into it ....

You then lie on the warm sand and feel happy that you thought about the environment ...

Remain with this good feeling...bring your attention to where you are at present...

Gently open your eyes.

8.5 Developing a Direct EHV Lesson

When preparing such a lesson, it is useful to brainstorm ways to present the explicit value being taught, the way to use the different techniques and their particular purposes, and the learning activities that might best allow the students to fully grasp the value in focus.

Some sample lesson outlines are given in Appendix 8.1.

It also helps to support these lessons by designing and creating positive reinforcement of the value. While the longer-term goal is to help the students to become intrinsically motivated and practising the values so as to become an integral component of their lives, such extrinsic motivators as are suggested here can play an initial role, but only to get the students to the stage where the intrinsic 'kicks in'. The following suggestions have been found to work well:

- ***Weekly Awards:*** Certificates awarded to children at assembly for displaying values as well as for academic success.
- ***Keys:*** Each week at assembly, a 'key' can be awarded to a child in each class who has been displaying the value in focus. This key is stuck on a special door in the hall titled 'The Door to Happiness'.
- ***Book Awards:*** At the end of each year, every student is awarded a book prize. Each book is inscribed inside with a value that the child has displayed most consistently throughout the year.
- ***Excellence in Human Values Award:*** Every year, on presentation night, a child who has been an outstanding role model and consistently displayed human values is awarded this special plaque. The child's name is engraved on the plaque, and it hangs in the school hall. The child also receives a replica of the award to keep.

Table 8.5 Example Direct Lesson Curriculum Year 7

EHV Curriculum Yr 7 Stg. 4					
	TERM 1			TERM 2	
	SELF AWARENESS				
WK	TOPIC	VALUE	WK	TOPIC	VALUE
1	Friendliness - values	L ove	1	Peer Pressure: Influences-family -1	
2	Spirit of Enquiry - values revision	Truth - Enquiry	2	Peer Pressure: +pos Influences-2	Love
3	Self knowledge1	Truth-Enquiry	3	Peer Pressure: Using Courage-1	
4	Self knowledge 2	Truth - Enquiry	4	Peer Pressure: Resisting-2	Truth
5	Self Esteem/Self Love	Love	5	Anti Bullying: Introduction-1	Right Conduct
6	Silent Sitting 1	Peace-	6	Anti Bullying: Bullying Stages - 2	Peace
7	Silent Sitting 2	Calmness	7	Anti Bullying: Cyberbullying -1	Non-Violence
8	Self Discipline 1	Right Conduct	8	Anti Bullying: Victim Assertiveness-2	
9	Self Discipline 2	Right Conduct	9	Anti Bullying: Bystander Courage - 1	Right Conduct
10	Self Analysis 1	Truth	10	Revision	Truth
11	Self Analysis 2	Truth			
	TERM 3			TERM 4	
	COMMUNITY/SOCIAL AWARENESS		ENVIRONMENT/GLOBAL AWARENESS		
WEEK	TOPIC	VALUE	Wk	TOPIC	VALUE
1	Anti Bullying - Bystander - 2	Right Conduct	1	Gratitude -1	
2	Anti Bullying 2 - Upstander		2	Gratitude - 2	Love
3	Social Awareness - 1	Non-Violence	3	Respect - 1	Right Conduct
4	Social Awareness(Skills) - 2		4	Respect - 2	
5	Harmony - 1	Peace	5	Care of the Environment - 1	Non-Violence
6	Harmony - 2		6	Care of the Environment - 2	
7	Compassion - 1	Love	7	Revision	All values
8	Compassion- 2		8	Service Activity	Love
9	Integrity - 1	Truth	9	Wed 6 EHV Activity in Hall - combined	Game Poverty
10	Integrity - 2				
	ISSEA 2018				

8.6 The EHV Direct Method in Secondary School

Direct EHV at primary school level (K–6) is concerned primarily with building up a language of values and showing how the values impinge on decisions and choices in life. The weekly lessons focus on one value at a time. The core of the lesson is the story, a cocoon containing the value and how it resolves daily situations.

By the time they reach secondary school (Grades 7–12), students will have acquired a large vocabulary of values, and repertoires of stories and songs to support this. It is important at this stage for them to engage in experiential situations that will challenge them. This helps them to realise that, in everyday life, we are faced with situations that require the balancing of clusters of values, because life is not simple. Individual values often need to be revisited in progressive years. Each time a value is reintroduced it provides the opportunity to relate it to a different context and to a greater depth. As the student matures the value can be presented in a broader context.

Here are some examples of curricula (Tables 8.5–8.7) for Years 7–9 as developed and used for the Sathya Sai College in Australia. (See Chapter 14 for more information about this school.)

Table 8.6 Example Direct Lesson Curriculum Year 8

EHV Curriculum Yr 8 Stg.4

	TERM 1			TERM 2	
	SELF AWARENESS			FAMILY/PEERS AWARENESS	
WK	TOPICS	VALUE	WK	TOPIC	VALUE
1	Values overview - focus on friendliness 1	Love	1	Respect Responsibility -1	Right Conduct
2	Values overvies focus on friendliness 2		2	Respect Responsibility-2	
3	Silent Sitting 1	Truth-Enquiry	3	Forgiveness-1	Love
4	Silent Sitting 2		4	Forgiveness-2	
5	Facing our Fears 1	Courage	5	Conscience Healthy Mind-1 - KF	Non-Violence
6	Facing our Fears 2		6	Conscience Healthy Mind-2	
7	Happiness 1	Peace	7	Compassion 1	Peace
8	Happiness-2		8	Compassion 2	
9	Self Confidence 1	Love	9	Cooperation 1	Right Conduct
10	Self Confidence 2		10	Cooperation 2	
11	Self Awareness Activities	Review			
	TERM 3			TERM 4	
	COMMUNITY/SOCIAL AWARENESS		ENVIRONMENT/GLOBAL AWARENESS		
WEEK	TOPIC	VALUE	Wk	TOPIC	VALUE
1	Choices in Life-1		1	Gratitude-1	Love
2	Choices in Life-2	Truth	2	Gratitude-2	Love
3	Humility-1	Truth	3	Respect-1	Right Conduct
4	Humility-2	Right Conduct	4	Respect-2	Right Conduct
5	Tolerance-1	Right Conduct	5	Care of the Environment -1	Non-Violence
6	Tolerance-2	Non-Violence	6	Care of the Environment- 2	Non-Violence
7	Sacrifice-1	Non-Violence	7	Service Activity	Love
8	Justice - Fair Go 1	Love	8	Revision	
9	Justice - Fair Go 2	Right Conduct	9	Wed 6 EHV Activity in Hall - combined	Game-Poverty
10	Revision				
	ISSEA 2018 - V3 MAY 2018				

Table 8.7 Example Direct Lesson Curriculum Year 9

EHV Curriculum Yr 9 2018 Stg.5

	TERM 1			TERM 2	
	SOCIAL AWARENESS			Positive Attributes	Right Action
WK	TOPICS	VALUE	WK	TOPIC	VALUE
1	Values overview and revision - 1	Right Action	1	Self Reliance 1	Self Respect
2	Values overview and revision - 2	Non-Violence	2	Self Reliance 2	
3	Silent Sitting - 1 revision	Truth	3	What is my purpose?	Truth(Role models-heroes)
4	Silent Sitting - 2 - research		4	Love of Learning	
5	Getting on with others - 1	Cooperation	5	Persistance	Right Action
6	Getting on with others - 2		6	Integrity	
7	Positive peer pressure - 1	Right Action	7	Citizenship	Right Action
8	Positive peer pressure - 2		8	Fairness	
9	Community Awareness - 1	Service	9	Leadership 1	Non-Violence
10	Community Awareness - 2	Influence on others	10	Leadership 2	
11	Social Awareness Activities	Review			
	TERM 3			TERM 4	
	Emotions - Pos & Neg			Global Communication	
WEEK	TOPIC - EMOTIONS	VALUE	Wk	TOPIC	VALUE
1	Self Regulation 1	Non-Violence	1	Communication	Love
2	Self Regulation 2		2	Relationship Choices	
3	Setting Goals	Truth	3	Identity Labels	Right Action
4	Pursuing Goals		4	Inner Voice	
5	Celebrating Goals		5	Life Journey - Inner 1	Truth
6	Resilience - Internal & External	Non-Violence	6	Life Journey - Inner 2	
7	Mindsets - 1 conditioning habits	Peace	7	Empathy - 1	Love
8	Mindsets - 2 conditioning habits		8	Empathy - 2	
9	Understanding Your Emotions	Truth	9	Service Activity	Love
10	Service Activity	Love	10	EHV Activity in Hall - combined	Game Poverty
				-	
	ISSEA 2018				

8.7 Concluding Comments

This chapter has focused on how the direct method of EHV aids in developing the language and concepts of the five core human values and their related value aspects. The purpose of this direct approach is to help students to consolidate their understanding and to recognise that human values are not just for use and consideration during the direct lesson; rather, they are for the whole of life. The goal is to develop the student's intrinsic awareness of values and their enactment in daily life. This goal is supported by integrating values across the curriculum. Ideally, every lesson has a values component, illustrating how the values discussed in the direct lessons are embedded in all aspects of life. This *integrated* approach is described in Chapters 9 and 10.

The direct method is used not only in conjunction with the integration of the human values into the school curriculum but also in the development of the whole ethos of the school. This will be described in Chapters 13 and 14.

8.8 Final Exercise

Before you proceed to Chapter 9, it is suggested that you spend some time, alone or preferably with a group of colleagues, to reflect on how you can incorporate some direct teaching of values concepts into your current classes.

Here are some suggestions for what you might do to put these ideas into practice, using the action learning model presented in Chapter 3 where appropriate:

- What are the values aspects most relevant to your context?
- How can you adapt the teaching techniques described in this chapter to your students' needs and interests?
- Develop a plan to implement some direct lesson activities into your teaching for at least two weeks. (*If you are unable to find a 30-minute block, you could spend 5–10 minutes per day, every day, which is a small amount of time to take from your day, given the benefits to be had.*)
- At the end of the fortnight, reflect with your colleagues on the feasibility and effectiveness of what you have tried.

Appendix 8.1: Examples of Direct Method Lesson Plans

This appendix presents examples of lesson plans for a single direct lesson. The intention is to illustrate what has been developed using the techniques described in this chapter. All are real lessons used in primary and secondary schools.

Lesson Plan Example Years 1 and 2

Value: Non-violence/Caring

Aim:

To raise the children's awareness of 'caring' in relation to their behaviours in the playground, classroom, and at home. To make children aware of subtle forms of bullying, e.g., name-calling and exclusion. Have the children realise that the value of 'caring' is absent in these behaviours.

Learning Outcomes:

Describe 'caring' and 'non-caring' behaviours.

Describe how others' caring behaviours make them feel and how their caring behaviours make others feel.

Quotation:

> Caring people help the world to be a better place.

Discuss:

- What do we mean by caring?
- How do we know when people are not caring?

Story:

Dinofours – I'm the Boss – by Steve Metzger – Scholastic 1998 (see https://www.amazon.com/Im-Boss-Dinofours-Steve-Metzger/dp/0590374583) – The bossy dinosaur learns how to share, listen, and, in turn, earn everyone's respect.

Discuss:

- Who wanted to play?
- Who wanted to be boss all the time?
- Why did each child leave in turn?
- Why do you think this happened?
- Did any of the children show caring behaviour?
- What non-caring behaviour did we see in this story?
- How could this have been changed to caring behaviour? How would this have made the children in the story feel?

Mind Map:

- A caring behaviour that makes us feel happy is when…
- An uncaring behaviour that makes us feel scared is when…
- We can make other people feel happy when we…
- We might make other people feel scared if we…
- A caring behaviour that makes us feel excited is when…
- An uncaring behaviour that makes us feel sad is when…
- We might make other people sad if we…

Creative Visualisation:

You are boarding a spaceship. It takes off very quickly and silently. You look out the window and are amazed to see planet Earth below, a beautiful white and blue planet. On it, you see all the children of the world, all races, colours, shapes, and sizes. They all have a light coming from their hearts. You see the same light in all. The lights all join together as one. You realise that we are all one in the light.

Song:

Stop Bullying song:
https://www.youtube.com/watch?v=NP4jRRb8nao (accessed 1-9-2022)

Lesson Plan Example Years 3 and 4

Value: Truth/Persistence/Making an Effort

Aim:

For children to realise that to be successful, they need to persist at difficult tasks. To have them realise that if they only look at all the reasons why they can't do something, the goal will be lost.

Learning Outcomes:

Describe the feelings associated with struggling with a difficult task and accept that these are natural feelings and a part of the process.

Describe the feelings after struggling with a difficult task and eventually succeeding.

Identify strategies that can help them to persist effectively (e.g., go for a walk, do silent sitting to help them to look at the task freshly).

Silent Sitting/Visualisation:

Think about a time when you have tried to do something that is new and difficult. It might be learning something (e.g., to ride a bicycle or to swim), making something, or trying to solve a problem.... Allow yourself to remember how you felt at that time .... Now remember when you finally succeeded. How did you feel then? Allow yourself to feel the good feeling of success for a few moments.

Discuss:

- What were some of the feelings you had when you were struggling to do the task?
- What were your feelings when you succeeded?
- *Values message:* Sometimes we need to accept that the bad feelings are a part of learning and not a reason to give up because eventually they give way to the good feelings of success.

Quotation:

Obstacles can be seen when we lose sight of the goal.

Discuss:

- What does this mean?
- How does this relate to the values message we learnt from the silent sitting?
- Help the children to realise that to be successful they need to persist at difficult work. If they only look at all the reasons why they cannot do something, the goal will never be reached.

Song:

Perseverance Song: https://www.youtube.com/watch?v=hhgHTe8GLWI (accessed 4-9-2022)

Story:

Out of Luck from the Program Achieve Manual by Michael E. Bernard: Australian Scholarships Group, 2001

Discuss:

- Discuss the real reasons Jonathon became successful.
- Discuss the types of obstacles we might put in our way to decrease our motivation.

OR '*The Most Magnificent Thing*' by Ashley Spires: Kids Can Press, 2015

Discuss:

- What did the girl do after she got really angry and frustrated? [*She went for a walk.*]
- What happened after that? [*She was refreshed and able to look at her project in a different way, and then she succeeded.*]
- Has something like this ever happened to you? If so, what did you do to refresh yourself, and what was the outcome? [*The teacher may be able to share some personal experiences to start this discussion.*]
- What are some other things we can do to refresh ourselves when we are suffering frustration and want to give up. [*Emphasise the importance of silent sitting as a tool for this purpose.*]

Activity:

Conduct an 'I Can't' Funeral

Rest In Peace: The I Can't Funeral - taken from *Chicken Soup for the Soul* by Jack Canfield and Mark Victor Hansen, Retrieved from https://william-bertrand.fr/rest-in-peace-the-i-cant-funeral-by-chick-moorman/ (accessed 4-9-2022)

The essence of this story is a group of students conducting a 'funeral' to bury all of the 'I can't' statements they found themselves making and replacing them with 'I can', 'I will', and 'I'm going to right away'.

Lesson Plan Example Years 5 and 6

Value: Self-Awareness

Aim:

To develop students' understanding that people can have different customs and ways of viewing things and that we should respect them for their differences. To encourage students to appreciate their own uniqueness, even if they may be different from others.

Learning Outcomes:

Identify what it is that everyone has in common (i.e., belonging, love, basic needs taken care of, to know who they are, feel fulfilled, have a purpose in their lives, to feel inner peace).

Emphasise the point that there are many different roads to the same destination, and we cannot judge whether one person's way is right and the other's is wrong.

Describe the importance of inner beauty/accepting our uniqueness being more important than outer beauty.

Identify their own uniqueness, which makes them special.

Story: '*Luke's Way of Looking*' by Nadia Wheatley, Walker Books Australia, 2012

This story is about a young boy who finds that looking at the world differently is not always accepted, but it is his way of finding his 'inner angel', his uniqueness.

Discuss:

- Was it fair that Mr. Barraclough punished Luke and that the other boys regarded him as weird?
- Why do people get teased, and what can we do to prevent it?
- Why do people have different coloured skins and eat different kinds of foods? (Emphasise that skin colour is a matter of what is appropriate for the climate into which our ancestors were born, as is the kind of food we eat. It is only for survival that we have developed different appearances and customs.)
- Does it matter the way you look, dress, behave, or see things? (i.e., bring out what does matter and what doesn't matter.)
- What can we do to encourage everyone to accept what we are discovering from this story, that everyone is the same on the inside and travelling on the same journey through life, but that it is our uniqueness that makes each of us special.

Creative Visualisation:

Allow a short time for students to practise deep, slow breathing and relax before beginning the visualization.

Imagine you are one of the children in Luke's class. Imagine the classroom and the other children sitting at their desks. You have been asked to paint an apple. You paint a beautiful red apple. The person beside you paints a beautiful green one. You look at Luke's painting and he has painted a bright blue one with a red stalk. Your teacher is angry, and all of the other children laugh. How does it make you feel, to see them laughing at him? Now imagine that you are looking at everyone in the class not from the outside but from the inside. Look closely at Luke. What are the beautiful, unique qualities you can see in Luke, that make him who he is? Now look closely at yourself. What are your beautiful, unique qualities that make you who you are?

Activity:

Children write their names on top of a piece of paper, and each child in the class writes something they like about that person or something they believe that student is good at below their name.

Discuss how it is important to be aware of what we believe about ourselves and also how others see us.

Song:

'*I am Beautiful*' by Christina Aguilera, 'Be True' EHV Vol. 1 https://www.youtube.com/watch?v=aoYEQgG4-JY (accessed 4-9-2022)

Another Story:

The Story of Gillian Lynne https://www.facebook.com/RunWildMyChildAdventures/photos/a.2456798864334525/4532058126808578/?type=3 (retrieved 26-8-2022)

This is the story of another child who was considered 'different' and 'difficult to manage' until she discovered that the uniqueness that made her different was her ability to dance. She went on to choreograph many performances, including the musical *Cats*.

Activities:

- Brainstorm about the similarities and differences between people of different races/different religions.
- Children draw around their bodies on large sheets of paper – emphasise drawing on the features that are the same for all of them. Alternatively, they can draw their own features but change something, e.g., skin colour or eye shape, to give the understanding that they are still the same person even if some external features are changed.
- This can also be a chance to focus on differences within our own community. For example, develop the understanding that we should treat people who are poor or people with disabilities as being the same as us on the inside.

Lesson Plan Example Year 7

Value: Self-Awareness/Love Lives as Self-Esteem

Aim:

To develop students' understanding of themselves by providing an awareness of their own unique gifts and talents. To expand the students' awareness of their own selves in society and that self-love, manifested as self-esteem, is important for their own happiness.

Learning Outcomes:

- Demonstrate greater confidence and greater self-respect.
- Compliment themselves and others lovingly.
- Increase confidence to be themselves.
- Identify their own unique strengths or talents and how they can use these to benefit themselves and others.

Silent Sitting:

To experience the calm, peaceful, restful real self – pure consciousness. Focus on the breath – hold – breathe out. Hold silence for one minute.

Song:

'*Greatest Love of All*' by Whitney Houston https://www.youtube.com/watch?v=mvCUZli0vSw (accessed 4-9-2022)

Discuss the content. Why is the greatest love of all to learn to love yourself? Is it selfish to love yourself?

Quotation:

I deserve love from myself.

I am good enough just being me.

To love others, I need to love and value myself.

The most powerful relationship that you will have is the relationship with yourself.

Discuss with the students the big picture of their existence:

- I live in a family.
- I live in a community with my peers and friends.
- I live in an environment of nature (air, water, plants, animals, etc.).
- But I am also a unique individual.

Conclusion: I need knowledge and skills to live in these four worlds of experience – first and foremost I need to start with understanding what it means to love myself, because then I can love others more effectively.

Discuss:
Knowledge and Skills to live as a unique, happy, and fulfilled human being: How I see myself, my strengths, and what I do well.

- My best subject at school
- My hobby or sport
- What I do in my free time
- What are my unique strengths/talents that are suggested by these activities?
- What do my peers/my parents consider to be my unique strengths/talents?
- How do I use these to benefit myself? (Ask students to brainstorm responses to the statement: 'When I engage in these activities, I feel good about myself. I feel ...' (e.g., happy, capable, confident)

- How do I/can I use these activities to benefit others? (People at home, people at school, people in my community, people in the whole world)

Discuss:
What is self-love?
Self-love is the belief you hold that you:

- are a valuable and worthy person
- have a positive view of yourself
- are confident in yourself
- are confident your place in the world
- know what your unique/special strengths/talents are and how to use them to feel happiness, confidence, and fulfilment to support yourself and others.

Group Activity:
Create a '*ME*' commercial:

- Each student is asked to write a 2–3 minutes TV commercial
- The topic is 'Why are you a unique and special person?'

OR

- In pairs, design commercials for each other, focusing on each other's positive qualities

Discuss:
What can we do to love ourselves? – brainstorm a list such as below, and discuss.

- STOP criticising ourselves
- Praise ourselves for our strengths/talents
- Forgive ourselves for our shortcomings
- Be gentle, kind, and patient with ourselves
- Take care of our bodies and our mental and emotional health

Videos:
'Who am I?' https://www.youtube.com/watch?v=UHwVyplU3Pg&t=167s (accessed 4-9-2022)
OR
https://www.youtube.com/watch?v=om3INBWfoxY (accessed 22-8-2022)
Summary:

- I am a unique individual. There is no other like me.
- I have unique strengths and talents that I can use to benefit myself and others.
- I can accept my weaknesses and use them as opportunities to grow, but I am not harsh on myself for having these weaknesses because they are a part of who I am.

- I can be happy to spend time with myself engaging in, for example, my hobby, reading a book, or walking in nature.
- It is not selfish to care for myself, because in doing so I can care better for my family, my friends, peers, and teachers.
- I am a capable person in charge of my life and my future.
- I am happy, contented with WHO I AM.

Lesson Plan Example Year 8

Value: Self-Awareness/Truth Lived as Self-Knowledge

Aim:

The aim is to explore the workings of the mind and how this can help us to understand better who and what we are.

Learning Outcomes:

Describe the different aspects of our awareness (thoughts, feelings, actions)

Identify the benefits of taking time to be aware of watching our thoughts/feelings/actions

Experience the power of creative visualisation to change our actions in positive and negative ways

Silent Sitting:

> Sit upright, place your feet on the floor. Clasp your hands loosely in your lap. Close your eyes and imagine you are out in the country, in a beautiful green pasture. It is a very safe place. Lie down and gaze up into the sky. See the billowing clouds racing across the sky. The clouds are the thoughts entering your mind. Don't follow them, let them drift across the sky of your empty mind. Focus only on the blue sky of your mind (allow one minute of silence). Now open your eyes and return to the class.

Discuss: You may elicit student comments on how successful they were in clearing the sky of clouds/thoughts.

Ask the students why we do silent sitting – what are the benefits?

- stills the mind
- promotes calmness
- improves memory and concentration

Discuss:

What is the mind?

In this lesson, we will explore the workings of our minds.

To answer this question, we need to have some understanding of who and what we are.

When we awaken in the morning and open our eyes, we have an awareness that we exist; we are aware of thoughts (get dressed, have breakfast, catch bus to school, etc.) and feelings, e.g., annoyance (didn't complete homework), happiness (will see my friends at school).

In other words, we are aware of three things:

- Our being aware (self-awareness)
- An outer world of action
- An inner world of thoughts and feelings

These three things that we all experience are embedded in our Consciousness and Mind.

Discussion

As a Conscious Being I can:

- Watch my mind (my thoughts)
- Watch my body (my actions)

What does this mean?

If there has been a time when you have been aware of watching your thoughts/your feelings/your actions, please share.

What are the benefits of taking time to watch your thoughts/feelings/actions?

How might this help you to respond in a more values-based way?

Watching my mind to see what happens:

Direct the students to close their eyes for a few moments, and then ask them to share what thoughts/feelings entered their awareness.

Categorise their replies into:

- Images
- Feelings
- Actions
- Desires

As a group, go for a walk around the school ground and focus on being aware of what you see/smell/hear/think/feel. After the walk, share your experiences. How does this add to your ideas about why this kind of awareness is important?

Video:

Thoughts Become Things

https://www.youtube.com/watch?v=8x4sVR67wCk (accessed 4-9-2022)

Discuss:

- Has there ever been a time when you have turned a wish/a thought into reality (either in a positive or in a negative way)? If so, please share your experience.
- Can I Control My Mind?

To answer this question, discuss the body/mind relationship as follows:

A thought enters the mind, and this leads to a feeling, and the feeling leads to an action. Invite students to suggest their own examples after considering those below.

- I was walking down some stairs in the dark and thought I might fall (thought). I felt anxious (feeling). I tripped and fell (action).
- I needed a new pair of jeans (thought). I imagined myself wearing my new jeans (feeling). A friend came to my house with *seven* pairs of jeans she had hardly worn but were too small for her, and gave them to me (action).
- I didn't want to go to a friend's birthday party (thought). I felt very negative about going (feeling). I fell over on the way and broke my arm (action).
- I was getting a headache (thought). I imagined myself relaxing beside a flowing river (feeling). My headache went away (action).
- We were all making fun of a boy who couldn't kick the football (thought). I imagined how he might feel (feeling). I stopped judging him and every lunchtime I went to the oval with him and helped him to learn how to kick (action).
- I was angry because my mother was insisting that I tidy my room (thought). I remembered how much she does for me (feeling). I happily supported her by tidying my own room (action).
- I thought I was going to fail my test (thought). I felt panicky (feeling). I did silent sitting and turned my panic to confidence (feeling). I was able to answer all of the questions (action).

- Give some sample thought scenarios (or invite students to suggest) and brainstorm what could be done to change their thoughts and feelings, in order to change their actions, for example:
  - you don't have any friends to play with
  - you aren't good at anything
  - you are always frightened to try new things
  - you are being bullied

Key Values Message:

- Thoughts lead to feelings which lead to actions
- Negative thoughts lead to negative feelings which lead to destructive actions
- Positive thoughts lead to positive feelings which lead to helpful actions

Conclusion: Can I control my feelings and actions?

- YES – by controlling my thoughts.
- If we are mindful of what we are thinking, we can change our feelings and actions.

Activity:
Homework Challenge:
For the next week, find one way in which you can be mindful of your thoughts and feelings and, by controlling your thoughts, change your feelings and actions.

Lesson Plan Example Year 9

Value: Truth/Positive Attributes

Aim:

To explore goal setting as a strategy for self-achievement and self-fulfilment.

Learning Outcomes:

Set some personal goals based on recognition of their own strengths and talents.

Explain why goal setting is important to give a sense of purpose and focus.

Creative Visualisation:[13]

Imagine that you are very, very tiny and you are walking inside your own mind. It looks like a library, with lots of shelves and books. Inside the books are all the things you have ever learned. You walk along the shelves until suddenly you find what you are looking for. It is a big book on a very high shelf. You take it off the shelf and look at the cover. On the cover it has your name, and it is called 'My Book of Goals'. Imagine that you open the book. On the first page there is a list of all the special strengths that you have, and all the things that you are good at. It might be words, or it might be a picture, or it might be like a movie. If you can't see anything don't worry because it will pop into your mind later. Have a good look at what is on the page and make sure you take careful notice of the information that is given to you…

Now imagine that you turn to the next page in the book, where it has the heading 'How I can use my special strengths to benefit myself and others'. On this page is a list of goals for using your strengths. Again, they might appear as words, pictures, or a movie. You might not notice anything at all. If you don't, there is no need to worry, because the ideas will probably come into your mind sometime later, often when you are least expecting it…

When you are ready, close the book and put it back on the shelf.

Discuss:

- Invite students who wish to do so to share the goals they identified.
- Discuss why it is important to have goals (i.e., so we can reach our full potential, be of service to ourselves and others, and thus achieve happiness and fulfilment. Also see Chapter 5).

Definition: *Goal:* an outcome to be aimed at, a winning part.

Discuss:

- Are there different types of goals, for example:
  - Short term, immediate, a few days
  - Medium term, days to months
  - Long term, years

Videos:

- https://www.youtube.com/watch?v=FFT6uP1fIFI (accessed 4-9-2022) Animated video reinforcing short-term and long-term goals.
- https://www.youtube.com/watch?v=nJRd-yzC5GI (accessed 4-9-2022) 'Where am I headed?' – video with teens talking about goals, includes values.

Also refer to article on Smart Goals: https://www.mindtools.com/pages/article/smart-goals.htm (accessed 4-9-2022)
Activity:

Think Tank:

- Use the five domains of the human personality, as discussed earlier in this chapter:
  - Cognitive Goals
  - Physical Goals
  - Emotional Goals
  - Social Goals
  - Spiritual Goals
- Put students in groups and have them write up their goals and place them in order of short, medium, and long term.
- OR have the students create their own personal mind maps of their goals – with paper and coloured marker pens.

Note: Goals must be achievable and realistic. In the discussion, bring out the range of goals that can be pursued. It may help the teacher to read Chapter 5 of this book for more background.
Activity:
Enemies of Achieving Goals
These four obstacles indicate a lack of purpose in life:

- Apathy – Lack of purpose in my life
- Laziness – Even a small effort is a challenge to me
- Poor health – I can't focus on goals, I am miserable and sick
- Fear – I can't face failure

On a scale of 1–5 have the students rate themselves for these four enemies. This will raise their awareness of their attitudes towards goal setting and achievement.

Lesson Plan Example Senior School (Years 10, 11, or 12)

Values:

Truth – Being honest about their usage of social media

Right action – Placing a ceiling on our desires to maintain our own inner peace

Aim:

To explore personal discrimination in the use of online resources and social media as a strategy for self-regulation, right actions, and peace in line with ceiling on desires (see also Chapter 11).

Note that this lesson actually requires a double class of 90 minutes, but if this is not possible it can be done in a 45-minute class, with less discussion.

Learning Outcomes:

- Set some personal boundaries and self-discipline based on recognition of the positive and negative aspects of Internet usage.
- Explain why ceiling on desires is important in managing Internet usage, in relation to social media, Internet gaming, and information gathering.

Silent Sitting:

Close your eyes and focus on your natural breathing pattern. Use your breathing to give you a feeling of calmness and relaxation. Now imagine that you are sending a very important, even urgent, message to a friend or friends. You can see that they are online. Because you consider your message to be very important, you are excitedly awaiting their reply.

You wait and wait and wait …

Nothing comes …. 24 hours go by ….still nothing!

How does this make you feel … about your friends not answering? ….about yourself? Can you pinpoint the location of these feelings in your body? What do you do? What are the thoughts going through your mind? Take a moment to listen to these thoughts…. Experience any feelings that these thoughts bring up… Just observe….

Now imagine that you have a bright light shining in the heart centre in your chest. Let the light slowly expand until it fills your whole chest cavity, then your whole body. Imagine that it is especially bright and strong in the parts of the body where you previously felt reactions to your friends not answering your messages. Allow the warmth of this light to burn away any bad or negative feelings, until you feel composed and powerful. Enjoy these feelings for a few breaths.

When you are ready, gently open your eyes.

Discuss:

- Invite students who wish to do so to share any feelings they identified.
- Discuss why it is important to have limits on Internet usage (i.e., so we can better concentrate on school/work, maintain healthy sleep patterns, limit exposure to negativity, appreciate the positive aspects of Internet usage, manage our time more efficiently, spend time with family and friends.)

Activity:

Personal Audit:

What different aspects of social media do you use and how? For example:

- How importantly do you rate its use in your life?
- What are the times of the day you usually access it?
- How much time each day do you access it?

Group Activity:

Using the five domains of the human personality, as discussed earlier in this chapter:

- Cognitive implications
- Physical implications
- Emotional implications
- Social implications
- Spiritual implications

Brainstorm the implications of excessive Internet usage.

Have the students create their own personal timetable of their time usage each week, placing realistic ceilings on their Internet and social media usage.

Group Activity:

- The following can be described as 'enemies' that can lead to excessive use of Internet activities:
  - ***Addiction*** – I find it difficult to limit my social media/gameplaying activities. Once I'm online, I find it difficult to get off.
  - ***Lack of focus*** – My work/study is rushed, minimalistic, or incomplete in order to spend more time online.

  - ***Poor health*** – I can't focus on goals or work; I am miserable, sick, and constantly tired.
  - ***Fear*** – I worry about what others say or think about me.

- Have the students truthfully rate themselves for these four negative outcomes on a scale of 1–5 (strongly disagree: somewhat disagree; neither agree nor disagree; somewhat agree: strongly agree). This will raise their awareness of their attitudes towards time management and achievement. These obstacles indicate a need for a ceiling on usage.

Activity:

Read the article at: https://www.itstimetologoff.com/2020/10/25/6-ways-to-beat-social-media-addiction/ (accessed 7-2-2023)

Have the students discuss the following five steps and how they might apply to them:

- Set boundaries, and stay mindful of them
- Have someone else keep you accountable
- Disable push notifications
- Delete the app – or decide whom to unfollow
- Reward yourself offline

Homework:

Carrying the values message into daily life:

- Practise the strategy/strategies that individual students think will be the most useful for them.
- After one month, share experiences with the class. Discuss, for example:

  - What you did to practise ceiling on desires for Internet use?
  - The positive outcomes and the challenges.
  - How you were able to spend the time saved from being on the Internet?
  - How the experience contributed to your sense of inner peace?
  - How your practice of ceiling on desires impacted on other people?

Notes

1 Education in Human Values, *Teachers Handbook* (Malaysia: Sri Sathya Sai Central Council, 1993).
2 *Ibid.*
3 Sathya Sai Baba, *Sathya Sai Speaks* (Prasanthi Nilayam, India: Books and Publications Trust, 1973–74), Vol. 12 (18).
4 The Sathya Sai Primary College, Murwillumbah, NSW. https://sathyasaicollege.nsw.edu.au/ accessed 3-6-2022.
5 *Ibid.*

6 L. Waters, A. Barsky, A. Ridd, and K. Allen, "Contemplative Education: A Systematic, Evidence-Based Review of the Effect of Meditation Interventions in Schools," *Educational Psychology Review* 27 (2014): 103–113. https://link.springer.com/article/10.1007/s10648-014-9258-2 accessed 17-11-2023.
7 Elbert Hubbard Quotes, BrainyQuote.com (n.d.). https://www.brainyquote.com/quotes/elbert_hubbard_377954 accessed 30-7-2022.
8 T. Buzan, *The Mind Map Book: Unlock Your Creativity, Boost Your Memory, Change Your Life* (London, UK: BBC, 2009).
9 Bloom's Taxonomy: See for example: https://www.simplypsychology.org/blooms-taxonomy.html#:~:text=Bloom%E2%80%99s%20Taxonomy%20is%20a%20system%20of%20hierarchical%20models,objectives%20into%20varying%20levels%20of%20complexity%20%28Bloom%2C%201956%29 accessed 30-07-2022.
10 For example, see: https://www.amazon.com/Im-Boss-Dinofours-Steve-Metzger/dp/0590374583 accessed 5-2-2023.
11 For example, see video: https://www.youtube.com/watch?v=bkLonu8sEdw accessed 5-2-2023.
12 Please note that the Sathya Sai School has these books, as do other schools, but they are no longer in print. Similar ones can be found by searching the web.
13 This has been adapted from a visualisation given in: M. Taplin, *Silent Sitting: A Resource Manual* (Institute of Sathya Sai Education of Hong Kong, 2010).

Chapter 9

Integrating Values into Current Practices

The 'Hidden' Curriculum

Margaret Taplin

9.1 Introduction

The language and concepts of values have to be taught (as described in Chapter 8) but then these values need to be inculcated through deliberately planned situations in all aspects of school life, including all curriculum subjects. Values can be imbibed consciously by linking them to curriculum areas, for example, through:

- Languages – stories and dramatisations about social evils
- Science – values behind scientific research and use of science
- History – facing historical issues and reacting to them
- Social Studies – how different living conditions affect cultures, value systems, and behaviours
- Physical Education – competition versus co-operation in sport, team spirit

When the indirect, or integrated, approach to Education in Human Values (EHV) is suggested, teachers typically ask questions like:

- How can I integrate values across my curriculum?
- Is it going to take time away from teaching my curriculum content?
- How will doing this benefit my students and me?

The aim of this chapter and the next one is to answer these questions and to suggest a range of strategies that can be used to achieve the dual purpose of teaching the subject content and eliciting a values message embedded in the topic. Examples have been included in this chapter and Chapter 10 to encompass all of the approaches to EHV that were described in previous chapters of this book. However, it needs to be emphasised that teachers are not expected to use all of these ideas in every lesson; rather, it is suggested to select the one or two that are the most suitable for a particular curriculum area and topic. Any of these strategies should only take up a few minutes of the lesson and

DOI: 10.4324/9781003478607-10

should enhance the topic learning as well as creating an opportunity to reflect on values.

Specifically, this chapter is designed to:

- Show how you can integrate values education effectively in just a few minutes.
- Suggest how you can do this by making some minor changes to your classroom management and interactions with students.
- Illustrate examples of values messages underpinning various topics to give suggestions about how to find your own ideas.
- Share some examples of questions to ask and words to use when giving praise or correction in a way that supports values education.
- Provide some examples of strategies used successfully by experienced EHV teachers.
- Recommend some ideas for making use of 'teachable moments'.
- Introduce some activities you might not have thought of using, such as silent sitting and guided visualisation (with sample scripts for visualisations).

We cannot promise, of course, but based on our experience, we suggest that, if you try out these activities, you will notice better student concentration, better understanding of the lesson content, and a more harmonious classroom environment.

It has been explained earlier in this book that it is important for students to be immersed in values-enriched environments throughout the whole day, and that the teacher has a crucial role to play as a living model of the human values. This chapter looks at those aspects of classroom practice, which can be termed the 'hidden curriculum'. The examples given include advice for the teacher's modelling of human values through body language, the use of praise and criticism, the use of reflective questioning to encourage students to think about the values in relation to themselves and their own lives, and capitalising on incidental opportunities that arise to bring in values messages. This chapter also suggests ways in which classroom displays can be used to reinforce the values messages in lesson topics.

9.2 Teacher Interactions with Students – Body Language and Facial Expressions

During everyday classroom interactions, there are various non-verbal ways in which teachers can show love and make students feel at peace, and even to acknowledge if they have tried to improve their characters. These can include:

- making eye contact with a student to acknowledge that 'we are engaged' fully and with empathy in listening, that we care, or that we appreciate what

they are doing, or acknowledging these behaviours with a gesture, a smile, a nod, or moving towards the student when listening to him/her
- not being angry if a student cannot understand something or makes a mistake because this can lead to fear of failure
- showing them how to recover from the mistake and try again
- telling them about famous people who were not afraid to make mistakes, or about some of the mistakes we have all made ourselves – but also encouraging accuracy and patiently asking them to correct their careless errors
- being careful not to frown if a student makes a mistake, and not allowing other students to frown or laugh if a classmate makes a mistake either
- giving full attention to the student receiving individual attention so that each one gets at least a few minutes of top-quality one-to-one time
- reflecting genuine pleasure with students' achievements

These all send messages to the pupils that they are *accepted* and *esteemed* by their teacher.

9.3 Values-Related Praise, Encouragement, and Correction

Teachers are engaged continually in praising or correcting students. With some small changes to the words we use, it is possible to enrich the values messages conveyed in the classroom. The ideas suggested in this section have been adapted from the work of Bartholomew.[1]

Why do we use praise in a values-enriched environment?

- to make students feel valued
- to show them we love them
- to acknowledge their uniqueness
- to describe the values we have observed in their behaviour
- to direct their attention to the positive aspects of their performance, so they can see some achievement even when other factors may be negative
- to encourage them: The linguistic root of 'encourage' refers to the heart; thus, to encourage students is to urge them to 'take heart' and 'have courage', to give them hope and inner strength.

Some examples of values-reflecting praise can include:

- Sarah, you did xxx accurately.
- Roger, that's the way.
- Bobby, you did all the xxx.
- Keep it up.

- You're on the right track.
- One more time and you'll get it.

Needless to say, there are times when praise can be counterproductive to achieving the purposes described above. These include when it:

- causes feelings of embarrassment
- makes students feel they are being manipulated to behave in a certain way
- is overused
- is empty, insincere, or praising where the praise is not deserved
- is motivated by wrong reasons
- is too general, e.g., 'good job'
- overdramatises – for example, always saying everything is 'the best', 'great', ...

Some of the words and body language to be avoided include:

- That wasn't very good.
- That was awful.
- You *never* wait your turn.
- You are *always* talking when you should be listening.
- You are stupid/lazy....

The following is an activity to consider in order to evaluate your own use of language for praise or correction. It could be useful to work in partnership with a colleague, to record each other's word use.

- List the 'praise' words you use in class.
- Categorise them according to:
    - words associated with *love*/acceptance/understanding
    - words associated with inner/outer *peace*
    - words associated with *right action*/right behaviour for the wellbeing of self and others

9.4 Using the Classroom Walls to Convey Values Messages (i.e., Displays of Subject-Related Work)

A key way to immerse students in a values-rich environment is to utilise display space on classroom walls and in corridors. This can include inspiring quotations and charts to monitor students' implementation of values-enriched behaviour. One of the most important ways to engage students with the displays is to use them to highlight the students' own work that reflects the values in their curriculum topics.

9.4.1 *Displays of Students' Work that Reflect Values*

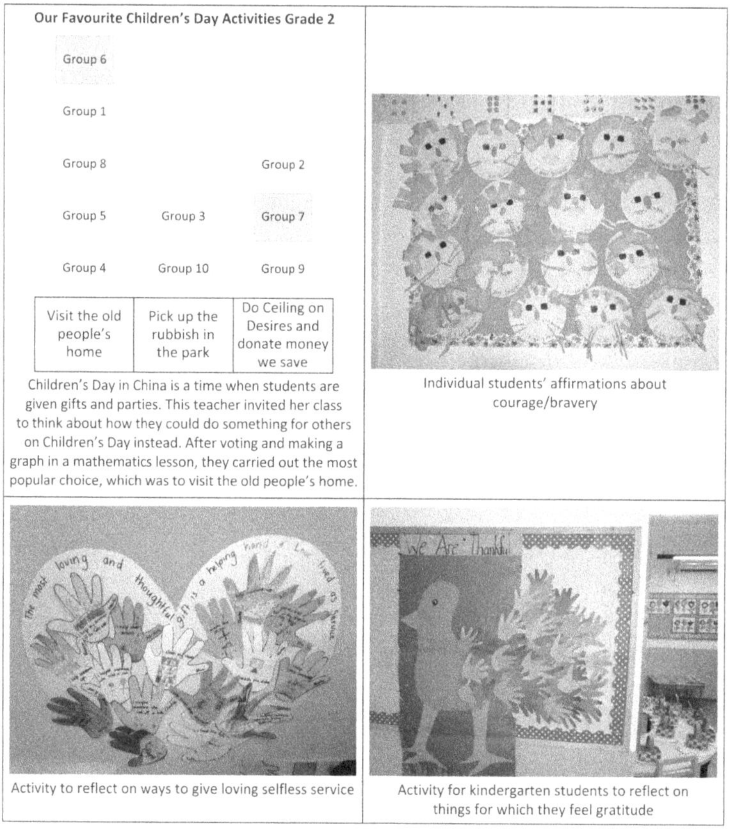

Figure 9.1 Examples of Student Work Demonstrating Values

Source: These displays were photographed with permission of Dimple Buxani, Gold Arch Kindergarten, Guangzhou, China.

9.4.2 *Monitoring Students' Behaviours and Feelings*

1 2

Figure 9.2 Displays of Student Behaviour and Feelings

Source: These displays were photographed with permission of Dimple Buxani, Gold Arch Kindergarten, Guangzhou, China.

9.4.3 Displaying Inspiring Quotations

Figure 9.3 Displaying Inspirational Quotes from Students

Source: Images 1–3: Institute of Sathya Sai Education of Hong Kong. Images 4 and 5 were photographed with permission of Sathya Sai School of Australia, Murwillumbah, Australia.

9.5 Capitalising on 'Teachable Moments'

Often opportunities arise incidentally in the classroom for unplanned values messages to be addressed by teachers who are astute to the opportunities. The following are two examples of teachers taking advantage of teachable moments to draw out values:

- In a mathematics lesson, a teacher conducted a whole-class quiz designed to reinforce the lesson topic. The students were eager to be chosen to contribute, particularly as prizes were given for correct responses. Repeatedly, the students who shot their hands up enthusiastically, and were not chosen, dropped their hands down with expressions of disappointment and sometimes glared jealously at the chosen winners. This created a perfect opportunity for a brief comment about the values message of wanting others to experience the same happiness that we want to experience and enjoying their success as much as if it were their own (Love).
- In another mathematics lesson, the students were seated in groups of four to complete a puzzle. One boy was looking very uncertain about what to do. The teacher asked the very bright little girl sitting next to him to help him. She gave him a nudge with her elbow to push him aside, reached over, and, in an instant, had completed his puzzle for him. This led to the opportunity to talk about the best ways to help others – facilitating them to do it for themselves and learn versus doing it for them.

9.5.1 Short silent sitting/visualisation activities

As a teachable moment, these can be conducted with the whole class to deal with issues that arise. For example, if students are unsettled or not listening during a lesson, it could be worthwhile to take a few minutes to settle them down with a visualisation such as the following:[2]

> Today we are going to use the light of the sun to help us to improve our listening. Imagine that you are sitting in a special, peaceful place and the sun is shining down on you. You are wearing a hat, so you are protected from being sunburnt, but the good effects of the sunrays are coming through your hat and into your head. Just enjoy sitting there with the warmth and the sunlight filling your head, until it is also a ball of light just like the sun.
>
> [Pause for a moment to let them reflect on this]
>
> Now imagine that the sunlight is running along the passages that connect your brain and your ears. You can feel the warmth and see the brightness lighting up all of these passages so the connection between your brain and your ears is clear and working well. Maybe there are some places where the

passage is blocked. If there are, you need to get rid of them because these can stop you from listening well. So let the sun melt any blockages, and then the passage is completely clear.

[Pause for a few seconds]

Now imagine that somebody is talking to you. It might be your teacher, or your parent, or one of your friends. Imagine that you can see their words as they come into your ear and then travel along the sunlit passage that you have just cleared and into your brain, where the message is received, and you can hear exactly what the person said to you. After you open your eyes and we start our work, keep remembering that you have these two sunlit passages and that whatever the person who is speaking says will now go straight into your mind.

9.6 Getting Started Using Action Learning

This chapter has presented a range of different ways in which values education through EHV principles and strategies can be integrated across the curriculum, through the 'hidden curriculum':

- Teacher interactions with students (body language, facial expressions)
- Values-related praise, encouragement, and correction
- Using the classroom walls (i.e., displays of subject-related work) to convey values messages
- Displaying inspiring quotations
- Capitalising on teachable moments
- Use of guided meditation to settle students

These do not all have to be introduced at the same time. We suggest that you select and focus on trialling one per month or until you feel that you have developed confidence to make it a regular part of your teaching repertoire.

Chapter 10 expands these ideas by exploring ways in which values messages can be integrated into existing curriculum subjects. At the end of Chapter 10, you will be invited to consider some action-learning tasks that will guide you to incorporate the principles of both the hidden and the overt curriculums into your existing programmes.

Notes

1 D. Bartholomew, "Effective Strategies for Praising Students," *Music Educators Journal* 80, no. 3 (1993): 40–43.

2 M. Taplin, *Silent Sitting: A Resource Manual* (Hong Kong: Institute of Sathya Sai Education, 2010), 32. Available for free download from: https://issea.org.au/wp-content/uploads/2020/08/Silent-Sitting-comp.pdf accessed 4-8-2022.

Chapter 10

Integrating Values into Current Practices

Overtly through the Curriculum

Margaret Taplin

10.1 Introduction

This chapter is a continuation of Chapter 9, sharing some examples to illustrate how the Education in Human Values (EHV) strategies can be used to integrate values messages into core subject topics. In particular, the aim of this chapter is to show that values can be integrated seamlessly and without taking time away from the lesson content, but, on the contrary, can enhance the quality of the subject learning. The chapter begins with some examples of values messages underpinning various core subject topics. The claim here is that every topic has an underpinning value. One of the easiest ways to integrate values is to change textbook or worksheet examples, and this is the next focus in this chapter, which then goes on to provide examples of using silent sitting, groupwork, storytelling, songs, and quotations (all described in Chapter 8) that simultaneously enhance the topic content and the values message. Reflective questioning is critical, and examples of this are given. The chapter then concludes with a discussion about how homework in the subject can also be used to carry the values into the students' lives outside school and to engage parents and families in EHV as well.

A great deal of effective values education can happen across the curriculum. With simple planning, it is possible to make values education an integral component of the lesson in ways that will not detract from the topic content, and that can, more often than not, actually enhance the content, and a range of strategies can be used, separately or in combinations, for this purpose.

Planning to incorporate values into subject topics needs to address the following:[1]

- *Knowledge* – making the learner aware of the inherent values or ethical issues linked to the topic
- *Judgements* – providing learners with conflicting situations to enable them to evaluate the implications of the relevant values
- *Believing* – emphasising relevant points that will help to develop the learner's faith in the related values

DOI: 10.4324/9781003478607-11

- *Actions* – encouraging the learner to practise the values in actual life situations as a result of change in behaviour brought about by relevant and meaningful experiences
- *Internalisation* – leading the learner to a stage where the practice of the acquired values becomes spontaneous and immediate.

The Appendices show some annotated examples of lessons to illustrate how the strategies described in this chapter can be brought together.

10.2 Finding Values Messages in Lesson Topics

The important first step to integrating values and subject topics is to identify the potential values message underpinning the topic. It is the contention of this book that every topic has such an underpinning message. We suggest that you streamline your school's set of values messages to make it easier to identify them in subject topics. These can be developed as a school (see Chapters 13 and 14), to ensure that consistent messages are being conveyed and everyone in the school community is speaking the same language of values (see Chapter 4). Please refer to Chapter 8 for examples of values messages appropriate for the five values of Truth, Right Action, Love, Peace, and Non-violence, and the following Table 10.1 gives examples relevant to various subject topics.

Table 10.1 Examples of Values Messages in Various Subject Topics

Subject	*Topic*	*Values message*
Science	Body Systems (Digestive System, Nervous Systems, Skeletal Systems, etc.)[2]	Teamwork: Each system working together to support the body. When working in a team, we should be aware of our responsibilities as team members and should work together to support each other so that the team can succeed.
	Chemical reactions: Atoms react to become stable either by sharing or donating their electrons.[3]	It is better to give away things to others that we may not need but maybe very useful to others. Discussion points: • Selfless service. • Love for others that you are willing to give and not expect anything in return.
Mathematics	Equations	Equations are about balancing the two sides of the = sign, and life is about us being balanced. What is a balanced person? When we have lots of desires and 'wants' these are clamouring inside us and we are open to feeling let down and disappointed, and balance is not possible. But, if we can happily accept everything that happens to us and see it as an opportunity to learn and grow into stronger people, we can become more balanced.

(*Continued*)

Table 10.1 (Continued)

Subject	*Topic*	*Values message*
		Balanced people are those who cope equally with things that flatter and things that hurt them – they accept praise and criticism equally, they treat friends and enemies the same, and they are not affected by events that happen around them that are either happy or sad.
	Addition and subtraction	What can we add and subtract in our lives? Add good qualities, e.g., love/sharing/compassion Subtract material desires/hatred/jealousy/competitiveness/dissatisfaction. There is never any end to this – even if we already have many good qualities we can keep adding more and continue to delete undesirable qualities.
	Average	Average – means the one who has more giving to the one who has less. (Discuss the idea of giving unconditionally to those who have less, without any expectation of anything in return.) Talk about what we can do to help people in difficulty. A student's comment: 'Average makes unfair become fair'. Tell the students that the idea of average helps us to appreciate each other's strengths. If we have a team in which one person is good at languages and another is good at mathematics, we can raise the average for the team by making good use of each person's strengths.
	Exponents	Illustrate the sequence of powers of 2. If one person (2^0) has love and peace in his/her heart and influences just one other, that will be 2 (2^1). If they each influence one other person, it will be 4 (2^2), then 8 (2^3), then 16 (2^4), etc. Graph these and show the effect of the exponential increase. We all think that we, as individuals, cannot make an impact, but this illustrates that if we change ourselves, 'one candle can light many lamps' or – in a more contemporary example – one social media posting can influence hundreds of people!
Geography/ Political Science	Conflict resolution	• Discuss what the people who live in areas of conflict should do: For instance, by being tolerant of other people's religions or political ideologies, understanding other races' cultures, not invading other people's rights, etc. • Discuss what people who live in areas beyond the conflict could do, e.g., to reconcile the conflicting nations or races, sending relief goods and volunteers, etc.

(*Continued*)

Table 10.1 (Continued)

Subject	*Topic*	*Values message*
Physical Education	Cricket[4]	• Each ball faced is an EXPERIENCE, a situation presented in the game of life – a chance to consider how you handle that experience – e.g., a lightning speed ball = a sudden event in life. • With each ball, you decide the type of stroke you need to play. Do you REACT, RESPOND, or simply let it go to the wicketkeeper? • What about sledging; is it fair, how would you feel if you were sledged, would you use sledging on others? • You are there to protect your wicket – the life force in you cannot just stand there, you were created for ACTION – the only weapon to handle the situation is your bat (mind) which is under your control. A good batsman RESPONDS not REACTS. • Each over you play is a chapter in your life. The balls hurtling towards you are the events or incidents that are your thoughts, desires, and destiny. What you think of comes to you, action follows thought.

10.3 Adjusting Textbook Examples

One of the quickest and easiest ways to integrate values messages into subjects is to change the wording of problems or exercises in textbooks or on worksheets. Here are examples:

10.3.1 *Mathematics*

Original problem: There are eight weeping willow trees in the school and three times as many pine trees. How many pine trees are there?

Suggested change: The students in xxx school were concerned about the damage that can happen to the environment if there are not enough trees. [Note – at the beginning of this lesson they could do a visualisation about the effects of a flood washing away the land because the trees had been cut down and were not there to hold the soil together.] They also know that planting even a few trees can help to reduce the poisonous carbon monoxide in the air. So, they decided to do something to help their local environment by planting more trees. They saved up their money, and, in September, they were able to buy eight trees to plant. By next April, they were able to plant three times as many trees as they planted in September. How many trees did they plant in April?

Original problem: There are 364 boys in the school and 1810 girls. How many students are there altogether?

Suggested change: There are 364 students in the school who are loving and caring and have good characters. There are 1810 who are still working on these qualities. How many students are there altogether?

Original problem: [for graphing] Which kinds of fruit do classmates like to eat?

Suggested change: All of our classmates are healthy students, and they know that it is good for their health to eat fruit every day. Which kinds of fruit do classmates like to eat?

OR: What are the special qualities of the students in this class? How many students are good at sports? at study? at creative things? at smiling and being kind to others?

Original problem: There were three old grandmothers in the old people's home. The one in the middle forgot the number of her room. The first grandmother said, 'I live in Room number 3'. The second one said, 'I live in Room number 5'. Can you think which room the forgetful grandmother lived in?

Suggested change: Tom was going to help in the old people's home. He was going to read to Mrs. Brown, but he didn't know her room number. There were two other ladies who said, 'She lives between us'. The first lady said, 'I live in Room number 3'. The second one said, 'I live in Room number 5'. Which room did Tom need to go to, to read to Mrs. Brown?

Original problem: In grade 6, 3 out of 30 students have perfect attendance. In grade 5, 3 out of 20 students have perfect attendance....

Suggested change: In grade 6, 3 out of 30 students managed to complete a whole week without getting angry. In grade 5, 3 out of 20 students managed to complete a whole week without getting angry......

Original problem: In the field, there are 30 milking cows. Each cow can provide 25,000 grams of milk per day. How many thousand grams of milk are provided in one day?

Suggested change: One person can affect 25 people per day by smiling at them. How many can 30 smiling people affect?

Original problem: A tank can be filled from a tap in 8 hours and can be emptied by a pipe in 10 hours. How long will it take to fill the tank if both the tap and the pipe are opened together?[5]

Solution:

Time taken by the tap to fill the tank = 8 hours
In 1 hour, the tap fills 1/8 of the tank.
Time taken by the pipe to empty the tank = 10 hours
In 1 hour, the pipe empties -1/10 of the tank
(since, empty is taken as negative)
Therefore, 1 hour's work done by the tap and the pipe = 1/8 – 1/10
= (5 – 4)/40
= 1/40
Therefore, when the tap and pipe are opened together the tank will fill in 40 hours.

Suggested change: (This is also the use of a quotation.)

Introduce the topic by discussing the following quotation:

We are like tanks that have the capacity to be filled with Love. We must endeavour to Love all. Love all, serve all. Hating everyone, feeling jealous of everyone – if you want to experience peace, how can you have it? Only if there is water in the tank can you get water in the tap. If the tank is dry, how can you draw water from the tap? If you fill the tank of your heart with Love, you can have Love towards everyone and receive Love from everyone.[6]

Imagine now that you are the tank in the problem, and you are filled with Love. What are the things in the pipe that can drain your tank? [get students to give the answer that our bad qualities like anger, jealousy, laziness....can drain us.] Now imagine there is a tap going into the tank, filling it with Love, Peace etc. If these good qualities could fill your tank in 8 hours but the bad qualities would empty it in 10 hours, how long now will it take to fill the tank? How many hours will have been wasted by letting the bad qualities drain away the good ones?

Original problem: A father and his sons equally shared an amount of $270. Then the amount each person had was $45. Taking the number of sons as x, construct an equation. Solve this equation and hence find the number of sons the father has.

Suggested change: A father and his sons decided to donate an amount of $270 to help buy food for some poor people. They wanted to do this because giving to others is one important way to help us to feel love and compassion. They believe in 'Love all, serve all'. The father and his sons each donated $45. Taking the number of sons as x, construct an equation. Solve this equation and hence find the number of sons the father has.

10.4 Using Silent Sitting and Creative Visualisation for Various Purposes during the Lesson

This can promote topic learning and reflection on the underpinning values. *Silent sitting* can be used in conjunction with curriculum topics for multiple purposes, such as:

- At the beginning of a lesson to settle the students and introduce the topic
- In the middle or at the end of a lesson to reflect on what has been learned
- To help students to get in touch with their 'inner computers' (their own wisdom/intuition) before tackling a problem/exam etc.
- To encourage students to reflect on the values message in the lesson in relation to themselves and whether or not they are showing these values in different situations in their lives.

Carefully designed ***visualisations*** can achieve the following three purposes:

- to introduce, revise, or reflect on the topic
- to invoke feelings associated with the topic
- to reflect on the values message underpinning the topic

Several examples are given in this section for various purposes and topics across the curriculum.

10.4.1 Visualisation for Problem Solving by Getting in Touch with Your Inner Computer

First read the problem. Then put it aside. Close your eyes and just listen to the inner silence of your mind for a few moments. Focus your concentration on the back of your closed eyelids at the point where your eyebrows meet. Don't try to think about anything – just allow your mind to be still and empty, and concentrate on the blankness behind your eyes. When you feel that your mind is completely still, think for a moment about the problem you need to solve. You can either repeat the whole question in your mind, or you can simply say,

I need to find the solution to the problem I am about to tackle.

Once you have asked this question, return your attention to focusing on the silent, blank emptiness of your mind behind your closed eyelids for a few more minutes. Then visualise your subconscious mind working like a computer. First it sorts the knowledge you already have to solve the problem. Then it sorts out what else you need to know. Next it puts this knowledge together in a logical way. Finally, it sends the output into your conscious mind so it can work on the problem. Take 3 slow, deep breaths, then open your eyes and start to work on the problem.

10.4.2 Visualisations to Reflect on the Topics and the Values Messages in the Topics

Science: Body Systems (Digestive System, Nervous System, Skeletal System, etc.)[7]

...Imagine a bright light entering your head and filling your head and your heart... Now imagine the light moving through your [insert name of the system you are working on]. ... Let the light fill your [one by one go through the parts of the system. You might need to remind them which part of the body each is in.]... Let the light join each system part together so they can work together in harmony for your health... Now imagine that you are sending the light to the person sitting on your right-hand side. From there it goes to the next person... and so on until you have sent light to every person in the room... Imagine the light connecting everyone in the room to everyone else. Say to yourself,

We are all a team and we support each other to be the best that we can be, so that the team can be healthy.

Science: Atoms – Atoms are made up of subatomic particles; neutrons, electrons, and protons.[8]

The values message is that we can deflect bad thoughts or allow them to go straight through us and that our hearts should be filled with positive thoughts surrounded by 'bright stars'. Do a shortened version of the light meditation, but concentrate particularly on the part where they are asked to send light to people who are being unkind to them or who they perceive to be unkind. Ask them to imagine that they are sending the light in the form of bright stars from their hearts to deflect the negative thoughts or words coming their way.

Share your own story about a time when you have used this technique successfully to improve a situation with somebody who has been sending negative thoughts to you.

Art: Colours

> What colour do you think of when you think of peace? When you think of love? When you think of anger? When you think of fear? etc. What happens when you mix your peace colour with your fear colour? With your anger colour?...
>
> Imagine a time when you felt a negative feeling. It might be anger, fear, jealousy, etc. Think about the colour this feeling reminds you of. Now think of the colour that peace reminds you of. Imagine that this colour of peace is filling your whole body, from your head to your toes. Let your whole self be filled with this colour of peace, so there is no more room anywhere in your body for the colour of your negative feelings.

10.4.3 Visualisation to Use in the Middle of a Lesson, to Evoke a Feeling and Think About an Answer to a Question

Literature:

This relates to an extract from a story about a disabled student called Nina. Here, a very short silent sitting/visualisation exercise was used in the middle of the lesson to get the students to feel empathy and to understand how their words could make Nina change from sad to happy. At the same time, the teacher is reminding the students about the values message that everyone has a special quality, an 'inner diamond'.

> Close your eyes for a moment and think about how we could help Nina to realise that she is also an important person with an 'inner diamond' and a contribution to make? What do you think might be some of her special strengths/talents that she can use to help her classmates? Think of something you would like to say to Nina... Now, with your eyes still closed, imagine that you are Nina. Imagine how she will feel when you say your words to her....

10.4.4 Visualisation to Reflect on the Subject Values Message in Students' Own Lives

Mathematics: Place value[9]

> We just learned that every digit in a number has a face value and a place value. The actual value of the number is the face value, and the place value depends on its place, or position, in the whole number. For example, in number 510, though 5 is smaller than 10, its place value is higher than 10, due to its position on the left side of 10. If 5 is placed instead, to the right

of 10 the place value of 5 decreases, even though the number 105 becomes greater.

Similarly, in this world, people initially get respect, fame, and popularity due to being rich monetarily. This is the face value of that person. If the same wealth is used only for selfish purposes and not for helping the needy, their place value in the society would decrease. It will also decrease if they are proud of their assets or wealth and look down upon a weaker group of people.

Famous personalities like [insert name of appropriate local people] are loved even today because they used their personal wealth to help the poor and needy by establishing many charitable Trusts. Their place value in the society will always be greater.

It is not the possession of material things that go to make persons great; it is their good, virtuous nature that makes them stand out in society.

Think about your own life. Are you more concerned about your face value or your place value? Think about a time when you really did have place value - i.e., when you put aside your need for fame or success and instead used your unique talents to give value to somebody else. Think about how this made you feel. How did it make the other/s feel?

10.5 Using Groupwork that Is Interdependent and Promotes Strength in Unity

There are many advantages in using group activities to enhance learning, and there are different ways to work together in groups. At one extreme, we see people who are trying to use their group for their own personal success or to take an easy ride and let the others do the work. At the other extreme, we see people working together to support each other as a team. In collaborative groupwork, students have opportunities to develop social skills of co-operating with others. In EHV groupwork, the aim is to achieve these goals, but also to be concerned with developing an understanding of the concept of 'strength in unity', brought about when individuals make their own unique contributions. The outcome will be better than if the individuals worked separately. As well as getting to know their own special qualities and have confidence in their contributions, students can come to respect other people's qualities. It is important that activities are structured in such a way as to encourage 'positive interdependence', with students being genuinely dependent on each other to be able to complete the task.

There is a simple activity that illustrates this concept. Take one sheet of paper from a packet. Tear it in half. See how easy it is to tear? Now take a book and try to tear it apart. What happens? This is the message about 'strength in unity'. If we all combine our individual strengths and skills, we can achieve much better results for ourselves and for others.

10.5.1 Examples of Collaborative, Interdependent Activities

In a mathematics lesson using the topic of nutrition, the students were asked to select pictures of dishes from a menu. Then they were given a chart showing the calories, protein, and other nutrients in the ingredients and they were asked to calculate how nutritious their chosen dishes were. This was a good group activity because:

- The group size was not too big, so all the students were active and engaged (ideal group size is 5–7).
- Every student had a job to do. One read the numbers from the chart, one did the calculations on a calculator, one checked the calculations by hand, one recorded, and one was the reporter so had to listen carefully.
- The students listened to each other's ideas.
- In some groups, the students disagreed and argued, but they found solutions to their disagreements.

The teacher told us that she had trained the students over some time to be able to work interdependently in this way. This was clearly an example of 'strength in unity'.

In responding to a story, each group member was assigned a different character to investigate. This included finding passages in the text that identified the character's values and predicting how the story's outcomes might have been different if the designated character had behaved in different ways. After collecting information individually, the group members then convened to share and discuss their findings.

A collaborative project in the Social Sciences involved some group members seeking information about designated aspects of the topic, others using their notes to write up the text, some preparing illustrations based on the text, and presenters to represent the group in a wider forum. In another case, the group brainstormed to break the topic into sub-topics, with each group member responsible for exploring one sub-topic and contributing the findings for discussion.

10.5.2 The Importance of Self-Reflection

It is critically important to have students talk about how well they contributed to the good of the team. It is also important to have them reflect on how their working as a team helped them to perform better as individuals. A checklist named 'What Did I Do in the Group?' can include such skills as listening, taking turns to speak, encouraging others, asking questions, explaining ideas, and checking each other's understanding. This analysis of the group's use of interpersonal skills and overall function as a group is essential if the pupils are to be aware that they are developing the desired qualities.

Questions such as the following should be asked often after group activities. They do not necessarily all need to be asked at once but can be used at different times to consolidate the message:

- Am I co-operative or competitive?
- Do I always have to win (or won't play unless I can)?
- Do I feel I am more valuable or less valuable than others?
- Do I have to have the last word?
- Do I argue frequently?
- Am I co-operating in order to improve something about myself or to please someone else?
- Am I interested in supporting the growth of the people I am with as much as in getting the job done?

10.6 Using Storytelling and Reflective Questioning in Various Subjects

Rowe[10] suggested a range of questions that encourage students to reflect on values messages in storytelling that expand on the reflective questions suggested above. These demonstrate how values or beliefs underpin people's actions and elicit different responses from students according to their personal values, sensitivities, and interests. They tap into emotions as well as knowledge and experience and provoke personal reflections as students identify with characters or feel they would act differently from them. Rowe specified three types of questioning:

- Questioning about moral analysis, which 'asks students to analyse the situation in moral terms, thinking about what is involved and what the characters ought to d*o*'.[11]
- Philosophical analysis questions that encourage them to think about rules and exceptions to rules as 'an essential component of moral reasoning'[12] and a way to develop empathy.
- Community building questions encourage thinking about rules and exceptions to rules as 'an essential component of moral reasoning'.[13]

Again, it is not necessary to use all questions at once, but rather to select as appropriate to the context. Table 10.2. presents the aims and associated questions for reflecting on values in stories.[14]

The following are some examples of stories related to various curriculum subjects, and reflective questions that can be asked.

Table 10.2 Aims and Associated Questions for Reflecting on Values in Stories

Aim	*Question*
To assess the students' understanding of an idea or concept	What do you think that means?
To find out about the students' concerns	Is there anything in the story that you would like to talk about? Let's share ideas and then decide on the best questions.
To discover the students' own understanding of the issues	What do you think of that? Why?
To encourage students to justify their opinions	Why do you think that?
To throw an issue back to the class rather than commenting oneself	Who agrees with that?
To encourage the students to make moral judgements	Do you think that was fair or right?
To encourage thinking about outcomes or consequences	What would have happened if …?
To encourage thinking about duties or obligations	What should he or she do in this situation?
To develop empathy	Who do you feel most sorry for in this story? Why?
To think about values	What was good or bad about that? Why do you think X did that?
To think about competing claims	What is due to this or that person? How should each person be treated?
To think about right action	In this situation, what do you think is the right thing to do?
To connect with students' own experiences	How would you feel if …? Has anything like that happened to you?
To encourage expression of feelings	How does that feel?

Science: Body Systems – Digestive System, Nervous System, Skeletal System, etc.

Values message: When working in a team, we need to be aware of our responsibilities as team members so as to work together to support each other, enabling the team to succeed.

Story:[15]

> Once upon a time the arms and the legs and the head made a plot against the stomach. They whispered together that they did all the work while the stomach did none. The legs said that they walked to get the food, the arms said they laboured for it, the mouth said that it received the food. The teeth said that they chewed it.
>
> So, they agreed not to do any more work, so as to prove to the stomach how helpless he was without them. The stomach heard what they said but pretended to take no notice.

And it came to pass that after a couple of days of idleness, the legs found they were growing very weak, the arms found they couldn't lift, the mouth was growing dry, the teeth were tired of doing nothing, and it was clear that the whole body was wasting away.

Then the legs, the hands and the head began whispering again, still thinking that the stomach didn't hear them. But he did.

The legs struggled to get some food, the hands struggled to lift it to the mouth, the mouth struggled to receive it. The teeth struggled to chew it. And slowly the body revived and became strong and hearty again. As for the stomach, he smiled to himself, but never said a single word.

Question for reflection: No parts of anything are of use unless they work happily with all the other parts. A family or a community is a poor sort of family/community unless all the members work together for the happiness of all. What are some examples, in our school community, of the 'parts' working effectively together? How can we do this better?

Mathematics: Equivalent fractions

Values message: We can have different names and appearances, but we are all the same (Non-violence/respect for diversity).

After pupils have looked at the patterns in equivalent fractions, tell the story of *Fraction Land*[16] and have them make up their own stories using equivalent fractions, that bring out the underlying value.

Story:

Once upon a time in Fraction Land there was chaos. All the fractions were constantly arguing with each other. 6/12 thought he was the best because he had the biggest numbers on both the top and the bottom, so he was cruel to the fractions with smaller numbers, like 2/4 and 3/6. 4/8 would not allow his students to play with the students of 3/6 because they always cut their food into 6 pieces and 4/8 believed that the only proper way was to cut it into 8 pieces – he did not want his students to learn any "wrong" ways of doing things. Mrs. 2/4 would shout at Mrs. 5/10 in the market because Mrs. 5/10 always bought 5/10 of a kilogram of everything and Mrs. 2/4, who only ever bought 2/4 of a kilogram, thought she was being very greedy. The 2/4 family would always cross the street if they saw anyone from the 3/6 or 4/8 families approaching them because they looked so different that they thought they must be very bad people indeed.

Things became so bad that the fractions all began to pray to their own gods to make their enemies go away. It was no longer a safe or happy place to be. One day a brilliant bright light appeared, and out of it stepped the most beautiful angel the fractions had ever seen. Her dress was painted with golden numbers that said 1/2. Suddenly everything went dark and when the lights came on again the fractions looked at each other in great surprise. They all looked exactly the same as each other. Everyone's tops had turned into a 1 and the bottom parts had turned into a 2.

Questions for Reflection
What had happened? Were they still the same Fraction Land people they had always been? Or had the angel turned them into different people?
Discuss the underpinning values message: We can have different names and appearances, beliefs, and customs, but we are all the same.
Students can write their own stories about how the *Fraction Land* people learned that we are all the same even if we look different.

Stories about great mathematicians or scientists – When teaching a topic related to such a person, tell a story of his/her character.
Maria Agnesi (Calculus)

Maria's use of silent sitting: Sometimes she would have trouble with a problem. But her mind went on working even in her sleep; she would sleep-walk to her study and back to bed. In the morning, she would find the answer to the problem waiting for her on her desk.

Her service to others: She had always worked with the poor people in her area, and she asked her father for separate rooms and turned them into a private hospital. She worked at the hospital until she died at the age of eighty-one.

Rene Descartes (analytic geometry; application of co-ordinate geometry to equations of curves)

Because Descartes was an unhealthy student, his teacher allowed him to lie in bed for as long as he wanted to in the mornings. From this, Descartes learned of the value of silence whenever he needed to think, and continued to do this for the rest of his life. These were the times when his great mathematical and philosophical insights came to him. One famous quotation of Descartes' was that he preferred truth to beauty. Descartes was not wealthy, but he was contented with what he had and felt that this was enough. He was moderate in his habits and was very kind to others. He continued to help with the welfare of his servants long after they had left his service.

English Literature

The Pearl (1947) by John Steinbeck

Here is a sample *multiple-choice* question that creates opportunities to talk about values and good character:

- What did the author say that led Juana to know that their old life had gone forever?

  a. because they were rich now
  b. because they were able to live in a bigger house
  c. because their student would be able to go to school and get a good job, to look after them
  d. because the jealousy and fear had ruined their happy way of life

Here are sample *open-ended* questions that create opportunities to talk about values and good character:

- This story has been described as a 'parable' – that is, a story that tells about good vs bad, black vs white, etc. and leaves people to take their own meaning from it. Write what you think is the main message/meaning of this story and share it with your class. Did they find the same message or a different one?

  It could be expected that students' answers could include:

  - Only bad things come from greed.
  - Greed brings out the worst qualities in people.
  - It is better to be poor and happy than rich and afraid.
  - Jealousy is a dangerous emotion that can cause a lot of trouble.

- Choose one character from the book and describe the good or bad qualities in him/her. Give evidence from the book to back up your ideas.

- Juana said the pearl was evil and they should get rid of it. Was the pearl really evil? If not, what was the evil? Share your ideas with your classmates.

  Students' answers might include:

  - The evil was jealousy and greed, brought about by Kino's owning the pearl. These bad qualities caused some very bad behaviour by the people in the village, and this is how the pearl came to cause the evil.
  - When they threw the pearl back into the water, they were saved from the evil, not because the pearl had gone but because the people had no reason to feel greedy or jealous anymore.

Tuesdays with Morrie (1997) by Mitch Albom

Sample *multiple-choice* questions that create opportunities to talk about values and good character:

1. What did the author mean when he said that he realised time is precious?

   a. We only have a certain amount of time in this life, and we should use it in the best possible way.
   b. We should spend as much of our time as we can working hard.
   c. We should only spend our time doing the things we want to do.
   d. If we are not busy all the time, we are wasting time.

2. When the author asked Morrie which 'side' always wins the game of life, what was the answer?

   a. Success always wins.
   b. Hard work always wins.
   c. Believing that you are right always wins.
   d. Love always wins.

3. What does Morrie tell the author is the best way to get meaning in your life?

   a. work hard and become rich and successful
   b. keep busy and occupied with lots of activities
   c. devote yourself to loving others, serving your community, and creating something that gives you purpose and meaning
   d. have a lot of friends

4. What did Morrie say that we should all do if we want to be at peace with ourselves?

   a. forgive ourselves and others
   b. become wealthy
   c. have lots of people around us
   d. that we should go to meditation retreats

Sample *open-ended* questions that create opportunities to talk about values and good character:

- When the author first went to visit Morrie, he asked him four questions:

  - Have you found someone to share your heart with?
  - Are you giving to your community?
  - Are you at peace with yourself?
  - Are you trying to be as human as you can be?

Imagine that you are talking to Morrie and answer these four questions about yourself. Try to make your answers as interesting as possible and give examples of the kinds of things you are doing.

- Morrie talks a lot about love. He says things like:

  Love is the only rational act.

  Love is when you are as concerned about someone else's situation as you are about your own.

  Love each other or die.

Give a talk to your class about the importance of love, emphasising the messages that Morrie has given us about it.

10.7 Using Songs across the Curriculum

Songs can be used effectively across the curriculum to reinforce a topic and to deliver a values message at the same time. The use of song was discussed in Chapter 8, and it is a valuable tool because it:

- can be fun and inspiring
- helps to remember important messages

- helps to remember new knowledge/skills
- can be something to draw on in challenging times
- conveys positive messages – especially at a time when a lot of songs these days have negative messages

Mathematics: Tessellations

Values message: What can we do to fit together as a class/a team/a family? Why is this important? How does it benefit everyone if we all fit together?

Song:

The more we fit together, together, together
The more we fit together
The happier we'll be.
For my joy is your joy, and your joy is my joy.
The more we fit together
The happier we'll be.

[see https://www.youtube.com/watch?v=lldmkrJXQ-E for the tune]

Other words to be substituted for *joy* can include *peace, friend, pain.*

Mathematics: Numbers that add together to make 10.

This is a rap song developed by a Grade 2 teacher to help students remember the pairs of numbers that add together to make 10. At the same time, she has incorporated values messages.

You say 1, I say 9. Good friends you and I.
You say 2, I say 8. Working together makes us great.
You say 3, I say 7. Helping others makes life better.
You say 4, I say 6. Speak honestly and don't play tricks.
You say 5, I say 5. To work together let us strive.

10.7.1 English as a Second Language (ESL)

This is an example of a song in the textbook that has been changed to reflect a values message, without changing the essential vocabulary introduced in the lesson. This song would be enhanced by a discussion about the qualities students admire in friends and the qualities they have to offer as friends.

Original song:

If your friend is tall and quiet, clap your hands,
If your friend is tall and quiet, clap your hands,
If your friend is tall and quiet, if your friend is tall and quiet
If your friend is tall and quiet, clap your hands.

New version with values messages embedded – These are just some examples. New lines can be added to reflect values messages currently being focused on.

- *If your friend is kind and helpful ...*
- *If your friend is always truthful ...*
- *If your friend helps his family ...*

10.8 Using Quotations

The reasons for using quotations have been described previously in Chapter 8. They can be used to inspire, to reinforce values messages, and to draw on in times of need. There are many instances when inspirational quotations can be drawn on to reinforce values messages across the curriculum. Different approaches can be used at different times to add variety. Some different ways to use a quotation can be as follows:

- Write it on a card and pin it to the wall so it can remain there for some time. Refer to it several times during the lesson when you introduce the related topic.
- Use it in the lesson as a basis for discussion. What do you think this quotation means? How can this help us in our daily lives? How can we use these words to help others in their lives? (Discussion can be with the whole class, in pairs or in groups of four – vary the group sizes each time you do this activity.)
- For homework, students can be asked to make a pledge of something they can do to put the quotation into practice in their own lives. Each pledge can be written on a card and pinned to the wall with the quotation.
- Some other, more challenging questions could include:
    - How would you explain this quotation to somebody who is too young to read it?
    - Is this quotation true for you? Is it true for most people?
    - Are there any times when this statement is not true?
    - Where do you see this in action in your own life?
- Have two quotations about the lesson topic and discuss how they are similar in meaning and how they are different.

Mathematics: Addition and subtraction
Discuss the quotation: 'Your net worth to the world is usually determined by what remains after your bad habits are subtracted from your good ones.' – Benjamin Franklin

Mathematics: Pythagoras' Theorem
Pythagoras was a philosopher as well as a mathematician. Students can be challenged to search for examples of his famous quotations which reflect his values and/or which reflect values the students see as important to themselves.

English: Phonics

Table 10.3 Values Words and Quotations Using Common Phonics

Sound	*Words*	*Quotations using the phonic sounds*
ai,ay	praise aid pain brain	*Use your brain to avoid giving others pain.*
al,au,all	all caught taught	*Love all, serve all.* *Good habits are caught, not taught.* [This means that other people learn good habits more from watching us than from us telling them what to do.]
ar	star are	*We are all stars in the same sky.*
h	head, heart, hands happy help harmony humility human habit	*Harmony of head, heart, and hands makes us happy.*
ea,ee	peace need see please speak clean	*Inner peace is a good feeling.* *Help people who are in need.* *See only the good things in others.*
ea	head health	*Head, heart, and hands.*
igh	light bright	*There is no light more bright than the light that shines within us.*
ir	first virtue	*Thinking first before you act is a virtue.*
oo	look	*Stop, look, and listen before you speak or act.*
ou,ow	power doubt our shower around	*We should not doubt our power to shower love all around.*
ur	hurt	*Help ever, hurt never.*
ch,tch	watch choice	*Watch your:* *Words* *Actions* *Thoughts* *Character* *Heart* *Is it a good choice or a bad choice?*
ll	well still allow	*Behave well.* *Use silent sitting to keep your mind still.* *Allow others to be the best they can be.*

10.9 Reflective Questioning

Teachers should be encouraged to ask students questions such as the following, to encourage them to reflect on the values message in the topic. The purpose of this is to draw out the students' own understandings of the message and to encourage them to reflect on how this value, if practised, can enrich their own lives and those of others.

- What does this remind you of in your own life?
- What can we learn from this? What is the human values message in what we have learned? (i.e., about ourselves, being better/happier people, helping ourselves and others, etc.)
- What can *we* do: (a) as individuals, (b) as a school, (c) as a society, and (d) as the whole world, to put this values message into practice?

From time to time, it is also important to ask the students what they have learned about human values from engaging in group activities and doing silent sitting.

A useful framework for reflective questioning can be to incorporate ***the Six Es*** into the teaching programme:[17]

- Engage students in the topic through questioning
- Explain the values and their place in real life, at the same time as explaining the relevant subject content
- Explore – i.e., look at the topic from different perspectives
- Elaborate – i.e., application to life
- Evaluate, post-discussion, through the use of discussion questions and reflections on the impacts of the value on students' daily lives
- Excel – ownership and development of the values lie with the learner, through a 'take-home message' or thought-provoking example

Table 10.4 shows some examples of questions that follow the ***Six Es*** model.[18]

Table 10.4 Reflection in Two Topics Using the *Six Es* Model

	Physical Education: Cricket	*Persuasive Writing: Friends vs Family*
Engage	1. How can cricket be equated to character building? What can the cricket pitch represent in your life? 2. What could the two wickets represent?	Which is more important, friends or family?
Explain	History, rules, and format of the game of cricket	Discuss what constitutes 'family' and what defines 'friends'

(*Continued*)

Table 10.4 (Continued)

	Physical Education: Cricket	*Persuasive Writing: Friends vs Family*
Explore	Explore the idea 'Cricket is a game of the mind rather than the body' (hint – game of decisions)	Discuss the meaning and implications of the quote – 'There are friends, there is family and then there are friends that become family' Write an exposition using genre structure
Elaborate	Each ball faced is an EXPERIENCE, a situation presented in game of life – chance to see how you handle that experience-lightning speed ball = sudden event in life. With each ball, you decide the type of stroke you need to play. Do you REACT, RESPOND, or simply let it go to the wicketkeeper? You are there to protect your wicket – the life force in you cannot just stand there, you were created for ACTION – the only weapon to handle the situation – your bat (mind) which is under your control. A good batsman RESPONDS not REACTS	Each student is to examine their home situation and explore the possibility of the quote – Have they experienced any friend being regarded as a family member? What characterises this type of person?
Evaluate	How can you relate the bat, three stumps, and the ball to life? Would you classify cricket as a team sport? Explain why cricket is a great team builder. Draw a poster of the CRICKET FIELD with players – label each component of the game as related to life	Which is more important – Family or Friend?
Excel	If you change your habits, you can become master of your destiny	Even though it is great to have friends, it is much better to have family. You might not be able to choose who they are, but you can certainly rely on them to be there and help you whenever you need them.

10.10 Using Homework to Consolidate Topic and Values Learning, and Involve Parents/Families

It is important for students to recognise that values are not just for practising at school but that they also enrich life outside school. Through extending the values message into homework relating to a topic, this can be reinforced. It also creates an opportunity for students to share values messages with their parents and families.

Science: Atoms are made up of subatomic particles; neutrons, electrons, and protons.

The values message is that we can deflect bad thoughts or allow them to go straight through us and that our hearts should be filled with positive thoughts surrounded by 'bright stars'. Challenge the students to choose somebody who they think is negative towards them and to practise this activity every day for one week. Suggest a timeframe, for example, two minutes per day, to focus on sending the stars from their hearts.

Remind them every day to do it.

At the end of the week, ask students to share any success stories.

To encourage them to do it, you could display stars on the wall with the names of the students who report a success story.

Science: Chemical reactions – Atoms react to become stable either by sharing or donating their electrons.

Challenge the students to do an activity that involves sharing or donating, for example, helping a family member secretly, or practising ceiling on desires, to save time, money, or some other items to donate to others (see also Chapter 12). At the end of the challenge, it is important to discuss with the students about how, like the atoms, they feel better about themselves (more stable) from doing these activities.

IT: Social media

Rather than just asking students to put a ceiling on the time they spend on social media (see Chapter 12), ask them to think about putting a ceiling on the *ineffective* time.

- Are you chatting effectively with your friends or just chatting indiscriminately? What does it mean to you to chat effectively? What is indiscriminate chatting? (Examples might include sending photos of everything you eat, reading everything that is posted by people you don't know even if it doesn't particularly interest you .... Ask the students to brainstorm about others.)
- As a class, decide some conditions to put onto your social media time to use it more effectively. For example, a condition might be that you will use your time to get to know your friends rather than indiscriminately chatting. What do you want to find out about your friend? What questions can you use to find out?
- As part of the Ceiling on Desires project (see Chapter 12), practise for a length of time decided by the class (e.g., 1 week, 2 weeks, 1 month), using the conditions agreed upon to use your time more effectively. Encourage students to report on their progress and to keep records (as above).

Mathematics: The tank-filling problem (see above in this chapter)

Homework Activity: Draw a diagram to explain this values message. On the 'in' pipe, write your good qualities that can fill your tank with love and peace. On the 'out' pipe, write the negative qualities that can drain your tank of its love and peace. Write down three things you can do to keep your tank from draining. Ask students to bring their work to class the next day and display their diagrams on the classroom wall.

10.11 Getting Started Using Action Learning

This chapter has presented a range of different ways in which values education can be integrated across the curriculum through EHV principles and strategies. Through overt values integration into curriculum subjects:

- Finding values messages in lesson topics
- Adjusting textbook examples
- Using silent sitting/visualisation for various purposes during the lesson
- Using groupwork that is truly interdependent and promotes strength in unity
- Storytelling
- Songs with the relevant values message
- Quotations
- Homework to consolidate topic and values learning, and involve parents/families
- The importance of reflective questioning was emphasised, to encourage students to think about what the values message means to them in their own lives.

It is important to realise that you do not have to use all of these approaches all of the time, but rather to select one or two that best match the topic. To start with, you could aim to prepare *three good values-integrated lessons* per week and gradually build up.

10.11.1 Action Learning

- Select one lesson/topic. Be creative to think of a values message suggested by this topic. Try to incorporate both interpersonal (social skills) and intrapersonal (inner feelings) values in your message.
- For this topic and your identified values message, choose 1–3 EHV strategies that are the most relevant.
- Pre-prepare your question/s to encourage the students to reflect on what the values message means to their own lives.
- If possible, consider planning a homework activity that extends their reflection on the values message along with their grasp of the topic.

You may wish to refer to the scripts in the Appendices for further ideas about the different ways in which values messages can be integrated into existing curriculum subjects.

As discussed earlier in the book, action learning can be more successful if done in pairs or small groups. Consider joining with one or two others to plan what you will do, discuss the outcomes, and decide what to do next (see the last part of Chapter 3).

10.11.2 Evaluation of Your Learning from Action

Keep a record of any insightful or unexpected comments or suggestions made by your students. Over time, look for changes or developments in their understanding and practice of values. You may find *Krathwohl's taxonomy*, discussed in Chapter 4, useful for looking at how your students are developing.

Appendices for Chapter 10

The scripts presented in these Appendices have been derived from teachers' integration of values messages, using the EHV approaches, into various curriculum subjects. The teachers' lesson plans have been annotated with comments to describe the EHV technique that was being used at different times during the lesson. Also included in the appendix are some lesson plan templates.

Key/Essential Aspects of EHV That Are Covered in These Scripts

1. Values messages drawn from the lesson topic
2. Changing the examples in the textbook to allow for a values message
3. Questioning to encourage the students to reflect on the values message in relation to their own lives
4. Silent sitting:
    - Teacher models using silent sitting in his/her own life
    - Talk to students about how silent sitting helps them
    - Silent sitting story about the values message in the lesson topic
    - Silent sitting to get in touch with your 'inner computer' to solve a problem
    - Silent sitting to reflect on what was learnt in the lesson
5. Storytelling
6. Songs that match the values message in the lesson topic; sometimes teachers change the words of a song that is in the textbook to have a values message, or they can use popular songs, as long as they have a values message
7. Groupwork
8. Use of famous quotations with the values message
9. Hidden curriculum (see Chapter 9):
    - Teacher talk/good EHV praise
    - EHV displays on walls in classrooms and corridors
    - EHV homework to introduce it to families
10. Projects to put the values into practice in their own daily lives
11. Inner diamond – we all have an 'inner diamond' that we need to polish and make shiny through practising the human values. Everyone has their

own special unique qualities that they can use to make the world a better place for themselves and others.

12. Selfless service – giving and helping others without expecting anything in return

Appendix 10.1: Sample Mathematics Lesson

Topic: Identifying the basic features of a circle: Understand the relationship and features of radius and diameter

Table 10.5 shows a sample lesson incorporating values messages with this topic.

Table 10.5 Values Lesson Plan for Basic Features of a Circle

Silent sitting: *Imagine that you are inside a golden circle. You can move around anywhere you like inside your circle and you feel very safe and happy. The other students are in their circles too. Sometimes you bump gently against each other, but you are inside your own circle, and nobody else can come in. Your golden circle is your own special space where you can go whenever you like.* ***Teacher:*** 'What is the difference between the circle and other shapes? A special property of the circle is that it is complete. We need to try to be like the circle – strong and complete in ourselves and not needing to rely on outer things to make us happy. Can you give an example of a time when you have been like a circle in your own life?'	What has happened in this part of the lesson? 1. Silent sitting is used to settle the students and introduce the topic of the lesson. But the silent sitting *ALSO* includes a deep values message, about being complete within yourself. 2. The teacher asked the students some questions to encourage them to think about their own sense of self-reliance. 3. Imagining enclosing hyperactive students in a golden circle helps them to define their boundaries. The golden colour represents security and purity.
Game – love others – [see the diagram below]: The circle has many radii. These can represent the rays of sunshine, and they can connect us to other people. How much love you have determines how much sunshine you will have and how much you will give. What kind of good deeds you have done will determine what virtues you have. Please fill these qualities in beside the radii marked on the circle. [Love: Heart-to-heart communication with other people; sharing and doing good deeds for others.]	What has happened in this part of the lesson? 1. The teacher reminds us of a strong values message that we can learn from the circle. 2. The teacher has introduced a game. This is fun for the students, *AND* it has an important values message. The teacher asks the students to think about their own virtues and how they use them in their daily lives.

(Continued)

Table 10.5 (Continued)

Teacher (after the activity): 'For example, in our class we have [Annie] who has a very warm and loving smile. [Annie] can spread sunshine to others by smiling at them. [Neil] has a very kind heart and will often go to sit beside somebody who he notices is feeling sad, and that is a way to spread sunshine too.' 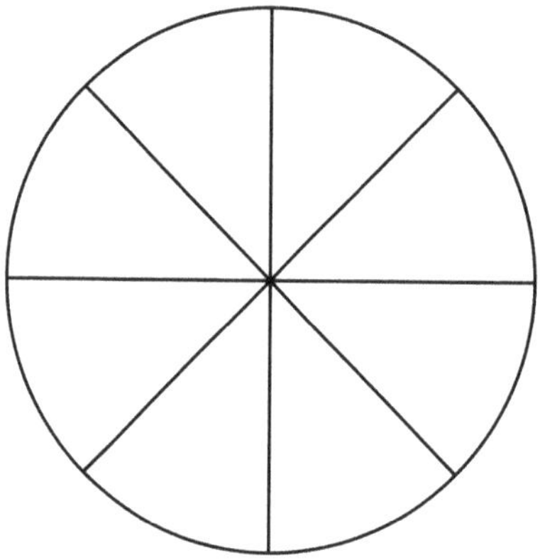 Teacher asks students to tell their partners briefly what good qualities they wrote on their radii.	3. It would be a good idea to display the students' circles from the game on the classroom wall as a reminder of the values message. 4. When introducing the game, the teacher gives some examples of the sunshine qualities of students in the class. These are genuine qualities that these students have, so the values praise is sincere and genuine. It is a good idea for the teacher to use some of the lesser-known students in the class as the examples. 5. After the game, the teacher reminds the students again about the values message.
Group activity – Give each student in the group a different-sized circle and ask them to explore the relationship between the radius and the diameter. They can record their findings as a group. From this, they can discover that the d = 2r rule is the same no matter what size the circle is. Teacher writes the quotation on the board: *'To want unwaveringly the welfare of another, both in the head and the heart, is the best help one can give.'* ***Teacher:*** 'Close your eyes for a moment and think about this quotation. Think of yourself sending out your good qualities like the radii of a circle coming from your heart at the centre and reaching out to help others. Think about how this makes you feel. Think about how it makes the others feel when you are reaching out like this to them.'	<u>What has happened in this part of the lesson?</u> 1. This is an interdependent group activity because each student is contributing an example to the group. Based on these contributions, the group can reach a consensus about the d = 2r rule. The quotation written on the board is a way to use classroom displays to reinforce values messages. It could be written on paper and displayed permanently on the wall. 2. The final silent sitting is very short but it reinforces the concept of the radii of the circle coming out from the centre and also reinforces the values message. So the students will take away the values messages and the concept of the circle and the radius in their long-term memories.

Appendix 10.2: Sample Reading Comprehension Lesson

Topic: Story about a mother cooking dumplings to show her love for her students

Table 10.6 shows a sample lesson incorporating values messages with this topic.

Table 10.6 Values Lesson Plan for Reading Comprehension

Read the text aloud, feeling between mother and sincere love. Listen to/sing a song about gratitude, e.g., **Louis Armstrong – What a Wonderful World, Andrew Gold – Thank You for Being a Friend; Celine Dion – Because You Loved Me (written as a tribute to her father)** ***Teacher talk:*** What is the values message in this song? I am very grateful for xxxxx. Please share with us some of the things you are grateful for. Do you think we can feel sad or angry at the same time that we are feeling grateful?	What has happened in this part of the lesson? • The teacher has identified a values message in the story topic: Learn to be grateful. As long as everyone has a thankful heart, the world will become so good, right? • The teacher used the song to introduce the values message. • Teacher shared with the students some of the things she is grateful for and asked them to share theirs. • Teacher asked the students to reflect on how it benefits us to feel grateful.
Read the text again and look for evidence of the mother's love. ***Teacher questioning:*** Has your mother/grandmother/another family member or friend ever done something like this to show her love for you? How did it make you feel?	What has happened in this part of the lesson? Teacher asked students again to talk about their own experiences when somebody has done something special to show their love for them and how it made them feel.
For homework: Write a letter of gratitude to your mother/father/grandparent/other family member to tell them some of their acts of love that you have appreciated and how these acts made you feel.	What has happened in this part of the lesson? 1. Teacher set a homework task to put the values into action in their daily lives. 2. A homework task is also a good way to bring the values messages into the home so students and their parents can talk about them.
Silent sitting to conclude the lesson: Listening to music and thinking about the love of the mother in the story for her students. Ask students to reflect on their own views about what love is. Finish with a quotation about love, e.g. *'Love is the one sunshine in the winter, to give people warmth; Love is the spring water in the desert, to give people hope; To give love is to give power.'*	What has happened in this part of the lesson? 1. The silent sitting invites the students to reflect on the message in the story and the feeling of the power of love. 2. Lesson finishes with quotation about love. (Note that this quotation can be left permanently on the classroom wall as a reminder.)

Appendix 10.3: Sample Reading Comprehension Lesson

Topic: A story about an earthquake in the Chinese city of Yushu

Table 10.7 shows a sample lesson incorporating values messages with this topic.

Table 10.7 Values Lesson Plan (2) for Reading Comprehension

Sing a song (Choose one from below) **<u>TO CARE TO SHARE</u>** To care, to share, Forgiving and giving. Is how we should be, To make life worth living. **<u>SHARE SHARE SHARE (Tune is Row row row your boat)</u>** Share, share, share and care, To everyone you see. Full of love and tolerance, That's how the world should be. ***Teacher questioning:*** What does it mean that caring and sharing and giving and forgiving make our lives worth living? [let some students suggest answers] Have you had a time when you felt your life was worth living because you cared and shared or forgave somebody? [Ask some students to suggest answers. Teacher can also give an example of a time in his/her own life.] ***Introduce the story:*** • Show the pictures of Yushu to indicate the extent of the earthquake damage and illustrate why the people are in need of help. • Introduce new vocabulary. • Read the text using various strategies (individual reading, reading to a partner, silent reading, etc.). • Read the text again and answer comprehension questions.	<u>What has happened in this part of the lesson?</u> • Teacher has introduced a song that has the values theme of the lesson. • The second song, Share share share is changed from the words of a well-known song, Row *row row your boat*. The new words have a better value meaning. • Questioning invites students to reflect on the value of selfless service in their own lives.

(*Continued*)

Table 10.7 (Continued)

Groupwork:
• Ask students to work in groups to discuss how to help the people in Yushu. Each student is invited to make a suggestion.
• Encourage group members to use vocabulary to support each other, such as:
  • What do you suggest?
  • Why don't you give them ...?
  • That's a good idea.
• Evaluation of performance in groups. ***Teacher:*** Please put up your hand if you gave everybody in your group a chance to speak. Put up your hand if you listened with your heart when the others were speaking. Put up your hand if you helped group members if they were stuck. Put up your hand if you praised your group members from your heart when you said, 'That's a good idea'. Can you suggest any ways you could be a better group member?
	What has happened in this part of the lesson?
	Students have been asked to practise using appropriate vocabulary for supporting group members.
	Teacher has asked questions to encourage students to reflect on their roles as group members and to think about how they can be better group members.

Silent sitting: Close your eyes and listen to the beautiful music. Imagine that you are in Yushu. Imagine you are standing in front of some students there. Now think about what you suggested in your group that you could do for them or give them. Imagine that you are really doing this now for the Yushu students standing in front of you. As you do it, feel love in your heart for them. They say thank you and go away. Now think about how it makes you feel in your heart to have helped the Yushu students. Think about the feeling in your heart that comes from helping somebody in trouble. When you open your eyes, try to hold this feeling in your heart for the rest of the day.	What has happened in this part of the lesson? Teacher has used silent sitting to consolidate what the students talked about in their groups and also to let them experience the feeling of love and happiness that comes from helping others.
Follow-up activity: Select one of the strategies suggested during groupwork and put it into action (e.g., Practise Ceiling on Desires for one month and donate money saved)	What has happened in this part of the lesson? Students have a chance to practise selfless service. Parents and families can also become involved in the values action.

Appendix 10.4: Sample Lesson Plan Template/s for Integrating Subject Topic Using EHV

Lesson Plan Template

Subject:

Topic:

Class:

Teacher

1. **Lesson aims and learning outcomes**

   Content to be taught:

   Learning outcomes:

2. **Values messages in topic**

   Values learning outcome:

   Values talk teacher will use in the lesson:

3. **Values messages in hidden curriculum and teacher behaviour**

   Values learning outcome:

   (e.g., confidence, co-operation, perseverance, etc.).

   Values talk teacher will use in the lesson
   [Be specific about what you will say to students, e.g., "Strength in unity": What does this mean? Why are we stronger if we work together? *Perseverance*: What happens if we do not succeed at first? How can we use our failures to learn and become better people because of them?

   Teacher's specific behaviours to focus on (e.g., communicate heart-to-heart, use of praise, attentive listening, etc.)
4. ***Rewording of textbook materials/problems to reflect a values message (if appropriate)***
5. ***Questions asked during lesson to draw out the pupils' own understanding of the values from the pupils:***
   For example:

- What does this remind you of in our own lives?
- What can we learn from this? What is the human values message in what we have learned? (i.e., about ourselves, being better/happier people, helping ourselves and others, etc.)
- What can *we* do: (a) as individuals, (b) as a school, (c) as a society, and (d) as the whole world to put this values message into practice?

Note that it is also important to ask students what they have learned about human values from engaging in group activities, doing silent sitting, etc.

Questions can be designed to reflect the ***6 Es:***

- **Engage** students in the topic through questioning
- **Explain** the values and their place in real life, at the same time as explaining the relevant subject content
- **Explore** – i.e., look at the topic from different perspectives
- **Elaborate** – i.e., application to life
- **Evaluate**, post-discussion, through the use of discussion questions and reflections on the impacts of the value on students' daily lives
- **Excel** – ownership and development of the values lie with the learner, through a 'take-home message' or thought-provoking example

6. ***Resources that reflect the values message*** (including music, pictures, etc.)
7. ***Lesson content***
8. ***Reflections on feedback***

Notes

1 G. Zukav and L. Francis, *Self-Empowerment Journal: A Companion to the Mind of the Soul: Responsible Choice* (New York, NY: Free Press, 2003).
2 Idea contributed by Gita Singh, Sathya Sai College, Murwillumbah, Australia.
3 *Ibid.*
4 Idea contributed by Raj Chandan Ram, Board Director, Sathya Sai College, Murwillumbah, Australia.
5 From Math-Only-Math.com. https://www.math-only-math.com/pipes-and-water-tank.html accessed 5-8-2022.
6 Sathya Sai Baba, *Sathya Sai Speaks* (Prasanthi Nilayam, India: Books and Publications Trust, May 29, 1988), Vol. 21.
7 Source: Gita Singh, teacher, Sathya Sai College, Murwillumbah, Australia. Cited in: M. Taplin, *Guided Visualizations for Integrating Education in Human Values into Curriculum Subjects,* ed. S. Parahakaran, A Human Values Pathway for Teachers (Singapore: Springe, 2021), 20.
8 *Ibid.*
9 Adapted from idea contributed by Vidya Vahini, *Integral Education for All, By All* (2023). www.srisathyasaividyavahini.org accessed 5-8-2022.
10 D. Rowe, *Talking about Values in the Classroom* (London: Citizenship Foundation, 2015), p. 3. https://gcedclearinghouse.org/resources/talking-about-values-classroom accessed 5-8-2022.
11 *Ibid.*, p. 5.
12 *Ibid.*, p. 5.
13 *Ibid.*, p. 6.
14 *Ibid.*, pp. 4–5.
15 Extracted from *Richards Topical Encyclopedia* (New York, NY: J. A. Richards Publishing Co., Inc., 1946).
16 Adapted from H. Dreux, "The Ghastly Deed," *Mathematics Teaching* (1973), 16–18.
17 Vahini, *Integral Education for All, By All,* 2023.
18 Ideas contributed by Sathya Sai College, Murwillumbah, Australia.

Chapter 11

Maintaining Positivity through EHV

Kevin Francis

11.1 Introduction

Positive Psychology is one of many ways to enhance life skills which promote character development through the teaching and practice of human values. Recently, it has been used increasingly in education and in self-help programmes. It has been found to be an effective way to promote mental wellbeing and increased concentration and cognitive performance. It has also been claimed that Positive Psychology strategies can help to alleviate many mental and emotional difficulties, including self-esteem issues, anxiety, depression, stress-related problems, and interpersonal issues. This is especially important in the 21st-century circumstances of calamities involving extremes of weather, which have led to droughts, bushfires, and floods, and the ongoing challenges of dealing with pandemics and their associated toll on the mental health and wellbeing of many (see also Chapter 1).

Whilst there are many references, online programmes, self-help books, and regimes available which promote an understanding of the benefits of Positive Psychology (sometimes referred to as *Healthy Optimism*), this chapter focuses on its understanding and application to the Education in Human Values (EHV) context.

In this chapter, you will be guided to first look at the elements of Positive Psychology in your own life, then relate this to *Character and Values Education*, in order to plan activities to develop the awareness of living with a positive disposition as a desirable part of character education. You will be able to find answers to the following questions:

- What do you know about Positive Psychology?
- Why is such a thing necessary in modern *society*?
- Is Positive Psychology just another name for being optimistic?
- How would you recognise a person who practices Positive Psychology?
- How does this help a person's Character to develop in terms of EHV?
- Do our schools currently develop this aspect of Character satisfactorily, *and if yes how? If no*, what could be done about this?

DOI: 10.4324/9781003478607-12

After completing this chapter, you will have insight into:

- Identifying your own understanding of Positive Psychology, and refining that by incorporating the views of selected others
- Describing how Positive Psychology can be used in practice
- Being able to explain the various aspects of *being positive*
- Having more awareness of your own emotional reaction to what you read, see, hear, or feel
- Developing ways to support the need for practising *a more positive outlook* in self and others
- Proposing ways of enacting your ideas
- Incorporating these outcomes into your life, work, and education with others to support both your practice and character development, and others through the exploration and integration of values

One aspect of Positive Psychology is the practice of *mindfulness*, which has been shown to change brain structure and function.[1]

As a successful secondary teacher and school counsellor for 44 years, I have used Positive Psychology effectively in both my teaching and counselling practices. This chapter describes an overview of my experiences. You can then further your own interest and research by exploring in greater depth the references at the end of this chapter.

The first part of the chapter gives a brief summary of recent theories about Positive Psychology and its related use of mindfulness practices, particularly describing the work of Martin Seligman. The next part then considers some commentary about Positive Psychology and its impacts. The relationship between Positive Psychology and the five basic human values of EHV, Truth, Peace, Love, Right Action, and Non-violence, is also explored. The final part describes some of the Positive Psychological principles personally used in counselling practice in both state and private schools and the wider educational community. These principles have been presented in a way that will allow the reader to follow them, either personally, during class time, or with others from all sectors of the education system.

11.2 What Is Positive Psychology?

Long before Positive Psychology became popular, Mahatma Gandhi had already shown the way to live through the following quote, *Keep your thoughts positive because your thoughts become your words. Keep your words positive, because your words become your behaviour. Keep your behaviour positive because your behaviour becomes your habits. Keep your habits positive because your habits become your values. Keep your values positive because your values become your destiny.*[2] This leads very nicely into one widely accepted definition of Positive Psychology: *Positive Psychology is the scientific study of human flourishing, and an applied approach to optimal functioning. It has also been defined as the study of the strengths and virtues that enable individuals, communities and organisations to thrive.*[3]

Positive Psychology is a reasonably modern trend (at least by western standards) in psychological thought, which focuses on the positive aspects of life generally and also on individual thoughts, feelings, and behaviours. Positive Psychology is used as a personalised aspect of optimism to enable higher levels of forbearance and resilience, which enable all to deal better with the fluctuating aspects of modern life.

When teaching Positive Psychology, students initially explore their own understanding of the benefits of being positive and then build on this by exploring other definitions and descriptors from a range of published sources. Readings add to the complexity of understanding how to plan action to improve personal practice and character – and hence Values Education, all in the context of personal relevance to the participant.

Positive Psychology involves the study and practice of all that makes life most worth living. It is a call for balance in dealing with strengths and weaknesses to enable building upon the positive things in life as well as dealing with the negative or the worst of life situations. In line with EHV, it is concerned with encouraging more fulfilling lives for people, to promote personal happiness and to see others in a more compassionate way. This is particularly relevant given recent contemporary events.

Contrary to a popular view that Positive Psychology is simply a naïve 'seeing the world through rose-coloured glasses' approach to life, it does not ignore or dismiss the very real problems that people experience. Instead, it looks for the learning experiences from life events, for which we can actually be grateful, as it allows a focus on the promotion of more resilience and forbearance in dealing with life's challenges; this fits in very neatly to the values of Right Action and Non-violence. Positive Psychology complements and extends the well-recognised and accepted problem-focused psychology that has been prevalent for many decades.

Seeing the good is neither illusionary nor simply ignoring problematic situations, but genuinely works on developing a balance, providing enthusiasm for life as it presents itself. It is also based on a great deal of scientific research, so it is more than just revamped positive thinking or the stuff of popular self-help programmes.

Turning to the concept of optimism, optimists generally keep their eyes on higher values, whilst pessimists slide down into dispirited attitudes leading to possible despair. The founder of the EHV Program, Sathya Sai Baba, once said:

> *Seeing a glass half filled with water, the optimist is glad that it is half full, whilst the pessimist is sad that it is half empty. Though both statements are correct, the optimist hopes to fill the other half too, whilst the pessimist gives up in despair. The one has faith; the other has no faith to sustain him. So we must develop faith by steady effort. Faith must lead to effort. Faith is essential for human progress in every field.*[4]

Positive Psychology can be viewed as one more practical method of Values Education, as a process by which people give purpose to their own lives to practise Right Action and develop a sense of inner peace as well as empathy towards others.

11.3 Recent Research

In 1996, when I was enrolled in a counselling-focused Graduate Diploma course, one aspect of the course was to look at theoretical models of Psychology as a basis for my own counselling practice. I was excited at the time and fully aware that having a positive outlook seemed to lead to better outcomes for clients. My research sought to show that a positive attitude leads to more productive interactions with clients and a greater likelihood of behaviour changes. It was at this time that I became aware of Gerald Jampolsky's[5] attitudinal approach to better life experiences and outcomes. My own experience suggested that those who had positive outlooks on life were happier in their work and had fewer mental health issues such as anxiety and fear about client behavioural changes. I found this positive approach worked very well with Ellis's *Rational Emotive Behavioural Therapy*[6] and Glasser's *Choice Theory*,[7] as neither methodology apportioned blame but looked at more positive thought processes and choices that were well within the scope and control of the clientele. As a direct result of this, I was invited on a regular basis to run many professional development workshops on Positive Psychology for other counsellors and people interested in this area, which incorporated a values-based approach to these two methodologies. These were well attended by teachers and parents, with excellent feedback. I continued to do this even beyond my retirement in 2016. I revisited many research papers and read many of the increasing number of books being released about attitudinal change and Positive Psychology to justify the research base of my practice.

In 2011, after years of practising and teaching Positive Psychology, in my role as a secondary school counsellor, I was invited by the Institute of Sathya Sai Education Australia (ISSEA) to conduct workshops for both staff and students of a values-based school in Murwillumbah, NSW. These interactive workshops were based on a three-pronged approach: Raising awareness, investigating any behavioural change necessary to become more content, resilient, and optimistic, and meeting life's challenges more productively to cope better by practising living a more values-based life. These are all components of the Positive Psychological approach.

Positive Psychology is a process involving six aspects:

1. Character strengths (forgiveness, kindness, gratitude, creativity)
2. A life with meaning and purpose (seeking Truth)

3. Happiness, positive emotions, and wellbeing (being at Peace)
4. Emotional and Social Intelligence (selflessly helping others, one aspect of Right Action)
5. Hope and Optimism (looking for peaceful solutions)
6. Not exploiting others (practising Non-violence and another aspect of Right Action).

In this context, Positive Psychology is more than just optimism, but a philosophical stand on personal attitude and discipline. By considering the research of one modern proponent of Positive Psychology, Martin Seligman, this can be explored further. Seligman's *Authentic Happiness Theory*[8] asserts there are three roads to the good life, which he described as a life with positive mental health and wellbeing. These are:

- The Pleasurable Life
- The Engaged Life
- The Meaningful Life

The Pleasurable Life deals with positive emotions, the Engaged life is about *flow* and *mindfulness*, and the Meaningful life relates to the meaning and purpose of a person's existence. Seligman said that the Meaningful life can lead to people experiencing authentic happiness.

This theory was revised further in 2011, to be renamed the *Well Being Theory*. This uses the PERMA Model as a basis for Positive Psychology:[9]

P	Positive emotions
E	Engagement
R	Relationships
M	Meaning
A	Accomplishment

According to Seligman, Positive Psychology focuses on six overarching virtues (values) from a core base of 24-character qualities, which are related below to the five Human Values of EHV (see Chapter 3).

• Wisdom	*(Truth)*
• Courage	*(Right Action)*
• Humanity	*(Love)*
• Justice	*(Right Action, Non-violence)*
• Temperance	*(Peace, Non-violence)*
• Transcendence	*(Love, Peace)*

11.4 Further Exploration of Positive Psychology

Based on these characteristics of Positive Psychology being linked to human values, as described above, one can pose the question: 'What are the qualities of a healthy, positively oriented human being?' Looking at the protective factors associated with Positive Psychology leads to the answer to this question, which is here defined as: 'A pattern of environmental or personal resources that help people fare better in the face of stressors'.

Having taught school Years 11 and 12 Psychology in South Australia from 2004 to 2016, my experience supports the use of the model of Psychology promoted by Spencer and Hartstone,[10] who break Positive Psychology into four general areas of understanding and study that will now be described.

11.4.1 The Biological Level

The first is at a biological level, which focuses on body systems, brain structures, and neurochemistry. From the biological perspective, physiological and psychological toughness mainly involves two classes of hormones secreted by the adrenal gland in the face of stress, *adrenaline* and *cortisol*, which both have negative effects if there are high and prolonged levels. Both of these neurotransmitters are key aspects of the flight and fight responses, which are so important to our survival. If adrenaline has a low resting level but a quick response to stress, followed by a quick return to resting levels, it is seen as protective. In the case of cortisol, it is more protective if it again has a low resting level but, this time, a low response level in the face of stress, so the person does not enter the exhaustion phase of Selye's *General Adaptation Syndrome.*[11] If high levels of adrenaline are maintained due to stress or even general anxiety, they can cause excessive wear and tear on the body, whilst continued high levels of cortisol lead to long-term depletion of the immune system, both of which are counterproductive to good physical and mental health. This can help to explain why exercise is considered health-enhancing, because it works on adrenaline response, not cortisol, and therefore promotes physiological toughness *and* stress resistance.

11.4.2 The Concept of Hardiness

The second understanding of basic processes that are common to all focuses on learning (and forgetting), cognitive processing and emotional reactions, which in turn lead to the Positive Psychological concept of *hardiness*. This is a stress-protective factor comprising three beliefs: *Commitment*, *control*, and *challenge*. Optimistic or positive people show commitment to work, family, relationships, religion, and other community involvements, all of which are seen as important. They have control over outcomes, with limited or no feelings of powerlessness. Demands and stressful or uncomfortable situations are viewed as challenges and opportunities for growth, not threats. Optimistic people display coping self-efficacy, a belief that they can perform the necessary behaviours to cope successfully, leading to optimistic expectations that things will turn out positively and/or for the best, thereby finding meaning in stressful life events and circumstances. They seem to have an inherent focus on achievements and problem-solving skills to get the best out of circumstances.

11.4.3 The Individual Level

On an individual or personal level, the focus is on the role of individual differences, unique biological factors, basic processes, and experiences that develop personality. The characteristics of individual personality traits determine whether a person is a workaholic, competitive, ambitious, or always taking on more than is feasible in the available time. This compares to a personality type which is less driven and more relaxed, and more positive in outlook. Not focusing on the positive creates constant pressure, leading to emotional reactions and hostility, which alienates social support mechanisms. An interesting aside to this is that a physiological overreaction to stressors in non-optimistic people leads to much higher risk of heart attack.

11.4.4 Sociocultural Level

At a sociocultural level, there is an emphasis on influences of close relationships with family, friends, peers, cultural norms, and societal expectations, which help to promote the positive. Positively oriented people rely on social support and the knowledge that others can be relied upon for help and support in times of crisis. We know that support from others, or even a belief in that support, enhances human functioning, whether the source of the support is a partner, a support group, or a psychotherapeutic group. Survivor rates in cancer patients or those enduring surgery can double with such support, which seems to give a greater sense of identity and meaning in life, allied with increasing control over stressors. Positive supports such as these can apply social pressure not to respond to stress in negative ways, thereby avoiding using maladaptive behaviours such as alcohol, other drugs, or high-risk behaviour, providing higher levels of security and stable harmony.

11.5 Resilience

Most systems to help people remain positive and cope better involve the development of Resilience, the capacity to cope with change and challenge, to bounce back relatively quickly in the face of adversity, and the ability to weather the negative effects of stress, either immediate or prolonged, insult, or injury. Resilience requires the development of competence, confidence in oneself, and caring in the face of risk and adversity. This certainly fits in with two of the EHV major values, Peace and Right Action.

This discussion of Resilience begs the question, 'What does a resilient person look like?' This can be answered from the two perspectives of *external* and *internal* assets.

11.5.1 The External Perspective

From an external point of view, resilient people are often in caring relationships, with strong connections to others in their lives who model and support healthy development and mental wellbeing. They also often have strong family ties, including extended family and other significant adults in 'parenting' roles. These significant others give consistent communication of direct and indirect messages of encouragement that the person can and will succeed responsibly. This self-regard from parents and significant others is often expressed in high, but at the same time realistic, expectations. Resilient people enjoy meaningful participation in relevant, engaging, and positive activities with opportunities for responsibility and contribution, and multiple opportunities to participate at home, school, and in other significant organisations.

11.5.2 The Internal Perspective

Internally resilient people show social competence by being able to communicate effectively and appropriately whilst demonstrating caring, flexibility, and responsiveness in social situations. They display skills in assertive behaviour such as cooperation, communication, empathy, problem-solving skills, and, where appropriate, a sense of humour.

At the same time, they display autonomy, a strong sense of personal identity and power, self-efficacy (belief in personal competence), and self-awareness. They generally have a well-developed sense of meaning and purpose, with a working belief and understanding of life's coherence. Their personal integrity and belief in their own ability to make a difference give them an optimistic outlook, which allows them to set realistic goals and carry them out. This allows them to develop coping skills by using Positive Psychology to manage taxing circumstances, by expending effort to solve or manage life's problems and seeking to master, manage, or reduce levels of stress.

Positive psychology provides people with a number of coping mechanisms. These allow them to become problem-focused and to use structured problem solving to identify problems and find available solutions. In this way, one could identify one or two best options and evaluate their effectiveness. Resilient people have effective assertive behaviours which enable them to set up a time for discussing issues of concern, state the problem in terms of possible consequences to the person, express their feelings clearly and seek out appropriate solutions.

11.5.3 The Resilient Person Is Healthier

The positive psychological approach provides a knowledge base that enables us to know where and when to seek help. Furthermore, it promotes a healthier perspective on issues through factual information using a cognitive rather than emotional approach about the dangers of catastrophising, a very common trap for young people when dealing with many of the issues which they face.

Mindfulness and Silent Sitting (see Chapters 8, 9, and 10) can be used effectively at this stage to visualise positive outcomes or a workable acceptance of a non-changeable situation, which can reduce physical arousal, thereby promoting a healthier immune system and orchestrating a break from thinking about the problem, or at least better compartmentalising of issues and putting them in perspective.

The use of positive self-talk allows modification of thoughts, feelings, ideas, and beliefs in order to foster confidence to use talents and skills effectively. Published research[12] suggests a strong connection between the use of positive affirmations and changed brain activity leading to new behaviours and beliefs; positive affirmations affect neurotransmitters and allow information to be continuously transmitted to the frontal lobes of the brain through a series of emotion-based filters. Psychologists have long linked emotions to cognitive processes (see Chapter 2) so it seems logical to suggest that positive thoughts will lead to more positive beliefs. We know that when we have any thought, there is a resultant burst of neurochemicals in the brain, forming patterns between brain cells, and creating neural pathways connected by synapses. The more a thought is repeated, the stronger these neural pathways become, and the faster the synapses work. The brain also makes emotional connections, which become more automatic and powerful the more the thought or information is repeated. This is the basis of a long-held adage of mine when advising students about study skills, the idea that constant practice eventually leads to a habit, which in turn becomes discipline, leading to an almost automatic response which can be called upon at will.

The same researchers drew the conclusion that: *Participants with greater stimulation in those sections of the brain – which control processing and evaluation – exhibited less sedentary behaviour afterward than participants who did not provide positive affirmations. This research indicates that future behaviour, as well as thoughts, can be improved by positive affirmations.*[13]

These same connections were investigated further by psychologists using MRI scans, which clearly showed more activity in the prefrontal cortex when positive affirmations were used.[14]

Thus, it can be said that, when we are emotionally stuck, a biochemical potential exists for positive change and growth by merely repeating positive intentions, which can eventually become a self-reinforcement of our thoughts, beliefs, and behaviour such that we can change negative aspects of our characters. I refer to this when dealing with clients as one aspect of their ability to respond and reflect, rather than react.

11.6 Positive Psychology and Challenges in Life

Modern teenagers live in an increasingly demanding and stress-generating world. They are constantly bombarded with many negative challenges of social media and other online activities which do little to encourage optimism or positive self-image. The increased rates of youth self-harm and suicide are testament to this. There are constant reminders in the media of young lives lost as a result of bullying, both direct and online. It has had a considerable impact on the mental wellbeing of today's youth, with increased mental health issues as a result of overt and covert online bullying, unhealthy social competition, and ever-increasing expectations, leading to much higher levels of anxiety and depression and reduced levels of resilience from the constant presence of high levels of stress. All of these clearly suggest that the need for better coping skills has never been greater.

11.6.1 Dealing with Bullying

Initially, most of my counselling interactions were related to bullying. Counselling sessions involved stilling the mind using the EHV technique of Silent Sitting and using the principles of Positive Psychology, including positive affirmations to help victims of bullying, students of Years 8–12 on three school campuses. It was also very important and necessary to work with the perpetrators of the bullying to change their behaviours. Both involved students who were not achieving at their peak academic abilities because of personal issues, resulting in low self-esteem and anxiety about attending school. The technique used was a relatively simple but effective one. Gentle non-frantic music would be playing as participants arrived (I used Steve Halpern's anti-frantic music[15]). When students either chose to attend the Wellbeing Centre, or were referred by parents or teachers, they would be greeted individually and then asked if they needed a glass of the cooled, filtered water provided. Positive affirmation posters were displayed prominently on the waiting room walls from such sources as *50 Great Life Skills*[16] and *50 Great Quotations Posters Philosophical Thoughts*,[17] as well as a regular rotation of a large collection of quotations and affirmations personally collected over my years as a secondary school counsellor. A few select ones were also displayed in my actual counselling room. The three which I never changed or rotated in all of my counselling years were:

- *Help ever, hurt never.*[18]
- *If you always do what you've always done, you'll always get what you've always got.*[19]
- *If you think you can or you think you can't, you're absolutely right.*[20]

These three were excellent starting points for discussion about most issues facing the clients who presented themselves to me, providing a foundation to introduce the concepts of Positive Psychology.

It is pertinent to give an example here. A smaller-than-average Year 9 boy, whose high levels of anxiety made him a target for ridicule and teasing by others in his year level, was quite a regular customer. When he arrived, mostly in a state of agitation, the first step in the Positive Psychological approach used was to get him to sit down, make himself comfortable, and engage in the practice of Silent Sitting. I would simply ask him to sit, close his eyes, and slow his breathing down, focusing on making his abdomen rise and fall with each breath. When his breathing pattern slowed, we would sit in silence for two to five minutes. I would then ask him to open his eyes, maintain the calm feeling, and articulate the reason for his visit. The change was always dramatic, with the side benefit of him displaying more empathy towards those giving him a hard time, and being able to articulate how he might make a mental resolution not to react emotionally to the situations in which he would find himself. We would explore the positive aspects that he could take out of each situation and the resultant character trait he might develop further. As mentioned in the introduction, mindfulness, through the use of Silent Sitting, provided a mechanism to highlight positive thoughts and behaviours to break the cycle of constantly focussing on the negative.

I would then ask him again to close his eyes lightly to minimise any peripheral visual distractions and become aware of his own breathing patterns, whilst acknowledging the sounds in the environment. This would then lead into slowing the breath down in an unstrained way by simply repeating the phrases.

> I am aware that I am breathing in (brief pause).
>
> I am aware that I am breathing out (brief pause).

at an ever-decreasing speed. If there were any other thoughts coming up, I directed him to simply observe them to refer to later, as if he was an outsider looking on, and come back to consciously watching his breath.

In this calm state, I would introduce a positive phrase about himself and his issue by asking him to repeat silently:

> I am worthy of respect. I can overcome setbacks and negativity by believing in my own inner strength of character. I reject the labels being used against me. Today and every day I will learn the positive thoughts and beliefs I need to be stronger and more resilient, knowing I am able to practise them at will. I am worthy of respect. I have inner strength of character.

I then instructed him to visualise himself as being stronger, to hold onto that vision for about 15 seconds, and then to go back to the breathing patterns of earlier. He would then be gently invited to come back to the present, return his breathing to its normal rate, and slowly and gently open his eyes.

From this relaxed state, the session would then explore Seligman's five aspects of positive wellbeing, PERMA[21] (introduced earlier in this chapter) and how they related to him and his issues. Seligman's ideas were explored in the following way. If he was being called a name, we would rationally examine the choices available to him regarding the name. I would firstly ask if he believed what was being said about him. Did he think it was true? I would then pick an object in the office, let's say a coffee table, and pointing to it, ask him what he thought of my new computer. A bland, bemused look would be the normal response. After repeating the exercise, I would then ask him what the object was, to which he would reply, 'A table'. The following question was then the key to the Positive Psychology process: 'So how many times do I have to call this table a computer for it to become one?'

His answer: 'It will always be a table'

> 'Ok. So, if you don't believe you are the name you are being called, then how many times must this person say it for you to become it?'

To keep things civilised in this chapter, let us use a term that is not too provocative, but has obvious offensive connotations and say he was being called a 'wanker'. The Collins Dictionary defines 'wanker' as a common vulgar insult used to imply, *An unlikeable person who is very stupid and unpleasant.*[22]

We would use an acronym breakdown to take the sting out of this word as follows:

W	Warm
A	Amicable
N	Natural
K	Kind
E	energetic
R	Reliable

In this light, the word 'wanker' could be turned around mentally to lose its sting as a pejorative term. This invariably brought a smile to the client's face, with a belief that he could do this in the future, at the same time practising the qualities we had chosen.

Everything changes when we learn to see life's challenges in a whole new light. What if we could learn to see them as highly beneficial experiences, adventures in learning, or even as a blessing in disguise? To even be grateful for them as gifts of potential personal growth? Wouldn't that be a welcome shift in perception?

One way to do this was to develop a personal reflection card. On one side of the card was a positive affirmation, often *Help Ever, Hurt Never*,[23] or *I can choose to respond and be at peace, or I can choose to react, and be upset and hurt.*[24]

The other side was an acronym of the student's name, with positive personal qualities for each letter that the students already recognised in themselves or would like to aspire to, which we would decide together. For confidentiality's sake, let us use the name 'Steven' as an example. The card could have the following printed on it:

S	Sensitive
T	Truthful
E	Empathetic
V	Virtuous
E	Enterprising
N	Non-violent

The truth is, with the right mental attitude, it is possible to reframe the way any challenge is experienced.

11.6.2 Reframing Experiences

Asking the right questions is one of the most effective ways to do this. With a little practice, daily challenges, even dealing with bullying, can be viewed as sometimes unpleasant but still valuable life experiences. Five questions anyone can ask themselves when facing challenges are as follows:

11.6.2.1 What Can Be Learned from This?

Challenges are viewed as irritating annoyances, when in fact they may present opportunities to learn and grow! Reflecting on the question, 'What can be learned from an experience?' allows an opportunity to discover something worth appreciating about the experience. It makes it possible to recognise opportunities that might have gone unnoticed, seeing possibility instead of inconvenience and annoyance. This leads to a sense of Peace and Right Action.

11.6.2.2 How Can What Is Currently Happening Be Seen as Strengthening?

One major reason why a challenge might be intimidating is a feeling of 'not being capable of handling it'. Due to limited perception of one's personal abilities, a challenge may seem bigger than it actually is. By seeing challenges as opportunities to become stronger and more capable, everything changes. Challenging situations can unlock untapped strengths and abilities. By doing this, confidence grows until most challenges become opportunities to harness personal power to an even greater degree. Again, Peace and Right action are positive outcomes here.

11.6.2.3 How Can the Challenges Being Faced Be Used for Personal Advantage?

Too often, challenges are viewed as disadvantages – but is that necessarily true? When something gets in the way, different strategies can be explored to accomplish more desirable outcomes. The challenge may help unlock better approaches to the situation. Asking, 'What advantage might be gained from this challenge?' opens possible alternatives that might otherwise have not been considered. This provides a new perspective on Truth and leads to Right Action.

11.6.2.4 Can This Be Used to Help in My Relationships with Others?

What is thought and felt, and ultimately done, impacts others. People who learn through modelling and replication and not letting challenges be intimidating can inspire and motivate others to do the same when they face obstacles in their lives as well as develop new coping skills. This could be seen as Love in action and lead to Non-violent choices.

11.6.2.5 What Would Make This a Worthwhile Learning Experience?

Sometimes, just being willing to recognise that a challenge may not be such a negative experience can be beneficial in itself. It enables personal empowerment by affirming choice of reacting (emotional) or responding (cognitive) to any situation. It also confirms the concept that challenges hold opportunities for further benefits and growth. This can also be interpreted as Love in action.

11.6.3 The Outcomes of the Example

Regular sessions were held with 'Steven' during his Years 9 and 10 study, which changed from several times a week in the early stages of Year 9 to once a month by the end of Year 10. He maintained these practices for the two years remaining in his secondary education after I had left the school, even becoming a popular school leader in his final year at school whilst successfully undertaking his Year 12 studies.

As a direct result of the perceived success of these changes, 'Steven's' teachers then invited me to run similar sessions with their classes. They had seen the changes in 'Steven's' attitude while also hearing that I was doing these practices in my own Senior School classes. Initially, these classes were in Philosophy, then Religious Studies, and indeed in my senior Chemistry classes, and of course, my Psychology classes, all with positive feedback from students and parents alike. In fact, the use of general positive affirmations continued in these teachers' classes even after I had finished working with them directly.

Incidentally, after my retirement, I visited the school during 'Steven's' final year and he approached me as a confident young man, at peace with his life circumstances and challenges, thanking me for my involvement in his life and even inviting me to his graduation as a guest of his family. His handling of his disappointment at my inability to attend was further evidence of his newfound character strengths.

11.7 Silent Sitting as an Adjunct to Positive Psychology Methodology

On a therapeutic level, the techniques of Silent Sitting were also incorporated very early on into my School Counselling practices as a way to promote Positive Psychology, both for incidental clients and for regular clients, particularly those on the autism spectrum. Over the years, the College (high school) had an ever-increasing number of students with diagnosed Asperger's Syndrome, who were regular visitors to the Wellbeing Centre, due to varying degrees of anxiety levels.

In 2004, when I started teaching Psychology to Year 11 and 12 students, I incorporated the Silent Sitting methodology into my own classes, particularly as it fitted well into the Positive Psychology philosophy upon which I based my teaching. The very nature of conducting Silent Sitting at the start of classes had an added benefit, in that I too gained significant clarity of thought and calmness in my teaching and counselling practices, a bonus often commented on by other teachers and students alike. This led to 'guest' sessions at student leadership camps and retreats, both for students and staff. The feedback was positive and also resulted in the opening of a whole new area of my counselling interactions. This was then followed by the compilation of several CDs (compact disks) which included Steve Halpern's music[25] (with his permission), to be used in classes without the need of my actual presence.

The practice of Silent Sitting with positive visualisation practices, particularly those involving imagining a successful outcome of goals for whatever task was causing anxiety or concern, then forming a mental picture of the steps needed to arrive at the desired outcome, was generally well received. Many staff members followed up the reference to Dr Ramesha Manocha's book[26] as well as his free website[27] which provides easy-to-follow guided wellbeing visualisations.

11.7.1 An Example

One particular example comes to mind. One day, a Year 11 student who had been clinically diagnosed with high levels of anxiety came rushing into my office before school had even started, and was in a highly agitated and incoherent state. I invited her into my office and gently conveyed to her that I could not understand what she was saying in her current state of agitation. I invited her to sit down so that we both could count our breathing down, in the same way we had in her previous visits. This was a technique which she had been practising with me over a period of several months on her regular counselling visits when times were less stressed. The change was almost immediate. I had taught her previously to become aware of her heart rate through measuring her pulse, so whilst she was slowing her breathing down, we would focus on remaining as still as possible. I invited her to just observe all the racing thoughts within her head as she watched her pulse rate. It was not uncommon for significant reductions to occur in her pulse rate. When her breathing became slower and more regular, she noted for herself that the initial agitation seemed to become less. In that stillness, she would calmly visualise the current issue upsetting her and, when ready, share it with me. She was able not only to express her feelings clearly but also to describe her reactions in some detail, analysing her emotions with increasing accuracy over time. Operating from such a relaxed and calm state made it easier for her to explore Positive Psychology strategies. She became very skilled in exploring other possible choices to respond to what had happened, allowing for more positive outcomes and significantly less anxiety.

11.7.2 *Using Art*

Over many years of practice, I have also found that artistic creative activity promotes a sense of centring or grounding. The Wellbeing Centre had a number of commercially available line-patterned colouring-in books and an array of good-quality coloured glitter gel pens and colouring pencils available to visitors. Whilst waiting for their appointments, students (and indeed staff members) were able to select any picture or pattern/s which appealed to them from one of the several books provided and to work silently on colouring them in any way they wished, with soft music in the background. A clearly delineated rule of the Wellbeing Centre was that no one else could complete an unfinished picture in the book if it was initialled. This rule was followed meticulously. Completed pictures could either be displayed in the Centre or taken home by the person who completed them. This concept of meditative colouring has become popular in recent times. Books of this type are readily available from news agencies and bookstores.

11.7.2.1 Outcomes

I found quietening the mind and gathering thoughts meant that clients using Silent Sitting before counselling sessions were able to express their thoughts and feelings better. On many occasions, they were even able to identify their own underlying issues and, with clarity and control, come up with self-generated strategies to deal with the situations in which they found themselves. They were often able to articulate possible misinterpretations of either the incidents which had upset them or their negative reactions to these incidents.

Sometimes, just by Silent Sitting and doing the colouring in, they were able to resolve their issues sufficiently without counselling intervention and to return calmly to the classroom out of which they had previously stormed.

The use of the colouring exercise was quite effective in dealing with students suffering from acute anxiety, ADHD, and also those on the Autism spectrum, particularly when coupled with Silent Sitting. On first reflection, focusing on breath might seem odd for someone whose very condition is about their inability to focus positively on any task for any length of time. I called the technique I developed the *PAUSE (see below)* method. As mentioned earlier, I often used acronyms in my work, which I printed out on small cards for the students, also laminating them so they could carry them in their pockets.

11.8 Using Focused Positive Psychology Exercises

In many of my workshops and written articles over my career, I have explained my use of acronyms, particularly of the word PAUSE. This was a simple technique which I worked out early in my counselling career, then printed on a small, laminated business-style card. I used PAUSE (along with a number of others) with many clients over the years, with a personal message on the back pertinent to the particular client who was using it.

P	put down any stuff you are using
A	assume a grounded position (feet firmly on the floor, shoulder width apart)
U	use your slow breathing count (4 in – 2 hold – 4 out)
S	still your body, then your mind
E	engage back into the task again when you feel ready

On the other side of the card was written either an acronym of the person's name or a positive affirmation they had chosen as pertinent to them (as outlined earlier in this chapter), such as: 'I choose to respond rather than react'.

The laminated card could be carried at all times by the client for easy reference when needed. Eventually, for many clients, it was enough to simply touch their pockets in which they had their cards, to reassure themselves and calm their minds, to the point that they could refocus in a positive manner and get back to what they had to do. Paying appropriate attention to confidentiality, this methodology was explained at many professional development days for teachers, ancillary staff, parents, and other counsellors. Many attendees contacted me after those meetings and workshops to ask if they too could have such a card, to remind them when they felt they were 'losing it'.

One of the fundamental essentials in resolution through counselling intervention using Positive Psychology is to be able to define the situation and explore possible alternative choices; choices which might avoid the repetition of problems or reactions to circumstances in the future, a major positive outcome of engaging in these techniques.

I used a similar approach with those difficult students whose lives easily spiralled out of control, and another example is pertinent here. It involved a Year-10 female student whose flight or fight response was interfering with her ability to control her explosive outbursts and the resultant lack of self-esteem and resilience. She had been asked to leave her previous school because of her outbursts, and her acceptance into our college was dependent on seeking regular counselling. After initial exploration of how we might work together, Silent Sitting and Positive Psychology became significant aspects used by this student to modify her attitude. In time, these were coupled with a 'numbered scale' which involved focusing on the moment at hand as well as accepting that her feelings were not only normal but also common to most people. The numbers on the scale were as follows:

1. I'm OK.
2. I'm starting to lose it. I need to still myself and practise my breathing and silence in order to go back to 1.
3. I need a break. I need help to calm down, in a quieter place.
4. It's all too much. I'm out of here.
5. I've totally lost it. I need to let off steam.

If I saw her in the yard, after sharing greetings, I would simply ask her for her number. I involved her teachers by encouraging them to do the same, and if she was higher than a two, she would be given permission to go to the Wellbeing Centre if she wished. She often took up this offer.

To incorporate the Positive Psychology approach, on the other side of her card was a positive affirmation, chosen by her, which read: *The difference between a flower and a weed is simply a matter of perception.*– Anon.

In later times, in her two years in my senior Psychology classes, she would categorise her days as either flowery or weedy, with a cheeky laugh.

We also regularly explored the principles of *The Four Agreements*[28] which are another expression of Positive Psychology. The four agreements are:

- Be impeccable with your word (our word is our power to create, express ourselves and communicate)
- Don't take anything personally (taking things personally sets us up for unnecessary suffering)
- Don't make assumptions (these create sadness and drama in our lives because we are afraid to seek clarification, fulfilling our need for justification)
- Always do your best (allows action of the first three, enabling them to become deeply ingrained habits).

Ruiz, the author of *The Four Agreements*, talked about three masteries:

- Awareness (who we are)
- Transformation (how to change)
- Intent (how loving and helpful we are with our choices)

Ruiz, like Seligman (see earlier in chapter), argued that the normal healthy human tendency is to enjoy life – to play, to explore, to be happy, and to love. When we break these agreements, we enter the blame game to justify why this is not happening in our lives. These clearly relate to the five human values of EHV, Love, Truth, Peace, Right Action, and Non-violence.

So back to my client. Over time, she would enter my office and immediately point to one of the four agreements, displayed as a poster on the wall, and say, for example, 'I think I'm making a few too many assumptions today' or 'I lied about so-and-so today and they got angry with me'. This gave a great starting point to look at possible choices which might be made to remediate the situation. I would ask her where this placed her on her five-point scale. We would then sit quietly for a few minutes before getting into the counselling session.

Coupled with this, in our early interactions, she and I explored the processes happening in her brain when she felt negative, hurt, or unhappy, which had then led to the development of her five-point card system. She often acknowledged her appreciation that someone was prepared to listen and understand her feelings and behaviour, something she believed had not happened at the school from which she had been asked to leave.

With regular practice and the better part of two years of regular sessions together, she was comfortably able to take personal responsibility for her erratic thoughts and behaviour, something she had not been ready or able to do at her previous school. She would leave the sessions much more relaxed and with a commitment to work on the agreement she felt she was not following. She became more settled and much less anxious, with fewer and fewer outbursts and much greater positive self-belief. As previously mentioned, she eventually became an enthusiastic and successful senior student in my Psychology classes.

Incidentally, some years later, we ran into each other at an overseas airport, and she joyfully told me that she was studying Psychology at university.

11.9 Concluding Comments

Having used the five-point scale, described in the previous section, with a significant number of students (dutifully modified and personalised for each specific client) over at least 20 years, I was surprised and delighted to discover eventually that this was a technique used by others.[29] I think the addition of focused Positive Psychology exercises and Silent Sitting enhanced its effectiveness.

Obviously, I am indebted to the college for its provision of a Wellbeing Centre during my professional life, a necessary place of retreat where students could come when needing time out or some structured guidance to do the Silent Sitting procedure and be immersed in Positive Psychology.

As well as the Four Agreements and Seligman's positive approach, the basic rules of the Wellbeing Centre further revolved around Jampolsky's *Seven Principles*,[30] a book about positive thoughts and attitudinal healing, which are really the principles of Positive Psychology simply expressed in a different way. It is worth listing them here:

1. Health is inner Peace
2. The essence of our being is Love
3. Giving is receiving
4. All minds are joined
5. Now is the only time there is
6. Decisions are made by learning to listen to the preference for Peace within us
7. Forgiveness is the way to true health and happiness[31]

I thoroughly recommend any interested readers of the Positive Psychological approach to read *Teach Only Love*, and each of the above seven points is able to be used as very powerful affirmational phrases during Silent Sitting. This, coupled with *Flourish*,[32] *Authentic Happiness*,[33] and *The Four Agreements*,[34] will provide a thorough grounding in the principles of using Positive Psychology and Values Education to enhance the development of individual character. Appendix 11.1 provides further resources for those interested in learning more about Positive Psychology.

Many groups of students successfully used the Wellbeing Centre to resolve their own friendship or other relationship issues by following Positive Psychology principles and the Silent Sitting protocols, with the counselling staff intervening only when absolutely necessary.

In my experience, such as described above, it is well worthwhile to practise Positive Psychology, particularly Silent Sitting, in the context of EHV and using positive affirmations, as a daily activity, since it can help to promote clarity of thought, inner peace, and reduced anxiety. Ultimately, these techniques can help students and teachers alike to cope with the current challenging times with greater resilience and strengthened character.

Appendix 11.1: Additional Reading/Resources

Books

Bush M. (2013) *Working with Mindfulness – Neuroscience at Work*, More Than Sound LLC

Bush M. (2013) *Working with Mindfulness: Research and Practice of Mindful Techniques in Organizations*, More Than Sound LLC

Csikszentmihalyi M. (1990) *Flow, Living at the Peak of Your Abilities*, Rider Press
The Dalai Lama et al. (1991) *Mind Science, An East-West Dialogue*, Wisdom Press
The Dalai Lama (2011) *The Mind's Own Physician*, Mind and Life Publications
Howell C. and Murphy M. (2011) *Release Your Worries*, Exisle Publishing Ltd
Jampolsky G. (2007) *Forgiveness the Greatest Healer of All*, Atria Books
Manocha R. (2008) *Does Meditation Have a Specific Effect?* A PhD Dissertation UNSW

Internet Resources

- Sathya Sai Education in Human Values: https://issea.org.au/resources/
- https://www.goodreads.com/quotes/1163097-keep-your-thoughts-positive-because-your-thought-become-your-words
- https://quotes.thefamouspeople.com/sathya-sai-baba-6338.php
- https://www.beyondthemind.com/
- https://www.thecut.com/2015/11/why-self-affirmation-works.html
- https://thebestbrainpossible.com/affirmations-brain-depression-anxiety/

Positive Psychology Resources and Videos

- https://positivepsychologyprogram.com/what-is-positive-psychology-definition/
- https://www.psychologytoday.com/us/blog/the-good-life/200805/what-is-positive-psychology-and-what-is-it-not
- https://www.ted.com/talks/martin_seligman_on_the_state_of_psychology?language=en
- https://www.youtube.com/watch?v=faT8jw17RHE
- https://www.youtube.com/watch?v=Mp8xN1K-ITs
- https://www.youtube.com/watch?v=Mp8xN1K-IT
- https://www.youtube.com/watch?v=Mp8xN1K-ITs
- https://www.youtube.com/watch?v=Mp8xN1K-ITs

Notes

1 R. Siegel, "The Science of Mindfulness: A Research-Based Path to Wellbeing," in The Great Courses (Virginia: The Teaching Company, 2014).
2 Mahatma Gandhi. https://www.goodreads.com/quotes/1163097-keep-your-thoughts-positive-because-your-thought-become-your-words accessed 22-2-2022.
3 Positive Psychology Institute (Apr 3, 2015). https://www.positivepsychologyinstitute.com.au/ accessed 9-8-2022.
4 Sathya Sai Baba, *Sathya Sai Speaks* (Prasanthi Nilayam, India: Books and Publications Trust, 1965), Vol. 5, p. 290.
5 G. Jampolsky, *Teach Only Love* (New York, NY: Bantam Books, 1983).

6 A. Ellis and W. Dryden, *The Practice of Rational Emotive Behaviour Therapy* (New York, NY: Springer Publishing, 2007).
7 W. Glasser, *Choice Theory* (New York, NY: Harper Collins, 1998).
8 M. Seligman, *Authentic Happiness* (Australia: Penguin Books, 2004).
9 *Ibid.*
10 P. Spencer and M. Hartstone, *Psychology for South Australia: Stage 2* (Milton: John Wiley & Sons, 2007). https://stage2psychatfaith.weebly.com/textbook.html accessed 25-2-2022.
11 Selye's General Adaption Syndrome (GAS). https://www.sciencedirect.com/topics/immunology-and-microbiology/adaptation-syndrome accessed 26-2-2022.
12 J. Manuello, U. Vercelli, A. Nani, T. Costa, and F. Cauda, "Mindfulness Meditation and Consciousness: An Integrative Neuroscientific Perspective," *Indian Journal of Psychiatry* 40 (2016): 67–78.
13 *Ibid.*
14 Christopher N. Cascio, Matthew Brook O'Donnell, Francis J. Tinney, Matthew D. Lieberman, Shelley E. Taylor, Victor J. Strecher, and Emily B. Falk, "Self-affirmation Activates Brain Systems Associated with Self-related Processing and Reward and Is Reinforced by Future Orientation," *Social Cognitive and Affective Neuroscience Journal* 11, no. 54 (2016): 621–629.
15 S. Halpern. *Inner Peace, and Gifts of the Angels* (New York, NY: Open Channel Sound Company, 1994).
16 https://loggerheadpublishing.co.uk accessed 27-2-2022.
17 *Ibid.*
18 Sathya Sai Baba, *Summer Showers 2000* (Prasnathi Nilayam, India: Books and Publications Trust, 2000), 15; *The Ideal Student* (Prasnathi Nilayam, India: Books and Publications Trust, 2000), 15.
19 Anonymous, Spectrum Education Poster.
20 Poster quotation by Henry Ford, Spectrum Education.
21 M. Seligman, *Learned Optimism* (North Sydney, Australia: William Heineman, 2011).
22 Collins School Dictionary.
23 Sathya Sai Baba, *Summer Showers,* 2000.
24 Kevin Francis, the author's own phrase.
25 Halpern, *Inner Peace, and Gifts of the Angels,* 1994.
26 R. Manocha, *Silence Your Mind* (Australia: Hachette, 2013).
27 https://www.beyondthemind.com/ accessed 1-3-2022.
28 Dom Miguel Ruiz, *The Four Agreements* (USA: Amber Allen Publishing, 1997).
29 K. Buron and M. Curtis, *The Incredible 5-Point Scale* (USA: Kansas APC Publishing Co, 2013).
30 J. Jampolsky, *Teach Only Love* (USA: Atria Books, 2008).
31 Jampolsky, *Teach Only Love,* 2008.
32 M. Seligman, *Flourish: A Visionary New Understanding of Happiness and Wellbeing* (USA: Atria Books, 2011).
33 M. Seligman, *Authentic Happiness* (Australia: William Heinemann, 2011).
34 Ruiz, *The Four Agreements,* 1997.

Chapter 12

Curbing Excesses

Placing a Ceiling on Desires

Kevin Francis

12.1 Introduction

This chapter looks at a particular aspect of Education in Human Values (EHV) called *Ceiling on Desires*.[1] This name is used as a personalised aspect of sustainability and conservation education and practice, while also having relevance in the development of character and human personality. The concept is more than relevant to the current social context of emphasis on self-centredness, consumerism, exploitation of increasingly limited resources, and the inequitable division and use of resources such as food, energy, wealth, and water, as discussed in Chapter 1.

The chapter initially explores the psychology of needs and desires and their relationship to the development of character and personality. It also explores other definitions and descriptors from a range of published sources. The Ceiling on Desires programme does not deny the human conditions of desiring a happy, healthy, and more contented and sustainable life. Rather, it suggests that a ceiling, or self-imposed limit, on individual desires, might curb the discrepancies between the 'haves' and 'have-nots' and lead to a more just and peaceful way of living, which ultimately benefits all people on the planet. By examining ways to curb our desires, through self-evaluation and appropriate research, it is hoped that this EHV practice will lead us to plan actions to improve both personal practice and character within a context of personal relevance. An added bonus to this approach is a more compassionate and socially just society. If values education is seen as the process by which people give moral values to their own lives and compassion towards others, Ceiling on Desires can be viewed as a practical aspect or method for doing this.

The chapter looks at how some others see the need to develop ceilings on desires, relating it to both psychological and philosophical theories. Philosophically, Ceiling on Desires is more commonly linked to excesses in materialism and indulgences in personal gratification, which seems to be one of society's ongoing major concerns. The chapter also explores aspects of the Ceiling on Desires approach, which involves examining our own habits and relating these to personality development, character, and values education.

DOI: 10.4324/9781003478607-13

A basic premise is that all human beings are driven by desires (needs) which generate conflict within us if the pursuit of these desires/needs is thwarted or denied. The Ceiling on Desires programme is not about stopping the necessary desires/needs but reining them in, not only to manage them but to enable us to live more contented lives by limiting their effects on us. Activities can be created to increase awareness of the need to place ceilings on our own desires as a necessary part of personal development and character education.

It is hoped that this chapter will stimulate reflection on the following questions:

- Why is such a concept as 'Ceiling on Desires' necessary in our current societal climate?
- In what areas might we need to have a ceiling on our desires?
- How would you recognise people who practise placing ceilings on their desires?
- What are the key aspects of this concept in reducing personal impacts on other people and the wider world?
- How does this help to develop character?
- Do our schools currently develop this aspect of character as you would wish?
- If it is being developed, how is it being achieved?
- Could more be done about this?

After reading this chapter, you will be able to:

- Understand the philosophy and psychology behind the concept of 'Ceiling on Desires'
- Identify your own understanding of the need to place ceilings on desires and refine this understanding by incorporating the views of others
- Explain the various aspects of Ceiling on Desires
- Describe how it can be used in practice
- Begin to propose ways to support the practice of Ceiling on Desires in yourself and others
- Develop ways of enacting their ideas
- Incorporate these ideas across the curriculum, where appropriate

12.2 The Neurological Basis of Desires

Lieberman and Long[2] explained human desires as a response to the 'up' neurotransmitter, dopamine, which makes us all desire what we do not yet have, driving us to constantly seek new things and experiences. They argued it is the source of: *The undeniable itch that drives scientists to find explanations and philosophers to find order, reason and meaning. It is fuel for the motor of our dreams: it is the source of our despair when we fail. It is why we seek and succeed: it is why we discover and prosper. It is also why we are never happy for very long.*[3]

Dopamine enables us to move beyond the pleasure of just 'being', so that we explore the myriad of developmental possibilities that come from our imaginations. The discovery of dopamine in the brain was relatively recent in 1957. Kathleen Montagu,[4] a researcher in the United Kingdom, made the link between it and norepinephrine, the form of adrenaline found in the brain when its presence was found to be related to experiencing feelings of pleasure. It was labelled 'The pleasure molecule' and was seen as an integral part of the reward circuit. Yet, after many further experiments, scientists concluded that, ultimately, dopamine is not about pleasure at all but is in fact the key to explaining and predicting behaviour across many human endeavours relating to future events in people's lives, connecting more to the realms of possibility. Dopamine seems to have a very specific job, to maximise resources to enable us to be happy or successful in the future, and always to pursue better things. These desire-driven impulses are somewhat of a roller coaster, as when the initial desire is fulfilled, unless there is a conscious change from anticipation to reasoned experience, the desire cycle is repeated over and over without any lasting satisfaction. Thus, the major setback of unfettered desires is inevitable disappointment. The rational and logical aspects of the mind need to be engaged if we are to gain lasting happiness and contentment.

Perhaps, after all, it would be better to define dopamine not as the 'pleasure' molecule but rather as the 'anticipation of desire' molecule. Lieberman and Long suggested that a more satisfying approach to contentment only comes about when we transition consciously from future-oriented dopamine to present-oriented chemicals such as serotonin, oxytocin, endorphins, and endocannabinoids such as anandamide, which give us pleasure from sensations and emotions. This leads to behaviour characterised by cooperation, compassion, and empathy.

As a professional counsellor, I have observed repeatedly that, unless it is reined in, this initial 'dopamine-chase' aspect of our desires, particularly in regard to relationships, frequently ends in unhappy, bitter, and broken individuals seeking help. The same could also be said when dealing with material possessions. I have often seen people caught up in the constant cycle of dissatisfaction with objects when, say, a new model of mobile phone or other electronic gadgetry is released. The perceived need for an iPhone 5 quickly became replaced by the iPhone 7, then the iPhone 10, etc, etc.; a marketing ploy well used by advertisers in these current times. We could, of course, link this to fashion, appearance, food preferences, and even to musical preferences as well.

It is not easy to detach from the dopaminergic thrill of anticipation of future pursuits or the challenges of passionate anticipation, but the ability to do so creates a more contented life and a major move towards lasting self-contentment and happiness. Placing limits on our desires and practising a disciplined approach to living in the 'now' provides a very real pathway.

This clearly defines the need for a Ceiling on Desires.

12.3 The Psychological Basis for the Need for a Ceiling on Desires: Desires and the Development of Personality

Let us now look at some personality development theories and how they relate to human desires. It will become self-evident that both theories indicate the need for modification of these desires to reach our full character and personality potentials; that is, effectively to place a ceiling on them.

12.3.1 Freud's Structure of the Mind

First, let us examine Freud's structures of the mind and their relationship to personality and character. Freud[5] divided the mind into three elements, which he labelled *Id*, *Ego*, and *Superego*. It should be noted that Ego and Superego have different connotations from the generally negative concept of ego in modern contemporary society.

Freud suggested that the Id consists of unconscious instincts and can be thought of as a reservoir of psychic energy to allow our desires to be expressed. We are all born with Id so that, as newborns, a significant majority of us have our basic needs met, pretty-well much on demand. This is the first human manifestation of desire, so the Id is known by Freudian psychologists as the 'pleasure principle', that is the quest for pleasure with no consideration for other demands of the situation.

Freud proposed the concept that the Ego develops to satisfy the needs of the Id. The Ego is the rational part of the mind, which develops out of an awareness that one cannot always get what one wants. It emerges within the first few years of life, when a grasp of reality demands constraints on life experiences through rational thought processes, eventually leading to internal negotiations between the Id and Freud's third concept, the Superego. Because the Ego relates to real-world situations, it is also referred to as the 'reality principle'.

The third component, Superego, is the moral branch of the mind/personality, which develops in response to moral and ethical restraints placed on the individual by parents and society, embodying parental and societal values. It enforces rules by creating anxiety and discomfort, leading to experiences of cognitive dissonance which require resolution. Superego is, therefore, known as the 'morality principle', equated with the conscience, thereby dictating and defining our philosophical concepts of 'right and wrong'.

A healthy individual is one who has these three elements in balance and harmony. An individual with a dominant Id can manifest as being bound up in self-gratification and uncaring of others. Such people are often overly competitive and possessive, to their detriment. Similarly, if the Ego is too strong, a person can become extremely rational and efficient but lacking in emotional connection. This can cause the person to be too cold, boring, or distant or to lack empathy. If the Superego is too strong, it usually manifests in one of two ways. It causes the person either to feel guilty all the time or to be unbearably saintly. Learning to place a Ceiling on Desires assists both the Freudian Ego and Superego to keep the Id in check or at least in balance.

12.3.2 Maslow's Humanistic Approach

Abraham Maslow's Humanistic approach to personality[6] and human character development clearly shows the influence of desires, which Maslow described as 'needs'. He stressed that a person's positive human qualities and capacity for personal growth, and freedom to choose one's own destiny are based on the natural fulfilment of a *hierarchy of needs*. According to Maslow,[7] personality is described in motivational terms as an individual's life, values, goals, and perceptions. Maslow saw these as being focused on the satisfaction of a set of needs, which he arranged as a universal hierarchy. The main drive in a person's development is to have one's lower-level needs met before one becomes aware of and tries to fulfil needs at the higher levels. The end result of such development is Self-Actualisation, leading to Transcendence.

The following representation is my interpretation of what each of these levels of development means in relation to my counselling young people about Ceiling on Desires, as represented by the words added to the right-hand side of Figure 12.1.

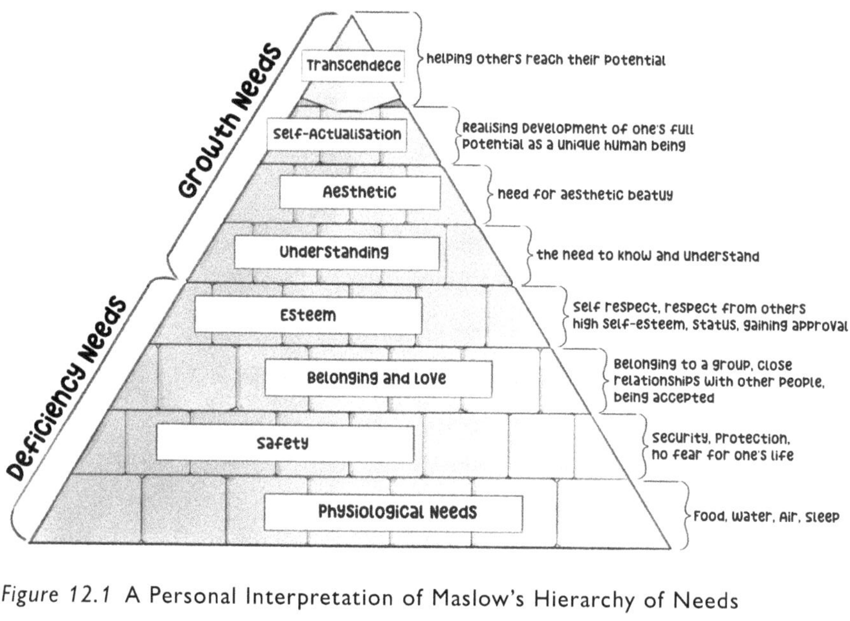

Figure 12.1 A Personal Interpretation of Maslow's Hierarchy of Needs

Maslow defined a self-actualised person as someone who is:

- reality centred,
- accepting of oneself and others,
- spontaneous and creative,
- independent of the environment (mentally), and
- an individual with a system of morality that is internalised.

As part of his theory, he recognised 'Peak Experiences' as a possible way of providing a route to achieving personal growth, integration, and fulfilment, so that ultimately the person feels at one with the universe, with a well-defined empathetic sense of purpose. Peak experiences are related to the fulfilment of desires and a recognition of their limits, which allows people to transcend or go beyond the limitations of the self.

Issues arise, including mental health issues, when the fulfilment of one's needs is frustrated, or when one gets stuck in any of the deficiency needs; this marries very nicely into the need to place a ceiling on these desires/needs at any of these levels. Self-actualisation (and transcendence) can only be achieved through discipline, and through placing limitations on desires, which may necessarily mean experiencing some levels of deprivation, frustration, pain, or loss. Indeed, these are often what constitute the 'peak experience', when they provide insight into our life purpose.

12.4 The Philosophical Basis for the Need for a Ceiling on Desires

Even though character development is examined in some detail in Chapter 6, it is worth referring to it briefly in this context as well.

The Jubilee Centre for Character and Virtue[8] links good character to human flourishing, which it defines as … *the widely accepted goal of life. To flourish is not only to be happy, but to fulfil one's potential. Flourishing is the aim of character education, which is critical to its achievement.*[9]

The founder of the EHV programme, Sathya Sai Baba, talked a lot about character and the need for its development. His writings link character with desires, *Students should develop good character along with acquisition of knowledge. Education without culture is useless. Just as the electric current flows when the positive and negative come together, likewise your life will be redeemed when education is coupled with culture. Students are good, but they do not know the right path. Some know what is good, but they do not follow because of limitless desires.*[10] Further, he linked culture and society to character, noting that *Character is based on good conduct. Only a young person with good qualities can become a good leader. He/she must take part in social service as a preparation for leadership. Everyone should realise that personal happiness is bound up with the happiness of society as a whole. Parents and teachers should develop such attitudes in the students.*[11]

The Scottish philosopher Alasdair MacIntyre[12] (see also Chapter 3) suggested that individuals can only function as modern life demands if desires are expressed and have a sense of order about them. He further suggested that desires need to be contained, implying the juxtaposition of placing some sort of ceiling on those desires. He claimed that *Desires....find their objects within lives structured by the needs, activities, responsibilities, and enjoyments of individuals, families and other groups, and we will not know how to think about desires until we are also able to think rightly about needs, activities, responsibilities, enjoyments, and the relationships between these. What individuals need is that without which they will be unable in adult life to engage in those activities and to discharge those responsibilities that are the mark of a fully participant member of their society.*[13]

MacIntyre further postulated that individuals whose needs are met also display a desire to find purpose in their pursuit of activities. He advocated that our attitudes, feelings, and desires are paramount to meeting our needs and engaging in selected activities which help to discharge our responsibilities and provide enjoyment.

This all fits in quite well with Maslow's concept of 'deficiency needs' which have to be met before we can consider more esoteric 'growth needs', aligned with MacIntyre's concept of desires. According to MacIntyre, our desires multiply, to the point when the need arises to make choices. An individual's powers of discrimination come into play here to make choices about which desires should be given priority, which are realistic, which are more fantasy, and which need to be made in dealing with conflicts arising from desires. The question arises as to whether the pursuit of one's own desires might interfere with other people's chances to satisfy or act upon theirs.

The practical realities are that life itself places limits on the human condition. We know that the body temperature is normally around 36.6–37.2 degrees Centigrade. If this goes beyond 38 degrees, fever has set in due to some disorder in the body. We inhale and exhale at a normal rate. If there is a slight increase or decrease in the rate, it indicates disorder in the body. Excessive food creates health issues such as high blood pressure. Changes in the pulse rate or blood pressure also indicate a possible health disorder. Eardrums also cannot tolerate hearing beyond a certain volume, and we close our ears or put cotton wool inside them when faced with excessive noise levels. If you cross such limits, even to a small extent, it can be dangerous or harmful to the body. Similar limits apply to many organisms in the natural world around us. Thus, it seems obvious that there is a need for ranking and placing limits or a Ceiling on Desires as well as some sort of societal standards in the pursuit of individual and societal happiness and a reduction in personal and community conflict. At the same time, it is important to acknowledge the need for a more sustainable and ethical approach to the fulfilment of needs and desires.

Understanding desire and placing a practical ceiling on one's desires is therefore necessary for human flourishing, building character, and moving towards a better society. The EHV practice of Ceiling on Desires provides a methodology to achieve this. The next section outlines this practical and achievable pathway.

12.5 A Practical Approach to Help Place a Ceiling on Desires

The *Ceiling on Desires* programme of EHV was outlined by Sathya Sai Baba, and initially involved looking at four aspects of everyday living, *Food*, *Energy*, *Money*, and *Time*, and how to place limits upon them. Phyllis Krystal,[14] an English psychologist, outlined the following approach to use discrimination with our desires and place a practical limit in relation to them. Each of these sections starts with a quotation from Sathya Sai Baba.[15] From the outset, it is pertinent to point out that these four elements are interrelated and overlap in many instances.

12.5.1 Food

Our first topic for this Ceiling on Desires programme, *food*, is also related to money, which in turn may possibly determine the quality and quantity of the food we eat. Despite this, we still have choices, within our monetary frameworks, as to the sort of food we eat, the amount of food we consume, whether we waste food or not, and whether we waste money when buying food.

The following quotes relate very specifically to the need to place a ceiling on our desires for food.[16]

> The quality of food intake by the well-to-do is now much beyond essential requirements. Overeating has become a fashion. The breakfast does not serve to break any fast, for there has been no fasting at all. It is as good as a full meal. Lunch is pressed in and consists of many dishes, chosen for the palate rather than to assuage hunger. Tea is tea only in name: it includes rather heavy fare, out of all proportion to the needs of the body. Dinner at night is the heaviest meal and includes the largest variety and so one goes to bed, weighted with unwanted stuff, to roll from side to side, in a vain effort to get a few minutes of sleep. The shortage of food grains is mainly due to bad and wasteful eating habits; it can be set right, and people can live longer and more healthily, if only they eat the minimum, rather than fill themselves with the maximum.

> The food that is required for sustaining the body is conducive to health only when it is consumed within limits. Overeating poisons the system. Food may give satisfaction or cause illness. By his food habits man is becoming prey to disease. Food is essential, but it must be taken within limits for it to be wholesome.

Even in Australia, despite the abundance of nutritious food, many are malnourished because they eat unsuitable food. Not only do people waste money on takeaways, but they also then waste more on dealing with the ailments derived from poor eating habits. People see takeaway food as convenient and time and energy-saving. But is it really? A number of questions arise about food. How often are people tempted into supersizing? Where is the balance? What about food used for comfort, or as a bribe? Or is the withdrawal of food being used as a method of control or as punishment? There are temptations to indulge in greed and gluttony.

Food can also be related to a number of undesirable character traits. For example, *pride* can be associated with food, whether exhibited by putting on an expensive dinner or by preparing it so as to show off our skills and receive excessive praise. *Laziness* and *slothfulness* from overindulgence speak for themselves.

There are negative emotions connected to the topic of food: *Fear* of not having enough, or enough of the foods we most desire, *anger* when not getting our favourite foods, *impatience* in waiting to be fed, *resentment* towards others with more than us, *anger* and *frustration* when we do not get the food we crave, and *addiction* to certain foods.

A very practical way of cutting the waste of food from our lives is to ask ourselves the following questions:

- What are our areas of waste?
- Do you plan ahead to avoid buying food you do not need?
- Are we impulse buyers?
- Are we impulse eaters?
- Do we buy so much that it spoils and needs to be thrown away?
- Do we buy fresh produce or processed food?
- Do we check ingredients for unhealthy content?
- Do we eat balanced, appropriately sized proportions of food, or indulge in seconds or supersizing?

In answering these questions, it is relatively easy to engineer a plan to place a Ceiling on Desires for our food consumption.

Now let us broaden the concept of food beyond that which we physically eat. Phyllis Krystal also spoke about the need to limit 'food' that is not physical food. She describes this as 'food for the mind', that is, those factors which affect our emotions and thought patterns, the things 'ingested' by our five senses. These include the music and words we use and hear, the movies and books we see and read, the odours we smell, the materials and objects we touch, and the actions we indulge in. Many studies have been conducted to explore the relationship between the music we listen to and our moods and frames of mind.[17]

One new area not investigated in Krystal's original writings relates to society's current relationship with the digital media we use, whether it is positive or negative, or constructive or destructive. This will be examined in more detail later in this chapter.

12.5.2 Energy

This section looks at *energy* from two perspectives: Internal or personal energy and external energy, and the ceilings that can be placed on both.

> Our physical, mental, and spiritual energies should never be wasted. You might ask me; 'How are we wasting our energies?' When you see bad things, your energy is wasted. Hearing bad things, speaking evil, thinking evil thoughts, and doing evil deeds wastes your energy. Conserve your energy in these five areas and make your life more meaningful.
>
> You are free to use as you like all the things given to you, subject to one condition: You will have to face the consequences of your actions. This means that you cannot abuse the freedom given to you to use the things that are provided for you. When you misuse anything, you have to bear the resulting misery. When you make good use of anything, you will enjoy the benefits therefrom.[18]

In contrast to the equal amount of time available to everyone, the amount of energy varies considerably from person to person. Whatever our energy levels, our energy should be used in productive and helpful pursuits, and it is in our best interests to avoid wasting it unnecessarily. There is a general consensus that the source of our energy is internal and is not just related to the food we eat. We also need appropriate levels of sleep, rest, relaxation, and exercise to maintain our balance and conserve energy. A recent Harvard Medical study[19] indicated that energy is best utilised by a fit and healthy body.

12.5.2.1 *Personal Energy Wasters 1 – Anxiety and Stress*

Anxiety, stress, and tension use vast reserves of our energy, even more than physical activity. Instead of merely feeling pleasantly tired, when tense, we may find our sleep disrupted or unrefreshing. This often also results in significant time wastage, with excessive worrying about both unlikely negative and even possible positive future events. For some, inappropriate use of food can be a consequence of stress and anxiety.

12.5.2.2 *Personal Energy Wasters 2 – Negative Emotions*

In my professional opinion, negative emotions are perhaps the greatest thieves of personal energy, robbing us of significant amounts of drive and motivation, and causing us to deal with the consequences for both ourselves and the recipients of our negative emotions.

Anger is perhaps the worst culprit, as it uses vast amounts of energy, apart from setting up situations which require significant amounts of time to remedy the consequences of angry outbursts. *Irritation* and *frustration* are milder forms of anger, relating to desires to control situations which may be beyond our control. *Resistance* to change is similar to *anger*, defined in this context as relating to insisting on our own wills at the expense of others.

'Fear, guilt, worry, indecision, and procrastination' all block the natural flow of energy while focusing excessively on the past and the future. This causes inertia and blockages in our abilities to carry out meaningful plans and solve problems.

What about excessive competitiveness? This is often disguised as exaggerated levels of ambition or disproportionate dedication to tasks. Further, I am sure we are all aware of the amount of energy and time wasted by perfectionists who do things over and over again with minimal task improvements. Then there can be the challenge, or striving, to win is a fine motivator for many people, but becomes an energy drain when it develops into *having* to win at all costs, which in turn can lead to cheating or undermining of others. Excessive praise and emphasis on winning can lead to an over-emphasis on ego (see above), which in turn means that when we lose, resentment and revenge cause further wastage of our energy, particularly when it is expressed as anger. One solution to curbing such energy wastage is to celebrate what is right with the world and rejoice in the actual competition, taking both winning and losing as simply part of life's twists and turns. There are many circumstances where cooperation and sharing of tasks have greater rewards than 'winning'.

Personal qualities such as looking for the positive in others, developing and showing empathy, and expressing gratitude for opportunities and experiences that enhance personal growth help to place ceilings on excessive outbursts of emotional energy. When we accept the idea that choosing to respond (cognitive) rather than react (emotional) takes excessive emotion out of situations, our energy remains on a more even keel. Rational thought also helps, for example, being able to accept that some things cannot be changed: It is just the way they are, so we can focus our energies on the things that we do have control over. Making time for personal reflection and practising Silent Sitting is another way not just to conserve personal energy but to build up reserves of it. A personal audit might be of use here. This could include such questions as:

- Do you work to a plan and set priorities?
- Are you a perfectionist?
- Do you expend unnecessary amounts of energy in order to please or impress others?
- Are you a procrastinator?
- Are you an impatient person?
- Do you plan groups of tasks to minimise internal and external energy wastage?

12.5.2.3 What about External Energy Usage?

This is probably a much easier task to address in terms of curbing energy use. I am sure all of us could outline ways to conserve fuel, electricity, water, and other physical resources of the planet and develop a personal plan of action. This plan could include simple practical things we might do to reduce our external energy consumption. The following three questions could serve as a starting point:

- How might we use less energy with transport?
- How could we cut down on electricity usage?
- How might we use fewer consumables thereby cutting down on energy costs in their manufacture?

Feel free to add your own questions to this list and to discuss these issues with family, friends, and work colleagues.

I find it helpful to also list resource requirements for better energy usage under the following headings:

- Personal
- Technology
- Media usage
- Finances
- Household
- Transport
- Workplace
- Normal duties
- Spiritual practices

Again, this list is not exhaustive, so feel free to add any that you think need to be addressed. You might want to explore these further under key issues with a possible time frame. You can do this by identifying key energy wastage areas that need immediate or near-term resolution and the consequences of not changing (emotionally, spiritually, physically, socially, and environmentally). Long-term energy wastage needs long-term resolutions.

12.5.3 Money

The amount of money, or lack of it, is a major focus in all societies around the world. Once again, it is pertinent to examine some comments about money made by the initiator of the *Ceiling on Desires* programme: *Money has to be given its own place of importance, it has to be used in the best way possible. Because you do not make the best use of any given thing, you cannot understand what it is there for. You should, for instance, use the power of intelligence to avoid the misuse of money*'. Next, he pointed out that '*Money is neither positive or negative; it depends on how it is used*'. '*Money comes and goes, morality comes and grows. …*

Man has been enslaved by money.... One should seek to possess only as much money as is most essential for living.[20] Then came this comparison, *Money is of the nature of manure. Piled up in one place, it pollutes the air. Spread it wide, scatter it over the fields – it rewards you with a bumper harvest. So too, when money is spent in all the four quarters for promoting good works, it yields contentment and happiness in plenty.*' ... '*But today, such deeds of renunciation and such holy thoughts are absent.*[21]

We need to determine how to discover where and how we waste money in our everyday lives and reduce this waste. It has already been noted that we potentially waste a lot of money when purchasing food. I am certain we could all list other purchases that are a wastage when it comes to money. Perhaps the first step is to answer these three questions:

- Do we budget?
- What do we understand by 'budgeting'?
- Why does this word have such negative connotations?

It is probably helpful to take some time to compile a list of weekly/monthly expenses!

There are simple ways to save money and conserve energy by limiting use of utilities, such as electricity, water, gas, and other resources. Limiting telephone calls, text messages, and social media usage can reduce energy usage, and completely switching off devices when not actually using them can be a great energy saver while also saving money. Taking a packed lunch rather than buying lunch is one obvious way to save significant amounts of money. Avoiding wasting food and refraining from buying impulsively rather than planning purchases can also save significant amounts of money. It might be a good time here to develop your own strategies to save money by considering the following list, and you might want to add items to this list to reflect your own situation:

- Food purchases
- Car usage
- Household items
- Clothing
- Energy usage
- Electronics
- Household costs
- Water

12.5.4 Time

Time is the commodity that we all have equally at our disposal, as every one of us only has 24 hours each day. This is the one aspect of our lives that we cannot save or stockpile. Wasted time is gone forever. In this regard, the founder of

EHV says, *Of all the precious things in the world, time is the most precious. Think over how you are spending your precious time. Health which is spoiled and lost can sometimes be recovered with the help of medicines. But time which has gone is lost for good; there is no way for it to ever come back and be used again.... You cannot know at what time, in what place and in what circumstances danger may present itself and come your way. Therefore, you have to sanctify the time at your disposal now and use it properly, recognising its sacredness and preciousness.*[22]

It is helpful to critically evaluate our usage of time. These questions might provide a good starting point:

- How do we budget time?
- How much of the day is unstructured or undefined?
- At what time of the day are we most productive?
- Are we morning, afternoon, or evening people?
- Is our 'spare' time wasteful?
- How much time do we dedicate to idle and unnecessary activities?
- Do we budget appropriate time for sleep?
- What are the key 'spending areas' of our time?

Answering these questions leads logically to a possible review of key objectives and critical success factors, such as identifying those things which make our time usage unique and effective and acknowledging our 'time wasters'.

Some possible time-wasting areas could include excessive use of television and digital media, overly worrying, daydreaming, and indulging in self-pity, idle chit-chat and overindulgence in sleep. Do we plan activities and trips to maximise our efforts? Do we choose the quickest and most economical routes, combining several errands at once?

It might be useful here to add any other areas which need attention and improvement, or a more cautious approach, in your life. Such critical evaluation can lead to more effective use of our time, such as time budgeting and maximising effective time usage. This could include reducing areas of wastage and adjusting committed time allocations for work, service to others, family time, rest time, and leisure. This can lead to better management and more efficient usage of both time and energy.

12.6 Human Values, Ceiling on Desires, and Sustainability

Sustainability can be defined as meeting our needs and desires without reducing the ability of others to meet their own.[23] Ideally, this 'others' needs to include all of nature, not just humans. Society most often relates this to life's physical, economic, and natural resource needs, but as a positive psychologist, I believe it also refers, equally importantly, to our social and emotional needs. This clearly relates to the need for a ceiling on those very desires which help to sustain us.

So how do we relate the five human values of Truth, Love, Peace, Right Action, and Non-violence to the concepts of sustainability through practising Ceiling on Desires? Let us examine each of the five human values in turn with this focus in mind.

12.6.1 How Does Love Relate to Ceiling on Desires?

Love in action supports a ceiling on our desires by encouraging sharing with others in all the areas previously discussed of money, food, time, and energy. It can also be expressed as loving the physical environment by paying attention to sustainable use of natural resources and reducing such things as our carbon footprint. This also includes respect for fellow creatures and their habitats.

12.6.2 How Does Peace Relate to Ceiling on Desires?

Peace in action involves reducing stress and anxiety about money, food, time, and energy. It also involves living in harmony with the physical environment and protecting the earth and its resources whenever and wherever possible. The lack of peace is also a possible consequence of inappropriate or excessive use of digital media and online social interactions. This will be examined in more specific detail later in this chapter.

12.6.3 How Does Truth Relate to Ceiling on Desires?

Truth in action manifests as being true to oneself when considering usage of the four aspects of money, food, time, and energy, and being consistent in thoughts, words, and actions. It involves committing wholly to a chosen plan of action when placing a ceiling on our desires, both for our own benefit and that of society.

12.6.4 How Does Right Action Relate to Ceiling on Desires?

Practical right action involves not being wasteful with money, food, time, water, or energy. This manifests as compassion and empathy in thoughts, words, and actions, and by following through with chosen plans of action for the betterment of others and the Earth itself. These are also actions of personal sustainability and integrity.

12.6.5 How Does Non-violence Relate to Ceiling on Desires?

Non-violence, in practice, means being helpful and refraining from causing hurt to others and caring for the physical environment in all its manifest areas.

This is brought about by kind thoughts, words, and actions, as well as by actively making a positive impact upon and improving the environment, both socially and physically.

12.7 Two Modern Time and Energy Wasters: Social Media and Screen Time

Young people have grown up with smartphones and other electronic devices that give us access to so much information and other contacts, not to mention making us accessible to others as well, yet for older people, it is very hard to recall life before the explosion of these technologies. We become easily distracted and face constant interruptions 24/7. This constant barrage of information and interaction has led to fragmentation of our powers of concentration. Indeed, it has been suggested that repeated interruptions seriously affect our ability to concentrate and remain focused. For example, research discussed by Griffey in a report found that those constantly distracted by emails, text messages, phone calls, and video linkups showed a 10% drop in their IQ scores, which was twice the effect of the impact of smoking marijuana. The report said that: *More than half of the 1100 participants said they always responded to an email immediately or as soon as possible, while 21% admitted they would interrupt a meeting to do so. Constant interruptions can have the same effect as the loss of a night's sleep.*[24]

Research from the UK's telecom regulator *Ofcom*[25] showed that people check their smartphones on average every 12 minutes during waking hours and a staggering 71% reported that they never turn their phones off, with 40% checking them within five minutes of waking. Furthermore, the average number of interruptions is six or seven per hour, or some 60 or so interruptions per day. The study also reported that it takes about 15 minutes to resume the previous levels of concentration on the task or activity that was interrupted.

The most common justification for this behaviour is a belief that we are becoming much better at multitasking. From a neuroscience perspective, however, we are simply switching rapidly from one task to another, involving increased levels of the stress hormones, adrenaline, and cortisol, which are well known to create and maintain a hyper-alert state towards stimuli and mirror a similar response to addiction.

The last few years have seen an explosion in the use and influence of social media platforms, both for legitimate and negative uses. So, what are the negatives related to social media use, apart from time wastage? First, as recent events have clearly shown, there are very few checks and balances as to the veracity of the information being presented. This means it is very easy to hurt others, with few barriers to block damaging information, and limited opportunities to correct false impressions. Visual information can be doctored, falsified, or enhanced to create whatever effect or message is required. Now, there is also AI-generated material through apps such as 'ChatGPT' that automatically generate content and video apps that generate false images. News reports constantly bombard us with the tragic consequences of online bullying and harassment. There are no 'time outs' from these, as the Internet is a 24/7 phenomenon, unlike physical safety, where there is the ability to remove oneself from a situation, at least temporarily.

Any written communication misses or ignores the major contributions of body language and paralinguistic cues such as emphasis on particular words, use of pauses, or loudness or softness of speech.[26] Here, instead, are what occurs with the written communication of social media:

- Information is read through the 'eyes' of how we feel at the time.
- There is no body language to give us clues.
- There is no tone of voice, so we do not know which words the sender has emphasised.
- We may misinterpret what someone else has said and so become disconnected, creating a lack of oneness.

Here is an example I have often used to illustrate this; the written phrase '*I didn't say you stole my smartphone*' can be read by emphasising just the underlined word as shown below. There are now seven different meanings to be derived when reading this sentence.

- ***I*** didn't say you stole my smartphone.
- I ***didn't*** say you stole my smartphone.
- I didn't ***say*** you stole my smartphone.
- I didn't say ***you*** stole my smartphone.
- I didn't say you ***stole*** my smartphone.
- I didn't say you stole ***my*** smartphone.
- I didn't say you stole my ***smartphone.***

Reflecting on these gives us a greater understanding of the potential stress the written word can create, as determined by the emotional state of the reader. Such examples can clearly produce discomfort, disharmony, a lack of connection or oneness. Two major challenging contributors to a lack of oneness, being an inability to place a ceiling on expressing both fear and anger.

12.7.1 *Looking at and Placing a Ceiling on Fear and Anger*

12.7.1.1 *Fear*

From an evolutionary perspective, fear is an emotion that has helped us survive by avoiding things which might hurt us, which is a healthy behaviour. This is sometimes identified as rational fear and is part of the 'fight or flight' response, necessary for our survival.

Irrational fear, however, is imagined and often leads to unfounded anxiety and distress. This type of fear is useful as an acronym that breaks down as:

- **F**alse
- **E**vidence
- **A**ppearing
- **R**eal

Once we are able to acknowledge this rationally, we can choose to respond in ways which are more realistic and conducive to promoting peace of mind and greater understanding. I think this type of fear is a major contributor to the disharmony created by our responses to multimedia and online usage and the resultant, often negative, behaviour it generates. We are all too aware of the devasting consequences that can occur when we feel constantly ridiculed, excluded, unworthy, and inadequate as a result of online targeting.

12.7.1.2 *Anger*

Anger is perhaps the biggest block to developing oneness and is a common first reaction when we are threatened, frustrated, or unhappy, with or without knowing why. When our 'fear emotion' takes over our thought processes and we react by feeling hurt or hurting others, we are displaying one of our strongest emotions of all, often inappropriately. To understand and place limits on such explosive reactions, I have found it useful when dealing with my own and then others' outbursts to pick a time when we are not angry and explore how our anger manifests.

Some words which describe the feeling of being angry include the following:

- Hot under the collar
- Letting off steam
- Seeing red

- Losing your cool
- Out of control
- Blowing your stack

Obviously, this list is not exhaustive by any means, but there is a common thread appearing; they all relate to temperature. Being angry does indeed raise our body temperature significantly, thereby increasing our internal use of energy. One technique I have used successfully to reduce the effects of anger is to teach (and use myself) breath awareness. When we focus consciously on gently slowing the breath, sometimes with a slow repetition of a two-syllable phrase, such as 'stay calm', 'be cool', or 'let go', to match the in and out breaths, the heart rate automatically slows, and the anger fog dissipates. In most situations, this results in a surprisingly rapid reduction in strong emotions. This is related to the old maxim of taking time out by moving away and slowly counting to ten or a hundred. From a neuroscience perspective, this disengages the amygdala and allows connections to the frontal cortex to re-establish engagement with the rational mind. Drinking a large glass of cool water slowly is also a useful way to cool the body physically and allow the high energy of anger to dissipate. Of course, both conscious breathing and drinking water may be used concurrently.

From a much calmer mind frame, the opportunity then arises to rationally and constructively explore issues which have triggered the angry reaction in the emotionally charged situation in the first place. This leads to the exploration of possible solutions and resolutions. The technique does not involve any evaluation of the rightness or wrongness of getting, or of being angry, it simply acknowledges anger as a common human emotion which exists within the emotional spectrum of human interactions.

12.7.2 Techniques to Help Place a Ceiling on Multimedia Usage

To help place a ceiling on multimedia usage, it is necessary first to critically examine our relationships with the media we use. These are some of the questions to ask ourselves:

- Are we drawing our happiness and self-validation from our social media or from inside ourselves?
- How do we handle criticism and negativity expressed through our online exchanges and exploration?
- What proportion of our interactions with others is through digital messaging?
- How emotionally charged do we become when viewing online media?

A technique from EHV to help limit our desires when interacting with social media is *Silent Sitting and Guided Visualization* (see Chapters 8, 9, and 10). These are methods that are available to us to critique our media usage. One example is as follows:

> Sit in a comfortable position with your spine straight. Gently close your eyes and become aware of your breathing, gently lengthening the in breath slightly, holding it for a mental count of three, then slowly exhaling. With each breath feel your body relaxing and your mind slowing down.
>
> When your breathing becomes regular and unforced, as you breathe in, repeat silently to yourself, 'I am aware of breathing in', as you breathe out, 'I am aware of breathing out' and count those breaths down from ten to zero. If you have disruptive thoughts during this countdown, start again from the number ten. You should become aware of a relaxed stillness.
>
> In this relaxed state, imagine your mobile phone. What does it look like? How does it feel? What are the sounds it makes when receiving a call or message? Focus on the tone it makes when you receive a message. .... As you imagine it, you hear that sound as a message arrives... What feeling(s) does it generate as you hear the message arriving? Where in your body do you feel the sensations it creates? Are these feelings positive or neutral, or does the anticipation of the message cause anxiety, even trepidation? .... Let us assume that the message is a very negative and personal one.... Ask yourself if the content of the message is true or not.
>
> If yes, question why it is upsetting, as it is something you already know about yourself, something which can be worked upon if it needs changing.
>
> If no, then remind yourself that, no matter how many times this message might be sent, it will never be true, so choose not to take it personally.... Detach yourself from the message and mentally send it to the trash bin.
>
> Refocus on your breathing again and your sense of relaxed stillness.

When this visualisation has been completed, it is worth asking participants if they are willing to share what they felt during the visualisation. Encourage them to express any feelings of frustration, annoyance, impatience, or hurt. See if they can articulate issues that arise within themselves and share the thoughts they have when this happens. Explore some responses (cognitive) rather than reactions (emotional) they might use when dealing with situations like this.

Now let us examine for a moment what it is that gives social media such power over us. Social media is often non-immediate, as people can be in different locations, even in other countries, when they receive or read a message, which may also be at a significantly different time from when it was sent. But using social media has promoted the false expectation of the 'instant response'. When we send a tweet or a message, we expect it to be answered or at least acknowledged immediately and often create strong and misguided emotions when this doesn't happen. Likewise, when we do not get a quick, if not immediate, reply, especially when we know the other person is online, we generate doubts and negative feelings and ask questions about ourselves and whether they like us, don't like us, etc. When we hear the chosen sound of a message coming in, it can release the anticipatory chemical dopamine, which makes us feel good, making it easy to become addicted to this feeling and become desirous of more and more messages to indicate their arrival into our in-boxes.

So how should we deal with such messages? From a positive psychological perspective, a reasoned, cognitive response is always preferable to an emotional reaction. Is the message kind? Is it true? Is it necessary? Does it help or hinder the issue?

Another exercise involving visualisation around social media can be found in the appendix at the end of Chapter 8 within the Lesson Plan Example for Senior School (Year 10/11 or 12), which offers a range of useful strategies to explore.

How might we resolve to deal with social media in future? It seems self-evident that the way to deal with the effects of modern electronic intrusions is to be disciplined and courageous in our approach.

12.7.3 A Ceiling on Desires Focus on the Use of Screen Time

Being mindful is a practical way to examine our media and screen use. This initially involves doing a time audit. Each day for one whole week, as accurately as possible, log the amount of time spent on all activities. As a counsellor, I found this to be very effective when advising students about creating study plans, where the first thing they logged was all the times that they did not study but were engaged in other activities. By placing reasonable limits on those activities which disproportionately consumed excessive amounts of time, and specifically ordering their priorities, they found it relatively easy to find the time needed to study. In this case, they could have logged the amount of screen time of any sort for each day, and the activity it related to, such as chatrooms, phone usage, games that were played, or other online communications.

Some personal examples might be pertinent here. During recent political elections, I found myself reading a lot of articles about the issues and polling, which were filled with teasers about related stories, to the point that, until I completed my screen time audit, I was not aware that it was taking up between two-and-a-half and three-and-a-half hours per day, with many of the stories I was reading quite repetitive. Furthermore, I also discovered that I was watching multiple news broadcasts on TV, one after the other, without any real difference in the stories and analyses being presented. As I consider myself a reasonably disciplined person who has been practising Ceiling on Desires for many years, it came as a rather confronting shock as to how much I was caught up in this time-consuming cycle. With the cold hard data before me, I realised that I was not being authentic to my values and practising what I preach, so to satisfy my urge to be informed, I restricted my news gathering to one hour total per day, such as a half an hour for e-news sources and another half an hour for TV news broadcasts. This meant up to two hours a day were freed up to engage in other activities.

Whilst I have enjoyed updating myself on recent research and studies for this chapter, again it was very easy to be seduced into over-reading pertinent academic journals and texts. I must confess that, as a result of this behaviour, it has taken longer than it should have to complete this chapter, with the consequence that I held up other contributors. The discipline of finding a balance of time to spend on such activities is a necessary way to improve efficiency and avoid time wastage. It is equally critical to predetermine the time and timing we choose to deal with answering electronic communications, which is clearly another area that can steal our time. It is very easy to be drawn into multiple series of back-and-forth interactions when just one might do. By taking time to consider seriously what we have written in an SMS, email, or tweet, the clarity of the message, and whether it fulfils the '*kind*, *true*, or *necessary*' criteria, we can, in most instances, also determine before sending our reply whether it is likely to be helpful or hindering.

If we look at emails as one example, most people seem to feel a need to respond instantly, particularly when the receipt of emails (and indeed other communication platforms) is now acknowledged with an audible cue on mobile phones. One work practice I found useful was to set a time each morning and spend half an hour answering emails which were pertinent to my activities or work of that day, then another ten minutes before my lunch break, and again at the end of the day to tidy up any further correspondence or loose ends. I would also negotiate a timeline for action with correspondence resulting from these communications, in achievable, mutually acceptable steps. I let people know that any urgent requests were better served by a direct phone call or a face-to-face meeting, if possible, again with a fairly specific time limit so as to be more efficient with time usage. Advertising and unsolicited emails went straight, unopened, into the trash, which was emptied immediately. I am sure readers have many other effective techniques for dealing with such messages.

When critiquing screen time generally, whether watching TV, browsing online, or playing e-games, again personal discipline is required, such as setting a specific time limit and sticking to it. This can involve a technique which I like to call the 'extra ten process'. The number can be any chosen amount, depending on the activity. An extra five push-ups when exercising, ten more pages when reading a text, two more paragraphs when writing an article, or one more website search' are all examples of this approach. It can even be one more game when relaxing. This could also involve taking a short break to leave the activity and physically get away for a glass of water, a cup of tea or coffee, a short walk, or a silent sitting activity.

Mindfulness breaks are useful here as well, so after a set period of predetermined time on a task, downing tools and taking even just a few seconds to become aware of breathing, then practising active recall to bring to mind five things that have been pertinent to the activity being undertaken can be helpful to refocus and maintain interest and efficiency.

12.8 Final Activities

The following ideas are some of the things that you can do to enhance a Ceiling on Desires programme. Select one of the following (or one of your own) and practise it for a week, then reflect on any outcomes:

1. Practise Ceiling on Desires yourself, thereby being able to share your own experiences with your students or family and friends, and empathise with their experiences.
2. Engage in non-judgemental discussions about social media and online usage and modern electronic devices; explore ways to place a ceiling on your desires to use them in ineffective or unproductive ways.
3. Encourage sound work practices and time management to limit time wastage and encourage discussion about productive ways to spend the time that is saved.
4. Research reading material and other media, including both fiction and non-fiction, that illustrate ways to enact limiting desires.

This list is open to being expanded by your own ideas and observations, as well as those of colleagues. When used in an educational setting, students can also contribute to appropriate strategies to make their lives more fulfilling and the life of the planet more sustainable.

12.9 Conclusion

If we practise *Ceiling on Desires*, we notice many benefits to ourselves and to those around us. As well, the practice helps us to understand better how the strategies work before introducing them to students or others. If we can share our own perspectives, ideas, and experiences of *Ceiling on Desires*, this will enrich the teaching process and our relationships with others.

Notes

1 Phyllis Krystal, *Ceiling on Desires* (Puttaparthi, India: Sai Towers Publications, 2007).
2 D. Lieberman and M. Long, *The Molecule of More* (Dallas, TX: Ben Bella Books, 2018).
3 *Ibid.*Introduction to Lieberman D, Long M (2018) *The Molecule of More*, Ben Bella Books
4 K. A. Montagu, "Catechol Compounds in Rat Tissues and in Brains of Different Animals," *Nature* 180, no. 4579 (August 1957): 244–245.
5 Sigmund Freu, *Simple Psychology Psychodynamic Approach.* https://www.simplypsychology.org/psychodynamic.html accessed 9-8-2020.
6 A. Maslow, *Toward a Psychology of Being* (Summit, NJ: Start Publishing, 2012).
7 A. Maslow, *A Motivation and Personality* (Prabhat Publishing, 2015 reprint).
8 The Jubilee Centre for Character and Virtues, Birmingham University, UK. https://www.jubileecentre.ac.uk/ accessed 9-8-2022.
9 *Ibid.*
10 Sathya Sai Baba, *Sathya Sai Speaks* (Prasanthi Nilayam, India: Books and Publications Trust, 2000), Vol. 33.
11 *Ibid.*
12 A. MacIntire, *Ethics in the Conflict of Modernity* (Cambridge, UK: Cambridge University Press, 2016).
13 *Ibid.*
14 Phyllis Krystal, *Ceiling on Desires* (Puttaparthi, India: Sai Towers Publications, 2007).
15 Sathya Sai Baba, *Sathya Sai Speaks, Ceiling on Desires* (Prasanthi Nilayam, India: Books and Publications Trust, January 19, 1983), Vol. 16 (3). https://saispeaks.sathyasai.org/discourse/ceiling-desires-i/?keyword=ceiling+on+desires accessed 3-3-2023.
16 Sathya Sai Baba, *A Compendium of the Teachings of Sathya Sai Baba* (Puttaparthi, India: Sai Towers Publishing, 1997).
17 S. Halpern, *Tuning the Human Instrument: An Owner's Manual* (Virginia, Ireland: Spectrum Research Institute, 1980)..
18 Sathya Sai Baba, *A Compendium of the Teachings of Sathya Sai Baba* (Puttaparthi, India: Sai Towers Publishing, 1997)
19 H. Ricciotti, *Harvard Medical School* (Harvard Health Publishing, July 2021). https://www.health.harvard.edu/staying-healthy/boosting-your-energy accessed 21-8-2022.
20 Sathya Sai Baba, *A Compendium of the Teachings of Sathya Sai Baba* (Puttaparthi, India: Sai Towers Publishing, 1997).
21 *Ibid.*
22 *Ibid.*
23 D. Meadows, 'Definition of Sustainability,' *Weekly Newsletter*, 1995. https://www.sustainabilityleadersnetwork.org/resources/definition-of-sustainability/#:~:text=Humankind%20has%20the%20ability%20to%20achieve%20sustainable%20development%E2%80%94to,and%20societal%20resources%20from%20which%20needs%20are%20met accessed 10-8-2022.
24 H. Griffey, *The Lost Art of Concentration: Being Distracted in a Digital World* (2018). https://www.theguardian.com/lifeandstyle/2018/oct/14/the-lost-art-of-concentration-being-distracted-in-a-digital-world accessed 10-8-2022.
25 Ofcom, *The Communications Market* (2018). https://www.ofcom.org.uk/research-and-data/multi-sector-research/cmr/cmr-2018/interactive accessed 10-8-2022.
26 K. Francis, *Unpublished Psychology Notes for Year 12 Students,* 2004–2016.

Chapter 13

Learning Partnerships to Enhance Values-based Education

Krish (Krishnamurthie) Naidoo, Kevin Francis, Margaret Taplin, and Roger Packham

13.1 Introduction

By accepting the EHV premise that 'the end of education is character', an obvious ancillary question becomes, 'so what influences the child's character?'. Can you teach happiness? Chapter 6 discussed Character and Character Education, and this chapter builds onto those ideas by considering the roles of the main stakeholders who influence a child's development in the home, the school, and the wider society and their potential impacts, positive and negative. This chapter discusses the importance of sound partnerships between these various stakeholders in implementing values education.

In the home, parents/caregivers are the main influencers, although siblings and other close relatives can also have an impact. The first section of this chapter explores different styles of parenting and possible resulting implications for the child. This supports the importance of having parents/caregivers participate in the values education so that the family is able to support and live the happy and peaceful life as promoted in a values-based school.

The chapter also examines some aspects of the school/teacher/parent or caregiver partnership while, at the same time, acknowledging how it is not a one-way process, as teachers also benefit from such partnerships. While the teachers' influences on character development is self-evident, it is certainly not intended that teachers should perceive values education to be yet another thing being added to their already overflowing plates. A transfer of values is already inherent in any teaching interaction as part of the 'hidden' curriculum (see Chapter 9). It is understandable that teachers might respond with, 'So you want me to teach all the academic content that I am required to cover, tutor students who need help, discipline students, be on committees, coach, volunteer after school, complete endless paperwork, work with parents and do values education as well?'. Here we suggest that EHV is not an additional source of stress and time consumption but rather a tool that can help students, and their teachers, to cope better with life's pressures.

The role of society in education is also explored in this chapter since the students of today are influencing not only tomorrow's society but also today's.

DOI: 10.4324/9781003478607-14

Businesses, religious institutions, youth organisations, and the immediate community all play pivotal roles in developing young people's values. Stakeholders in the health and success of communities, businesses, and other organisations are in a good position to support initiatives that strengthen the character of youths. It is vital to create opportunities for businesses and community organisations to participate in the school community's values education programme.

The following scenario highlights the need for partnerships. It also suggests the difference between focusing just on academic excellence and including character development, with academic performance a consequence rather than the only focus:

> Assume you are either a parent, grandparent, aunt, uncle, or friend to 15-year-old Emma. While shopping at the local supermarket, a friend comes up and engages you in conversation. He mentions that you must be proud of Emma's academic achievement. You state, with all possible modesty, that you and others are very proud of her.
>
> A week later, another friend, who happens to be a nurse in the local hospital, engages you concerning Emma's social and moral excellence. 'You can always count on Emma to be at the hospital to volunteer on time. She is the best volunteer who holds and softly strokes the children born prematurely in the nursery. She even comforts some of the parents. We consider her to be a valued member of our staff.'

Now, which compliment means the most to you: The first one regarding Emma's academic achievement or the second one involving her character? For many, the second one would resonate more. This does not suggest we should minimise any child's academic achievement. Excellence in academic performance and improvement should always be celebrated and recognised. But, as adults, we understand that a child can be a 'high distinction' student in school and still fail in coping with the ups and downs of life and relationships with others, and that one's character is important in shaping one's future. Both are surely important, with character influencing how academic excellence may be used to benefit both the individual and society.

13.2 Values Begin at Home

As the home environment is where children spend most of their time, its influence on them cannot be underestimated. There are various actors associated with home life that have differing levels of influence, but, generally speaking, parents or other primary caregiver/s are significant architects of their children's characters. Many of the world's great leaders have attributed their success to one or both of their parents. For example, Mahatma Gandhi spoke and wrote about the influence of his mother,[1] and David Beckham, one of the greatest soccer players of all time, might never have touched a ball if his father had not shared his passion for the sport with his son.[2]

13.2.1 *Guidelines to Assist Parents and Caregivers*

The following guidelines are seen as 'ideal' practices in children's upbringing and the establishment of their developing characters:[3]

- Boost your child's self-esteem
- Catch kids being good
- Set limits and be consistent with your discipline
- Make time for your kids
- Be a good role model
- Make communication a priority
- Be flexible and willing to adjust your parenting style
- Show that your love is unconditional
- Know your own needs and limitations as a parent

These are the ideals to aim for, as far as is possible, in a range of contexts, recognising that no one can be perfect all the time, yet everyone can strive to improve once there is a standard to achieve.

13.2.2 *Parenting (Caregiver) Styles*

Raising children is universally acknowledged as one of the most challenging tasks facing humanity, but at the same time it is one of life's richest experiences. It is a balancing act between support and control, affection, and discipline. According to prominent Australian psychologist Dr Michael Carr-Gregg,[4] there are four main parenting (caregiver) styles:

- Authoritarian
- Neglectful
- Laissez-faire
- Authoritative

The *authoritarian* is highly demanding and unresponsive. Such parents/caregivers attempt to mould and control the behaviour and attitudes of their children according to a rigid set of standards. They tend to emphasise obedience, respect for authority, and order. Authoritarians also discourage verbal give-and-take with children, expecting rules to be followed without further explanation. The impact of this behaviour on children's development has been documented in many studies to which Carr-Gregg referred. This style is characterised as rejecting, avoidant, withdrawn, intolerant, coercive, and punitive. Carr-Gregg reported that poor parenting/caregiver practices are also related to lower school achievement. Both a lack of parental control (see next section) and excessive levels of it may lead to improper social attitudes and behaviours ranging from truancy to drug abuse and lower school achievement, suggesting that harsh and indulgent styles may result in children becoming anti-social and aggressive, and developing maladaptive styles of processing social information. Children from authoritarian families tend to get into less trouble than those from permissive or uninvolved parents/caregivers. The numbers of children from authoritarian families involved in drug and alcohol use and risky behaviours like driving a car without a seat belt or being disruptive and aggressive are less when compared to children from permissive families.

Neglectful parents or caregivers tend to be uninvolved, detached, or dismissive towards their children. This type of parenting style appears to have low levels of control and affection. The basic needs of the child may or may not be met. Also, such parents and carers do not seem concerned at all about their children's lives. There is a distinct lack of supervision, little or no discipline, no communication, and limited warmth, love, or affection. This type of parent or caregiver rarely attends school events, such as parent-teacher interviews. The children from this type of home usually have higher risks of substance abuse and other types of serious problems later in life. Unfortunately, these children often tend to replicate this style of parenting and lifestyle.

Laissez-Faire is a French term meaning 'to let them do as they please'. These parents adopt a permissive style in which they avoid providing guidance and discipline. They are usually skewed more towards affection rather than control. There is a distinct lack of boundary setting and enforcement. There is a tendency to want to be 'friends' rather than to parent from a position of authority. Their children are likely to be impulsive, disobedient, rebellious, and to crave independence from their parents. As adolescents, they may have poor self-control, poor school performances, and higher rates of drug use.

The *Authoritative* style of parenting or caregiving is found to be the most effective style. The authoritative style maintains an effective balance between high levels of expectation and responsiveness. These parents or caregivers establish clear and consistent boundaries and firmly enforce necessary rules and standards for their children's behaviour. They consistently monitor the conduct and use non-punitive strategies or appropriate discipline when rules are violated. Socially responsible, mature behaviour is expected and reinforced. Authoritative parents or caregivers are also warm and supportive. They encourage bidirectional communication, validate the child's point of view, and recognise the rights of both themselves and their children. The warm and affectionate relationships between children and parents or caregivers foster cognitive growth in children. The influence of the authoritative style does not diminish during adolescence; adolescents who are reared in an authoritative environment consistently score higher on measures of psychological competence and school achievement and lower on measures of internal distress and problem behaviour than do those from non-authoritative families. An authoritative style therefore creates a warm, loving, and mutual understanding in the family and fosters stable children's behaviour and personality.

So, what are the implications of these parents' styles for the development of their children's lifelong values frameworks? According to Carr-Gregg, children from *authoritarian* families may not always be as well-grounded in personal moral development and behaviour as children from *authoritative* families.[5] It seems that those from *authoritarian* families do not fully internalise the values deployed by their parents or caregivers. Further, adolescents with *authoritarian* parents are less likely to feel socially accepted by their peers. They are also rated as less self-reliant, less resourceful, less competent, less helpful, and less popular. They have low self-esteem and experience depersonalisation: That is, how they relate to themselves, since it can make them feel as if they aren't real. Children from *authoritarian* families are more inclined to simply follow values and rules set up by their parents whilst in their presence, but they may choose to reject those values in a new environment, such as in the classroom when their 'parent or caregiver figures' are absent.

13.2.3 Parental Involvement in Schools

There are three main areas through which schools can involve parents and caregivers in their character/values education development agendas:

- as information recipients
- as partners
- as clients

Let us now consider these ways in which parents and caregivers can be engaged in school values education cultures.

13.2.3.1 As Information Recipients

This is the least interactive way in which parents and caregivers can become involved in character and values education. They are informed about school events through regular newsletters that also share information about the values being focused on in the school or information sessions being offered. Many schools incorporate articles extolling values-related practices as regular contributions to such newsletters, with appropriate referencing included for further enquiry. School websites can also share information about values policies, approaches, and successes.

The examples in Appendix 13.1 are from the Sathya Sai College, Australia,[6] illustrating how a school's values ethos can be portrayed in school newsletters.

The first examples show how the school's current values foci are highlighted in the school leaders' messages for the primary and secondary schools. The second example in Appendix 13.1 is from the secondary school newsletter, illustrating how values-related activities are reported and celebrated for each class.

13.2.3.2 Parents/Caregivers as Partners

Ideally, the best approach is to engage parents and caregivers as partners in their children's character education. There are indeed many parallels between parenting and teaching, but parents and teachers also have different roles and responsibilities; hence, there is strength in having them work together. This means going beyond the traditional, but limited, roles typically assigned to parents and caregivers, such as helping with reading or other classroom activities, checking homework, and supporting extracurricular activities. For example, homework tasks or class/whole-school challenges can be set that encourage parents, caregivers, and other family members to participate in values-related activities. To encourage strong partnerships, it is important that the parents or caregivers have a clear appreciation and understanding of the values programme the school has adopted, and why it has chosen to do this. An example of how to achieve this is the *Values Awareness for Parents Programme*[7] (VAPP) that has been used in one school.[8] This VAPP was initially developed[9] to introduce parents and caregivers to the key values concepts of this school, which was using EHV for all its activities. The parents and caregivers, it was hoped, would then support the values education in the home environment. This school had a policy of compulsory attendance at a VAPP for all new parents or caregivers of children enrolled at the school, but this may not be possible for all schools. The VAPP has been offered in a number of educational settings around Australia for different groups and can be presented in three sessions of one-and-a-half hours each, two sessions of two hours, or one longer session. The programme has been well received by parents, many of whom have asked for more workshops to develop the ideas further.

The workshops focus on three areas:

- Awareness of the need for and use of values in our daily decision-making.
- Awareness of the language of values and a deep understanding of their impact on achieving our life's goals.
- The need for self and social awareness and an understanding of the obstacles we face in daily life that prevent us from practising values consistently and universally.

The workshops are interactive, consisting of guided discussions and group activities. The facilitator guides the discussion with carefully designed questions. The collective responses are then used as a basis for drawing conclusions. In the following box are some examples of questions used in the discussion sessions and an activity that the participants undertake.

Examples of Workshop Activities

Sample Discussion Questions

- What are your concerns about raising children in the modern world?
- What positive attributes/values do you want your child to have?
- What are the obstacles? – What prevents us from achieving these goals?

Sample Activity

- Place participants in pairs. Sit quietly, close eyes, and think of someone who had a significant influence on you, e.g., a parent, teacher, or friend. List the qualities that this person displayed. Share your list with your partner.

In Chapter 10, some examples were given of homework tasks that can be set for different subjects that incorporate values. Students can be encouraged to introduce strategies such as silent sitting (see Chapter 8), WATCH (see Chapter 8), and Ceiling on Desires (see Chapter 12) to their families and reflect on and report on the impacts on themselves and their families.

Parents and caregivers can be encouraged to report on evidence of their children putting the values into practice at home. Whole-class or whole-school challenges can be introduced to encourage families to practise values together, for example, by engaging in service projects. Parents and caregivers can be encouraged to share with their children their experiences of putting values into practice in their own lives and can be invited to talk to class groups or school assemblies. The three examples to illustrate how parents and caregivers can be involved in the child's character development are presented in the following box; they can also be encouraged to help with setting up values-related displays around the school. EHV promotes and strives for as much parental involvement as possible.

Ways Parents Can Be Involved in the Child's Character Development

My Helping Diary

Ask the children to take these diaries home. Teachers, other children, and their parents and caregivers can all help them to identify their unique, special strengths. Then the parents and caregivers can write a comment in the diary each week to describe what the child has done to utilise these strengths to help in the home or the wider community.

How Have I Lived My Values Today?

With the class, or the whole school, decide what value/values you want to put into practice during the week. Ask children to keep their values diaries for the week and record how well they lived the values each day. Ask parents to record which values they saw their children practising.

Values in Television Programmes

Students and their families can analyse commercials and the messages sent by watching television together. What are the values messages in the cartoons? Share their ideas in the next class.

13.2.3.3 Parents as Clients

Another way schools can positively bring parental influence to bear on values education is by providing resources to parents and caregivers. Ever-increasing numbers of schools also provide training on topics related to child rearing; for example, helping them to understand how practising values can help through using positive discipline, drawing on their values to deal with bullying, minimising risky behaviour, or dealing with anxieties and stress, and offering help in navigating the online media world.

Another example comes from the USA, where one particular values education programme provides schools with a parent-training video and discussion guide that can be used to teach parents about the same social and emotional skills that their children are learning at school.[10] This further encourages school principals or counsellors to engage families through a six-session programme designed to help parents apply the same social skills within the family.

13.3 Values Education Initiatives in Schools

This section describes just a few of the many values education initiatives that have been implemented in schools and that can be adapted effectively to other contexts.

13.3.1 Acknowledging, Sustaining, and Enhancing Values Education Initiatives in Schools

As mentioned at the start of this chapter, values education should not be seen as yet another programme to be added to the educator's plate but rather as an exciting initiative that, in many schools, is already at least partially infused into the school culture to make it a more pleasant place to be and to reduce the pressures currently faced by many teachers and students. If the school management and leadership commit to modelling and leading the initiative, they can potentially bring about big changes in the quality of the community. This works best when the major stakeholders in the school share a common commitment to modelling and teaching a culture of ethical and social excellence. Acknowledging values education as a crucial part of education for all students is important, so it should be given more than just a mention in the school plan.[11] Please refer to the Appendices to this chapter and to Chapter 14 for examples of how values can be integrated into school documents. Even if the major purpose of a school is to improve the students' academic outcomes, this will be achieved better when attention is focused on developing the social, emotional, and ethical climate of the school through values-based practices Teachers and students can create an environment conducive to better teaching and learning, as was found in the Australian 'Values Education Project' discussed earlier in Chapter 2.

Some strategies to model and teach values include:[12]

- Identify values inherent in any current school development plan and ways they might be further enhanced and delivered.
- Encourage interested teachers to try common projects involving these values in their classes (such as the impact of regular silent sitting) over a period of time, so they have similar experiences to share and discuss.
- Create opportunities in staff and department meetings to share the outcomes of values education initiatives with colleagues, as they are crucial in setting the tone for the school.
- Involve the entire school community, including parent and student representatives, in developing a values education vision for the school.
- Provide a framework and vocabulary (see Chapters 4, 6, and 8) for reinforcing good character in staff and students, particularly to reflect values education concepts when disciplining students.[13] See the following box for an example.
- Allow time and activities in staff meetings for teachers to share their ideas about the teaching of values throughout their subjects (see Chapters 10 and 14).
- Encourage whole-staff discussions and professional development about values to encourage staff to support the modelling of values behaviour in all interactions and to acknowledge it in students (see Chapter 14).
- Engage relief teachers, ancillary staff, including caretakers, cleaners, and, where possible, others such as bus drivers, in the reinforcement of good character through whole-staff discussions about suitable strategies and vocabulary.
- Form a values education wellbeing group/committee comprised of a core of individuals in the school who are interested to establish a values education initiative, and to explore how modelling EHV strategies can help to improve their own lives. It is easier and more enjoyable for teachers to work together in a *community of practice* to investigate best practice examples of successful implementation of values education, rather than trying to do it in isolation.[14]

13.3.2 *Establishing a School Values Education/Wellbeing Group/ Committee*

In all schools, good school leadership can make the difference between a character-development effort that occurs in a few classrooms and an initiative that influences the entire school community. A school-level values education (or wellbeing) committee (or group) can provide this needed leadership and direction. A school EHV committee can play an important role in addressing the goal of creating a respectful and responsible school community and in enabling teachers to feel that they are working in a supportive team to implement EHV, rather than alone in a vacuum. Ideally, an EHV initiative has the same priority as academic and behaviour expectations, so that it provides a foundation for improved academic performance and behaviour while underpinning the whole school culture as well as its curriculum. Often, values education initiatives are led by school counsellors and/or wellbeing coordinators. Whilst EHV could be seen as intrinsic to the job specifications of school counsellors, it is most effective when it is 'owned' by a partnership of the whole community and is directed by teachers, administrators, parents, and students. Through an effective and active committee, the school's EHV initiative can provide a definite and deliberate direction that supports a positive school climate.

13.3.2.1 Strategies for Establishing a Group that Directs the School's Values Education Initiative[15]

The most important strategy is the creation of time and opportunities for all staff to discuss and share their strategies, their successes, and their challenges, enabling learning from each other's experiences. Examples of how this can be achieved are given in Chapter 14 for the Australian Sathya Sai school. Some strategies are:

- Include stakeholders from both the school and the wider community
- Invite members from each main area of the school
- Invite a parent and at least two students from each grade/year level to serve on the committee
- Include the school principal as an active member of the committee
- Hold committee meetings regularly, possibly twice per term
- Share the ideas and initiatives discussed with all staff members
- Rotate committee members on and off, leaving a core group that has a history of directing the values education initiative while new members are acclimatised to the initiative.

Above all, it is important to remember that it is not enough just to tell teachers and other stakeholders that their school is going to be an EHV school, also tell them what they need to do, or even how to do it, and expect that they will do it when they are in their classrooms. If a school is to become truly a values-rich one, the important starting point is for it to touch the teachers' and other stakeholders' hearts first so they can experience and understand how it enhances their own lives, so they do it because they can see the benefits themselves and not because somebody told them to do it.

13.3.3 Formulating a Values Education Action Plan

As action plans are ongoing, usually spanning a three- to five-year period, regular infusions of new strategies *during this time* can keep the initiative fresh. A school can tailor its own plan based on a needs assessment before the action plan is written. The results of this assessment could start with the most troublesome area and expand to eventually have the whole school benefit from the improved climate. Regular evaluation and adjustments to these goals can keep the plan current. The following are some examples of school-based action plans developed to address whole-school issues and needs:

- A group of teachers made a commitment to doing silent sitting together before class every morning for one month. At the end of the month, they shared their experiences of how this activity impacted upon themselves and their classes.
- The first ten minutes of the school day were devoted to activities titled 'Start the Day with Love'. Examples included describing classmates' admirable qualities, sharing stories about loving acts they had done for others, singing songs about self-love and love for others, focusing on loving thoughts in silent sitting, and discussing stories and quotations.
- In a boarding primary school, the younger or new children were homesick and finding it difficult to adjust. The school instigated a 'Caring in the Dormitory' initiative, in which all boarders and supervising staff were encouraged to engage in specific values-based activities to show love and caring for the boarders.

13.3.3.1 Strategies for Formulating a Values Education Action Plan

- Complete a needs assessment for the school to pinpoint the areas the EHV action plan should address first and those in which it is most feasible to implement (e.g., use direct or indirect methods and 'hidden' curriculum – see Chapters 8, 9, and 10).
- Once the needs assessment is complete, use the results, along with input from the EHV Committee members, to write an action plan.
- When writing the plan, create achievable strategies that directly relate to the goals established by the needs assessment results.
- Span the action plan over three to five years to ensure quality strategies and activities are added each year.
- Assess the new strategies implemented each year, as well as the original strategies, to determine if the EHV goals are being met.
- Adjust strategies and activities annually based on the evaluation results.

Examples are presented in Appendix 13.2 to illustrate how school policy documents can be adjusted to incorporate a school's values focus.

13.3.4 Relationships Are at the Core

A crucial element[16] of a culturally competent school is its ability to build and sustain relationships among its stakeholders. Values education researchers[17] have supported this idea by emphasising the importance of adults building relationships centred on respect, responsibility, and caring for each other and for students. In today's world, students, as well as adults, need positive role models of civility and caring. Many students are living in homes and communities that have few examples of positive models, so role models are needed to help them to build the habits and attitudes essential for academic and social competence. Given that learning by imitation is still one of education's most powerful and productive learning mechanisms (see Chapter 2) it is imperative for our own wellbeing, as educators and role models, that the value traits that have contributed to our success as caring, committed educators are taught and modelled. It is also important to integrate into the school culture ways to use values strategies to support and enhance staff and collegial relationships to maximise their wellbeing.

13.3.4.1 Strategies for Focusing on Relationships

- Emphasise all the benefits that arise from positive staff-to-staff, staff-to-students, and student-to-student relationships in forging a positive school climate.
- Create opportunities for all to share and discuss personal benefits that have occurred.
- Conduct specific activities to encourage staff to appreciate the role of values in their own lives and put them into practice with colleagues; e.g., the activity of writing something you respect about each other – for example, one teacher who did this in a staff meeting said, 'If my house was on fire, I would rescue that list, because I had no idea my colleagues had thought such nice things about me'. (See Chapter 14 for some other specific examples.)
- Discuss regularly, in teams and at staff meetings, the importance and the benefits of modelling when teaching values.
- Remind teachers and staff to be 'warm demanders'. Teachers want to build wonderful relationships with their students, but they must also expect rigour in all they do. Excellence, whether social or academic, is contagious. It is a common misunderstanding that a school culture based on human values, particularly Love, means a laissez-faire environment when, in fact, discipline and rules have a very important place in a values-based environment. The difference is that discipline is also values-based and done from a position of Peace and Love, rather than anger or frustration,[18] and teachers who are loving towards their students do not cross the boundary between friendliness and familiarity.

- Recognise students for demonstrating good values behaviour, for example helping a student in need, standing up to peer pressure or not engaging in behaviours that they think are wrong, and showing significant improvement in dealing positively with a negative behaviour such as anger.
- Provide students with opportunities, through literature and narratives, to observe and discuss their own character strengths and flaws (see Chapters 8, 9, and 10).
- Encourage staff members to get to know their students, their dreams, and their aspirations.
- Teach to the students' learning styles and intelligences so that every student can feel successful. Encourage every child to recognise their own unique qualities and support them to use these qualities for their own benefits and those of others.
- Set high but realistic expectations for students. Empower them to make positive decisions and set goals.
- Encourage positive relationships among students by rejecting bullying and promoting tolerance and respect for themselves and others.
- Regularly remind staff that positive and negative teacher attitudes and expectations have profound effects on their own wellbeing and on their students, and that caring prompts effort and achievement.
- Identify disconnected students and create a mentoring programme within the school to support them.
- Remember to maintain professional integrity in all relationships.

13.3.5 Establish a Cross-Curricular Approach to Values Education

Students are most likely to appreciate the place of values in everyday life if these values are connected throughout the curriculum, with teachers of all subjects taking advantage of 'teachable moments' that relate to values and character (see Chapter 9). Creating a school culture of values takes more than a few posters and several morning announcements, even though these are an important component of the overall school values environment and are helpful in creating a common sense of direction. Integrating values education into the vision and life of a school requires a whole-school cross-curricular approach so students see that values have a place in every aspect of their lives, not only in specific 'values education' lessons. Ideally, values education components are woven into the curricula for all subjects, as all are replete with authentic examples and opportunities to expand a student's understanding of life's social and ethical issues (see Chapter 10).

13.3.5.1 Strategies for Implementing a Values Education Community

- Share the purpose, goals, and concepts of values education so that they may be reinforced throughout the school community.
- Align all aspects of the character education initiative (see Chapter 6) to the curriculum so that there is a congruence of core values.

- Build a collection of resource materials, including activities that support the common core values. This could include a quotation list, profiles of 'heroes' of male and female role models, and a collection of relevant contemporary articles from newspapers, magazines, and the Internet.
- Create a professional library that includes values education resources.[19]
- Correlate the values education programme to the achievement standards set by the relevant State Education Authority. Examples of how this can be done, from two schools, are presented in Appendix 13.3.
- If necessary, rewrite, in values language, conflict resolution, violence prevention, anti-bullying, and anti-harassment activities. An example of an anti-bullying policy is shown, along with other policies, in Appendices 13.2 and 13.3.
- Empower students by giving them opportunities to establish goals, engage in service initiatives, plan activities and actions, and explore career, skills, and higher education options.
- Recognise that the inevitable occurrence of breakdowns and transgressions of values are also 'teachable and learning moments' and add authenticity to the idea that values are for all and require persistent practice.

13.3.6 *Ensure Values Education Efforts Are Clearly Visible*

Visual representations of excellent work provide exemplars to members of the school community as they walk through hallways and enter classrooms. One can recite a pledge and listen to thoughtful words about a certain trait, but displays and visual testimonials of one's actions echo louder and reach further. Such displays can be a valuable way to celebrate the core beliefs and practices of the school and the standards of values to which students are held. Examples include:

- Pictures of individual school community members accompanied by written statements explaining why these individuals are being recognised and giving specific examples of their positive behaviour.
- Activities such as a 'Peace Wall', on which school community members are encouraged to write their understanding about the importance of inner and outer peace.
- A 'Compliment Tree' in the school and/or classroom, where individuals can thank others who have made positive impacts on their lives.
- Posters showing values quotations and messages.
- Photographs of school community members 'caught in the act' of practising good values.
- Examples of students' work that build their values reflections into their academic tasks (see Chapter 10 for some examples).

13.3.7 *Morning Meetings*

During morning meetings of either the whole school or the class, put values into practice by encouraging adults and students to share and respect each other's social and emotional needs, through using experiences from both inside and outside of school. It is worthwhile to consider how to start the day to ensure a positive experience for all in the school. If done well, these meetings can help students connect with their peers as well as the adults in the school. However, the development of a connection requires more than just a few announcements; it should be a time to gather to greet each other and address the concerns that arise in any close-knit group. As described by one experienced teacher,[20] students in a primary classroom can even sit on a rug and lean back on comfortable floor pillows, with the teacher seated nearby. This is the time to make announcements and give students any information they need to take home, also, to share and celebrate good news or bad – both are important parts of a caring group. This process is a real community-builder within a class. Another example of values-related class meeting activities is presented in the following box:[21]

Examples of Values-Related Class Meeting Activities Used Typically in the Values-Based Toogoolawa Schools in Queensland, Australia[22]

The teacher reminds the students of the *Thought for the Week*. One student reads it aloud, and the students are asked to explain what they think it means and how they can apply it at home, school, or in the community. (Teacher asks questions to draw out their understanding further.)

Students are invited to contribute to the Circle of Acknowledgement, e.g., 'I acknowledge John for being kind, when he helped me....', to acknowledge the human values they have observed in others during the day.

Students are encouraged to talk about the feelings of happiness that they experience from doing selfless service.

Circle of Restorative Justice

This is held before school each morning before the quiet time. The purpose is to provide a safe, controlled framework for challenging and changing inappropriate and hurtful behaviours by students (and sometimes by teachers) – always with the reminder that we all have the five human values within us and that we all love and accept each other regardless of what we have done wrong.

Restorative justice does not include scolding, labelling, judging, blaming, or verbal abuse. Rather, it is an opportunity for those who have hurt or offended others to hear from the sufferers how they have been affected by the other's behaviour. The aim is not to punish or shame the offender but to facilitate him to empathise with his victim and to look into his own essential goodness to see if there is any way he can repair the harm that has been done.

A great strength of this format is that it is easily customised to address each school's unique needs. A common misunderstanding is that morning meetings are just for primary schools, when clearly high school students can also benefit from this opportunity to connect with other students and adults, to share and reflect on values practices.

13.3.7.1 Strategies for Putting Morning Meetings into Practice

- When morning meetings are not held, use time at the beginning of a class, before the formal lesson, to review classroom norms, share feelings and thoughts, and set goals. Establish procedures and a time limit to keep these sessions productive and efficient.
- Invite students to thank anyone in the class who helped them the day before or that morning.
- Invite students to share one positive thing that has happened to them in the past day. Be willing to share one positive thing as a teacher if asked by the students.
- Share important information. Be sure to plan time for discussion if the topic merits elaboration.
- Consider this a good time to discuss current events that could be influencing the students or their community, and particularly to discuss the values underpinning these events.
- Develop service projects that may be sponsored, or participated in, by the students. Service projects can be particularly valuable if they are linked to the curriculum, so they are learning about the subject and putting values into practice simultaneously. For example, IT students could help senior citizens to develop their skills or offer workshops on cyber safety and etiquette for younger children. (See Chapter 12 for an example of how students can discuss the dopamine effect of social media.)
- Use the morning meeting to discuss issues that may arise within the life of the classroom. Have students share some of their concerns. This can be done in the actual meeting or by writing concerns on cards and placing them in a container beforehand, then discussing them during the meeting. This anonymity may help more students to express their concerns. In discussing these group concerns, be careful not to use individual names, and seek input from students on how to resolve the issue by applying the values they have been discussing across the school.
- Take time to celebrate good news and accomplishments. For example, recognise students who have improved their grades, won an art award, or been selected for a school sports team, or engaged in activities providing service to others. Use this as a 'teachable moment' to talk about feeling jealous of others' achievements versus feeling as happy for the other person as you would for yourself if it were your achievement.

- Consider meeting at other times during the day. Although the term 'morning meeting' is often used, schools may find success using this type of strategy throughout the course of the day. For example, a school that has a mid-morning break might combine the break with a meeting time, using the time to celebrate successes and intervene in conflicts and other issues.

13.3.8 Morning Announcements

A focus on a quote, character trait, idea, or thought-provoking concept is an excellent way to start the day and to instil a common thought about a value throughout the school. Everyone spends a few minutes reflecting on the message that can frame the day and be reinforced throughout the day. The values message during the morning announcements becomes a powerful method for maximising impact in a short amount of time. An added benefit is that the message reaches the entire school, and its positive impact can be reflected in the actions and attitudes of both adults and students in the school.

It needs to be emphasised that this is just one component of a whole-school values programme and that much more is also required to promote a values-based development of character. Using morning announcements to focus all stakeholders on the school's character goals is just one tool for reminding stakeholders of what is important in the school.

13.3.8.1 Strategies for Integrating Values into Morning Announcements[23]

- Make positive affirmations, character quotes, daily words of wisdom, or thoughts of the day, a part of every daily announcement.
- Invite a staff member, school visitor, student, custodian, or office staff member to deliver the daily message. Personal examples or interpretations of the message can be added and expanded upon. For example, a message about caring may be presented by, or about, a person working within the school who continually demonstrates a loving, compassionate, and empathetic attitude towards others.
- A meaningful phrase relating to the school vision statement, or the school's motto, can be repeated by students and staff members alike at the end of morning announcements.
- A principal's daily message to staff may include a monthly value focus along with examples and suggestions for practising the value during the day.
- As a follow-up to a weekly values lesson, consider inviting students to present their own skits, poems, stories, etc. during the morning announcements.
- Incorporate the use of relevant music into the announcements, as music can capture the attention of students.

- Use music or songs with values messages, rather than bells or sirens, to demarcate breaks during the day, or while waiting for morning assembly to start.
- Occasionally, use the morning announcements to identify and highlight students and staff who display exemplary value-based characters.
- Consider designating students exhibiting positive behaviour as the 'Character Hero' of the Day (or week, month, etc.), making sure to encompass other behaviours such as a peaceful resolution of a conflict, or a particularly good service project.
- Use the morning announcements as a time to teach students about national holidays, important historical events, and individuals in history who have shown positive character traits.
- Alert parents to a child's upcoming 'performance' during the morning announcements. This generates an enthusiasm that is carried home and reinforces the value traits established at school. Parents are more likely to buy into values education when they see a direct connection to their child, and that their child and their family environment are being enhanced by the practice.

13.4 Values Education and Communities

Partnerships with businesses and communities support values-building efforts. If values education can be extended beyond the school, this will make the most significant positive differences in the teachers' and students' lives. Parents, families, businesses, and communities can all join the effort to develop good character.

Partnerships between schools and businesses are useful in developing a school's values initiative as well as having many other benefits. Families, teachers, students, government leaders, business leaders, clergy, and civic organisations can work together to ensure that students are exposed to positive role models. When their overlapping involvement is woven into children's lives, they receive the support needed to grow into healthy citizens and productive members of the community.

Partnerships give business leaders and civic organisations opportunities to contribute to the values education process, yet to be effective, the partnership needs to be beneficial to all parties. There are many ways for businesses and community organisations to contribute to schools, and here are just a few:

- participating in joint service projects
- mentoring in a values-based way, for example, sharing how using values in business and professions leads to better outcomes
- joining the school's values education team or committee

- expanding school-based projects (e.g., Ceiling on Desires, Chapter 12, and W.A.T.C.H.[24]) into their workplaces and comparing experiences with student
- The practice of 'Ceiling on Desires' (see Chapter 12) can be an effective way to bring partners together in joint, values-based projects. For example, the community can be encouraged to practise this for a week or a month and save money, that would otherwise be spent on overindulgence in the 'desires', to donate to a worthy cause.

Mentoring with a values-based focus is a powerful way for communities to support a school EHV programme because it provides an opportunity for positive and authentic role modelling (as discussed in Chapter 6), academic support, and the forming of relationships with new individuals based on trust and caring. This is a different focus from the conventional school mentoring programmes, as it creates opportunities specifically for mentors to share with students their own experiences of living human values in their workplaces or daily lives. It is often said that children learn best by example, and a relationship developed through mentoring has as its foundation the principle that the mentor will provide leadership and guidance for the mentored. Last, it is important periodically to evaluate any community partnership programme from both a student and community perspective.

13.5 How Does the Implementation of EHV Make a Better School?

Is the school one where teachers are stressed, unable to cope with juggling everything they have to do, dread going into the classroom, try to put colleagues down to make themselves look good, and are too exhausted when they go home to interact with their families in positive ways?

Or is it a school in which teachers go into the classroom with calm, positive mindsets, and engage in practices that encourage students to be settled and concentrate, can cope with the pressures because of this underlying calmness, take time for self-compassion when needed so all can feel more peaceful to interact with their families at home, respect and support each other, respect the students and deal with issues in calm, values-based ways, and have a healthy acceptance that things can go wrong at times, but that strategies can be developed to accept mistakes and learn from them as part of a values-based approach?

We would all choose the second type of school. In all schools, there are relationships between all stakeholders. The teachers, administrators, students, and other adults in the school community who are in a values-focused school, such as one using EHV, are all glad to be there. This does not mean that every day is perfect. This would be unrealistic and unlikely, as all schools have their struggles and difficult times. But EHV teaches and models how to persevere through these and work towards values-based common goals. They know where they are going and how to lift each other up when a lift is needed. There are high academic, social, moral, and ethical standards for all in these schools. Educators believe their students can and will achieve their highest potentials in all aspects of assessment. They also believe that EHV-based social and moral actions are a prerequisite to meeting their academic goals; the school climate is a precursor for academic, artistic, and even athletic excellence. They have consistent rules and, more importantly, procedures or practices for how to live their lives in harmony with others. These procedures are practised until they become habits.

The adults in this type of school have experienced that practising human values in their own lives helps them to cope more easily with their professional and personal challenges and thus automatically becomes a moral compass for students in their school. This is not easy, and sometimes, being humans, we fail, but we can be honest about sharing our mistakes with our students in an authentic manner and show them how we can learn and grow from mistakes by adhering to the EHV principles. This compass helps guide students in their actions towards others. The adult stakeholders truly care about the students. They care, as parents care for their own children, firmly but with fairness, trying to love their students and being able to recognise that they are all 'diamonds' at different stages of emerging from the rough core, even at times when they behave in unlikeable ways.

Parents or other caregivers are considered important in helping students reach their goals. However, the staff members in this school do not blame the children if their parents or caregivers fail to attend meetings or programmes. They acknowledge the presence and assistance of connected parents and caregivers and feel that the social and ethical development of their students is as important as their academic development. They may have to accept reluctantly that some parents and caregivers will not come to the school despite their best efforts to encourage them to do so, and some may even not always act in the best interests of their children. This provides an opportunity for teachers to further practise their own values of compassion, tolerance, and understanding.

Of course, we have presented here an ideal scenario of a values-based school, and this chapter has suggested a wide and deep range of philosophies, beliefs, and strategies to be put into place in order to achieve such a school. We do not want readers to feel overwhelmed at the thought of having to put all of this into place at once in order to create a values-rich environment. Implementing any one of the aspects discussed in this chapter will help to bring about positive changes to a school culture, so it is quite reasonable to start with small steps towards establishing the aspects that are the most easily achievable. Naturally, the more that are implemented the better the outcome will be. Chapter 14 describes some of the outcomes that have been achieved for schools and teachers who have implemented steps, whether small or large, to establish EHV schools. We encourage you to try one or more of the ideas of this chapter in your own school. While it is always preferable to do this with others, please do not underestimate *The Power of One*.[25]

Appendix 13.1: Examples of School Newsletters Promoting Values (see Earlier Section 13.2.3)

Sathya Sai College

Character Development & Academic Excellence

Term 4 / Week 8/ November 2023

Truth lived as Integrity

"Say what you mean, mean what you say..."

Week 7 Assembly Song: We are love

Week 8 Assembly Song: Integrity song

Integrity is doing the right thing, even when no one is watching

- C.S. Lewis

Principal's Message

The value of focus for weeks 7 & 8 was Integrity.

Integrity is not a single action, it is a state of mind that is developed. It comes from the mind and heart of a person, it shows who you really are and what you really believe is right or wrong, good or bad. Integrity is exhibited in not just one act of goodness, but in your whole character.

To nurture children to instil integrity as part of their character, we must be their role model. Children need to be able to trust that true words have been spoken. This echoes the reality that we need to be careful to let our "yes" be yes and our "no" be no.

Thank you

As we creep closer to concluding the year, I would like to thank all our volunteers from far and wide for your support throughout the year. To all the people who made lunches, organised dances and picnics, attended working bees, constructed outdoor furniture, weeded and mowed the garden, restored furniture, repaired equipment, rejuvenated the Kindy Garden and tended to so many other tasks throughout the year, at both campuses, it is greatly appreciated.

The work completed by volunteers (P & F, parent helpers, Sai Organisation volunteers, past staff and friends of the school) has made our school safer, improved functionality as well as making it look more appealing. Those who have worked tirelessly to maintain our school inside and out have also reduced the maintenance and operational costs significantly. We all have busy lives and donating time can be difficult, but it assists the school in many ways and the benefits are far reaching. Thank you again and I hope to work alongside many more volunteers next year.

Cal Atkins
Principal

Figure 13.1 Examples of Values-Based School Newsletters[26] *(Continued)*

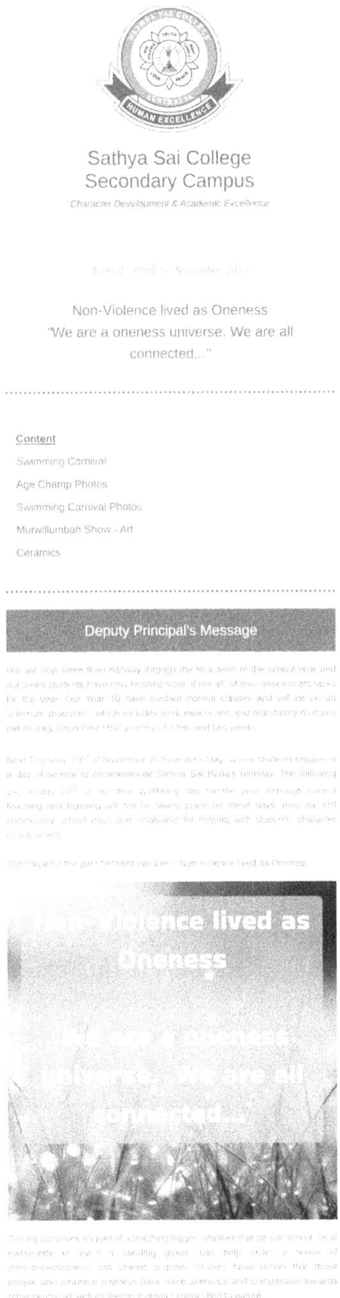

Figure 13.1 (Continued)

Appendix 13.2: Examples of School Policies Reflecting Values Frameworks (see Earlier Section 13.3.3)

School Philosophy[27]

Sathya Sai Preschool – Rongomai

Statement of Philosophy

The Sathya Sai Preschool has been established for the purpose of providing quality, value-based, free education to our community through the Sathya Sai Educare programme.

Our teachers will exemplify the values of Right Conduct, Peace, Truth, Love, and Non-violence and will draw these innate Human Values from the children using the Educare teaching method and by imbuing the lessons in classes with Human Values.

Parents, family, whanau, volunteers, and persons who choose to work in the Preschool in a supporting role will do so with an understanding of these values and a willingness to make them the basis of all interactions, thus making the Preschool, and its wider community, a Human Values learning and practising one. Through this values-based practice, values will become a meaningful experience both within our community and to those with whom we come into contact.

Figure 13.2 Statement of Philosophy for a Values-Based Preschool

School Action Plan[28]

Vision

'Character Development with Academic Excellence' has been the governing principle of all endeavours in the school. The school at every step, big or small, is guided by the comprehensive educational philosophy of Sri Sathya Baba who emphatically advocates, 'Education should be for life; not for mere living'.

Mission

The relentless pursuit of the school is:

To lay the foundation of a noble character in the young minds by instilling in them the eternal and universal values of brotherhood, patriotism, sacrifice, and moral integrity so that they grow up as ideal leaders who can shape the destiny of the nation and the world.

Figure 13.3 School Action Plan (*Continued*)

To fulfil our mission, we aim to:

1. Work together with our wider school community to create an environment, culture, and ethos permeated by the active practice of the five inherent human values; Truth, Right Conduct, Peace, Love, and Non-violence in daily life.
2. Select competent staff with good character and support them in being excellent team members and exemplars of the human values.
3. Maintain a student population that reflects local and national culture.
4. Provide a curriculum that meets state registration requirements and integrates the philosophy of *Sathya Sai Educare* using the teaching method of *Integral Education* (see Addendum).
5. Maintain recognition by the Sri Sathya Sai World Foundation as a Sathya Sai College by ongoing review and renewal in line with the Sathya Sai College Guidelines (see Addendum).
6. Provide the environment, resources, and opportunity for each child to achieve their best academic potential.
7. Provide education which is experiential and transformational in character, in addition to imparting knowledge and skills.
8. Encourage the unity of thought, word, and deed.
9. Develop an active social conscience in students and an inclination to provide service to others.

The school does not charge tuition fees but only a low resource fee to cover the cost of resources provided to students.

Curriculum

The philosophical cornerstone of Sathya Sai Education is the concept of *Sathya Sai Educare*. Sathya Sai Baba says,

> *Educare has two aspects, the worldly and the spiritual. Worldly education brings out the latent knowledge pertaining to the physical world. Spiritual education brings out the inherent divinity in man. So, both worldly and spiritual educations are essential, without which the human life has no value.*

The guiding principles of the term *Sathya Sai Educare* in the context of *education* are:

- Divinity is love and it is manifested as the universal human values;
- *Sathya Sai Educare* enables men and women to navigate the world and to realise their spiritual heritage;
- The purpose of education is for living a fully human and spiritual life;
- The end of education is character, and character manifests itself as the unity of thought, word, and deed.

Figure 13.3 (Continued)

The school provides a balanced curriculum that maximises the opportunity for all students to achieve the outcomes described in the Board of Studies Syllabus and *Sathya Sai World Foundation* guidelines.

Educare

The founder of the school Sri Sathya Sai Baba has fostered a unique approach to education called ***educare***, drawing out divine qualities of truth, right-conduct, peace, love, and non-violence which are latent within the individual. *Educare* aligns the heart, head, and hands. True education must in Sai Baba's words, 'broaden the heart and expand one's love'. True education is 'that which fosters the sense of oneness, draws out one's divine qualities and promotes the blossoming of human personality'.

To enable the adaptation of the above the Sathya Sai College:

- provides **Integral Education** by combining value-based education with academic excellence
- provides holistic learning experience that is **I**nsightful, **I**nspiring, **E**njoyable and **P**articipative **(IIEP)**
- create a domain of influence to learning interactions in **C**lassroom, designing learning spaces in **C**orridors, learning culture in the **C**ampus and through **C**ommunity outreach **(4Cs)**

Figure 13.3 *(Continued)*

School Code of Ethics[29]

Each one of the teachers, volunteers, and directors involved with Toogoolawa Schools makes a personal commitment to go through an ongoing transformation to become ideal role models of the Human Values for the students in their care. To assist us in this endeavour, we have the 'Code of Ethics for Teachers (Figure 13.4)'.

Love can be expressed by:

- Relating to the 'wise inner-goodness' of each student
- Whenever possible, putting the interests of the student ahead of one's own
- Using caring and respectful words
- Developing compassion, so that the student's pain and frustration is felt and understood

Figure 13.4 Code of Ethics for Teachers at a Values-Based School *(Continued)*

Truth can be expressed by:

- Practising honesty in dealing with students, staff, friends, society and encouraging honesty in the students
- Recognising that we are more than a body which moves, thinks and feels – that we are all kings and queens in disguise
- Learning to discover and trust one's own intuition
- Developing self-confidence and having trust is a higher power

Peace can be expressed by:

- Being a good listener
- Taking time to explain things carefully, sometimes more than once
- Showing patience and tolerance, even when provoked
- Moving without hurry or haste

Right conduct can be expressed by:

- Behaving towards others (particularly students) as one would like others to behave towards oneself
- Demonstrating personal tidiness, punctuality, and integrity
- Being true to the dictates of one's own conscience
- Having respect for society's laws, the elderly, and one's parents and for the customs and practices of other cultures and faiths

Non-violence can be expressed by:

- Refraining from using hurtful words or actions
- Not speaking (or thinking) badly about others
- Speaking gently and kindly, even when firmness is required
- Avoiding the expression of one's own anger, resentment, bitterness, jealousy, and selfishness – changing them into love and peace as much as we can

Figure 13.4 (Continued)

Extract from School Bullying Policy[30]

Rationale

Children will tend to explore past the boundaries of acceptable or appropriate behaviour and the teacher's role is to set and teach them the boundaries through the philosophy of the Sathya Sai School Rongomai.

Figure 13.5 Extract from School Bullying Policy *(Continued)*

When children achieve appropriate behaviour, acknowledgement and reinforcement are paramount.

Aim

To use positive methods and appropriate values-related vocabulary to help children take responsibility for their own actions, learn to respect the rights of others, control inappropriate emotions, and reflect on the consequences for themselves and others of applying appropriate values.

Procedures

- Remind the child of appropriate behaviour.
- Refrain from bribery and threats.
- Roleplay preferred action.
- Use storytelling where appropriate to make children aware of appropriate values choices.

Teachers ensure that:

- Every child deserves respect and dignity.
- Every child is encouraged to display appropriate social competence and values, taking into consideration the child's age and stage of development.

Every child is given positive guidance strategies, and teachers:

- Role model praise and encouragement,
- Avoid blame and harsh language, and
- Avoid belittling or degrading responses.

Figure 13.5 (*Continued*)

Appendix 13.3: Examples of Relating EHV to Curricular Criteria (See Earlier Section 13.3.5)

- The following is an example from *Wellbeing Criteria* set previously for Grade 2 by the Tasmanian Education Department.[31] The left-hand column lists these criteria, and the right-hand one illustrates how the values education programme relates to them:

Table 13.1 Example of a Wellbeing Criteria Set for Grade 2

Criterion	*Illustration of EHV relationship*
Encouraged to use relevant 'values' language	Children are encouraged to focus on 'wellbeing' terms including inner peace/not being disturbed if upsetting things happen around them/appreciating having a place of silence and solitude where they can feel free to be themselves, etc.

(*Continued*)

Table 13.1 (Continued)

Criterion	*Illustration of EHV relationship*
Significant value in class of group meetings to identify issues, pose problems, and provide strategies to reinforce personal and social responsibility	A weekly meeting is held for children to share what they have done to help others, for the 'diamond of the week' to reflect on how the experience has helped him/her, and for the incoming 'diamond of the week' to discuss helpful strategies.
Self-directed, adaptable, and resilient, and recognise the interdependent factors that contribute to wellbeing	As a result of regular discussions, children are aware of the power of everyone combining forces to help somebody who wants to change, but that it is important to do this in the way that person wants.
'stop', 'think', 'do' strategies	Children respond very well to the idea of 'head, heart and hands' – that is, whenever an idea comes into our heads, we should examine in our hearts whether or not it is a good thing to do before we put it into action with our hands.
Developing a sense of belonging to a group	Children develop a sense of group solidarity as they begin to recognise the powerful effect of everyone helping and supporting each other.
Key concept of 'space'	It is very important for young children – particularly hyperactive ones – to have a sense of their own space. Psychologists have made effective use of visualising a golden circle or bubble enclosing the child to promote this sense of personal space. This is used regularly (preferably daily) in silent sitting.
Understand what is involved in making health decisions and in managing and maintaining a healthy and balanced lifestyle	As children fill in the space in their weekly diaries about 'helping myself' they become increasingly aware of the factors that are important to them for their wellbeing (getting enough rest, being happy with themselves, playing a musical instrument to make themselves feel happy, playing sport because it makes them feel good, etc.). This has been particularly successful if their parents become involved.
Starting to identify differences in other people and begin to understand that others do not necessarily share the same perspective on issues that they do	Emphasis is placed on the fact that EVERYONE has special strengths and talents and that it is important for us to recognise and celebrate these.
Friendship groups – understanding how to be a good friend and keep friends	Diary entries have included comments such as 'I invited somebody who was lonely to join in a game we were playing'. This kind of emphasis on how to be a good friend can be encouraged through the diary entry on 'helping my friends'. Children become aware of consciously putting into practise strategies to help their friends.

- The following extract[32] is another illustration of a school's alignment with the national curriculum and the school's values philosophy. The first column shows criteria from the New Zealand preschool curriculum.[33] The middle column shows how the school has aligned these criteria with Māori and Pacific Islander values since the school caters mostly for children from these cultural groups. The third column shows alignment with Sathya Sai Education in Human Values.

Sathya Sai Education in Human Values Integrated with Te Whariki		
Te Whariki	**Maori/Tangata Pasifika**	**SSEHV**
Empowerment – Whakamana Protecting and promoting children Respecting and responding to the cultures, identities, and languages of the children attending the school Develop self-esteem and confidence about their identity, language, and culture	Protecting the Mana of childrenWhakamana is understood and reflected. It is embedded within cultural perspectives and the ways these perspectives are expressed in the learning programmes and wellbeing of the children in the preschool	Honouring the beingness of the child as an embodiment of Love, Truth, Beauty, and GoodnessLearning environment is inclusive of children's' identity, culture, and language
Family and Community – Whanau Tangata Teachers make connections across the settings in children's lives, including their homes Fostering culturally and linguistically appropriate ways of communicating with whānau, parents, extended family, and community	Whānau Tangata Learning environment depicts elements of children's cultureCulturally inclusive and appropriate ways of interacting and communicating	Teachers will demonstrate an attitude of enhancement and strengthening to all children. Learning programme will include the five Human values – Love, Peace, Truth, Right conduct and Non-violence and related values common to Maori/ Pasifika and other cultures in the centre *See notes for definition of values

Figure 13.6 A School's Alignment of the National Curriculum and the School's Values Philosophy (*Continued*)

Holistic Development – Kotahitanga Identities, languages, and cultures are important aspects of children's lives and their relationships with their worlds and others. Cultural understandings influence perceptions of the cognitive, social, cultural, physical, emotional, and spiritual dimensions of human development. The ways in which these dimensions of children's lives are interwoven is therefore shaped by the identities, languages, and cultures of children, whānau, and kaiako.	Children's learning and development is enhanced thought Tikanga Maori, Kaupapa Maori/ Pacifika Centre reflects and connects to Tikanga and whenunatanga are important feature of this connectivity. The identities, languages, and cultures of whānau and communities influence child-rearing patterns, beliefs and traditions, and the ways different knowledge, skills, and attitudes are valued.	Teachers will validate and weave features of the cultural learning mat through the values of respect of all cultures and promote the holistic development of the children through inclusiveness and culturally appropriate right conduct and the value of right conduct.
Relationships – Ngā Hononga The development of culturally and linguistically appropriate ways of communicating with parents, whānau, and community supports the development of meaningful, trusting relationships. These relationships may acknowledge the past, present, and future, the importance of place and land, and engagement with people, places, events, and taonga. It also requires understandings of, and respect for, whānau aspirations for their children.	Build on trusting, respectful relationships of Rangimaria, and respect Whanau aspirations that the child is the taonga and the centrepiece of the school in all aspects.	Teachers are aware of parents' aspirations and children are respected as the most important treasures of the nation. Human values of treasuring the children to be embodiments of love and knowledge. Programmes and interactions allow for children to discover their hidden treasure. Build on the knowledge horizon that PARENTS ARE THE FIRST TEACHERS (PAFT).

Figure 13.4 (*Continued*)

- The next set of extracts is from the policy documents of the Australian Sathya Sai College (SSC). These have been extracted to illustrate the emphasis on human values in the policies, and the way in which this emphasis is represented in the actual documents.

Extract from Bullying Policy

The SSC community aims to prevent bullying by modelling and promoting appropriate behaviour through the college's five Human Values of Love, Peace, Truth, Right Conduct, and Non-violence and encourages all SSC members to engage in respectful relationships.

SSC staff have a responsibility to:

- respect and support all students,
- model and promote appropriate behaviour and Human Values,
- have knowledge of SSC's policies relating to bullying behaviour, and
- respond in a timely manner to incidents of bullying according to SSC's Antibullying Plan.

Extract from Student Code of Conduct

All students shall be treated with dignity, respect, and fairness by other students and staff. They shall be provided with a learning environment that is free from physical, emotional, and social abuse.

In return, students at the Sathya Sai College are expected to:

- Show respect for authority, parents, elders, others, and their property, values, and ethnic backgrounds.
- Strive for academic excellence.
- Be disciplined and apply the five Human Values in daily life.
- Follow good study and work habits such as concentration and time management.
- Be friendly and cooperative by forming positive relationships with peers and adults.
- Report any incidents, including those in the nature of bullying, to the attention of staff immediately.
- Show initiative and a willingness to accept responsibility.
- Take responsibility increasingly for their own choices, through their own conscience.
- Be punctual and follow school attendance, uniform, and other policies.
- Develop an attitude of selfless service to the community.

Figure 13.7 Extracts from school policy documents *(Continued)*

Extract from Procedure for Wellbeing and Self-Discipline

The Sathya Sai EHV model is based on the premise 'the end of education is character'. Therefore, every opportunity is used to enhance character. While implementing a disciplinary action, the teacher adopts the use of 'To Teach, Not to Punish'; a practical Human Values Approach to Discipline model which uses key vocabulary that can be used in explaining to the child the purpose of the correct exercise and where it adds to the value of the process. The following is an outline of the school's discipline procedures.

Classroom rules:

- Display the five human values: Love, Truth, Right action, Peace, and Non-violence.
- Listen to the teacher and follow directions.
- Show respect for yourself and all others.
- Put up your hand when you wish to say something.
- Give your best effort.
- Keep your classroom and belongings clean and tidy.

Each class teacher is to implement an appropriate reward system for his/her class. The important ingredients for a healthy classroom interaction to occur come from students showing or promoting the five universal, secular human values behaviours such as:

- Responsibility through hard work
- Peace through calmness, displaying outwardly as clear speech
- Non-violence through treating peers with care and love

Students to focus on values vision:

- The school culture and ethos encourage reflective behaviour and understanding.
- A student must be able to articulate and give reasons why his/her behaviour was deemed inappropriate.
- The values are the core basis for explaining inappropriate behaviour, and teachers should always ask three questions to elicit understanding. These questions include:
  - Was your behaviour loving?
  - Was your behaviour peaceful?
  - Were you practising truth?

Figure 13.7 (Continued)

Notes

1 https://www.speakingtree.in/blog/influence-of-mother-on-gandhiji accessed 30-12-2021.
2 https://www.familius.com/the-dad-influence-famous-people-and-how-their-dads-made-a-difference/ accessed 30-12-2021.
3 Nemours Kids Health Medical Experts (n.d.). https://kidshealth.org/en/parents/nine-steps.html#:~:text=9%20Steps%20to%20More%20Effective%20Parenting%201%201.,That%20Your%20Love%20Is%20Unconditional%20...%20More%20items accessed 12-3-2023.
4 M. Carr-Gregg, *Strictly Parenting* (Melbourne, Australia: Penguin Group, 2014).
5 *Ibid.*
6 Sathya Sai College, Murwillumbah, NSW. https://sathyasaicollege.nsw.edu.au/newsletters/ accessed 30-12-2021.
7 For more details about the VAPP workshop please contact Institute of Sathya Sai Education, Australia, info@issea.org.au
8 The Australian Sathya Sai College, Murwillumbah, NSW.
9 The VAPP was developed and implemented by Bob and Roz Molloy while Bob was the Principal of the Sathya Sai School (now College), Australia.
10 Maryland State Department of Education, *Character Education by Design. A Blueprint for Successful District and School Initiatives* (Baltimore, MD: Maryland State Department of Education, 2007). https://files.eric.ed.gov/fulltext/ED509093.pdf.accessed 12-3-2023
11 These values education initiatives have been adapted from: Maryland State Department of Education, *Character Education by Design. A Blueprint for Successful District and School Initiatives* (Baltimore, MD: Maryland State Department of Education, 2007).
12 Maryland State Department of Education, *Character Education by Design*, 2007.
13 For example, see: M. Taplin and A. Devi, *To Teach, Not to Punish: A Practical Human Values Approach to Discipline* (Hong Kong: Institute of Sathya Sai Education, 2004). https://issea.org.au/wp-content/uploads/2020/08/To-Teach-Not-to-Punish.pdf.accessed 27-1-2024
14 For an example of a community of practice in action, please see the professional development section in Chapter 14.
15 Maryland State Department of Education, *Character Education by Design*, 2007.
16 G. Gay, "Preparing for Culturally Responsive Teaching," *Journal of Teacher Education* 53, no. 2 (2002): 106–116.
17 *Ibid.*
18 For a deeper discussion of values-based discipline, please refer to Taplin and Devi, *To Teach, Not to Punish*, 2004. Available for free download from: https://issea.org.au/resources/creating-a-values-rich-environment/ accessed 27-2-2023.
19 For some examples, please refer to the website: https://issea.org.au/ accessed 2-12-2021.
20 D. A. Brown, *Growing Character: 99 Successful Strategies for the Elementary Classroom* (Chapel Hill, NC: Character Development Publishing, 2003).
21 Taken from: R. Farmer, *Love Changes Everything. Toogoolawa Schools: Stories from the Real Education Revolution* (Australia: McPherson, 2009).
22 *Ibid.*
23 See: www.issea.org.au for a collection of free, downloadable posters and associated activities suitable for this purpose.
24 W.A.T.C.H. is an acronym as mentioned in earlier chapters. Its use is described with students on the verge of expulsion: see project (2) at this website: https://issea.org.au/projects/completed/.accessed 27-1-2024

25 B. Courtenay, *The Power Of One* (UK: Popular Penguins, 2010).
26 From Sathya Sai College, Australia, 2023
27 From *Sathya Sai Preschool, Rongomai*. Auckland, New Zealand, 2021.
28 From Sathya Sai College, Australia, 2021.
29 Taken from: R. Farmer, Love Changes Everything. Toogoolawa Schools: Stories from the Real Education Revolution (Australia: McPherson, 2009).
30 Bullying policy adapted *from Sathya Sai Preschool, Rongomai*. Auckland, New Zealand, 2021
31 Department of Education and the Arts, Tasmania. *Our Children: The Future. A Curriculum for Children* (1991).
32 From *Sathya Sai Preschool, Rongomai*. Auckland, New Zealand, 2021.
33 Ministry of Education, *Te Whāriki: Early Childhood Curriculum* (New Zealand, 2017).

Chapter 14

Character Education through EHV in Practice

Roger Packham and Margaret Taplin

14.1 Introduction

The goal of this chapter is to demonstrate the application and benefits of values education through Education in Human Values (EHV) in a number of real-world contexts. The *Educare* philosophy and the integration of the EHV teaching techniques are the key features, and the success of these schools depends on a whole-school philosophy in which all stakeholders have a constant and integrated awareness of practising human values (see Chapter 13), including ongoing teacher professional development.

The chapter gives some specific examples of how EHV impacts upon teachers and students. It also introduces some background about model Sathya Sai Schools around the world that have been established to demonstrate EHV. Also included is a snapshot of a teacher professional development session conducted in one such model school in Australia.

14.2 The Model for a Sathya Sai School

The founder of EHV said, *A school should not be considered to be just a commonplace arrangement designed for teaching and learning. It is the place where the consciousness is aroused and illumined, purified and strengthened, the place where the seeds of discipline, duty and devotion are planted and fostered into fruition.*[1] Around the world, there are 'Sathya Sai Schools' that have been established for the purpose of demonstrating how to create whole-school EHV models and to demonstrate the benefits of doing so. The first ones were established in India starting in 1968, and from the early 1990s, Sathya Sai Schools were then established in other countries. By 2021, there were around 40 Schools in around 30 countries. Institutes of Sathya Sai Education (ISSE) have also been established in each of these countries to train teachers and ensure the quality of the EHV approach. All Sathya Sai Schools practise EHV, particularly by integrating *Educare* with the curricula of their respective countries. Their broad aim is to graduate students with both good characters and skills in academic areas, developed

DOI: 10.4324/9781003478607-15

through the integration of EHV using both direct and indirect methods (see Chapters 8, 9, and 10).

All Sathya Sai Schools are independent private schools and are non-denominational, but are aligned with the cultural and/or political ideologies of the countries in which they are established. They operate within the legal, cultural, and educational frameworks of their respective countries of location. They are subject to government oversight, follow the official curricula of local or national educational authorities, and prepare children for national examinations at different academic levels. They have an open-door policy of admission and are often located in disadvantaged areas of cities, towns, or rural areas so that they may provide quality education to children who would otherwise not receive it.

14.2.1 *Aspects of Values Education in Sathya Sai Schools*

There are many schools conducting excellent values education programmes. There are, however, some differences, often subtle, between what these schools are doing and what takes place in a Sathya Sai School. There are some particular characteristics that make Sathya Schools distinct and unique. These include:

- While a good school with a values education programme is concerned with character development, a Sathya Sai School is concerned with the transformation of children, teachers, and all others involved in the five dimensions of health – physical, intellectual, emotional, social, and spiritual. This implies that teachers need to understand these five dimensions (see Chapter 7 for more discussion about these).
- While conventional values programmes focus on values that are relevant to the local culture or those determined by local education authorities, in Sathya Sai Schools these same values are addressed but they are classified into the five categories of *Truth, Right Action, Peace, Love*, and *Non-violence*, not only as social skills but also as internal, intrapersonal values (see Chapter 4).
- Sathya Sai Schools utilise some unique concepts, including *3HV*, which is a play on the acronym EHV and refers to the harmony of head, heart, and hands; Ceiling on Desires; and *W.A.T.C.H.*; all of which were described in earlier chapters.
- While typical values education programmes are based on a culture of respect, Sathya Schools are founded on a culture of Love. This implies specific activities put in place to facilitate the development of this culture, with students, teachers, school management, and parents working together to develop loving cohesion as a group (see Chapter 13).
- While values are generally present in the environments of all good schools, in Sathya Sai Schools they permeate the total school environment – which implies that all personnel need to understand the concept of constant integrated awareness (CIA) of the values (see Chapter 13).

- In any good school, academic achievement is the goal. In a Sathya Sai School, academic achievement and values are given equal focus – with improved academic achievement nearly always turning out to be a by-product of the values permeation.
- Experiential education and active learning are key approaches in many good schools. In Sathya Sai Schools, experiential education is expanded to include not only the subject content but also to explore the human values through action, experience, and reflection (unity of thought, word, and deed) – this implies that teachers need to know how to create opportunities and encourage reflection (see Chapters 8, 9, and 10).
- Service learning is a phenomenon growing in popularity in many good schools. In Sathya Sai Schools, this plays a major role, and the emphasis is not only on the subject learning that takes place through service activities but also on the personal transformation that is brought about through service learning.
- Good schools have strong discipline policies. Sathya Sai Schools' discipline policies reach deeper than 'good behaviour', with an emphasis on using disciplinary situations to deepen students' reflections on their practise of appropriate values.
- It is common for good teaching practices to incorporate the techniques used frequently in Sathya Sai Schools; including groupwork, stories, inspiring quotations, songs, and various forms of silent sitting (see Chapters 8, 9, and 10). In Sathya Sai Schools, these techniques are designed specifically to encourage practice and reflection on the human values – this implies that teachers need to be equipped not just to use these techniques but to use them effectively for this purpose.
- While regular self-review, peer-review, and review by teachers are key to good evaluation practices, in Sathya Sai Schools this includes regular reviews of individuals' personal transformation (teachers as well as students).
- Co-curricular activities such as sport, music, and the arts are standard in most good schools, as they are in Sathya Sai Schools. In the latter, these activities are used to reinforce the philosophy of values in action and in reflection.

In Sathya Sai Schools, the local national curricula are followed, but values are ingested into all curriculum areas (see Chapters 8, 9, and 10). As well, regular timeslots are made available for the direct teaching method (see Chapter 8). These are supplemented further by the integration of values into the whole school community (see Chapters 9, 10, and 13), that is, all school stakeholders including students, teachers, support staff, cleaning staff, groundskeepers, and parents. Parents participate in training and other activities (see Chapter 13) to ensure understanding and involvement in the EHV philosophy.

Stakeholders:	Staff, Students, and Community
Base:	Constant Integrated Awareness – that is living the human values in all aspects of daily life
Where to Implement Values:	Classroom, Corridor, Campus, and Community
Tools:	Staff meeting presentations, professional development, planning to incorporate values into all lessons, practice of the values (fortnightly schedule), signage and displays, and use of the seven teaching techniques. Values Awareness Programme for Parents (VAPP) and other support staff held at regular intervals.

Figure 14.1 A Hierarchical Overview of a Model for a Sathya Sai School

14.2.2 *An Example of EHV Implementation*

Figure 14.1 presents a hierarchical overview of a model for a Sathya Sai School, this one having been developed by the Sathya Sai College in NSW, Australia.[2] More information on the establishment and development of the Australian Sathya Sai College is presented in Appendix 14.1.

The key here is that all stakeholders need to be onside with regards to the school's values-based philosophy. Once they are engaged, they are able to move towards a state of 'constant integrated awareness' (CIA, see Chapter 13), in which they are encouraged to live the human values in all aspects of their daily lives, so that it becomes automatic to respond to situations in values-related ways and to see and utilise opportunities to reflect on values that arise both in and out of the classroom. With their own appreciation of how their lives can be enhanced by this constant awareness and practice of values, it becomes important to utilise every aspect of the school environment as a vehicle for recognising and reflecting on these values; this gives rise to the '4Cs' – classroom, corridor, campus, and community. This reinforces the importance of constant reminders about values in all of these venues through displays of students' work that reflects on their own CIA (see Chapters 9 and 10), inspiring quotations and stories, and recognition of values-based behaviours. The bottom row in the table above describes the tools that can be used to bring about a values-permeated school (see Chapter 13).

14.3 EHV Outcomes from Sathya Sai Schools

This section presents some selected examples of Sathya Sai Schools and partnership schools in a range of continents that include Africa, Asia, Europe, and Australasia, as illustrations of typical outcomes of these schools.

14.3.1 Zambia

The Sathya Sai School of Ndola, Zambia, was started in 1991. The initial intakes were students from the poorest socio-economic areas. Many of them were school dropouts whom other schools in the district refused to accept. Within the first year, the school had achieved a 100% pass rate for the national exams. The Sathya Sai School in Zambia has received many awards and much acclaim. Its students continue to achieve 100% pass rates in Grades 7, 9, and 12.

The school[3] has adopted six government schools and six villages to participate in EHV and service activities. The school farm produces bags of maize and provides free weekly medical services and medical camps each term. Other service opportunities in which the students have been involved are assisting the blind and community-development activities like maintaining roadside drainage, painting zebra crossings, and caring for the environment. To ensure that the students receive the same messages at home and at school, regular workshops are held for parents as well as training seminars for teachers.

The following is the testimony of one student who studied at the school: *The human values of Sathya Sai have greatly enlightened me. They have taught me not to steal, and to have a good attitude towards work. Discipline, character, and behaviour are the most important things at school.*[4]

Another Year 7 student said, *My teachers were always interested in character. I thought they were going to make me a monitor because I was bigger than most of the boys. I was surprised to see that my teacher chose a boy who was medium sized but with good character. I learnt that to be a leader, you have to lead by example and not just be physically big while you are small in character.*[5]

14.3.2 Thailand[6]

The Sathya Sai School in Thailand has had a profound and positive influence on the Thai Education system. Building the school commenced in 1990, and it opened to the first class of nine children in 1992. Since then, hundreds of children have graduated from this institution and have taken the message of EHV into society.

The school has attracted widespread interest in EHV throughout Thailand. In the past 20 years, it has been visited by thousands of teachers, university professors, and students, as well as television and other media crews. The school's philosophy and teaching methods have also become a focus for several PhD and MA research dissertations.[7]

The Thai school has had an impact on a global basis, with seminars conducted by school leaders Dr Art-ong Jumsai and Ms Loraine Burrows, in more than 35 countries over a 20-year period. The school has become very well known as a leader of values education. The result of all this exposure has led to many changes in the Thai Education system, the most important being that morals or values should be a part of all classes.[8] The school's leaders have developed many books and other publications about teaching EHV, as well as an international residential teacher training programme based at the school: This course covers both the theory and practice of EHV, with classroom teaching a key aspect of the course.

14.3.3 Kenya[9]

The director of the district within which the Sathya Sai School Kisaju, Kenya, is located, viewed the EHV programme as a solution to various educational challenges in the whole of her school district, thanks to her experiences of the teachers, students, and school management. The director thus desired and requested that the schools in the education district embrace the EHV programme within their school curricula. Subsequently, in April 2017, Mrs Elizabeth Otieno, the District Education officer for the Kajiado District of Kenya, was a guest at the EHV Teacher Training Course at the Sathya Sai School. In her address at the opening ceremony, she expressed the pride she felt whenever she visited the Kisaju Sathya Sai School as it stood out for its consistently high academic performances and its serene and disciplined environment. She saw the programme as being especially relevant and timely as a new *Framework for Basic Education* had just been launched in Kenya in 2017.

A comparative study of the EHV model and this new framework was prepared and served as a discussion paper. Government officials agreed that the relevance of the EHV model and its associated teacher training programme would play an important role in preparing teachers to embrace the new framework, which stressed the importance of values education. The director of the nearby international teacher training college, who was also a private school principal whose school was chosen as a pilot school for the new framework, expressed interest in having the full EHV training for all her teachers, as well as becoming a 'partnership' school. There was a follow-up programme for 200 selected participants, specifically school managers and senior teachers. The district was on its way to developing its own trainers to further promote the EHV programme amongst its thousands of teachers in its schools.

14.3.4 South Africa[10]

In 2018, Mrs G.L. Myende, the Superintendent of Education for the Karanja and Burlington Education Circuit, Durban, South Africa, was a regular visitor to the Chatsworth Sathya Sai School in Durban as part of her professional development programme. The school was well known in her district as it always excelled in the annual matriculation (Grade 12) examinations. She also had one of her own children enrolled in the school. This led to an invitation to present the EHV programme to all school managers within her district. Approximately 150 educators attended, and feedback was highly positive, with many requesting EHV teacher training for their teachers. The programme was recognised immediately as a solution to the critical issue of student discipline in schools. Mrs Myende then approved a series of follow-up EHV training programmes in various school clusters.

14.4 Outcomes of EHV in Other Contexts

14.4.1 *Republic of Ireland*[11]

This is an example of a school that is not a Sathya Sai School, but one in which one teacher's use of EHV in one class developed into its being adopted by the whole school and beyond. It began in 2016 when Ann Moran, a primary school teacher, introduced the EHV method into her curriculum. The other teachers in the school noticed the transformation of her students and adopted it in their own teaching. The principal of the school became aware of the transformation of the students and adopted the philosophy to become a Human Values School. Being the first Human Values School in Ireland, and because of the remarkable achievement with using the EHV programme, it was featured on Ireland's national television.[12] Interest spread. An EHV training course was developed for other schools in 2018 to share with teachers and principals how to integrate EHV principles into their teaching and learning. Participants have included the principals of nine different special schools (for children with special educational needs) across Ireland. As a result of the training course (which is approved by the Department of Education in Ireland), there are at least 30 other schools to date that are incorporating EHV into their schools.

14.4.2 *The Toogoolawah School, Australia*

The Toogoolawah School[13] is a special school in Queensland that is based on EHV and the Educare philosophy and caters for teenage and pre-teen boys who are unable to fit in with mainstream schools due to social and emotional problems. The school reports significant positive impacts on the character development and academic achievement of the students: *Since Toogoolawah began operations in 1998, over 1580 students have benefited from the education programme. Of these, about one third of the boys have integrated back into mainstream schooling. Others enter traineeships or TAFE [vocational training] courses. Around 85% of the students leave Toogoolawah and take on some form of work or study.*[14]

14.4.3 *Partnership Schools*

Many Sathya Sai Schools have 'partnership' schools in which the entire school, public/government or private, is implementing EHV with the assistance of a Sathya Sai School. The Sathya Sai School assists with the EHV training, with some or all of the partnership school's teachers trained to deliver the EHV programme. An international survey conducted in 2018[15] identified 55 such schools in 22 countries, with programmes lasting from 1 to 13 years and having catered for an estimated total of around 30,000 students.

14.4.4 *Human Values in Water Sanitation and Hygiene Education Programme of UN-Habitat (HVWSHE)*

In the late 1990s, the Sathya Sai School of Zambia responded to water shortage in the school and its surrounding area, caused partly by selfish and corrupt behaviours, with a programme of education based on EHV. The programme's goal was to help the community to value water and become more honest and careful with its use. This programme was very effective and improved the situation for both the school and the community. News of this success quickly spread, and, as a result, the school was invited to share the project at a meeting of the United Nations (UN). Following this, the school's principal was recruited to help the *United Nations Human Settlements Programme* (UN-Habitat) develop a similar programme for their wider use. A primary focus of the work of UN-Habitat at that time was to support efforts by governments in developing countries in their pursuit of the (then) *Millennium Development Goals* (MDG) for water and sanitation. The new programme's rationale was the realisation that improvements in water management and use cannot be accomplished by technical or regulatory measures alone but need to be complemented by initiatives aimed at changing people's attitudes and behaviours towards water, sanitation, and hygiene. This was to be achieved through educational means in schools and communities, using EHV. In the view of UN-Habitat, EHV had the potential both to influence the behaviour of young children at primary school and to change attitudes in small local communities.

The programme was started under the leadership of both the Zambian Sathya Sai School Principal, Dr Victor Kanu, and Mr Kalyan Ray who, in 2000, was the head of the Urban Basic Services branch of UN-Habitat in Nairobi, Kenya. The programme commenced in six African cities in 2001, and, after a favourable external review in 2004, it was modified and expanded into a further eleven African cities in nine countries.

In 2003, an Asian component was started under the auspices of the Southeast Asian Ministers of Education Organization (SEAMEO) and the Government of the Philippines. HVWSHE then became an integral component of UN-Habitat's Water for Asian Cities Programme. Dr Art-ong Jumsai and Ms Loraine Burrows, from the Sathya Sai School and Institute of Sathya Sai Education of Thailand, led the EHV teacher training component in Asia, and the Sathya Sai School of Thailand developed a 'water classroom' and eco-house to demonstrate human values in action for the environment. These facilities received more than 1000 visitors each month. A set of videos in English became available on the Thai Ministry of Education website to support this programme.[16] Subsequently, Latin American and Caribbean programmes were started.

14.5 Outcomes for Students Using EHV

There are many anecdotes about the beneficial impacts of EHV on students. As just one set of examples, in the Australian context, the following comments are from Grade 6 students in a Queensland public primary school who had completed just one year of EHV.[17] In particular, the comments illustrate how their teacher's frequent 'values talk' and activities such as silent sitting and singing inspirational songs had an impact on the students and helped them to make significant changes in their behaviours and thinking.

Student A: Grade 6 girl

What realisation/'aha moment' led me to change?
Selfish love and selfless love – means don't fake love, be truthful.
Ceiling on desires – you always need to have your desires sealed.
Discrimination – distinction between right/wrong.
Always stay calm.

Student B: Grade 6 girl

What was my behaviour like at the start of the year?
My behaviour at the start of the year was very poor. I really had no respect for anyone, and I hated school. I was restless, loud, annoying, stupid, and uneducated about what life really meant and the purpose of it.
Where am I at the moment?
My behaviour is improving, and I have more respect for people. I now love school and want to come every day because we do the values education. Now, I know the purpose of it, and I'm starting to get it.
What has led me to that transformation?
The song ('I am Light') has really helped me; I listen to it all the time, and also the silent sitting has helped me a lot.

Student C: Grade 6 girl

I realised that if I don't stand up for myself that I would be taken advantage of and lead to the wrong path and that I would be pushed around. I realised that crying wouldn't solve anything either.
What has led me to that transformation?
Knowing how to act like a human being and also how to self-control your behaviour.
Self-control knowing you can but deciding you won't.

Student D: Grade 6 boy

What helped me:
My teacher, Mr Ram, and the phrase he has: What is the point of tomorrow if today is the same as yesterday? I knew I needed to change!

Student E: Grade 6 boy

My behaviour was terrible at the start of the year, but Mr Ram taught me how to be in the *now* and why I am here; the same with the journey of life. I've changed a little, bit but I believe by the end of high school I'll have changed, with his voice showing and guiding me to the way of life. Example: 'If you are on a boat and you're in a bad storm, what would you do?' What Mr Ram is trying to say is that you should keep your cool when bad things are happening around you.

Student F: Grade 6 girl

My teacher, Mr Ram, has taught my class and me a lot of importance, including things to do with behaviour, life, yourself, and what you really don't have to worry about!

I have been taught that I'm the B=beauty, the diamond within myself and, if I try, I can succeed. These messages have really brought out the best in me, and I'm now more like a true human being.

Student G: Grade 6 girl

I was a little bit behind in some areas, and I was very confused about what was going on and I got into trouble a little bit more than often.

I'm back on track quite a lot. All the human values made me the person I am now, and also silent sitting and the song 'I am Light' got me through a lot. Inside of us, there are two wolves. One is anger, envy, sorrow, regret, greed, etc. And the other is joy, peace, love, serenity, etc.

Student H: Grade 6 girl

The lotus flower first starts off in disgusting dirty mud but comes out beautiful. This shows us that if we are brought up with bad stuff around us, we can ignore that and come out with the diamond within us.

14.6 Teacher Professional Development in EHV

When we personally reflect on our own teachers who had the strongest impacts on us, we usually find that the most memorable were the ones who inspired us. It is often said that these kinds of teachers are 'born not made'; however, it is our belief that the right kind of professional development in human values can help most teachers to become the kinds of teachers who inspire and whom their students will remember for life. Furthermore, we strongly believe that human values professional development can be a very effective instrument for teacher wellbeing, nurturing teachers to better cope with the challenges of their professional lives. It is for this reason that this description of Sathya Sai School professional development programmes begins with an emphasis on 'putting the teachers first'.

14.6.1 Putting the Teachers First

The following two quotes from the founder of EHV acknowledge the importance of teachers nurturing themselves first and foremost: *Teachers are reservoirs from which, through the process of education, students draw the water of life. Only if there is water in the tank can you get water in the tap. If the tank is dry, how can you draw water from the tap?*.[18] Further, he said *You have it in your power to make your days on Earth a path of flowers, instead of a path of thorns.*[19]

We want to emphasise strongly here that EHV is not intended to be an add-on extra to teachers' busy lives or to create a sense that this is just one more thing that teachers are expected to do. Teachers, by their very nature, are already practising human values in their lives. Nevertheless, as the quotations above suggest, it is necessary for teachers to nurture themselves; if they try to keep giving and giving without doing so, it is likely that they will eventually become drained and empty, which is what many refer to as 'burnt out'. A major purpose of the ideas and strategies shared throughout this book is to help teachers (and others, such as parents and caregivers) to understand these values better and to use them to benefit themselves first and foremost.

The comments below are from teachers[20] who have put EHV into practice in their own lives, as well as with their classes, and found that they were able to cope much more easily with their professional and personal lives. The more the teachers integrated the practices of the values into their own lives, the more the transformation extended to their students, with the whole school environment becoming more harmonious for everyone. This is the aim of CIA.

Teacher A: Since participating in the values education, the children in the class and I have grown together, letting me realise the value of the human values. Their forgiveness, loyalty, sympathy, love, selflessness, peace, patience, and so on have given my own life a focus and have caused me to have warmth, forgiveness, and love.

Teacher B: I think that we have to improve ourselves … if we persist in forming good habits, our thinking and behaviour will be improved … if our hearts are kind, our children will be positive and, in this condition, we can all feel happy.

Teacher C: I have no problems these days because I have changed my mood, so life is easy for me.

Teacher D: I can look at things from another perspective when I communicate with children or parents. I am more tolerant.

Teacher E: If we feel happy, then we can deal with the exhaustion and other problems – even if the problems don't go away, we can deal with them better.

Teacher F: Before, it took too much time to deal with problems – now I feel I am more tolerant – emotionally better, more communicative with children, positive changes in the children have made me happier, and this has had positive effects on my health.

Teacher G: The children in my Grades 1 and 2 classes like to do silent sitting at the beginning of the lesson – this can settle them and also can give me the strength to calm down and be peaceful, so I will not be influenced by the children's behaviour.

Teacher H: Every day, early in the morning, I close my eyes and breathe deeply three times and fully concentrate on the day's work … Then the day's work goes smoothly – everything is under control, and I feel full of joy.

And the teachers' practice of the values even has effects on families:

Teacher I: In the year of the EHV, I have gradually changed from impatient to tranquil. Even if my husband does not come home for his meal, I am tranquil. I will watch television, prepare a lesson, and perhaps practise writing some calligraphy. I no longer get into a rage or slam down the telephone, but look at it from his point of view, understand, and forgive him.

Teacher J: As an average teacher, I think that the values education has changed me in many ways. The values education has changed my disposition when I encounter a difficulty. Instead of being irritable or having a fit of temper, it has helped me to learn to endure patiently and be tolerant.

Teacher K: In my family, I am the only daughter; therefore, I was often impulsive, did not consider others' feelings, and always expected to be the 'centre'. If something happened to not meet my expectations, I was unable to recover after a setback. But after participating in the values education, I changed. I have become magnanimous, open-minded, and forgiving. I say frequently to myself that others must feel happy and joyful because of my existence. If I can make others joyful, I will.

While the human values are already inherent within us, it does take time and practice to develop the habit of CIA. Regular EHV staff meetings can be a valuable opportunity for teachers to share their stories and experiences and inspire each other. The excerpt below illustrates how the teachers learn and grow together in regular meetings at the Sathya Sai College, Australia.

14.6.2 Regular EHV Staff Meetings

Figure 14.2 is the school's weekly staff meeting schedule. The highlighted boxes are the fortnightly EHV Staff Meetings. (Teachers' names have been changed for anonymity.) This schedule illustrates the frequency of EHV meetings, which are given the same amount of attention as the Key Learning Activity (KLA) meetings held in the alternative fortnights, and the range of values topics covered (see also the values schedule, Chapter 8).

WK	*TERM 1*	*TERM 2*	*TERM 3*	*TERM 4*
1	**25/1 –** First day of the year – whole staff welcome and allocation of roles & responsibilities, etc	**20/4** –Staff meeting Jane* sharing Love lived as Caring	**15/7 –** KLA/Team meeting	**7/10 –** No Staff meeting – Yr 12 P & T interviews
2	**4/2 –** EHV meeting Joe sharing Right Conduct lived as Courage	**29/4 –** EHV meeting Doris sharing Right Conduct lived as Determination	**22/7 –** EHV meeting Sally sharing Truth lived as Discrimination	**14/10 –** EHV meeting Ange sharing Love lived as Service
3	**11/2 –** KLA/Team meetings	**5/5 – P & T Interviews** **6/5 –** Staff meeting Erin on minutes	**29/7 –** Staff meeting Greg on minutes	**21/10 –** KLA/ Team meetings
4	**18/2 –** EHV meeting Greg sharing Peace lived as Optimism	**13/5 –** EHV meeting John sharing Non Violence lived as Understanding	**5/8 –** EHV meeting Karen sharing Love lived as Sharing	**28/10 –** EHV meeting Joe sharing Right Conduct lived as manners
5	**25/2 –** Staff meeting Karen on minutes	**20/5 –** KLA/Team meeting	**12/8 –** KLA/Team meeting	**4/11 –** Staff meeting Sally on minutes
6	**4/3 –** EHV meetings Sally sharing Non Violence lived as Restraint	**27/5 –** EHV meeting Helen sharing Peace lived as Flexibility	**19/8 –** EHV meeting Jane sharing Peace lived as Patience	**11/11 –** EHV meeting Rob sharing Non Violence lived as Justice
7	**11/3 –** KLA/Team meeting	**3/6 –** Staff meeting Ange on minutes	**26/8 –** Staff meeting Joe on minutes	**18/11 –** No meeting Report writing

Figure 14.2 Staff EHV and KLA/Team Meeting Schedule 2021 Staff, EHV and KLA/ Team Meetings Schedule 2021 Thursdays **3:00 pm – 5:00 pm** In Room 2 *(Continued)*

8	**18/3** – EHV meeting Beth sharing on Truth lived as Truthfulness	**10/6** – EHV meeting Geoff sharing Truth lived as Honesty	**2/9** – EHV meeting Sue sharing Non Violence lived as Humility	**25/11** – EHV meeting Ange sharing Truth lived as Unity
9	**25/3** – Staff meeting Helen on minutes	**17/6** – No staff meeting – report writing	**9/9** – KLA/Team meeting	**2/12** – Staff meeting Karen on minutes
10	**1/4** – EHV meeting	**24/6** – EHV meeting Doris sharing Right Conduct lived as Cleanliness	**16/9** – EHV meeting Kate sharing Peace lived as Resilience	**9/12** – KLA/Team meetings

Figure 14.2 (Continued)

14.6.3 A Snapshot of an EHV Staff Meeting

Most of the following ideas have been taken from the Sathya Sai College, Australia, with a few other ideas, such as starting the meeting with silent sitting and ending it with a song, drawn from other schools:

- It is 3 p.m. and the school echoes with the silence that always settles when the children have gone home. The teachers are gathering in the staff room for the EHV Staff Meeting that is held instead of regular staff meetings every second week.
- As usual, they start with the Light Visualisation (see Chapter 8). This week it is Jane's turn to lead it. At first, some of the teachers thought it was a somewhat strange way to start a staff meeting, but they have come to look forward to it as a way of re-energising themselves after the day's work, and they feel that it creates a sense of harmony and collegiality that makes it easier for them to work together on the meeting's tasks.
- John, a fairly new teacher, uses the opportunity to share an experiment he has been trying for the past week. 'I have started doing this visualisation by myself for a few minutes every morning when I first get into in my classroom before the children arrive. I feel so much calmer after rushing around to get here. I finish by imagining that I am sending light to each child in the class – even to the ones whom I don't particularly like or the usual troublemakers. I don't know if it's because this affects my mindset or why it happens, but I am finding that the troublemakers are less troublesome, and the less likeable students are so much easier to get along with. There seem to be fewer problems during the day, and when they do arise, I seem to be able to cope with them so much better.'

- 'What a great idea', Joe responds. 'I'd like to start doing that too. It would probably encourage me to remember to do it if we made a time each morning to do it together.' Others agree, and in no time a group of six teachers has formed, agreeing to meet daily and do the visualisation together.
- This fortnight, it's Ange's turn to introduce the meeting on the topic of Truth, expressed as Acceptance, which is to be the whole-school value for the next fortnight (Figure 14.3). Ange is a fresh graduate, and the concept of EHV is very new to her, but she is learning quickly. She has thought carefully about this topic and presents her ideas for addressing this value in direct EHV lessons (see the 6Es description, Chapter 8).

	Sathya Sai College EHV – Lesson Plan Template			
Level	Grade: 5 & 6	Created By:		
Schedule	Term 1		Weeks: 7 & 8	
Value	**Truth**			
Sub-Value	**Acceptance**			
Format	**6 E's – (incorporating the current techniques to further enhance the effectiveness and sharpness of the delivery)** **When preparing the lesson plan give attention to the following Domains – Classroom, Corridor, Campus, and Community**			
A. Silent Sitting – USE what may be appropriate for the class/Change after a period.				
The 'blossoming heart' visualisation				
B. Quote – USE quotes that are easy to remember and are inspiring.				
'Acceptance is the road to all change...'				
C. INQUISITIVE QUESTIONS – Mind Mapping – ENGAGE				

Figure 14.3 Draft Direct Lesson Plan for 'Truth, Expressed as Acceptance'

(Continued)

Key questions

- 'What is acceptance?
- How can we show acceptance?
- What are some related values?
- What are the benefits/challenges of acceptance?
- Examples of where you have lived or seen the value of acceptance in action
- How do we/others feel when we show acceptance?
- What does acceptance look like?
- How do I feel when I have to accept that some things just are the way they are, because it is not possible to change them?
- How do others feel when I accept things about them that they can't change?
- What usually happens if I don't accept things? Do I get frustrated and then sometimes even angry?
- When should I not accept something?

D. Spirit of Enquiry – Main Script -Story/discussion – EXPLAIN

Attitude is Altitude (Nick Vujicic – No arms, no legs, no worries) https://www.youtube.com/watch?v=Fk5EAxFCczM

E. ACTIVITY– **role play/group activity/song – EXPLORE**

Teacher to give scenarios where students have to show acceptance and students role play their solutions

- You lose the big grand final of your weekly sport activity
- The umpire makes a decision that is final and you believe it is wrong
- Your mum and dad throw away your homework without realizing while cleaning up
- You kick a ball in the house and break a very special ornament. Your parents tell you that you're no longer allowed to go to school camp.

F. INTERESTING ASIDE – Follow up activity/Application in life -ELABORATE

- Discuss these scenarios with students and how they responded in their role plays.
- Does anyone disagree with the role play?
- How would you have reacted?

G. QUESTIONS TO ASSESS – Post discussion -EVALUATE

Have discussion with students to check their understanding of the value and explain further if required.

H. HUMAN VALUE CONTENT– Take home message/thought provoking example -EXCEL

We need to accept others for who they are and the consequences to our actions. If we can do this, we can move on quicker and shine our inner diamonds again.

Cross-curriculum links:

Reflection, feedback, and notes:

Figure 14.3 (*Continued*)

- She has also suggested some ideas for integrating the values message into her curriculum. 'Wow', exclaims Greg. 'I'd never thought of linking that to the topic of fractions. I'm definitely going to use that idea.'
- The time passes quickly as other teachers make suggestions, and Sally, the secretary for this meeting, adds them to Ange's original notes.
- 'I am having a problem with some of the girls in my Grade 6', mentions Doris. 'Some of them have been getting very catty towards each other lately, and I suspect there is some unkind behaviour happening through social media outside of school. Does anyone have any ideas about how we can use this value topic to deal with this situation?' A lively discussion evolves, and some useful suggestions are made about how the values programme can be modified to address the dynamics of this particular situation that has arisen in Doris' class. Doris thankfully agrees to try these suggestions and share her experiences in the next meeting.
- It is time for a break. The teachers are divided into three groups and given 15 minutes to brainstorm about the tree in the school carpark. They had recently been asked not to park underneath it because it has been dropping large seed pods that are heavy and tough enough to have cracked a staff member's windscreen. The group's challenge is to identify a values message relating to the tree and suggest how they could introduce the message to their students and relate it to their own lives and their students' lives.
- This is not a new activity for the teachers. At first, they found it to be quite difficult, but they do this kind of brainstorming session in every EHV staff meeting, and now they have become much quicker and more efficient at seeing the values in everything around them, in daily life, and in the subjects they teach. It is important for them to be able to do this so they can be continuously aware of 'teachable moments' to bring about transformation in their students and be able to respond to these moments almost automatically.
- The lower primary school group is the first to share their idea. 'The seed is of value because it can grow into a massive tree, that gives shade, provides fruit to eat, helps to clean the air, and makes us feel happy when we look at it because of its beauty. And it gives these things to everyone, it doesn't pick and choose. We all aspire to be like this tree, because it gives so much, without discrimination.'
- 'But' chips in the upper primary group, 'there's still the problem of the seed pods breaking windscreens. So, despite the good things, the tree can also cause destruction'.
- 'I suppose, then', calls one of the secondary teachers, in a flash of inspiration, 'the tree is a lot like us. We all have the potential to be helpful and let our inner beauty show, or to be destructive. I guess it's up to each one of us to decide which we are going to choose'.
- After the groups have shared their ideas, Raj, the professional development facilitator, uses the opportunity to share some further examples of 'teachable moments' when values messages can be emphasised.

- The final part of the meeting becomes an informal discussion about ideas that the teachers have tried over the past fortnight, what worked, and what needs to be modified. This is a favourite time of the meeting for most of the teachers, new and experienced alike, because it is the time when they can learn so much from each other's experiences, and it strengthens their own understanding of the human values and their effects on their own lives in a way that top-down direction can never achieve as well.
- Recently, it has become a custom to end the EHV staff meeting with the whole staff singing an uplifting song with a human values message, in the same way that they encourage this kind of singing with the students across the school. It has become quite a challenge for the teacher responsible to find a song that is suitable for the teachers in a particular moment. This week it is Jane's turn to finish the meeting with a song, as she started it with the Light Visualisation, and she has chosen Whitney Houston's 'The Greatest Love of All'.

Further examples of other activities that can be used in staff meetings to develop EHV are included in Appendix 14.2.

14.7 Conclusion

This concludes not only this chapter but also the whole book. One's character is the distinctive mark that differentiates oneself from others. People of good character are individuals who 'know good, love good, and do good'. Knowing the good includes coming not only to understand right and wrong but also being willing to make the choice to do what is right, even under peer pressure or if they know they are not being observed (see Chapter 3). It means developing the ability to sum up a situation, deliberate, choose the right thing to do, and then doing it. Loving the good means developing a full range of moral feelings and emotions, including a love for the right and a contempt for the wrong, as well as a capacity to empathise with others. Doing good means that, after thoughtful consideration of all the circumstances and relevant facts, a person is able to make the decision to act in the right way.

The above characteristics are what most people strive for, but they are not easy to develop and maintain. There is always the possibility that individuals may sometimes choose to do that which they know they should not do. How they resolve such relapses, with adjustments to their behaviour and actions over time, gives a truer picture of their characters and the effectiveness of the human values education. The development of children who will possess and act upon ethical sensibilities ideally begins when they are very young. Since parenting styles are not homogeneous, schools often represent hope for students of fulfilling their potentials to become flourishing, contributing members of society.

The influencing power of the school for all students is quite pronounced, as they spend, on average, between 7 and 10 hours each day involved with schooling and for approximately 200 days in the year. Hence, schools and their teachers have a significant influence on the social and ethical development of their students. The important question that needs to be answered is concerned with the quality of that influence. Therefore, the task facing the teacher is twofold:

- To help the students succeed in becoming the best they can be in whatever academic, artistic, athletic, or vocational tracks they may pursue, and
- To have a substantial influence on the kinds of people they will become, making it vital to establish a foundation for this to occur.

Students need to be able to see their teachers putting into practice their own values of importance, as well as having opportunities to practise and reflect upon the greater significance of establishing human values in the lives of all stakeholders. How adults face the challenges to their own values and the authenticity of their responses may very well be the compasses that guide them to make a major difference in the lives of their students.

Teachers may feel this is another thing that is being added to their already overflowing plates. As mentioned in Chapter 13, the likely comment might be, 'So you want me to teach all the academics that I am required to cover, tutor students who need help, discipline students, be on committees, coach, volunteer after school, work with parents and do values education – and on top of it all, you are telling me to love my students when sometimes I find it difficult even to like them?'

The response is yes! Teachers are already in the business of imparting values, whether they are aware of it or not. Think of EHV as not another thing to be added to the plate of the teacher; rather, consider the character development of students as the plate on which all else is placed. Sound character development of students is essential. Teaching becomes more difficult without a good classroom or school climate. Students who are constantly late to class, disruptive, and uncivil towards others, including adults, in a school, seriously impact the learning environment for others. Values education through EHV will promote wellbeing in all who use it: Teachers, students, parents, caregivers, other staff, and other stakeholders.

Clearly, some schools seem to have better teaching and learning climates than others, and the socio-economic demographic is not always the predictor of which schools can succeed and which will fail. If, as teachers, we ask ourselves the reason why we became educators in the first place, the most likely answer will be that we wanted to make a difference in the total lives of our students, for them to be both happy and successful as educated people of good character. The curriculum is the tool used, but as educators, the best possible development of personhood is what we want to achieve with students. As teachers, we want to help students become smart, compassionate, and ethical people, not just because somebody writes a book telling us that we should do so, but because this reflects the kind of people we are and why we became teachers in the first place!

Appendix 14.1: The Development of the Australian Sathya Sai College

To illustrate further the development and nature of a Sathya Sai School, an overview is presented here of the Australian Sathya Sai College's establishment and development.[21] The school was first established in 1997 and located near Mount Warning in northern New South Wales (NSW), on the grounds of a property owned by a family who were committed to the ideals of EHV. There was no cost to attend the school, and it commenced with nine children. The first teacher was a volunteer, and costs were met by donations of goods or money. This is how many Sathya Sai Schools have started.

After the first year, the school moved into rented premises in the nearby town of Murwillumbah, and then, as student numbers grew, a full-time teacher was employed, along with a part-time volunteer principal. Again, as has been the case up to the present, shortfalls in finances were met by donations from a community of people who believed in the philosophy of EHV and wanted it demonstrated in Australia. Soon after relocating, the school was registered as an accredited private school with the NSW State Government and hence attracted subsidies from the State and Federal Governments (as do all private schools in Australia) on a per capita basis. As numbers grew, these subsidies soon met the costs of employing the teacher. By this time, a recently retired deputy school principal, from a government secondary school in Victoria, had decided to move to the area to become the full-time volunteer principal, while his wife also volunteered to be the school bursar. They continued in these roles for many years, allowing the school to grow and develop at minimum cost while also training the teachers in EHV and ensuring the integrity of the EHV programme. The only fee the school charged to students was, and continues to be, a small 'consumables' fee to cover the costs of paper, pens, books, and other direct consumables used by the students. If a student came from a family that was unable to meet this fee, a welfare fund was available to provide support, so no child was disadvantaged or excluded by a lack of ability to meet these costs.

Like all Sathya Sai Schools, the main role of the Australian Sathya Sai College is to model EHV to the wider Australian community, with a focus on graduating students of character who have also achieved their respective academic potentials.

Several years after the school's establishment, a nearby hall and grounds in the town came up for sale, and another supporter generously gave a sufficiently large donation to enable the school to purchase this hall and grounds as a permanent location. Similar large and small donations allowed the school to expand as needed as the enrolments kept growing; an adjacent block of land was bought, and eventually all new classrooms were built for K-6 single-stream classes.

The Sathya Sai College expanded in 2015 with the purchase of buildings and grounds from a private school that had closed in the nearby village of Dungay. This became the new secondary school campus that took its first Year 7 intake in 2016 and reached Year 12 in 2021.

During the establishment of the school, financial costs could be met primarily because the full-time principal and the bursar were both volunteers, and other volunteer staff also helped to defray costs. As the number of students grew, most staff became full-time professionals. The funds coming from the government covered salaries, but the provision of resources for other purposes, particularly new buildings, has continued to come from donations of money and time: These come mainly from the Sathya Sai International Organisation (SSIO) of Australia that has the school as a major service project to support and expand the use of EHV in Australia.

At the time of writing, the college is at near maximum capacity with full classes and a waiting list in the primary school, K-6. The secondary school campus has grown year by year, graduating its first Year 12 cohort in 2021. It has started a second stream of Year 7 due to increased demand. Again, this secondary school has been funded through government grants and large and small donations and is still expanding as finances allow.

The Australian Sathya Sai College and the Institute of Sathya Sai Education of Australia (ISSEA) maintain a collaborative relationship, as is the case for all Sathya Sai Schools. The ISSEA, like ISSEs in other countries, is also responsible for supporting schools and community organisations to incorporate EHV in their activities and for providing training and professional development as required.

Appendix 14.2: Further Activities for Staff Meetings or Professional Development Sessions

We believe that one of the best ways to support teachers to use EHV as a tool to benefit their pupils and themselves is to create opportunities for collegial discussion. We have prepared the following suggestions for professional development workshops, or for discussions over a period of time, in staff meetings. We suggest that short, regular discussions will help teachers to consolidate their understanding of EHV principles and how to apply them in their teaching and in their own lives.

Silent Sitting

Session 1:

What kind of teacher would you really like to be? What do you want your students to remember you for? (Brainstorm on board)

Use the words they come up with as a basis for a *silent sitting visualisation.* For example, they could sit quietly for 1–2 minutes, silently repeating one of the words, for example, 'loving' or 'inspirational'.

- Before they start give them a list of strategies to help them, such as the following:
  - sit comfortably, with a straight back
  - close eyes lightly to reduce distractions
  - try not to let the mind become distracted by other thoughts, but keep returning it to the word if the mind strays
- Suggest they can use this at the beginning of every day. Choice of words is personal and individual.

It would be a very good idea to do this activity for a couple of minutes at the start of each staff meeting, with each individual repeating a word of his/her own choice.

Ask teachers to share their experiences of how things go for them if they do this regularly or if they stop doing it.

Lead this into other group support visualisations, such as supporting each other as a team, visualising filling the classroom with loving feelings before the start of the day, etc.

Ask teachers to try this in their own lives and with their students for the next week/fortnight.

Session 2:

- Share their experiences: What effects have you noticed on yourself? On your relationships with other people (adults and children)? If you have tried it with your students, what effects have you noticed?
- Share their research findings that support their own experiences.
- Have you had any disappointments or things that haven't worked out as you expected or would have liked (e.g., making time to do it, 'monkey mind' where the mind is jumping around from one thought to another?). Remind them that it is important to be loving with themselves and not be self-critical or disappointed if it does not work out as expected.
- Introduce using silent sitting with students and the different ways it can be used. Ask teachers to select the method/s that they think is/are the most appropriate for their children and try it for a week or fortnight.
- Suggestions:
  - Use headphones for students who need some time out or to give them silence; set up a silent sitting place in the classroom with different options for students.
  - Broaden the idea from exploring the value of silent sitting to the value of silence in other contexts as well. For example, students can be asked

to work collaboratively on a project, such as creating a piece of artwork, in silence.

- Ask some students' opinions and bring them to share in the next meeting.

Session 3:

- Reflect on which formats of silent sitting teachers have used and what the effects have been.
- Share that they can do more for themselves. Introduce the light visualisation. Do this together in staff meeting or as a group before the beginning of the school day.

Service – First to Yourself, and Then to Other Colleagues, Children, and Parents

Session 1:

- Silent sitting is one way to help yourself and can often be used to lead into other transformative experiences, such as service activities. Use silent sitting first to visualise and then suggest other ways you can support/nurture yourself. Are there any ways the school can support you to support yourself? Ask teachers to write letters to themselves, promising what they will do. These can be collected, but not read, by another person and given back to them at the end of a period of time to re-read their own promises.
- Use silent sitting to visualise supporting each other. From this, go into the activity of writing good things about each other. Each teacher writes his/her name at the top of a blank sheet of paper. The paper is passed around the group, and each person will write something they admire about the person whose name is at the top. On completion, the papers are returned to their original owners. Discuss the importance of finding positive things to think about others, and then to say them. Reflect on how you can support each other and how this helps you to support yourself better.
- Reflect on: What do I need from my colleagues? What do they need from me? Set up a 'graffiti board' in the staffroom of ways we can support each other.
- 'Secret friend' where every day you do something, anonymously, to make a colleague feel good; once in a while do something to make all your colleagues feel good.
- Talk about attitudes towards service/doing service with the right frame of mind.

Session 2:

- How can you extend these ideas to encourage children to support each other?

- Try out the ideas and collect anecdotal evidence of how students have changed.
- Create some time for teachers to share the ideas they are already using.

Music

- How are you already using music, both in and out of specialist music classes?
- Why do we teach music/use music, both formally and informally, in our teaching?
- Talk about the development of children's musical intelligence in a particular age group.
- How can we use music in values education?
- Teachers singing together in staff meetings, and students singing together in assembly: How does this uplift us, and what benefits does it have?
- Find and use songs that can provide support and upliftment in different situations; for example, 'I have Confidence' from 'The Sound of Music' can be sung by somebody who is feeling nervous.

Inspirational/Uplifting Quotations and Stories

The starting point of this activity is for the teachers themselves to do this in staff meetings (perhaps they can take it in turns for one teacher to provide a quote or story each week).

- Leader reads the quote/story (this could be something general, such as the quotes attached, or an inspirational story from the Internet about teaching).
- Read it a second time. Ask the group if there is a particular word or phrase that jumps out for them.
- Repeat the word or phrase over and over, allow it to sink in and then act on your heart, noticing any feelings, thoughts, questions arising, and allow these to touch your life.
- Read it for the third time. This time, ask the group to start to think about what the message is really saying to them. Reflect on: What am I hearing? How is this touching me? What am I being invited to do? How will I respond?
- Discuss how this idea could be used with students of different ages – e.g., with stories that have a moral. For example, if the story is about friendship, you could ask the students to sit quietly and think, 'Is this true? Why is it true?' Alternatively, you could make up simple quotations and ask them to reflect on 'Is this true?' 'Why is it true?' 'What can we do today to ... [e.g. be kind to others]?' At the end of the day, reflect again on the quote, 'What did we do today to be kind to others?'

Making Promises and Commitments

- Invite staff members to discuss which of the following commitments they are prepared to make and support each other with on a daily basis as a part of their own self-nurturing and nurturing of each other. Discuss whether there are any obstacles that might prevent you from meeting your commitment, and discuss as a group how you might support each other to overcome these obstacles and keep your commitment:
  - a commitment to the practice of silent sitting each day
  - a short reading and reflection of some sort of uplifting/spiritually enriching quotation or story daily
  - a commitment to share your experiences and support each other (e.g., you might come across a particularly useful quotation or saying that you could share with your colleagues by writing on the whiteboard in the staff room, etc.)
  - a commitment to behave towards somebody else every day that reflects the values of an EHV teacher
  - a commitment to help other teachers with the job of teaching
- Please add your own further suggestions for commitments that can help with your self-nurturing and your nurturing of each other as colleagues.

Reflecting on Inspiring Teachers

- What were the values that made you decide to become a teacher in the first place? Make a list and discuss which of these values still hold true and which have changed. Have you been disillusioned in any way? Have your values been particularly inspired in any way by your teaching experience?
- What do you want your students to gain from having been taught by you?
- Has there ever been an incident in your classroom that you've regretted or that you wish you had handled differently?
- How does your teaching affect your health?
- Create a vision statement for yourself, for your colleagues, or for your classes (create together) – not where you are but where you want to be. Use 'I am' …

Effects of Your Own Past Teachers

The purpose here is to examine and question your own experiences as pupils at school, the way your own former teachers taught, punished, and reacted to mistakes, and the effects these behaviours have had on 'programming' you as a teacher.

Teachers as Models of Values

- *As the teacher, so the pupil.*[22]
- *There is no greater teacher than your heart.*[23]

- *Teachers are the sun, which encourages the lotus buds to bloom and scatter fragrance.*[24]
- *Teachers are the sculptors who shape the rocks into things of beauty and significance, of utility and inspiration.*[25]

The above quotes by the founder of EHV suggest that teachers' impacts on pupils and colleagues can be enhanced if they become models of the values that are important to them and to their particular society. We would like to suggest that teachers become able to examine the extent to which they become not just role models for the human values but also are able to live their own values within the classroom context.

- After critical self-reflection, in what ways do you think that you fall short of being a model/living example of these values?
- What are your feelings about modelling these values? Is it something that comes easily to you and makes you feel good about yourself, or is it something that causes you stress because it's expected of you rather than being the real you? What, if anything, can you do to change things so that it becomes a part of the real you, and not something you have to strain at?
- Do you think it is important for teachers to be constantly examining and developing their own values, or do you believe this is something static which cannot be changed? Perhaps you might wish to share your experiences with your colleagues.

Group Mini Action-Research Projects

Teachers working in isolation to implement initiatives such as EHV can often feel lonely, but teachers working in grade-level or subject teams of two or three can divide the labour and provide support for each other.

Mini action-research projects of a month or so duration (see also last section of Chapter 3) can be very valuable ways for these teams to explore solutions to common problems. For example, a team can experiment with implementing silent sitting (see Chapter 8) at least three times per week for two or three months and monitor the effects on students' behaviour, concentration, and even academic outcomes.

Mini projects can also be conducted at school level. For example, the whole school can engage in a Ceiling on Desires project (see Chapter 12), and, at the end of the time, teachers can share their experiences of the impact on their students, their environment, and themselves.

Some More Examples of Values Messages in Everyday Items

- The window is firm, because it blocks wind and rain at any time, allowing the temperature to remain constant. The window is upright because it allows people to see the real scenery outside. The window is loving because it allows sunlight to shine through itself into the room.

- A book is fair because it communicates with all readers in an equal manner. A book is generous because it gives knowledge to the reader without reservation.
- A chair reminds me of reliability and stability because it can bear dozens of times its own weight. It reminds me of elasticity because the cushion on its surface can change shape according to a person's weight or sitting posture. It reminds me of harmony because people usually feel relaxed when sitting on a chair, and it is also necessary in a scene of family reunion or friends chatting. It also reminds me of dedication, because it has changed from a tree to a chair, leaving its familiar environment in order to serve mankind.
- A washing machine is selfless because it accepts everything that needs to be washed.
- A woollen pullover is friendly and dedicated because it can provide warmth, comfort, and the feeling of being loved.
- A trash can has a strong spirit. No matter how others treat it, it silently endures all kinds of trash thrown away by others. It never complains. It silently dedicates itself to the cleanliness of the environment. The rubbish bin has a high tolerance, whether it is filled with dry garbage or wet garbage. The rubbish bin is friendly to everyone, even those who dislike it. As long as others need it, it is there to deal with the garbage that others don't want.
- A candle has the quality of selfless dedication because it illuminates others by burning itself. It is also full of love because it can provide warmth in the cold night.

Notes

1 Sathya Sai Baba, *Global Overview of Sathya Sai Education*, 2007, Ch. 2, p. 21. https://www.sathyasai.org/education/globaloverview/Chapter2_30Jun07.htm accessed 3-3-2023.
2 Kindly provided by the Sathya Sai College Principal, Murwillumbah, NSW, Australia.
3 Adapted from: http://www.sathyasaiehv.org.uk/Zambia.htm accessed 24-9-2021.
4 Personal correspondence with Victor Karnu (School Principal), August, 2001.
5 *Ibid.*
6 This section is based on personal communication from Ms Loraine Burrows who helped establish and develop the Sathya Sai School in Thailand under the leadership of Dr Art-ong Jumsai.
7 Loraine Burrows, personal communication.
8 *Ibid.*
9 This section is based on information provided by Professor Lalini Reddy, past Director, South African Institute of Sathya Sai Education (SAISSE).
10 *Ibid.*
11 Provided by Jacqui Robinson from Western Australia.
12 The Irish TV programme can be viewed at: https://twitter.com/news2dayRTE/status/930112528482418688 accessed 3-3-2023.
13 R. Farmer, *Love Changes Everything. Toogoolawah Schools: Stories from the Real Education Revolution* (Australia: McPherson, 2009).

14 https://www.toogoolawa.com.au/facts.html accessed 3-3-2023.
15 Sathya Sai Education in Human Values Global Compendium. Sathya Sai International Organisation, 2018.
16 This set of videos of the HVWSHE training programmes is available at: https://protect-au.mimecast.com/s/bUrCCwV1GxiXvp15fq1ekf?domain=aus01.safelinks.protection.outlook.com accessed 9-3-2023.
17 Contributed in 2019 by Raj Chandan Ram, then a government primary school teacher, Queensland, Australia.
18 Sathya Sai Baba, *Sathya Sai Speaks* (Prasanthi Nilayam, India: Books and Publication Trust, May 29, 1998), Vol. 21.
19 Sathya Sai Baba, *Sathya Sai Speaks* (Prasanthi Nilayam, India: Books and Publication Trust, May 11, 1975), Vol. 13.
20 M. Taplin, Unpublished comments from primary school teachers, collected by herself and postgraduate students during a project to implement EHV in schools in a district of China.
21 The Australian Sathya Sai College. https://sathyasai.nsw.edu.au/ accessed 4-3-2023.
22 Sathya Sai Baba, *Sathya Sai Speaks* (Prasanthi Nilayam, India: Books and Publications Trust, Nov. 20, 1979), Vol. 14.
23 Sathya Sai Baba, *Sathya Sai Speaks* (Prasanthi Nilayam, India: Books and Publications Trust, July 17, 1997), Vol. 30 Prasanthi Nilayam, India.
24 Sathya Sai Baba, *Sathya Sai Speaks* (Prasanthi Nilayam, India: Books and Publications Trust, June 14, 1983), Vol. 16.
25 Sathya Sai Baba, *Sathya Sai Speaks* (Prasanthi Nilayam, India: Books and Publications Trust, Jan. 3, 1974), Vol. 12.

Index

Note: Page references in *italics* denote figures, in **bold** tables and with "n" endnotes.

For Product Safety Concerns and Information please contact our EU representative GPSR@taylorandfrancis.com
Taylor & Francis Verlag GmbH, Kaufingerstraße 24, 80331 München, Germany

www.ingramcontent.com/pod-product-compliance
Ingram Content Group UK Ltd.
Pitfield, Milton Keynes, MK11 3LW, UK
UKHW020154200926
475702UK00016B/2708
9781032764733